Inflation Dynamic

This book explains inflation dynamic using time series data from 1960 for 42 countries. These countries are different in every aspect – historically, culturally, socially, politically, institutionally, and economically. They are chosen on the basis of the data availability only and cover the Middle East and North Africa (MENA) region, Africa, Asia, the Caribbean, Europe, Australasia, and the United States.

Inflation reached double digits in the developed countries in the 1970s and 1980s, and then central banks successfully stabilized it by anchoring inflation expectations for decades, until now. Conditional on common and country-specific shocks such as oil price shocks, financial and banking and political crises, wars, pandemics, and natural disasters, the book tests various theoretical models of the long- and short-run relationships between money and prices, money growth and inflation, money growth and real output, expected inflation, the output gap, fiscal policy, and inflation, using a number of parametric and non-parametric methods, and pays attention to specifications and estimations problems. In addition, it explains why policymakers in inflation-targeting countries, for example, the United States, failed to anticipate the recent sudden rise in inflation. And it examines the fallibility of the Modern Monetary Theory's policy prescription to reduce inflation by raising taxes.

This is a unique and innovative book, which will find an audience among students, academics, researchers, policymakers, analysts in corporations, private and central banks, and international monetary institutions.

Weshah Razzak is Honorary Research Fellow at the School of Economics and Finance, Massey University, Palmerston North, New Zealand.

Routledge International Studies in Money and Banking

Digital Finance and the Future of the Global Financial System
Disruption and Innovation in Financial Services
Edited by Lech Gąsiorkiewicz and Jan Monkiewicz

Sovereign Debt Sustainability
Multilateral Debt Treatment and the Credit Rating Impasse
Daniel Cash

Environmental Risk Modelling in Banking
Edited by Magdalena Zioło

Money, Debt and Politics
The Bank of Lisbon and the Portuguese Liberal Revolution of 1820
José Luís Cardoso

The Digital Revolution in Banking, Insurance and Capital Markets
Edited by Lech Gąsiorkiewicz and Jan Monkiewicz

Activist Retail Investors and the Future of Financial Markets
Understanding YOLO Capitalism
Edited by Usman W. Chohan and Sven van Kerckhoven

Banking, Risk and Crises in Europe
From the Global Financial Crisis to COVID-19
Renata Karkowska, Zbigniew Korzeb, Anna Matysek-Jędrych and Paweł Niedziółka

Inflation Dynamic
Global Positive Economic Analysis
Weshah Razzak

For more information about this series, please visit: www.routledge.com/ Routledge-International-Studies-in-Money-and-Banking/book-series/SE0403

Inflation Dynamic
Global Positive Economic Analysis

Weshah Razzak

LONDON AND NEW YORK

First published 2023

by Routledge
4 Park Square, Milton Park, Abingdon, Oxon OX14 4RN

and by Routledge
605 Third Avenue, New York, NY 10158

Routledge is an imprint of the Taylor & Francis Group, an informa business

© 2023 Weshah Razzak

The right of Weshah Razzak to be identified as author of this work has been asserted in accordance with sections 77 and 78 of the Copyright, Designs and Patents Act 1988.

All rights reserved. No part of this book may be reprinted or reproduced or utilised in any form or by any electronic, mechanical, or other means, now known or hereafter invented, including photocopying and recording, or in any information storage or retrieval system, without permission in writing from the publishers.

Trademark notice: Product or corporate names may be trademarks or registered trademarks and are used only for identification and explanation without intent to infringe.

British Library Cataloguing-in-Publication Data
A catalogue record for this book is available from the British Library

Library of Congress Cataloging-in-Publication Data
Names: Razzak, Weshah, author.
Title: Inflation dynamic : global positive economic analysis / Weshah
    Razzak.
Description: 1 Edition. | New York, NY : Routledge, 2023. |
    Series: Routledge international studies in money and banking |
    Includes bibliographical references and index.
Identifiers: LCCN 2022056680 (print) | LCCN 2022056681 (ebook) |
    ISBN 9781032465449 (hardback) | ISBN 9781032465470 (paperback) |
    ISBN 9781003382218 (ebook)
Subjects: LCSH: Inflation (Finance)—Case studies. | Inflation (Finance)—
    Econometric models. | Macroeconomics.
Classification: LCC HG229 .R399 2023 (print) | LCC HG229 (ebook) |
    DDC 332.4/1—dc23/eng/20230130
LC record available at https://lccn.loc.gov/2022056680
LC ebook record available at https://lccn.loc.gov/2022056681

ISBN: 978-1-032-46544-9 (hbk)
ISBN: 978-1-032-46547-0 (pbk)
ISBN: 978-1-003-38221-8 (ebk)

DOI: 10.4324/9781003382218

Typeset in Times New Roman
by Apex CoVantage, LLC

To my family, and all my teachers

Contents

List of Figures	x
List of Tables	xx

1 Introduction   1
Theories of Inflation 4
Inflation Is Bad 6
Hyperinflation 8
Objectives 9
The Findings in Brief 10
The Organization of the Book 11

2 The Price Level and the Inflation the Data at a Glance: 1960–2021   13

**3 The Quantity Theory of Money, Prices, and Output:
The Equation of Exchange – the Quantity Theory of Money**   26

4 Testing the Relationship Between Money and Prices   29
Appendix 4.1: Dynamic OLS (DOLS) 56

5 Money Growth and Inflation   57
The MENA Countries 59
The Latin and South American Countries 66
The African Countries 77
The Asian Countries 81
The Caribbean Countries 88
The Developed Inflation-Targeting Countries 89
*The Cross-Sectional Evidence for Money Growth–Inflation
Relationship 106*
Appendix 5.1: Unit Root Tests with Break 107

viii *Contents*

6 The Neutrality of Money 113
A Formal Representation of Money Neutrality 114
Does the Increase in the Quantity of Money Increase
  Real GDP in the Long Run? 115
Does the Increase in the Quantity of Money Increase
  Real GDP in the Short Run? 120

7 Why Do Central Banks Print More Money? 135
Seigniorage Revenues 136
Government Consumption Expenditures 142
Excess Money and Asset Prices 162

8 The Phillips Curve, Anticipated Inflation, and Output 172
Short-Run and Long-Run Phillips Curves 176
No Long-Run Money Illusion 179
The Phillips Curve Is a Mirage 190
Formation of Inflation Expectation Is a Challenging
  Specification Problem 192
Endogeneity 193
The Mismeasurement of the Output Gap and Expected
  Inflation 193
The Rational Expectations (RE), Policy Issues and
  the Phillips Curve 194
The Assumption of Price Stickiness 195
The Micro-Foundation for Sticky Prices 196
The Lucas Critique 197
Time Consistency and Inflation Bias 199
Reputation 200
Rational Expectations and the Rules versus
  Discretion Argument 201
The Variance of Demand Management Policy 202
Estimation of a Single-Equation Phillips Curve 202
The Stability of the New Keynesian Phillips Curve
  Specification – Change in Inflation and the Output Gap 207

9 Estimating the Phillips Curve 217
Measuring Expected Inflation 218
The Estimation of the Phillips Curve 222
Appendix 9.1: Order and Rank Conditions for Identifying
  the System 245
Appendix 9.2: The Solver of the Model 247

Contents ix

10 The "Newer" Theories and Models of Inflation 248
The New Phillips Curve 248
The Sticky Information Model 252
The P Model 252
The Fiscal Theory of Price Level and Inflation –
  FTOPL and FTOI 253
The Government Budget Constraint 254
The Central Bank Budget Constraint 254
The Consolidated Government Budget Constraint 254
The Intertemporal Government Budget Constraint 255
The Fiscal Theory of Inflation – FTOI 256
The Fiscal Theory of the Price Level – FTOPL 257
The Modern Monetary Theory – MMT 258
  The Household 260
  The Firm 260
Appendix 10.1 280
  Table A10.1 UK Cointegration Summary Statistics
    of a Number of Different Specifications 280
  Table A10.2 Norway Cointegration Summary Statistics
    of a Number of Different Specifications 281

11 Reducing Inflation 283
The Model 284
  The Household 285
  The Firm 285
r_t^* *for the United States 289*
Appendix 11.1: Data Appendix 293

12 Summary and Conclusion 295

References 300
Index 312

Figures

1.1a	The US Quarterly Inflation Rate: Consumer Price Index for All Urban Consumers, All Items in US City Average, Percent Change from Year Ago, Quarterly, Seasonally Adjusted	3
1.1b	The US Core Inflation Rate: Personal Consumption Expenditures Excluding Food and Energy (Chain-Type Price Index), Percent Change from Year Ago, Quarterly, Seasonally Adjusted	4
1.2	US Real Wealth–Real GDP Ratio Declines with Inflation	7
1.3	US Real Wealth–GDP Growth Rate and Inflation Negatively Correlated, 1960–2020	7
1.4	Russian Successful Disinflationary Policy after the Fall of the USSR	9
2.1	Consumer Price Index (2015 = 100)	14
2.2	Inflation in the MENA Group Is High at All Times	14
2.3	Inflation in the Latin and South American Countries Is Historically High	16
2.4	Africa Too Has a Very High Rate of Inflation, 1960–2020	18
2.5	Asian Countries' Inflation Rates	19
2.6	The Caribbean Countries' Inflation Rates	20
2.7	Conquering Inflation by Explicit Targeting	21
2.8	The EU Inflation-Targeting Success	23
2.9	Average Inflation Rate, 1960–2021	23
2.10	New Zealand CPI Quarterly Inflation Rate, March 1988 to June 2022	25
4.1	Broad Money – Real GDP Ratio (Percent)	30
4.2	Broad Money – Real GDP Ratio (Percent) – Including Bolivia and Japan	30
4.3	Broad Money – Real GDP Ratio (Percent) – Including Sudan	31
4.4	Consumer Price Index (2015 = 100)	32
4.5	45° Scatter Plots of Log (CPI) and Log (Broad Money – Real GDP Ratio): MENA Countries	33
4.6	45° Scatter Plots of Log (CPI) and Log (Broad Money – Real GDP Ratio): Latin and South America	34

4.7	45° Scatter Plots of Log (CPI) and Log (Broad Money – Real GDP Ratio): African Countries	35
4.8	45° Scatter Plots of Log (CPI) and Log (Broad Money – Real GDP Ratio): Asian Countries	36
4.9	45° Scatter Plots of Log (CPI) and Log (Broad Money – Real GDP Ratio): The Caribbean Countries	36
4.10	45° Scatter Plots of Log (CPI) and Log (Broad Money – Real GDP Ratio): The Inflation-Targeting Countries	37
4.11	Estimated DOLS Slope Coefficients for all Countries, 1960–2020	55
5.1a	Significant Relationship between Money Per Unit of Output Growth Rate and Inflation in MENA Countries, 1961–2020	60
5.1b	Money Per Unit of Output Growth Rate and Inflation Time Series in MENA Countries, 1961–2020	61
5.1c	The Goodness of Fit of the Inflation and Broad Money Per Unit of Real Output Model in MENA Countries	64
5.2a	Significant Relationship between Money Per Unit of Output Growth Rate and Inflation in Latin and South American Countries, 1961–2020	67
5.2b	Money Per Unit of Output Growth Rate and Inflation Time Series in Latin and South American Countries, 1961–2020	68
5.2c	The Goodness of Fit of the Inflation and Broad Money Per Unit of Real Output Model of Latin and South American Countries	74
5.3a	Significant Relationship between Money Per Unit of Output Growth Rate and Inflation in African Countries, 1961–2020	75
5.3b	Money Per Unit of Output Growth Rate and Inflation Time Series in African Countries, 1961–2020	76
5.3c	The Goodness of Fit of the Inflation and Broad Money Per Unit of Real Output Model in African Countries	80
5.4a	Significant Relationship between Money Per Unit of Output Growth Rate and Inflation in Asian Countries, 1961–2020	81
5.4b	Money Per Unit of Output Growth Rate and Inflation Time Series in Asian Countries, 1961–2020	82
5.4c	The Goodness of Fit of the Inflation and Broad Money Per Unit of Real Output Model in Asian Countries	84
5.5a	Reasonably Significant Relationship between Money Per Unit of Output Growth Rate and Inflation in Caribbean Countries, 1961–2020	86
5.5b	Money Per Unit of Output Growth Rate and Inflation Time Series in Caribbean Countries, 1961–2020	86
5.5c	The Goodness of Fit of the Inflation and Broad Money Per Unit of Real Output Model in Caribbean Countries	88
5.6a	Significant Relationship between Money Per Unit of Output Growth Rate and Inflation in Inflation-Targeting Countries, 1961–2020	90

xii *Figures*

5.6b	Money Per Unit of Output Growth Rate and Inflation in the Inflation Time Series in Inflation-Targeting Countries, 1961–2020	92
5.7a	Scatter Plots of New Zealand Year-on-Year *Quarterly* Data from March 1988 to June 2022	93
5.7b	New Zealand Year-on-Year *Quarterly* Time Series Data from March 1988 to June 2022	93
5.8a	Australia's Actual, Fitted Values and the Residuals	96
5.8b	Denmark's Actual, Fitted Values and the Residuals	97
5.8c	Norway's Actual, Fitted Values and the Residuals	98
5.8d	New Zealand's Actual, Fitted Values and the Residuals	99
5.8e	Sweden's Actual, Fitted Values and the Residuals	100
5.8f	The UK's Actual, Fitted Values and the Residuals	101
5.8g	The US Actual, Fitted Values and the Residuals	102
5.9	DOLS-Estimated Slope Coefficients: 1960–2020	103
5.10a	45° Scatter Plots of All Countries' Ten-Year Averages of Growth Rate of Broad Money Per Unit of Real Output and Inflation, 1960–1969	104
5.10b	Ten-Year Averages of Growth Rate of Broad Money Per Unit of Real Output and Inflation, 1970–1979	104
5.10c	Ten-Year Averages of Growth Rate of Broad Money Per Unit of Real Output and Inflation, 1980–1989	105
5.10d	Ten-Year Averages of Growth Rate of Broad Money Per Unit of Real Output and Inflation, 1990–1999	105
5.10e	Ten-Year Averages of Growth Rate of Broad Money Per Unit of Real Output and Inflation, 2000–2009	105
5.10f	Ten-Year Averages of Growth Rate of Broad Money Per Unit of Real Output and Inflation, 2010–2022	106
6.1	45° Line Scatter Plot of the Full-Sample 10-Year Average Money Growth and Real GDP for all 42 Countries	119
6.2	Ten-Year Average Money and Real GDP Growth Rates: The MENA Countries	120
6.3	Ten-Year Average Money and Real GDP Growth Rates: The Latin and South American Countries	121
6.4	Ten-Year Average Money and Real GDP Growth Rates: The African Countries	122
6.5	Ten-Year Average Money and Real GDP Growth Rates: The Asian Countries	123
6.6	Ten-Year Average Money and Real GDP Growth Rates: The Caribbean Countries	124
6.7	Ten-Year Average Money and Real GDP Growth Rates: The Inflation-Targeting Countries	124
6.8	45° Scatter Plot with 95 Percent Chi-Squared Confidence Ellipse Test of Money and Real Output in MENA Countries, 1960–2020	126

Figures xiii

6.9	45° Scatter Plot with 95 Percent Chi-Squared Confidence Ellipse Test of Money and Real Output in Latin and South America, 1960–2020	127
6.10	45° Scatter Plot with 95 Percent Chi-Squared Confidence Ellipse Test of Money and Real Output in Africa, 1960–2020	128
6.10a	Gabon's Cyclical Broad Money Fluctuations and the Real Output Gap	129
6.10b	South Africa's Cyclical Broad Money Fluctuations and the Real Output Gap	129
6.11	45° Scatter Plot with 95 Percent Chi-Squared Confidence Ellipse Test of Money and Real Output in Asia, 1960–2020	130
6.11a	Singapore's Broad Money Fluctuations and Real Output Gap	130
6.12	45° Scatter Plot with 95 Percent Chi-Squared Confidence Ellipse Test of Money and Real Output in the Caribbean Countries, 1960–2020	131
6.12a	Trinidad and Tobago's Broad Money Fluctuations and Real Output Gap	131
6.13	45° Scatter Plot with 95 Percent Chi-Squared Confidence Ellipse Test of Money and Real Output in the Developed Inflation-Targeting Countries, 1960–2020	132
6.14	45° Scatter Plot with 95 Percent Chi-Squared Confidence Ellipse Test of New Zealand *Quarterly* Money and Real Output, March 1988 to December 2021	132
6.15	45° Scatter Plot with 95 Percent Chi-Squared Confidence Ellipse Test of Money and Output Gap in Inflation-Targeting Countries, 1992–2020	133
6.16	The US *Quarterly* Fluctuations of Broad Money and the Real Output Gap	134
7.1	US Money Base Increasing and (Seigniorage/GDE)	138
7.2	New Zealand Quarterly Money Base and (Seigniorage/ Nominal GDP)	138
7.3	UK Money Base and (Seigniorage/GDE)	139
7.4	Korea's Money Base and (Seigniorage/NGDE)	140
7.5	Malaysia's Money Base and (Seigniorage/NGDE)	140
7.6	Turkey's Money Base and (Seigniorage/GDE)	141
7.7	Gabon's Money Base and (Seigniorage/GDE)	141
7.8a	UK Real Budget Surplus (Real Tax Revenues Less Real Government Expenditures)	143
7.8b	UK Nominal and Real Government Consumption and the CPI	143
7.8c	45° Line Scatter Plots and 95 Percent Chi-Squared Confidence Ellipse Test for UK Data Before Inflation-Targeting, 1960–1992	144
7.8d	45° Line Scatter Plot of UK Inflation-Targeting, 1993–2016	144

xiv *Figures*

7.8e	Growth Rates of the Monetary Base in the United Kingdom During Inflation-Targeting, 1993–2016	145
7.9a	45° Line Scatter Plot of Government Consumption Expenditures and the Monetary Base of New Zealand, March 2002 to December 2020	146
7.9b	45° Line Scatter Plot of New Zealand *Broad Money* and Government Consumption Expenditures, March 2002 to December 2020	146
7.10a	US Real Surplus (Deficit)	148
7.10b	US CPI, Nominal, and Real Government Consumption Expenditures	148
7.10c	45° Line Scatter Plot of US Monetary Base and Government Consumption Expenditures, 1970–2020	149
7.10d	45° Line Scatter Plot and 95 Percent Chi-Squared Confidence Ellipse Test of US Broad Money and Government Consumption Expenditures, 1971–2020	149
7.11a	95 Percent Chi-Squared Confidence Ellipse Test for Turkey Monetary Base and Government Consumption Expenditures, 2002–2020	150
7.11b	95 Percent Chi-Squared Confidence Ellipse Test for Turkey Broad Money and Government Consumption Expenditures, 1960–2020	150
7.12a	Korea CPI and Nominal and Real Government Consumption Expenditures	151
7.12b	95 Percent Chi-Squared Confidence Ellipse Test for Korea Monetary Base and Government Consumption Expenditures Before Inflation-Targeting, 1961–2002	151
7.12c	95 Percent Chi-Squared Confidence Ellipse Test for Korea Broad Money and Government Consumption Expenditures, Full Sample, 1961–2016	152
7.12d	95 Percent Chi-Squared Confidence Ellipse Test for Korea Broad Money and Government Consumption Expenditures, Full Sample, 1961–2020	152
7.13a	Malaysia CPI and Nominal and Real Government Consumption Expenditures	153
7.13b	45° Line Scatter Plot of Malaysia Monetary Base and Government Consumption Expenditures in Inflation-Targeting Period, 2000–2020	153
7.14a	Gabon CPI and Nominal and Real Government Consumption Expenditures	154
7.14b	45° Line Scatter Plot of Gabon Monetary Base and Government Consumption Expenditures, 2002–2019	154
7.15	95 Percent Chi-Squared Confidence Ellipse Test and 45° Line Scatter Plot of MENA Countries' Broad Money and Nominal Government Consumption Expenditures, 1961–2020	156

Figures xv

7.16	95 Percent Chi-Squared Confidence Ellipse Test and 45° Line Scatter Plot of Latin and South America's Broad Money and Nominal Government Consumption Expenditures, 1961–2020	157
7.17	95 Percent Chi-Squared Confidence Ellipse test for African Countries' Broad Money and Nominal Government Consumption Expenditures, 1961–2020	158
7.18	95 Percent Chi-Squared Confidence Ellipse Test for Asian Countries' Broad Money and Nominal Government Consumption Expenditures, 1961–2020	159
7.19	95 Percent Chi-Squared Confidence Ellipse Test and 45° Line Scatter Plots for Australia's Broad Money and Nominal Government Consumption Expenditures, 1961–2020	160
7.20	95 Percent Chi-Squared Confidence Ellipse Test and 45° Line Scatter Plots for Denmark's Broad Money and Nominal Government Consumption Expenditures, 1967–2020	160
7.21	95 Percent Chi-Squared Confidence Ellipse Test and 45° Line Scatter Plots for Norway's Broad Money and Nominal Government Consumption Expenditures, 1971–2020	161
7.22	95 Percent Chi-Squared Confidence Ellipse Test and 45° Line Scatter Plots for Sweden's Broad Money and Nominal Government Consumption Expenditures, 1961–2020	161
7.23a	Standardized Growth Rates of Real Money Balances and Real Stock Price in the United States, 1973–2020	164
7.23b	45° Line Scatter Plot of US Standardized Growth Rates of Real Broad Money and Real Stock Prices, 1973–2020	165
7.23c	95 Percent Chi-Squared Confidence Ellipse Test of US Standardized Growth Rates of Real Broad Money and Real Stock Prices, 1973–2020	165
7.24	45° Line Scatter Plot of UK Standardized Growth Rates of Real Broad Money and Stock Prices, 1961–2020	166
7.25	Housing Prices and Broad Money – Real GDP Ratios in Inflation-Targeting Countries (Except Australia)	167
7.26	45° Line Scatter Plot of Cyclical Fluctuation of Broad Money and Housing Prices in Inflation-Targeting Countries	168
7.27	95 Percent Chi-Squared Confidence Ellipse Test of Cyclical Fluctuation of Broad Money and Housing Prices in Inflation-Targeting Countries	169
7.28	New Zealand Quarterly Business Cycle Fluctuations of Broad Money and Housing Prices	170
7.29	95 Percent Chi-Squared Confidence Ellipse Test of New Zealand Cyclical Fluctuation of Broad Money and Housing Prices in Inflation-Targeting Countries, March 2002 to September 2021	170
8.1	Nominal and Real Wage Growth Rates in the United States	178

xvi *Figures*

8.2a	95 Percent Chi-Squared Confidence Ellipse Test of the New Keynesian Preferred Specification of the Phillips Curve of the United States, 1960–2021	181
8.2b	95 Percent Chi-Squared Confidence Ellipse Test of the New Keynesian Preferred Specification of the Phillips Curve of the United States, March 1960 to June 2022	182
8.2c	95 Percent Chi-Squared Confidence Ellipse Test of the Original Specification of the Phillips Curve of the United States, March 1960 to June 2022	183
8.3	95 Percent Chi-Squared Confidence Ellipse Test of the New Keynesian Specification of the Phillips Curve of the Japan Inflation, 1960–2021	183
8.4	95 Percent Chi-Squared Confidence Ellipse Test of the Phillips Curve Specifications of the MENA Countries, 1960–2020	184
8.5	95 Percent Chi-Squared Confidence Ellipse Test of the Phillips Curve Specifications of the Latin and South American Countries, 1960–2020	185
8.6	95 Percent Chi-Squared Confidence Ellipse Test of the Phillips Curve Specifications of the African Countries, 1960–2020	186
8.7	95 Percent Chi-Squared Confidence Ellipse Test of the Phillips Curve Specifications of the Asian Countries, 1960–2020	187
8.8	95 Percent Chi-Squared Confidence Ellipse Test of the Phillips Curve Specifications of the Caribbean Countries, 1960–2020	188
8.9a	95 Percent Chi-Squared Confidence Ellipse Test of the Phillips Curve Specifications of the Inflation-Targeting Countries Before Inflation-Targeting, 1960–1990	188
8.9b	95 Percent Chi-Squared Confidence Ellipse Test of the Phillips Curve Specifications of the Inflation-Targeting Countries Under Inflation-Targeting, 1992–2021	189
8.10	95 Percent Chi-Squared Confidence Ellipse Test of the Phillips Curve Specifications of the US Quarterly Data for Inflation-Targeting Period, March 2012 to December 2021	190
8.11	95 Percent Chi-Squared Confidence Ellipse Test of the Phillips Curve Specifications of the New Zealand Quarterly Data for Inflation-Targeting Period, June 1988 to December 2021	191
8.12	Sample Generalized Variance for the MENA Countries' New Keynesian Phillips Curve Specification, 1962–2020	210
8.13	Sample Generalized Variance for Latin and South American Countries' New Keynesian Phillips Curve Specification, 1962–2020	212
8.14	Sample Generalized Variance for the African Countries' New Keynesian Phillips Curve Specification, 1962–2020	213
8.15	Sample Generalized Variance for the Asian Countries' New Keynesian Phillips Curve Specification, 1962–2020	214
8.16	Sample Generalized Variance for the Caribbean Countries' New Keynesian Phillips Curve Specification, 1962–2020	215

8.17	Sample Generalized Variance for the Inflation-Targeting Countries' New Keynesian Phillips Curve Specification, 1962–2020	215
8.18	Sample Generalized Variance for New Zealand's New Keynesian Phillips Curve Specification, March 1989 to December 2021	216
9.1	Actual CPI Inflation and US Survey of 1-Year-Ahead CPI Inflation	219
9.2	45° Line Scatter Plot of US Money and Nominal GDP Growth, March 1961 to March 2022	223
9.3	45° Line Scatter Plot of the US Inflation and Nominal GDP Growth, March 1961 to March 2022	223
9.4	Quarterly Growth Rate of the Variables Used to Estimate the US Phillips Curve System (%)	227
9.5	45° Line Scatter Plot of Money Growth and Inflation in the United States, March 1961 to March 2022	230
9.6a	Residuals – Model Specification (1)	232
9.6b	Residuals – Model Specification (2)	233
9.7a	Actual and Mean Dynamic Stochastic Projections of Quarterly US Inflation: Model (1) – RE Specifications: Phillips Curve	234
9.7b	Actual and Mean Dynamic Stochastic Projections of Quarterly US Inflation: Model (2) – New Keynesian Specifications: Phillips Curve	234
9.8	Actual Inflation and Mean Dynamic Stochastic Projections for Model (1) and Model (2)	235
9.9a	45° Line Scatter Plot of New Zealand's Broad Money Growth and Inflation, March 1992 to December 2021	238
9.9b	95 Percent Chi-Square Confidence Ellipse Test of New Zealand's Broad Money and Nominal GDP Growth Rates, March 1992 to September 2021	239
9.9c	95 Percent Chi-Square Confidence Ellipse Test of New Zealand's Growth Rates of Nominal Government Expenditures and GDP(e), March 1992 to December 2021	240
9.9d	95 Percent Chi-Square Confidence Ellipse Test of New Zealand's Slope of the Yield Curve and the Output Gap, March 1992 to December 2021	241
9.10a	Actual and Mean Dynamic Stochastic Projections of New Zealand Quarterly Inflation: Model (1) – RE Specifications: Phillips Curve	242
9.10b	Actual and Mean Dynamic Stochastic Projections of New Zealand Quarterly Inflation: Model (1) – New Keynesian Specifications: Phillips Curve	243
9.10c	Actual and Mean Dynamic Stochastic Projections of New Zealand Quarterly Inflation: Model (1) – RE and Model (2) New Keynesian Specifications: Phillips Curve	243

xviii   *Figures*

10.1	Cyclical Fluctuations of Real Wages and Real Output in the United States	251
10.2	The UK Variables of the VAR	264
10.3	UK Generalized Impulse Response Functions of the Baseline VAR	266
10.4	UK Mean Baseline Dynamic Stochastic Projections of *Log Nominal* Debt	267
10.5	UK Mean Baseline Dynamic Stochastic Projections of *Log Real* Surplus (Log Real Taxes and Log Real Government Expenditures)	267
10.6	UK Mean Baseline Dynamic Stochastic Projections of *Real C/Y*	268
10.7	UK Mean Baseline Dynamic Stochastic Projections of Hours Worked	268
10.8	UK Mean Baseline Dynamic Stochastic Projections of the CPI	269
Sketch 10.1	Effect of Doubling the Tax Rate on Real Output and the Price Level	270
10.9a	UK Mean Dynamic Stochastic Projections of Annual Average Hours Worked Per Worker, 2018–2040	270
10.9b	UK Mean Dynamic Stochastic Projection of Annual Average Hours Worked Per Worker: *Deviations from Baseline Mean*	271
10.10a	UK Mean Dynamic Stochastic Projection of CPI, 2018–2040	271
10.10b	UK Mean Dynamic Stochastic Projection of CPI: *Deviations from Baseline Mean*	272
10.11	Norway Variables of the VAR	273
10.12	Norway Generalized Impulse Response Functions of the Baseline VAR	274
10.13	Norway Mean Baseline Dynamic Stochastic Projection of Nominal Debt	275
10.14	Norway Mean Baseline Dynamic Stochastic Projection of Log Real Deficit	275
10.15	Norway Mean Baseline Dynamic Stochastic Projection of *C/Y*	276
10.16	Norway Mean Baseline Dynamic Stochastic Projection of Hours Worked	276
10.17	Norway Mean Baseline Dynamic Stochastic Projection of the CPI	277
10.18	Norway Mean Dynamic Stochastic Projection of Hours Worked: *Deviations from Baseline Mean*	277
10.19	Norway Mean Dynamic Stochastic Projection of CPI: *Deviations from Baseline Mean*	278

10.20	Comparing the Deviation of Average Annual Hours Worked from Baseline Doubling Taxes in Norway and the United Kingdom, 2018–2040	279
10.21	Comparing the Deviation of CPI from Baseline Doubling Taxes in Norway and the United Kingdom, 2018–2040	279
11.1	The US Federal Fund Rate – r* Gaps	290
11.2	Chi-Square Correlation Test of Real Rate of Return on Stocks and the Natural Rate r_{1t}^*	291
11.3	Chi-Square Correlation Test of Real Rate of Return on Stocks and the Natural Rate r_{2t}^*	291
11.4	Computed r_t^* for Selective Advanced Countries	292
A11.1	The US Data Growth Rates Required to Compute r^*	294

Tables

2.1	Descriptive Statistics: Inflation in Latin and South American Countries, 1960–2021	17
2.2	Descriptive Statistics: Inflation in Africa, 1960–2021	19
2.3	Descriptive Statistics: Inflation in Asia, 1960–2021	20
2.4	Descriptive Statistics for the Caribbean Inflation, 1960–2021	20
2.5	Descriptive Statistics: Developed Inflation-Targeting Countries, 1960–2021	22
4.1	Trend of the CPI and the Money–Output Ratio Is Stochastic in MENA Countries	37
4.2	Trend of the CPI and the Money–Output Ratio Is Stochastic in Latin and South America	38
4.3	Trend of the CPI and the Money–Output Ratio Is Stochastic in the African Countries	39
4.4	Trend of the CPI and the Money–Output Ratio Is Stochastic in the Asian Countries	39
4.5	Trend of the CPI and the Money–Output Ratio Is Stochastic in the Caribbean Countries	40
4.6	Trend of the CPI and the Money–Output Ratio Is Stochastic in the Inflation-Targeting Countries	40
4.7	OLS and Dynamic OLS for the MENA Countries: Relationship between Log (Broad Money – Real GDP Ratio) and Log CPI Is Consistent with the QTM	43
4.8	OLS and Dynamic OLS for Latin and South American Countries: Relationship between Log (Broad Money – Real GDP Ratio) and Log CPI Is Consistent with the QTM	44
4.9	OLS and Dynamic OLS for the African Countries; Relationship between Log (Broad Money – Real GDP Ratio) and Log CPI Is Consistent with the QTM	47
4.10	OLS and Dynamic OLS for the Asian Countries; Relationship between Log (Broad Money – Real GDP Ratio) and Log CPI Is Consistent with the QTM	49
4.11	OLS and Dynamic OLS for the Caribbean Countries: Relationship between Log (Broad Money – Real GDP Ratio) and Log CPI Is Consistent with the QTM	51

Tables xxi

4.12 OLS and Dynamic OLS for the Inflation-Targeting Countries: Relationship between Log (Broad Money – Real GDP Ratio) and Log CPI Is Consistent with the QTM 53

4.13 Summary Statistics of the DOLS Estimates of the Intercepts and the Slopes 55

5.1 Descriptive Statistics for Broad Money – Real GDP Ratio Growth and Inflation in MENA Countries, 1960–2020 62

5.2 Are Mean Inflation and (Broad Money – Real GDP Ratio) Growth Equal in the MENA Countries in 1960–2020? 63

5.3 Are Variability of Inflation and (Broad Money – Real GDP Ratio) Growth Equal in the MENA Countries in 1960–2020? 63

5.4 Dynamic OLS Estimated Broad Money – Real GDP Ratio Growth–Inflation Relationship in MENA Countries 65

5.5 Descriptive Statistics for Broad Money – Real GDP Ratio Growth and Inflation in Latin and South American Countries in 1960–2020 69

5.6 Are Mean Inflation and (Broad Money – Real GDP Ratio) Growth Equal in the Latin and South American Countries in 1960–2020? 69

5.7 Are Variability of Inflation and (Broad Money – Real GDP Ratio) Growth Equal in Latin and South American Countries in 1960–2020? 70

5.8 Dynamic OLS Estimated Broad Money – Real GDP Ratio Growth–Inflation Relationship in Latin and South American Countries 71

5.9 Descriptive Statistics for Broad Money – Real GDP Ratio Growth and Inflation in African Countries, 1960–2020 77

5.10 Are Mean Inflation and (Broad Money – Real GDP Ratio) Growth Equal in the African Countries in 1960–2020? 77

5.11 Is Variability of Inflation and (Broad Money – Real GDP Ratio) Growth Equal in the African Countries in 1960–2020? 78

5.12 Dynamic OLS Estimated Broad Money – Real GDP Ratio Growth–Inflation Relationship in African Countries 78

5.13 Descriptive Statistics for Broad Money – Real GDP Ratio Growth and Inflation in Asian Countries in 1960–2020 82

5.14 Are Mean Inflation and (Broad Money – Real GDP Ratio) Growth Equal in the Asian Countries in 1960–2020? 83

5.15 Are Variability of Inflation and (Broad Money – Real GDP Ratio) Growth Equal in the Asian Countries in 1960–2020? 83

5.16 Dynamic OLS Estimated Broad Money – Real GDP Ratio Growth–Inflation Relationship in Asian Countries 85

5.17 Descriptive Statistics for Broad Money – Real GDP Ratio Growth and Inflation in Caribbean Countries, 1960–2020 87

5.18 Are Mean Inflation and (Broad Money – Real GDP Ratio) Growth Equal in the Caribbean Countries in 1960–2020? 87

5.19 Are Variability of Inflation and (Broad Money – Real GDP Ratio) Growth Equal in Caribbean Countries in 1960–2020? 87

xxii *Tables*

5.20	Dynamic OLS Estimated Broad Money – Real GDP Ratio Growth–Inflation Relationship in Caribbean Countries. Dependent Variable is Inflation	88
5.21	Descriptive Statistics for Broad Money – Real GDP Ratio Growth and Inflation in Inflation-Targeting Countries (*Annual* Data 1960–2020)	94
5.22	Are Mean Inflation and (Broad Money – Real GDP Ratio) Growth Equal in Inflation-Targeting Countries in 1960–2020?	94
5.23	Are Variability of Inflation and (Broad Money – Real GDP Ratio) Growth Equal in the Inflation-Targeting Countries in 1960–2020?	94
5.24a	Dynamic OLS Estimated (Broad Money – Real GDP Ratio) Growth–Inflation Relationship in the Inflation-Targeting Countries: Australia	96
5.24b	Dynamic OLS Estimated (Broad Money – Real GDP Ratio) Growth–Inflation Relationship in the Inflation-Targeting Countries: Denmark	97
5.24c	Dynamic OLS Estimated (Broad Money – Real GDP Ratio) Growth–Inflation Relationship in the Inflation-Targeting Countries: Norway	98
5.24d	Dynamic OLS Estimated (Broad Money – Real GDP Ratio) Growth–Inflation Relationship in the Inflation-Targeting Countries: New Zealand (Quarterly Data)	99
5.24e	Dynamic OLS Estimated (Broad Money – Real GDP Ratio) Growth–Inflation Relationship in the Inflation-Targeting Countries: Sweden	100
5.24f	Dynamic OLS Estimated (Broad Money – Real GDP Ratio) Growth–Inflation Relationship in the Inflation-Targeting Countries: The United Kingdom	101
5.24g	Dynamic OLS Estimated (Broad Money – Real GDP Ratio) Growth–Inflation Relationship in the Inflation-Targeting Countries: The United States	102
A-5.1	ADF Tests of Unit Root with a Break	108
6.1	Ten-Year Averages of Broad Money and Real GDP Growth Rates in the MENA Countries	116
6.2	Ten-Year Averages of Broad Money and Real GDP Growth Rates in the Latin and South American Countries	116
6.3	Ten-Year Averages of Broad Money and Real GDP Growth Rates in the African Countries	117
6.4	Ten-Year Averages of Broad Money and Real GDP Growth Rates in the Asian Countries	117
6.5	Ten-Year Averages of Broad Money and Real GDP Growth Rates in the Caribbean Countries	118
6.6	Ten-Year Averages of Broad Money and Real GDP Growth Rates in the Developed Inflation-Targeting Countries	118

Tables xxiii

7.1	Descriptive Statistics of (Seigniorage/NGDE) in Selected Countries	142
7.2	Descriptive Statistics: New Zealand Government Growth Rates of Consumption Expenditures, Broad Money, and the Monetary Base in March 2002 to September 2021	147
8.1	Descriptive Statistics of the MENA Countries: Change in Inflation and the Output Gap, 1960–2020	203
8.2	Descriptive Statistics of the Latin and South American Countries: Change in Inflation and the Output Gap, 1960–2020	204
8.3	Descriptive Statistics of the African Countries: Change in Inflation and the Output Gap, 1960–2020	204
8.4	Descriptive Statistics of the Asian Countries: Change in Inflation and the Output Gap, 1960–2020	205
8.5	Descriptive Statistics of the Caribbean Countries: Change in Inflation and the Output Gap, 1960–2020	205
8.6	Descriptive Statistics of the Inflation-Targeting Countries: Change in Inflation and the Output Gap Before Inflation-Targeting, 1960–1992	206
8.7	Descriptive Statistics of the Inflation-Targeting Countries: Change in Inflation and the Output Gap Under Inflation-Targeting, 1993–2021	206
8.8	The MENA Countries' Sample Generalized Variance	209
9.1	OLS Regression Test of the US CPI Inflation Survey Data	220
9.2	OLS Regression Test of the Residuals	221
9.3	Maximum Likelihood Estimates of the *Quarterly* US Phillips Curve, September 1960 to March 2022	228
9.4	Descriptive Statistics of Dynamic Stochastic Projections of Models (1) and (2): Actual and Mean Dynamic Stochastic Projections	235
9.5	Maximum Likelihood Estimates of the *Quarterly* NZ Phillips Curve, March 1992 to June 2022	241
9.6	Descriptive Statistics of New Zealand Actual Inflation and Mean Dynamic Stochastic Projections of Models (1) and (2), March 1993 to June 2022	244
A10.1	UK Cointegration Summary Statistics of a Number of Different Specifications	280
A10.2	Norway Cointegration Summary Statistics of a Number of Different Specifications	281
11.1	Computed r_t^* and Interest Rate Gaps for the United States	290
11.2	Descriptive Statistics of Computed r_t^* for Selective Countries, 2000–2019	292

1 Introduction

It is rather important to understand at the outset what inflation is in order to avoid the confusion between the increase in *relative prices* and the *general price level* and between *inflation* and a *one-off* increase of the price level. In this book, inflation is defined as the *steady and sustained rise in prices* (Henderson, 2021).[1] Barro (1993, p. 165) defines inflation as the c*ontinuing upward movement* or *continuing increase* in the *general* price level. The US Federal Reserve Board of Governors also agrees with this definition.[2] For example, if the general price level this year, P_t is 100 units and it increases next year, that is, P_{t+1}, to 120 units, then the rate of increase will be 20 percent. Typically, we use last and current years to measure it. However, this one-off increase in the price level is still not inflation. If the price falls again next year, then what we had last year was not inflation. *Secular* inflation describes a *prolonged period of continuing price increases*. Secular inflation continues to persist over a long period of time. It is the gradual, rather than extreme, increase in the general price level.

We should not confuse the causes of inflation either. Excess demand for goods and services does not cause inflation; it results in an increase in the price level. Furthermore, global shocks such as the main oil price shocks in 1973 and 1979, Global Financial Crisis (GFC), and country- and region-specific shocks such as adverse supply shocks, droughts, earthquakes, wars, political unrests, and pandemics reduce real output by shifting the aggregate supply curve to the left, causing real output to fall and the *price level* to increase, and none of these shocks cause inflation. They do, however, if they occur during periods of relatively loose monetary policy or high expected inflation. Persistent price increase might be at the heart of the issue here. Central bankers usually look through the rise in the general price level, which is due to an adverse supply shock, and care more about *second round effects*, that is, the effect on inflation. However, when the rise in oil price, for example, feeds into other prices and wages and persists, the intervention, or not, becomes a serious policy issue. Rising nominal wages do not *cause* inflation either. The most recent evidence about the price–wage spiral confirms it (see Alvarez *et al.* [2022b]). Some central bankers are still obsessed with it though.

---

1 He attributed this definition to Milton Friedman.
2 www.federalreserve.gov/faqs/economy_14419.htm

DOI: 10.4324/9781003382218-1

2 Introduction

Continuous or persistent increase in prices and a decline in output (increase in unemployment), that is, *stagflation*, result from supply shocks over the business cycle. Rising general price level (e.g., Consumer Price Index, CPI) relative to the long-run trends, or a target, over the business cycle is a concern for the central bank. Deviations from equilibrium, or long-run trends, are due mostly to random shocks. However, it is rather difficult to identify the nature and the permanency of the shocks. The deviations of inflation from its anticipated level and output from its potential level or unemployment from its natural level are reasons for *active monetary policy*, whereby the monetary authority intervenes in the market, either to fight inflation or to increase employment and output. We will study these deviations in depth. Potential output is the maximum number of goods and services an economy can produce at full capacity. The deviation of real GDP from potential is the output gap, which plays an important role in the models of inflation. The natural rate of unemployment is the rate of unemployment arising from all sources, except fluctuations in aggregate demand. Estimates of potential GDP are based on the long-term natural rate. This is often used interchangeably with the Non-Accelerating Inflation Rate of Unemployment, but they are not the same thing. Both potential output and the natural rate of unemployment are unobservable; hence, they must be quantified econometrically. We will discuss these issues in more detail later.

Trend, too, is very difficult to predict (Phillips, 2003). It is also controversial to identify its nature, whether it is linear and deterministic or stochastic using the commonly used tools we have. There might be reasons to believe that we experience a stagflation today after a series of adverse supply shocks. We do not have sufficient data to analyze the macroeconomics of such shocks.[3] If, indeed, we have stagflation then monetary policy is in a pickle because central banks, particularly in developed countries, manage aggregate demand by raising interest rates to fight inflation. However, higher interest rates will reduce real output more and could cause a recession and increase unemployment.

Various shocks affect the variation in inflation. Monetary policy targets the inflation rate and reduces its variability; however, it cannot reduce variability below the *natural variation level* in the data.[4] For example, in the United States, inflation was below 3 percent since March 1959; it jumped over 3 percent in June 1966

---

3 It is outside the scope of this book, but the Trump's tariffs on China and the EU and the Chinese retaliatory tariffs on the United States, the EU, and Australia are still in effect. Their effects on trade, commodity prices, intermediate good prices, and finished goods prices might have had some effect on domestic prices. COVID-19 effects on production, disruption of global supply channels, and labor cost among other supply-side effects must have affected domestic prices. The Ukraine–Russia war reduced supply and pushed food and energy prices up. These shocks do not cause inflation *per se*; however, they could persist and affect inflation in countries with expansionary monetary and fiscal policies.

4 A random variable x_t has an observed mean square around its mean, $= \frac{1}{n}\sum_{i=1}^{n}\left(x_t - \bar{\mu}_x\right)^2$, where $\bar{\mu}_x$ is the mean of x_t. The expected value of this function is $\left(\bar{x} - \bar{\mu}_x\right)^2 + \sigma^2$. This is minimized if the mean of x_t and $\bar{x}$ is set equal to $\bar{\mu}_x$. Thus, the expected value of the observed mean squares cannot be reduced below the inherited natural variance σ^2.

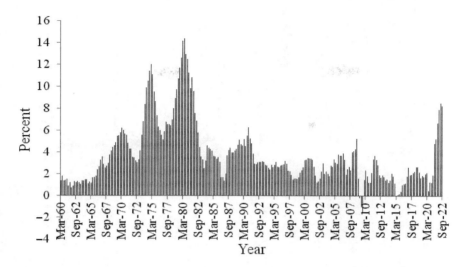

Figure 1.1a The US Quarterly Inflation Rate: Consumer Price Index for All Urban Consumers, All Items in US City Average, Percent Change from Year Ago, Quarterly, Seasonally Adjusted

Data Source: FRED

and kept increasing until it hit 8.3 percent in September 1973 and 12.2 percent in December 1974. It peaked at 14.5 percent in June 1980. The Fed then began the so-called Volcker's disinflation policy, which saw inflation falling rapidly. Then, inflation stabilized for decades until now. In 2012, the Fed announced an explicit inflation target of 2 percent over the long run.

An example of the time series data of inflation are in figures 1.1a and 1.1b, which plot the year-on-year *quarterly* CPI inflation rate of the United States (all items and core inflation, which excludes food and energy) and OECD Countries (all items). The US and OECD inflation data show that the oil and food prices are the reason for the volatility of the CPI. Visually, the volatility of the core inflation measure is significantly smaller than the CPIs. The standard deviations of core inflation, OECD, and US CPI inflation rates are 2.62, 3.70, and 2.95 respectively.[5]

Inflation was similarly high in most advanced countries during the 1970s and 1980s, and it was evidently out of control in many developing countries in Africa and Latin and South America. Inflation has increased lately in many countries. We will display the data and stylized facts in the next chapter.

---

5 In New Zealand, a rise in the price of tomatoes in winter could cause a spike in the CPI. A purchase of a large military item by the government surely causes a spike in the CPI.

4 Introduction

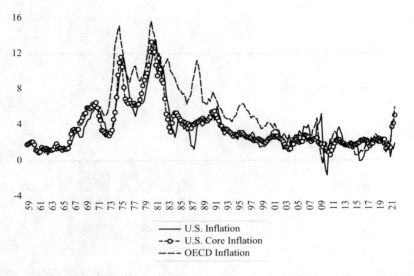

Figure 1.1b The US Core Inflation Rate: Personal Consumption Expenditures Excluding Food and Energy (Chain-Type Price Index), Percent Change from Year Ago, Quarterly, Seasonally Adjusted

Data Source: FRED and OECD

Theories of Inflation

There are a few theories and models of inflation, but only two are considered important in the sense that they dominated the literature and have been taken seriously by policymakers; the Quantity Theory of Money (QTM) (Fisher, 1911) and the Phillips curve (Phillips, 1958). The main objective of this book is about testing the predictions of these theories empirically. We will also examine newer theories.

The QTM theory of money and prices, however, might have been recognized and studied a long time ago. The Polish mathematician Nicolaus Copernicus (1517) formulated the idea, see (Lowry, 1996). The British philosophers John Locke and David Hume, and the French Jean Bodin, restated the theory in the eighteenth century, which was developed in by (Newcomb, 1885). Generally, the story of the QTM is truly simple. In any economy, households and governments buy goods and services from the sellers in the markets. For the aggregate economy, the value of sales must be equal to the value of receipts. The value of sales is equal to the number of transactions (volume) conducted in a period of time multiplied by the average price. The value of purchase, on the other hand, must be equal to the amount of money in circulation in that economy multiplied by the average number of times it changes hands – the velocity – during the same period. This story is written as an algebraic identity that should hold true in the *long run*.

In addition to the QTM, we also discuss and carefully test the Phillips curve (Phillips, 1958), which is a negative relationship between inflation and unemployment

Introduction 5

or a positive relationship between inflation and output. Also, we study the *accelerationist* Phillips curve (Phelps, 1967), whereby inflation is a function of expected inflation and the deviations of the unemployment rate from the *natural rate of unemployment*, or the *output gap*, that is, the deviation of output from its potential level, not the quantity of money. There is no role for money as the main explanatory variable of inflation in this theory. It is rather important to stress that unlike money, both explanatory variables in the Phillips curve are unobservable. They are estimated, computed, or constructed; hence, measurement errors could have significant effects on the coefficient estimates of the Phillips curve equation. We will focus more on the implications of the specification of expected inflation, that is, specification errors, on the projections of inflation.

There are of course significant policy implications for not foreseeing rising inflation. Policy wise, if the Phillips curve is the *modus operandi*, central banks increase the short-term nominal interest rate (the only policy instrument), which supposedly increases the *real* short-term interest rate, reduces aggregate demand, then reduces inflation. The dynamic of such a process is complex and depends on the accuracy of expected inflation. The central bank ought to set the policy interest rate at time t based on an anticipation of high inflation at time $t + k$ and because the policy lags are *long and variable*; it takes time for the increased short-term real interest rate to reduce aggregate demand, which in turn reduces inflation. Being surprised by high inflation may induce a strong tightening and for a long time as we witness today. We witness a big increase in interest rates in all advanced countries.

"Newer" theories of inflation include the New Phillips curve (see Clarida *et al.* [1999] and Gali *et al.* [2001]); the Sticky Information Phillips curve (see Mankiw and Reis [2002, 2007]); and the P* model (see Gerlach and Svensson [2003]), which attempt to explain inflation. All of the aforementioned theories and models, although empirically testable with obvious specifications and estimations problems, have been challenged on a theoretical ground too. For example, the Fiscal Theory of the Price Level (see Leeper [1991], Cochrane [2000], Sims [1994], and Woodford [1994, 1995, 1998a, 1998b]) predicts that under certain conditions, the price level could be pinned down by fiscal policy rather than money or other monetary factors. We will test the implications of a new theory called the Modern Monetary Theory (MMT) (Mitchell *et al.*, 2019), which does not seem to have been tested widely so far.

As in any other economic story, the difficulty always, however, is in capturing the dynamic. A complex dynamic between *now* and the *long run* may exist. The long run is not a calendar date. In economics, the long run is the time when all expectations are validated; the growth of all variables ceases; and at the full employment level of income there is a fixed ratio of the volume of transactions to the level of output. In this story, money is assumed to be produced by the central bank, that is, fiat money. It is supplied on demand presumably, and it must be willingly held at any moment in time. The quantity of money per unit of real output drives the average general price level in the economy. It predicts a one-to-one relationship in the long run. It is, however, an empirical question, which may or may not be accepted by the data.

6 *Introduction*

Of course, there might be many reasons for the evidence to fail the tests, which we will study in this book. For example, in the 1980s and 1990s, the Japanese economy was in a deep recession. The central bank of Japan injected lots of money into the economy to induce people to spend (a stimulus of aggregate demand), but people chose not to spend.

Another example is the case of successful inflation-targeting countries, where the correlation between money growth and inflation all but disappeared because monetary policy altered the time series properties of the data, that is, rendered inflation stationary.

Inflation Is Bad

Inflation is a tax. If inflation goes up mainly because of the rise in food and energy prices like what we observe today, it might have a worse effect on the low income and poor people than on the rich because the share of food consumption in total expenditures is higher than that of the richer people (the Engel curve). When nominal wages increase, the tax brackets are pushed up too. People are taxed more. The continuing, or persistent, increase in the price level also reduces real money balances, real wages, the real interest rate, real wealth, the real value of money, real gross debt, and welfare.[6] High inflation distorts optimal investment plans too. Inflation is bad. The optimal level of inflation is controversial. Economists seem to argue about whether it should be negative, zero, or positive. We will discuss these issues further even though this issue is beyond our objectives.

Robert Shiller (1997) showed that ordinary people have different views about inflation from economists. He asked people whether or not they agree with the statement that the biggest gripe about inflation is that it hurts my real buying power; it makes me poorer. Seventy-seven percent of the people agreed with the statement, compared with only 12 percent of economists. Shiller suggested that the fear of inflation might be psychological. Real income is nominal income adjusted for inflation. If inflation increases, real income declines. How is that not a problem? When inflation is high, money becomes like a "hot potato" – no one wants to hold it. People hold money willingly; therefore, when they expect inflation, they hedge against it by buying assets, gold, land, housing, etc.

By definition, higher inflation reduces *real* wages, the *ex-post real* interest rate, and *real* wealth among many real variables. Figure 1.2 plots the total wealth–GDP ratio for the United States, and Figure 1.3 is a scatter plot of the growth rate of wealth–GDP and inflation. As inflation rose in the 1960–1980 period, real

---

6 In the models of the exchange rate in the 1970s and 1980s, an increase in the relative quantity of money in a country depreciates its currency relative to the others. Thus, it reduces the purchasing power. People, whether they are rich or poor, understand that high inflation is not a good thing. For the rich, it could turn their financial wealth into dust in no time. For the poor, it makes life expensive if not impossible.

Introduction 7

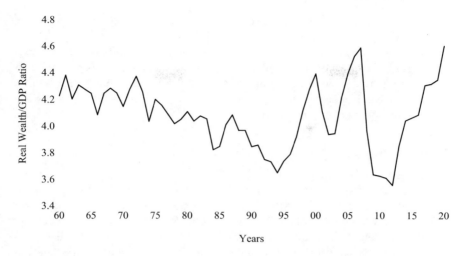

Figure 1.2 US Real Wealth–Real GDP Ratio Declines with Inflation
Data Source: FRED

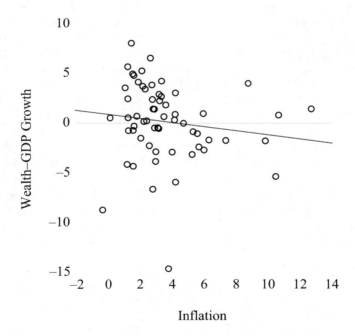

Figure 1.3 US Real Wealth–GDP Growth Rate and Inflation Negatively Correlated, 1960–2020
Data Source: FRED

8 *Introduction*

wealth declined. A 1 percent increase in inflation reduces wealth–GDP growth by 0.20 percent.[7]

Not only economists are concerned about inflation. Psychologists as well have investigated the effect of rising inflation on suicides and found a positive relationship.[8] So inflation is not a good thing at all, and most reasonable people seem to agree that the evidence points to this fact.

Inflation could go out of control.

Hyperinflation

A significantly damaging inflation is called *hyperinflation*. It is a devastating case of rapidly rising inflation, that is, by the day or by the hour. The Cato Institute published the Hanke–Krus table, which shows that Hungary's hyperinflation reached 13,600,000,000,000,000 percent in 1945. The inflation rate doubled every 15.6 hours. In Zimbabwe, it doubled every 24.7 hours. The table lists more than 50 cases of worldwide hyperinflation. An economist friend of mine showed me his favorite example of hyperinflation; an envelope he received from his parents in Argentina during the 1980s, where stamps covered the front and the back of the envelope fully. Horror stories from faraway places are told about this phenomenon. In 1920s Germany, the wives of the workers waited outside the factory gates on paydays in order to get the salaries of their husbands and quickly buy food because food prices rose so quickly that they needed to conserve shopping time. Banknotes printed on one face only; the back of the note was blank because the press was running nonstop. In Iraq during the UN sanction in the 1990s, banknotes were printed so quickly and cheaply, that the ink stuck on the hands when handling the banknotes. The highest denomination Iraqi banknote before the Gulf War was 25 dinar. The highest denomination note now is 50,000 dinars. These examples are real cases of people's fear of inflation. The fear of hyperinflation is real.

It seems like not all economists agree that inflation is always and everywhere a monetary phenomenon. Henderson (2021) says that Friedman stated this famous sentence in a talk in India in 1964. His point is that *nothing else* but printing money at accelerating rates causes inflation. However, Friedman and Schwartz (1963), who studied the history of monetary policy in the United States, made the case that the Great Depression in 1929–1932 was a result of a monetary policy error. That was the argument they made against the Federal Reserve Board in the years leading to the Great Depression; the Fed did not increase the money supply *when*

---

7 We regress inflation on a constant term and the growth rate of the ratio of total wealth–GDP in the United States from 1960 to 2020 using OLS with Newey and West's (1994) corrected variance–covariance matrix.

8 For example, see (Solano *et al.*, 2012) who investigated the effect of unemployment and inflation on the number of suicides in Italy from 2001 to 2008. They reported a significant association between inflation and suicide attempt. Agrrawal *et al.* (2017) also show positive significant association between rising inflation and suicides in the United States (1980–2016).

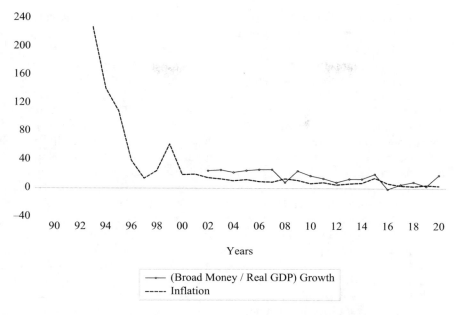

Figure 1.4 Russian Successful Disinflationary Policy after the Fall of the USSR
Data Source: World Development Indicators

needed. Right after the fall of the Soviet Union, inflation exceeded 200 percent. The Russian central bank reduced inflation by reducing money and credit growth significantly.[9] Figure 1.4 plots the CPI inflation rate in Russia, which was above 200 percent after the fall of the USSR, and the growth rate of broad money to real GDP ratio.

In 1989, New Zealand was the first country to explicitly target inflation. Many countries followed suit, which were Australia, the United Kingdom, Canada, the EU, and so on. They recognized the importance of price stability in the law.

Objectives

The first main objective of this book is to empirically explain the inflation dynamic using annual and quarterly time series from 1960 to 2020, 2021, and to June 2022 in 42 countries conditional on global and regional and country-specific shocks such

---

[9] For more details, see (Wachtel and Korhonen, 2004) among others on this issue, although fiscal policy and exchange rate policy also played a role in disinflation. South Africa is another example. In 1992, inflation was a double digit. They adopted an inflation-targeting policy in 2000. They were able to bring inflation down to 3 percent in 2020. Disinflation brought it down via tight control of the growth rate of money. A team of central bank economists from the South African Reserve Bank visited the Reserve Bank of New Zealand and explained to us that the way they targeted inflation was by squeezing money and credit growth.

10 *Introduction*

as oil price shocks, GFC, the Asian Financial Crisis (AFC), debt and banking crisis, political crisis, invasions, wars, earthquakes, draughts, and pandemics. The data, which are required to test the theories of inflation such as real GDP or unemployment (quarterly), are always published after the publication of inflation and money (monthly). Developing countries publish data at least a year later. The countries in our sample cover the Middle East and North Africa (MENA) region, Africa, Asia, the Caribbean, Europe, Australasia, and the United States. These 42 countries are chosen on the basis of *data availability* only and considering no other factor. The countries are very different in every aspect, historically, culturally, socially, politically, institutionally, and economically. We use data from the World Development Indicators of the World Bank, the Organization of Economic Constructions and Development (OECD), the International Monetary Fund (IMF), and the Federal Reserve Bank of St. Louis (FRED), and some other central banks.

We will empirically test the long-run and short-run relationship between money and prices, money growth and inflation, money growth and real output, expected inflation; the output gap and inflation using a number of parametric, for example, Dynamic OLS and Maximum Likelihood (ML) for system estimation, Vector Autoregression (VAR), Dynamic Stochastic Projections; and many non-parametric methods, and we pay attention to specifications and estimations problems, especially the specification of expected inflation.

The second main objective is to explain why the recent rise in inflation was unanticipated by central banks, especially in the developed countries, for example, the US Fed and the Reserve Bank of New Zealand among others. The Chairman of the Fed said publicly that they did not anticipate this increase in inflation. The Secretary of the US Treasury, herself a prominent economist, said publicly that *I think I was wrong then about the path that inflation would take*.

The third objective is to test the inflation policy implications of the MMT, which proposes to use fiscal policy, that is, tax policy to be specific, to reduce high inflation that follows from the theory's quite liberal printing of money to finance the budget deficit.

Finally, we provide a method to compute the *natural rate of interest* as a statistic using observable data, which could make monetary policy less uncertain and less daunting.

The Findings in Brief

Conditional on global and country-specific shocks, the quantity of broad money and the general CPI price level share a common trend in all 42 countries in our sample, and the quantity of money and the CPI have a significant one-to-one relationship. The growth rate of money and the inflation rate are highly correlated. This correlation is insignificant in developed countries during the periods of successful inflation-targeting. We pay attention to estimating the dynamics of these relationships. Furthermore, we show very strong evidence that money is neutral and in many cases super-neutral, that is, money has no significant effect on real output in the long runs. Given this evidence, we ask why central banks keep print money at high rates. We test three hypotheses. The relationships between inflation and the

Introduction 11

output gap and that between the change in inflation and the output gap are statistically unstable in the majority of countries. There is evidence that the expectation-augmented Phillips curve fit the data in a few countries. We provide evidence that the specification of expected inflation in the Philips curve explains why central banks failed to predict the recent rise in inflation. Furthermore, we explain the reasoning. Finally, we test the policy implication of the MMT to reduce inflation.

Our analysis indicates that there is one main cause of inflation and that is bad policies which propagate through the quantity of money and inflation expectations mostly and, to a lesser extent, through other variables such as the output gap. Bad luck (bad shocks), for example, global and country and regional-specific adverse supply shocks, such as oil price shocks, amplify inflation if they coincide with highly expansionary fiscal and monetary policy.[10]

One should not be surprised to learn that monetary policy in developed countries is not entirely evidenced-based. Edmund (Phelps, 2006) says that a notorious example of nonevidence-based policy is postwar macroeconomic policymaking under radical Keynesians. The radicals, he said, relied on Keynes' untested theory that unemployment depended on effective demand in relation to the money wage, but their policy ignored the past about wages and sought to stabilize demand at a high-enough level to ensure full employment. My own view is that central bankers have strong economic views, and there is a lot of *gut-feeling* stuff among policymakers.

Alan Blinder's (1997) "Distinguished Lecture on Economics in Government: What Central Bankers Could Learn from Academics – and Vice Versa" stated that while working at the Fed, he used to say that there are two basic ways to obtain quantitative information about the economy: you can study econometric evidence, or you can ask your uncle. To him, he says, the choice was easy despite all the well-known pitfalls of time series econometrics. But he said that he believes that *there is far too much uncle-asking in government circles in general and in central banking circles in particular*. Blinder put his finger on the spot.

The Organization of the Book

The book is organized as follows. The next chapter presents the inflation data. Chapter 3 lays out the QTM predictions. In Chapter 4, we examine the long-run

---

10 The policymaker's job is to interrogate the data, as they arrive, in an attempt to identify the nature and the permanency of the shocks. It would be a mistake that leads to a policy error if the policymaker fails to identify the shock (e.g., demand versus supply, permanent versus transitory, and anticipated versus unanticipated). Furthermore, the policymaker could make the wrong assumption about the specification of expectations (e.g., forward looking versus backward looking, rational versus adoptive) and as a result fail to foresee inflation. Forecast errors could translate into policy errors. These policy errors are notoriously persistent. It is costly to undo their effects (e.g., changing policy at the wrong time, acting late, or acting earlier). Forecast errors typically increase around the economy's turning points because of rising uncertainty. All nonevidence-based policies, that is, policies based on gut feelings and prejudices, are bad policies. We would anticipate more policy errors when policies are discretionary in nature.

12   *Introduction*

relationship between the CPI and the quantity of money. Then, we test the relationship between the CPI inflation rate and the growth rate of money in Chapter 5, and we focus on the deterioration of the relationship under successful inflation-targeting. In Chapter 6, we formally present the neutrality of money. We examine the long-run and the short-run effect of money on real output. Chapter 7 asks the question that why do central banks print more money if they know that money is neutral and that monetary policy cannot stimulate the economy unless it surprises people and only in the short run. We test three hypotheses – increase seigniorage revenues, finance deficit spending, and propping asset prices. Chapter 8 is reserved for the Phillips curve and the expectation-augmented Phillips curve and for all the theoretical policy-issues that arose because of the Phillips curve: Short-run and long-run Phillips curves; no long-run money illusion; the stability of the Phillips curve; the formation of inflation expectation that is a challenging specification problem; endogeneity; the measurement of the gaps; the rational expectations (RE); policy issues and the Phillips curve; the assumption of price stickiness; the micro-foundation for sticky prices, the Lucas critique; time consistency and inflation Bias; reputation; rational expectations and the rules versus discretion; the variance of demand management policy; and estimating a single-equation specification of the Phillips curve; and test the stability of the New Keynesian Phillips curve specification – change in inflation and the output gap – the Sample Generalized Variance test. Chapter 9 is the estimation of the Phillips curve. In Chapter 10, we discuss the "newer" models of inflation, which we alluded to earlier, and provide an empirical evaluation of the inflation's policy recommendation of the MMT. Chapter 11 explains how central banks reduce inflation. Economists postulate a mechanism by which the central bank sets the short-term overnight interest rate higher than the *natural rate of interest a la* (Wicksell, 1898). This natural rate of interest is unobservable, hence must be estimated econometrically. We are unsure how many central banks do rely on such estimates, however, we are sure that there are serious estimation and specification issues. We therefore, present a different, much easier, approach. Ours is based on an analytical solution of a structural micro-foundation model, which boils down to computing this New Keynesian natural rate as a statistic. This natural rate requires computing the growth rates of the consumption – leisure ratio and the capital – labor ratio. Finally, chapter 12 sums up and concludes.

2 The Price Level and the Inflation the Data at a Glance

1960–2021

Abstract

The Consumer Price Index (all items) for 42 countries has a positive trend. The inflation rate defined as the percentage change in the CPI is, on average, positive for all countries. In most of the developing countries, the average of inflation from 1960 to 2021 is a double digit and very variable. There are exceptions, however. The Latin and South American countries have relatively higher inflation on average, followed by the MENA countries and Africa. The Asian countries have remarkably relatively lower average inflation rates. Japan, Singapore, and Malaysia have very low inflation rates. The seven developed countries, which we have in our sample, Australia, Denmark, Norway, New Zealand, Sweden, the United Kingdom and the United States, have successfully targeted low and stable inflation rates around 2–2.5 percent since the early 1990s. Totally unanticipated by policymakers, inflation has increased in 2021, and it has been rising ever since, more so in the developed inflation-targeting countries. As a result of inflation-targeting, the price level keeps rising, has a stochastic trend, and is indeterminate.

Figure 2.1 plots the CPI for all the countries. The base year of the CPI is 2015, hence the data intersection at this point. Egypt and Ghana have the highest CPI level followed by Turkey, Uruguay, Haiti, Nepal, Pakistan, India, and none of the developed inflation-targeting countries are close. Japan has the lowest level of CPI. In the low cluster, you find the United States, Korea, Sweden, Norway, Gabon, Costa Rica, and so on.

Annual inflation rate in this book is measured as $\Delta lnP_t \times 100$, and P_t is all-items CPI. The annual data are from 1960 to 2020, but some countries' data are up to 2021. The data are taken from the World Bank World Development Indicators, which are originally taken from the IMF data. The developed countries have quarterly up-to-date data on the websites of the central banks.

Figure 2.2 plots the inflation rate for the MENA country group in the sample and an arbitrary 5 percent level reference point. We will include this 5 percent in all graphs as a reference point. The vertical axis says it all. Inflation is quite high and variable historically. With the exception of Algeria and Turkey, which were able to reduce inflation in recent years, all five countries have histories of high inflation. For Algeria, the mean is 8.02 percent. It was as high as 27.5 percent in

DOI: 10.4324/9781003382218-2

14 *The Price Level and the Inflation the Data at a Glance*

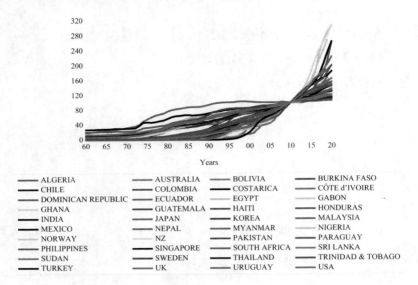

Figure 2.1 Consumer Price Index (2015 = 100)
Data Source: World Development Indicators

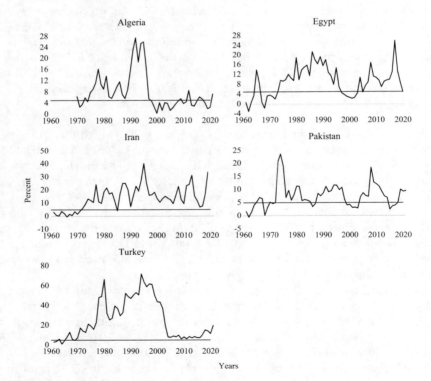

Figure 2.2 Inflation in the MENA Group Is High at All Times
Data Source: World Development Indicators

The Price Level and the Inflation the Data at a Glance 15

1992, albeit the central bank managed to bring it down below 5 percent by 2020. In 2021, inflation was 7.2 percent and rising. In Egypt, the mean is 9.2 percent. It was always high, and it reached 25.85 percent in 2017 before it came down to 5 percent in 2020. Iran's inflation history is high. The mean is 14.01 percent. The maximum was 40 percent. However, it was negative early in the 1960s before it started to shoot up in the early 1970s. Pakistan's inflation average is 7.65 percent; however, it was as high as 23.6 percent in 1974. In 2020, inflation was 9.5 percent. Finally, Turkey is a good example of a very high and variable inflation. The mean is 25.66 percent. Inflation was 71.8 percent in 1994. In 2010, it reached 19.6 percent. Inflation targeting was implemented later. However, inflation is still in double digits. Note also that there is a visually apparent trend in inflation.

Figure 2.3 plots the inflation rate for the Latin and South American countries in the sample, and Table 2.1 reports some descriptive statistics. Latin and South American countries have experienced massive random supply shocks such as wars, military copes, foreign invasions and interventions, political and banking and financial crises, and debt crises. These shocks left some significant effects on inflation. The inflation rates have been extremely high. There is a spike in Bolivia's inflation, which dominates the graph. Inflation exceeded 450 percent. Its inflation average is 25.7 percent, which is quite an achievement. It has been less than 3 percent since 2017. In 2021, the inflation rate was less than 1 percent, which is astonishing.

Chile's inflation rate was as high as 180 percent in 1974, but Chile became an inflation-targeting country and managed to stabilize inflation. The inflation rate is highly volatile in Chile. From 1999 to 2021, inflation fluctuated below 5 percent, except during the GFC in 2008, where it climbed to 8.3 percent then fell to less than ½ a percent in 2009 probably because of the recession. In 2021, it rose to 4.5 percent. Their inflation-targeting does not seem to deliver a stable inflation.

Colombia also managed to target a lower inflation rate over the past few years. It began a single digit inflation rate in 2000, relatively high but significantly declining year-on-year. The average over the period 2000 to 2021 is 4.7 percent.

Costa Rica has lower average inflation than the aforementioned countries and managed to bring inflation down to less than 2 percent in 2015. In 2021, inflation increased to 1.7 percent, which is relatively low. The Dominican Republic has a relatively lower and stable inflation on average. It has been kept below 5 percent since 2012. However, in 2021, inflation rose to 8.2 percent. Ecuador is similar to the rest of the countries; it has a high average inflation. It brought inflation down from a double digit in 2002. The inflation rate remained in the single digit ever since. Inflation shot up to 8 percent in 2008, during the GFC. It was kept below 5 percent from 2010 to 2021. Despite Guatemala's political crisis, its average inflation is significantly lower than all other countries, which is a little puzzling. It has been a single digit inflation rate since 1997. It was 10.75 percent during the GFC in 2008, fell below 2 percent in 2009, and below 5 percent since then. Honduras' inflation is similar to Guatemala's on average. The inflation rate has been a single digit since 2001, increased to 10.8 percent in 2008, and has been below 5 percent since 2015. Mexico has a history of debt and banking crisis. The 1980s were turbulent.

16 *The Price Level and the Inflation the Data at a Glance*

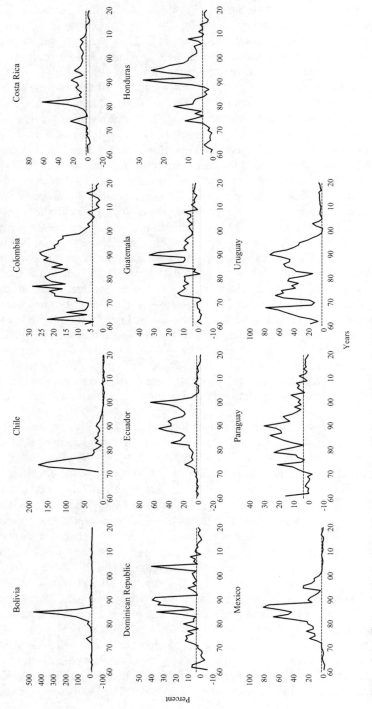

Figure 2.3 Inflation in the Latin and South American Countries Is Historically High

Data Source: World Development Indicators

Table 2.1 Descriptive Statistics: Inflation in Latin and South American Countries, 1960–2021

Country	Mean	Max	Min.	Std. Dev.	Obs.
Bolivia	25.77	477.5	−0.70	71.50	61
Chile	23.03	179.9	0.35	40.26	51
Colombia	12.89	29.3	1.99	8.14	61
Costa Rica	10.28	64.2	−0.66	10.24	61
Dominican Republic	9.49	41.5	−3.97	10.69	61
Ecuador	15.18	67.3	−0.34	15.66	61
Guatemala	7.33	34.5	−0.80	7.01	61
Honduras	7.67	29.2	1.08	6.08	60
Mexico	15.39	84.0	0.59	19.21	61
Paraguay	9.710	31.6	−0.86	7.71	61
Uruguay	29.47	81.2	4.26	22.49	61

Some countries' data are from 1960 to 2020, and some have missing data.

Inflation was as high as 85 percent in 1987. In 2000, inflation stabilized at a single digit and did not even increase during the GFC. Mexico's inflation rate fluctuated between approximately 2.5 and 5.5 percent since 2002. Paraguay has a single-digit average over the sample. Inflation has been below 5 percent since 2012. However, Uruguay's inflation average is nearly 30 percent. Its inflation rate, although in the single digit since 2004, remained relatively high. Here, too, trend inflation is apparent in many countries.

Figure 2.4 plots the inflation rate for the African countries in the sample. Table 2.2 provides descriptive statistics. Except for Côte d'Ivoire, Gabon, and South Africa, average inflation rates are high and similar to Latin and South America. The lowest rate is in Burkina Faso. The high rates are double digit and extremely high. Variability is high too. These are, by all means, very high tax rates. Similar to the MENA countries and the Latin and South American, inflation rates in Africa have trends.

Figure 2.5 plots the Asian data. Table 2.3 reports the descriptive statistics.

Although the inflation rates are high, they are relatively lower on average than the inflation rate in the MENA countries, Latin and South America, and Africa. Myanmar, a very unstable country, has an average inflation lower than many countries. Japan had low inflation rates historically. Japan experienced deflationary periods, and Singapore, of course, is exceptional. Malaysia's average inflation rate is also as low as Japan and Singapore.

Figure 2.6 and Table 2.4 report the two Caribbean countries' inflation data.

These figures are not significantly different from the inflation rates in the rest of the developing countries. Certainly, a few countries in the aforementioned sample of 35 countries managed to keep a very low inflation average; Japan is an industrial G7 country; Singapore and Malaysia are among the emerging countries. In Africa, only Burkina Faso has an average inflation of less than 4 percent.

This brings us to the last block of countries, the inflation-targeting, which are Australia, Denmark, Norway, New Zealand, Sweden, the United Kingdom, and

18   *The Price Level and the Inflation the Data at a Glance*

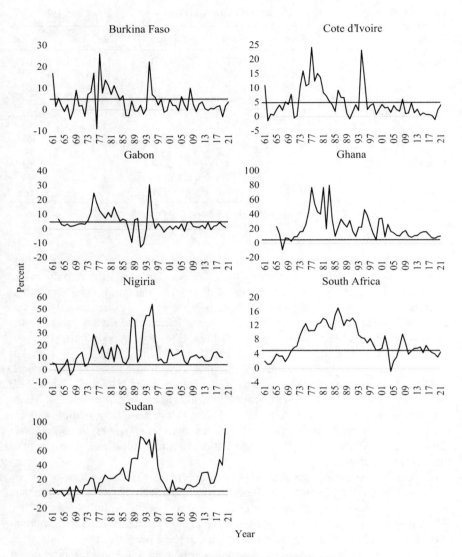

Figure 2.4 Africa Too Has a Very High Rate of Inflation, 1960–2020
Data Source: World Development Indicators

United States. These countries stabilized consumer price inflation successfully although their money printing continued to increase as we have shown earlier. In late 1980s, New Zealand adopted a legally binding monetary policy regime for price stability, which involved an explicit inflation target. Many countries did the same, for example, Canada (1991), the United Kingdom (1992), Australia (1993), Sweden (1993), Norway (2001), the EU (1999), and many other countries around

Table 2.2 Descriptive Statistics: Inflation in Africa, 1960–2021

Country	Mean	Max	Min.	Std. Dev.	Obs.
Burkina Faso	3.88	26.22	−8.77	6.22	61
Côte d'Ivoire	5.02	24.23	−1.35	5.47	61
Gabon	4.46	30.83	−12.43	6.95	58
Ghana	22.10	80.14	−8.79	18.18	57
Nigeria	14.08	54.71	−3.79	12.05	59
South Africa	7.49	17.10	−0.69	4.26	61
Sudan	25.00	91.75	−10.57	23.38	60

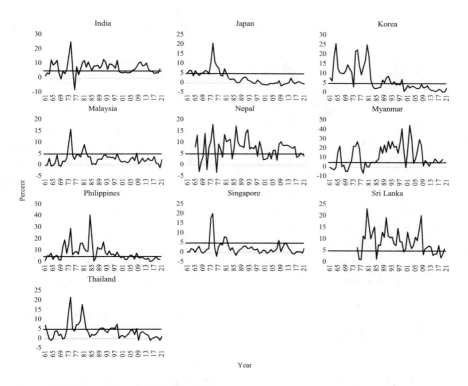

Figure 2.5 Asian Countries' Inflation Rates
Data Source: World Development Indicators

the world. The Federal Reserve Bank adopted an explicit 2 percent inflation target late in 2012. The targets vary across countries. Some countries used a fixed target, and others, for example, New Zealand, used a range of an upper and lower level inflation. The target was 0 to 2 percent in 1990, changed to 0 to 3 percent in 1996, then to 1 to 3 percent in 2002. Central banks also have different time horizons when targeting inflation. Some target inflation over the business cycle, whatever that meant, is unclear. Others such as the United States targets inflation in the long

20   *The Price Level and the Inflation the Data at a Glance*

Table 2.3 Descriptive Statistics: Inflation in Asia, 1960–2021

Country	Mean	Max	Min.	Std. Dev.	Obs.
India	7.15	25.15	−7.94	4.52	60
Japan	2.80	20.87	−1.34	3.84	61
Korea	7.19	25.82	0.38	6.48	61
Malaysia	2.87	15.98	−1.14	2.72	61
Nepal	7.44	18.07	−3.16	4.49	57
Myanmar	11.8	45.15	−6.23	11.8	59
Philippines	7.94	40.77	0.67	7.03	60
Singapore	2.37	20.18	−1.86	3.66	61
Sri Lanka	8.96	23.22	1.21	5.05	46
Thailand	3.95	21.76	−0.90	4.22	61

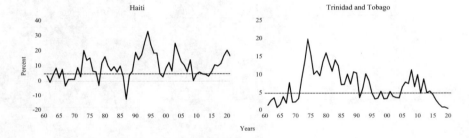

Figure 2.6 The Caribbean Countries' Inflation Rates
Data Source: World Development Indicators

Table 2.4 Descriptive Statistics for the Caribbean Inflation, 1960–2021

Country	Mean	Max	Min.	Std. Dev.	Obs.
Haiti	9.66	33.16	−12.16	8.06	61
Trinidad and Tobago	6.89	19.90	0.59	4.43	60

run, also unclear what they meant. Still others suggest maintaining the target over the medium term. None of these are rules by any means. Figure 2.7 plots the data and Table 2.5 reports the descriptive statistics. The shaded areas are the periods of inflation-targeting.

The developed inflation-targeting countries successfully targeted a low and stable inflation rate from about 1992 onward. Their inflation rates are significantly lower than all the rest of the 42 countries in the sample, except for Japan, Singapore, and Malaysia. The United States began an explicit inflation-targeting of 2 percent in 2012; yet its average inflation is lower than all other inflation-targeting countries. In 2021, Australia's inflation was 2.9 percent, which is above the target; Denmark's inflation was 1.9 percent, which is an increase closer to the target;

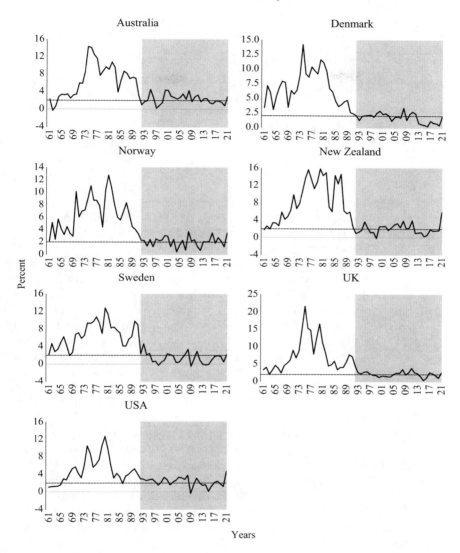

Figure 2.7 Conquering Inflation by Explicit Targeting*

*The United States started an explicit inflation-targeting in 2012 although the Fed was implicitly targeting lower inflation rate.

Data Source: World Development Indicators

Norway's is 3.5 percent, which is a breach of the target; New Zealand's inflation reached 5.9 percent, a significant jump above the target and it is climbing; Sweden's is 2.2 percent, with the United Kingdom's 2.5 percent and the United States' 4.7 percent. These numbers have been rising through the first and the second quarters of 2022, and expectations look at much higher rates.

22　The Price Level and the Inflation the Data at a Glance

Table 2.5 Descriptive Statistics: Developed Inflation-Targeting Countries, 1960–2021

Country	Mean	Max	Min.	Std. Dev.	Obs.
Australia	4.50	14.34	−0.32	3.55	61
Denmark	4.29	14.214	0.25	3.35	61
Norway	4.32	12.79	0.45	3.03	61
New Zealand	5.25	15.83	−0.11	4.68	61
Sweden	4.11	12.843	−0.49	3.49	61
UK	4.89	21.673	0.36	4.42	61
USA	3.63	12.703	−0.35	2.60	61

Figure 2.8 plots the harmonized CPI inflation rate for the EU. Inflation was kept around 3 percent for a long time, but it has increased significantly in 2020. In 2022, the European Central Bank data reported 8.2 percent in 2022.

To sum up, the averages of the inflation rates from 1960 to 2021 (to 2020 for some countries) are plotted in Figure 2.9. With the exception of Burkina Faso and Gabon, all developing countries have a high average inflation. The Latin and South American countries have relatively high inflation, about 15 percent on average. The developed countries have low average inflation. The MENA and African countries have high inflation on average, lower than Latin and South America and higher than Asia. The Asian group's average inflation is about 6.3 percent because Japan, Malaysia, and Singapore have had very low inflation rates historically. The developed countries have the least inflation.

The log-difference is a filter; it removes stochastic trends from the data. The log-difference of the CPI, that is, inflation, however, has a visually visible trend in *some* countries. There is a huge literature on the econometrics of trend inflation, which lies outside the scope of this book, but one must examine and proceed with caution. We will examine this issue later before we test any theory about inflation.

There could be different interpretations or explanations for trend inflation. Why log-differenced data have trend? One possibility is that inflation might be a fractionally integrated time series with $d > 0.5$, that is, nonstationary.[1] All commonly used tests for unit root, such as the (Dickey and Fuller, 1979), the Augmented Dickey–Fuller test (Said and Dickey, 1984), the (Phillips and Perron, 1988) test, the GLS – ADF (Elliot *et al.*, 1996), the (Ng and Perron, 2001) test, and (Kwiatkowski *et al.*, 1992), the KPSS test, are weak against stationary alternatives. There is a huge econometrics literature on this issue, which is beyond the

---

1　(Baillie *et al.*, 1996) study fractional integration of inflation. Shimotsu and Phillips (2005, 2006) provide estimation's methods for fractional integration. An ARIMA (p,d,q) process with d > 0.5 means inflation is a nonstationary *long-memory process*, but not necessarily a unit root process. Thus, rendering it stationary requires less than first-differencing the data. Atsushi Inoue wrote many papers on these issues; (Diebold and Inoue, 2001), for example, provide evidence that structural breaks in time series could be confused with fractional integration. Razzak (1994) tests the New Zealand's inflation data and finds evidence for fractional integration with d>0.5 for the period before 1994.

The Price Level and the Inflation the Data at a Glance 23

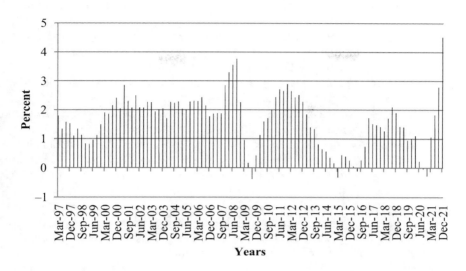

Figure 2.8 The EU Inflation-Targeting Success
Data Source: International Financial Statistics – IMF inflation is $\Delta ln P_t \times 100$ and P_t is the CPI

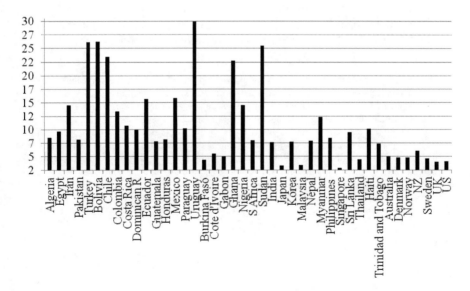

Figure 2.9 Average Inflation Rate, 1960–2021

24   *The Price Level and the Inflation the Data at a Glance*

scope of this book. A weak test is one that fails to reject the null hypothesis of unit root more often.

The other concern is that these tests might have difficulty distinguishing a root of 1 from 0.98; see Rudebusch (1993), Cochrane (1991), Christiano and Eichenbaum (1990), and Stock (1991), among many others, for example.[2]

We will test the inflation data for unit root with a break later in the book. Breaks in the data might confuse the linear unit root tests, which are linear OLS regressions. Such regressions confuse the breaks with unit root. Quite possible, isn't it? Nonlinear unit root test might be useful.

There is perhaps another interpretation, however. Such a trend in inflation may suggest that the CPI is an I(2) time series, that is, *integrated of order 2*, not an I(1), that is, *integrated of order 1*, to begin with. Differencing the log of the CPI *twice* produces an I(0) inflation rate. The economic interpretation of an I(2) process means that shocks that affected the price level in the *distant past* have more effects *now* than the *more recent* shocks that hit the CPI. Older shocks have more effects today than newer shocks! This sounds strange, but there is no other economic interpretation to an I(2) process. What old shocks might those be? For example, the first oil price shock in 1973, the second oil price shock in 1979, the Asian Financial Crisis in 1997, and the GFC in 2007 have more impact on the CPI *today* than, for example, the *recent* shock to oil prices.

We plot more up-to-date *quarterly* data for inflation in the developed inflation-targeting countries in Figure 2.10 plotting New Zealand. For New Zealand, the inflation target was 0 to 2 percent up until 1996. The target has been 0 to 3 percent from 1996 to the end of sample. There is a clear jump in inflation in the late quarters in 2021 and 2022, which we will analyze more in this book.

---

2   One must be careful labelling these tests "weak" when these unit root tests reject the null hypothesis of unit root because the weakness of these tests is an irrelevant argument in case of rejection. A test statistic is said to be weak only if it fails to reject the null very often, not when it rejects it. Therefore, one could argue that rejection of the unit root in this case renders the weak test argument irrelevant. Razzak (2007) gives the following example. Think about the null hypothesis: the windshield of your car is unbreakable. Say that you have two tests: one is powerful, where you hit the windshield with a sledgehammer; and the other is weak, whereby you hit the windshield with a plastic or a rubber hammer. Say that you hit the windshield with the weak plastic/rubber hammer and you break the windshield. Therefore, you reject the null hypothesis that your car's windshield is unbreakable. Does it matter for the result whether you used a plastic hammer, a mallet, or sledgehammer? The answer is definitely no. Thus, the power of the test is not an issue when the test rejects the null. It is only an issue when null cannot be rejected more often.

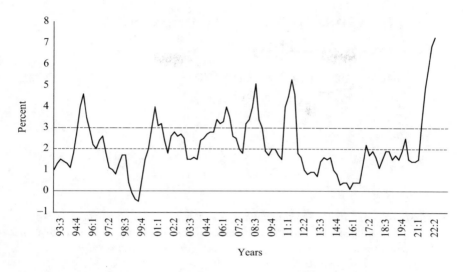

Figure 2.10 New Zealand CPI Quarterly Inflation Rate, March 1988 to June 2022

3 The Quantity Theory of Money, Prices, and Output

The Equation of Exchange – the Quantity Theory of Money

Abstract

The first obvious starting point to explain prices and the change in prices is to examine the quantity of money. Money has been known to be the main explanatory variable of prices since the sixteenth century. Therefore, we begin our investigation of inflation from the Equation of Exchange – the Quantity Theory of Money.

The twentieth century's theory of money and prices was formulated by (Fisher, 1911). However, it might have been recognized and studied a long time ago. The Polish mathematician Nicolaus Copernicus (1517) formulated the idea (see Lowry [1996]). The British philosophers John Locke and David Hume, and the French Jean Bodin, restated the theory in the eighteenth century, which was developed in (Newcomb, 1885).

The price level is a key variable in economic theory. In the simplest form, at the microeconomic level, the demand and supply of any good are functions of the price and the quantity of the goods. Money has been the medium of exchange for a long time. It is used primarily to pay for the purchases of goods and assets. Fiat money is the money produced by the central banks. It consists of narrow money including cash, that is, the monetary base (high-powered money), which is the liability of the central bank. Central banks must know exactly the quantity of their liability. Money also includes broad aggregates, which include demand deposits and savings accounts. The OECD defines broad money as currency, deposits with an agreed maturity of up to 2 years, deposits redeemable at notice of up to 3 months, repurchase agreements, money market fund shares/units, and debt securities up to 2 years.

Henderson (2021) placed Milton Friedman's famous statement, "Inflation is always and everywhere a monetary phenomenon," in a speech he gave in India in 1964. The famous quote implies that inflation can be produced *only* by a more rapid increase in the quantity of money. The theory that makes the cornerstone of the Monetarist view is the Quantity Theory of Money (sixteenth to seventeenth centuries) as we mentioned earlier.

To think about the relationship between money, prices, and output, we begin with the Quantity Theory of Money – QTM. It states that the general price level of goods and services is proportional to the amount of money in circulation. There are some important issues regarding this theory. It is primarily about the effect of

DOI: 10.4324/9781003382218-3

The Quantity Theory of Money, Prices, and Output 27

money on the economy in the long run. It assumes that people (i.e., households, firms, and the government) want to hold money in order to pay for the purchases of goods and services and assets. The word "quantity" literally refers to the number of units of currency be it dollars or any other currency exchanged in the economy.

Fisher (1911) explains the Equation of Exchange, which states that every transaction requires a buyer and a seller. Therefore, for the aggregate economy, the value of sales must be equal to the value of receipts. The value of sales must equal the number of transactions conducted in a period of time multiplied by the average price. The value of purchase, on the other hand, must be equal to the amount of money in circulation in that economy multiplied by the average number of times it changes hands during the same period. The equation is an *identity*, given by:

$$MV = PT \tag{3.1}$$

where M is the *quantity of money*; V is the *velocity of money* or the transaction velocity of money, which measures the rate at which money circulates in the economy. P is the average price level, and T is the total number of transactions (volume), which could be taken as given. It is assumed that at the long-run equilibrium of any economy – at full-employment levels of income, there is a fixed ratio of the volume of transaction to the level of output. Fisher also treated velocity to be independent of the other variables in the equation and thought it is a *constant*, which might vary over a time, but it returns to a constant equilibrium value in a short period. Furthermore, if both T and V are assumed to be constants, e.g., $\overline{T}$ and $\overline{V}$, then if the demand for money is equal to the supply of money, the equilibrium price level is determined by the quantity of money, which is assumed to be exogenous and constant.

Replacing T by real output Y, and because real output is determined by factor inputs in the production process, and velocity is constant, therefore, when the central bank changes the quantity of money, the price level must change by the same amount to keep the identity unchanged. All these assumptions and predictions are testable, which have been tested over and over in the past 100 years.

We could write the QTM identity as a stochastic equation in a log form as:

$$ln(P_t) = ln(V) + ln\left(\frac{M}{Y}\right)_t + \varepsilon_t \tag{3.2}$$

The implications of the QTM is that a one-unit increase in the money per unit of income (output) increases the general price level by one unit. Therefore, if the government keeps printing money, presumably to spend, the price level keeps going up one to one.

A more testable stochastic form is:

$$\ln\left(P_t\right) = \alpha_0 + \alpha_1 ln\left(\frac{M}{Y}\right)_t + \varepsilon_t \tag{3.3}$$

28   *The Quantity Theory of Money, Prices, and Output*

Such that α_0 is a constant equal to $ln(V)$ and could be positive, negative, or zero. We test $H_0 : \alpha_1 = 1$. If α_1 is 1, then broad money per unit of real output affects prices 1:1 in the long run.

Next, we test the theory, first, by testing the relationship between the levels of the CPI and the level of broad money per unit of real output for each of the 42 countries in our sample. These countries are grouped by regions, the MENA, Latin and South America, Africa, Asia, the Caribbean, and the last group is a number of developed and mainly OECD inflation-targeting countries, which includes Australia, Denmark, Norway, New Zealand, Sweden, the United Kingdom, and United States. The United States has just more recently become an explicit inflation-targeting country. The rest had begun inflation targeting for much longer. Then, we test the relationship between the inflation rate and the growth rate of broad money per unit of real output.

4 Testing the Relationship Between Money and Prices

Abstract

We test the correlation between the quantity of broad money and the CPI in levels in our sample of 42 countries from 1960 to 2020. There is a positive trend in both variables in all countries. The relationship is significantly tighter in some countries than others; however, a number of commonly used (weak) unit root tests with different specifications do not reject the unit root. Dynamic OLS regressions for every country show that the relationship between money and the CPI, however, is not exactly one-to-one in all 42 countries; it is very close to that in many cases.

We estimate the QTM, Eq. (3.3), using the data of the 42 countries in our sample over the period 1960 to 2020, because the *annual* data for real output reported in the World Development Indicators are available from 1960 to 2020 only. Broad money is taken from the International Financial Statistics (IMF) and defined as the sum of currency outside the banks, demand deposits other than those of the central government, the time, savings, and foreign currency deposits of resident sectors other than the central government, bank and traveller's checks, and other securities such as certificates of deposit and commercial papers.

The majority of governments and central banks have been printing money at high rates, more so recently after COVID-19. Figure 4.1 plots broad money per unit of real output (percent) for the 42 countries representing all continents from 1960 to 2020 (World Development Indicators) to show that the amount of broad money per unit of real output (GDP) has a positive significant trend, sometimes explosive.[1] Bolivia, Japan, and Sudan are excluded from this graph because they have very high money–output ratios that are above the scale of magnitudes of the other countries. The highest in 2020 in the bunch of jumbled time series are Honduras, Thailand, Pakistan, Turkey, Korea, Nepal, the UK, Singapore, Malaysia, and so on, and the lowest is Côte d'Ivoire and Gabon. Figure 4.2 includes Bolivia and Japan, but not Sudan because its ratio is explosive. Figure 4.3 includes Sudan.

---

1 The Dickey–Fuller test statistic in (Dickey and Fuller, 1979) tabulated for explosive roots in addition to unit root. A value of $\rho > 0$ indicates an explosive root assuming that we have the correct lag-specification of the regression equation.

DOI: 10.4324/9781003382218-4

30 *Testing the Relationship Between Money and Prices*

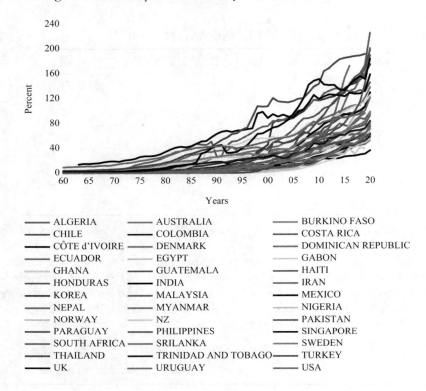

Figure 4.1 Broad Money – Real GDP Ratio (Percent)

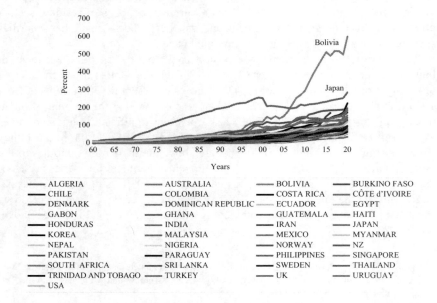

Figure 4.2 Broad Money – Real GDP Ratio (Percent) – Including Bolivia and Japan

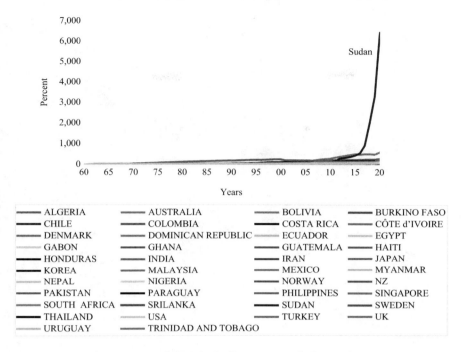

Figure 4.3 Broad Money – Real GDP Ratio (Percent) – Including Sudan
Data Source: World Development Indicators

Figure 4.4, which we printed earlier, plots the CPI for these countries. The trend is positive. A country-by-country 45° scatter plot of the log-level of broad money per unit of real output and the log of CPI shows that there is a very strong positive association between these two variables in all countries. There is a trend in the data, which masks the true underlying relationship. This trend has to be examined and accounted for. Identifying the nature of trend and accounting for it is not straightforward. Figures 4.5 to 4.10 are scatter plots of the log (the natural log) of the data.

For robustness, our strategy in this book is to test for the nature of trend using a number of commonly used tests such as the (Dickey and Fuller, 1979), the Augmented Dickey–Fuller test (Said and Dickey, 1984), the (Phillips and Perron, 1988) test, the GLS–ADF (Elliot *et al.*, 1996), the (Ng and Perron, 2001) test, and (Kwiatkowski *et al.*, 1992), the KPSS test. There are more tests for unit root, but we doubt it very much if the results would change significantly. However, the most concerning issue, which we do not address here, is whether the true Data Generating Process (DGP) of either the CPI or money is *nonlinear*, thus a nonlinear unit root test is required. We say that because the unit root tests given before fit a linear line through the data; they would confuse breaks in the data, if any, with nonlinearity. Nonetheless, nonlinear unit root is a probability (e.g., see Kapetanios *et al.* [2003]).

32 Testing the Relationship Between Money and Prices

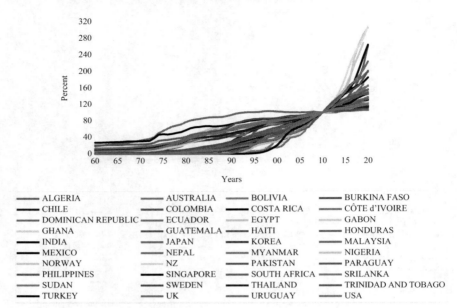

Figure 4.4 Consumer Price Index (2015 = 100)

A second important issue is to test for unit root conditional on a deterministic trend especially for the quantity of money, not the CPI, because its trend may be deterministically determined by the monetary authority in each country.

For more robustness, in each of the aforementioned tests, we use a number of specifications. We use regressions without an intercept and linear trend, with an intercept only, and with an intercept and linear trend. In each test and each specification, we use a number of Information Criteria to determine the number of lag differences in the regressions. Remember that those different specifications have different distributions. We do not report the results of all these tests and specifications because the output is very large and takes a lot of space; however, the results of the various regressions across all different tests are not different in any significant way. They all indicate that the trend in the data is stochastic, that is, the time series data have unit root. Cautiously, the reason is perhaps that these tests are weak, that is, have low power. A weak test fails to reject the null hypothesis of a unit root more often. I cited at least one paper earlier, but there is a huge econometrics literature on the statistical power of these unit root tests, which is beyond the scope of this book; nevertheless, it is important to be aware of it. These tests may vary a little by power, but they are all essentially low power – commonly used tests.[2]

---

2 We cannot compare the power of these unit root tests with the power of the KPSS because the KPSS test's null hypothesis is "no unit root" or I(0) while the other tests null is I(1); hence power comparison is not inapplicable.

Testing the Relationship Between Money and Prices 33

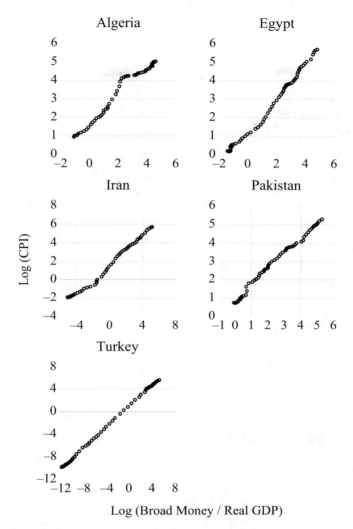

Figure 4.5 45° Scatter Plots of Log (CPI) and Log (Broad Money − Real GDP Ratio): MENA Countries

Data Source: World Development Indicators

Tables 4.1 to 4.6 report the ADF test statistics for the MENA countries, Latin and South America, Africa, Asia, the Caribbean, and the developed inflation-targeting countries. Remember that these are Ordinary Least Squares estimators (OLS). The results as we said earlier fail to reject the null hypothesis that the log of the CPI and the log of broad money per unit of real output have unit roots.

34 Testing the Relationship Between Money and Prices

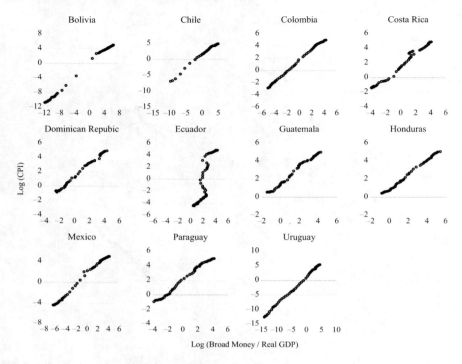

Figure 4.6 45° Scatter Plots of Log (CPI) and Log (Broad Money – Real GDP Ratio): Latin and South America

Data Source: World Development Indicators

The ADF results suggest that we cannot reject the unit root in the CPI and broad money per unit of real output in all cases, except for the CPI in Pakistan, which is not a unit root process. In a regression specification with an intercept only, and in a specification without an intercept and trend, the unit root hypothesis could not be rejected. The *P*-values of the ADF tests are 0.9380 and 0.9892, respectively. For Iran, the ADF test's *P*-value for the CPI specification with an intercept only is 0.9998. It is 0.4624 without an intercept and a trend, which indicates nonrejections of the null hypothesis of unit root. All these time series exhibit a trend, which is probably stochastic, that is, unit root, albeit we caution the reader again that these tests are weak and tend not to reject the null hypothesis of unit root most often. We fit a linear trend in the regressions in order to condition on it, and it was found to be significant in all regressions.

We could not reject the null hypothesis of unit root. The same caveats regarding the power of the tests that we discussed earlier remain. The null hypothesis of unit root could not be rejected by all other tests that we used and not reported.

We tested the EU (15) countries too – Austria, Belgium, Denmark, Finland, France, Germany, Greece, Ireland, Italy, Luxembourg, Netherlands, Portugal, Spain, Sweden, and the United Kingdom – even though the sample is relatively short. Again, just like every other country in the data set, the log of the CPI and log broad money

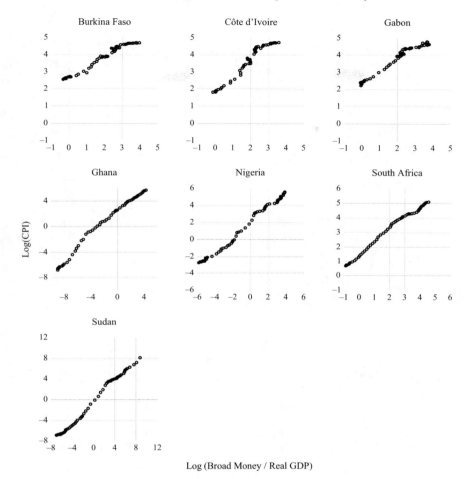

Figure 4.7 45° Scatter Plots of Log (CPI) and Log (Broad Money – Real GDP Ratio): African Countries

Data Source: World Development Indicators

per unit of real output probably has a unit root. This result suggests that testing the QTM in log-levels has to account for these unit roots. There are options for the choice of the estimator to estimate and test the QTM, but they depend on whether these two variables are cointegrated, that is, share a common long run trend, or not. If they are, an OLS estimator suffices. However, we choose the Dynamic OLS estimator, which we describe in Appendix 4.1, because it accounts for endogeneity and serial correlation in the residuals, and it is highly efficient if not the most efficient estimator.

Tables 4.7 to 4.12, where the results are reported, have two regression results, OLS and DOLS (Dynamic OLS). Under OLS, the first column lists the countries, followed by the sample size in the second column, the estimated intercept α_0 is in the third, the estimated slope α_1 is in column four, then R^2 (the measure of the

36 Testing the Relationship Between Money and Prices

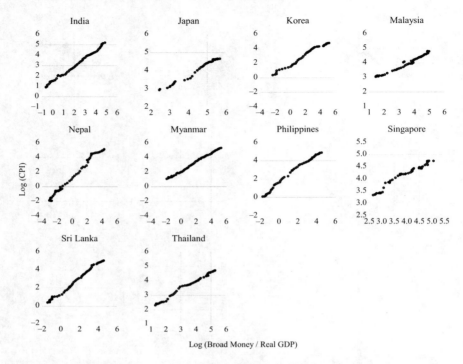

Figure 4.8 45° Scatter Plots of Log (CPI) and Log (Broad Money – Real GDP Ratio): Asian Countries

Data Source: World Development Indicators

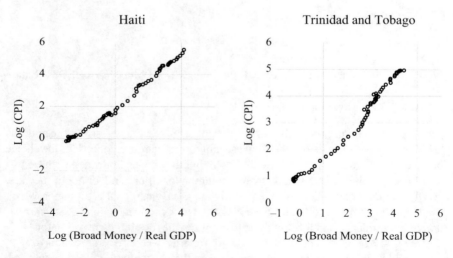

Figure 4.9 45° Scatter Plots of Log (CPI) and Log (Broad Money – Real GDP Ratio): The Caribbean Countries

Data Source: World Development Indicators

Testing the Relationship Between Money and Prices 37

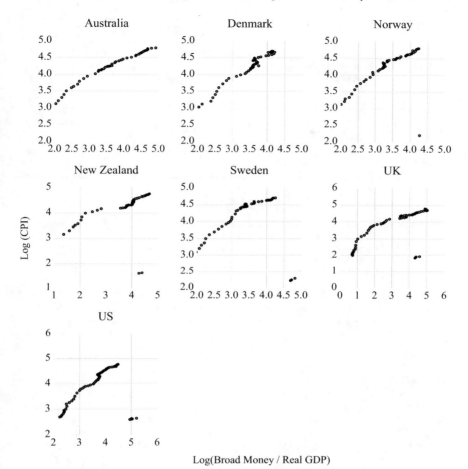

Figure 4.10 45° Scatter Plots of Log (CPI) and Log (Broad Money − Real GDP Ratio): The Inflation-Targeting Countries

Data Source: World Development Indicators

Table 4.1 Trend of the CPI and the Money–Output Ratio Is Stochastic in MENA Countries: OLS − $\Delta \ln(y_t) = \alpha + \beta\, trend + \rho \ln(y_{t-1}) + \sum_{i=1}^{k} \delta_i \Delta \ln(y_{t-i}) + e_t$

	CPI			Broad Money–Real GDP		
	Sample	τ_ρ	k	Sample	τ_ρ	k
Algeria	1971–2020	−1.74 (0.7190)	1	1965–2020	−0.14 (0.9928)	0
Egypt	1971–2020	−2.70 (0.2390)	10	1962–2020	−2.18 (0.4895)	1
Iran*	1963–2019	−3.24 (0.0860)	2	1968–2016 i	−4.60 (0.0994)	7

38 *Testing the Relationship Between Money and Prices*

	CPI			Broad Money–Real GDP		
	Sample	τ_ρ	*k*	*Sample*	τ_ρ	*k*
-	-	-	-	1968–2016 (ii)	−5.08 (0.0648)	7
-	-	-	-	1968–2020 (iii)	−4.08 (0.4668)	5
Pakistan	1962–2020	−4.10 (0.0105)	1	1964–2020	−2.33 (0.4071)	3
Turkey	1962–2020	−2.19 (0.4835)	1	1964–2020	−2.61 (0.2755)	3

- τ_ρ is the ADF statistics. $H_0 : I(1)$
- MacKinnon (1996) one-sided *P*-values are in parentheses.
- Lags are automatically determined by the AIC.
- *Iran's broad money – real GDP ratio has two missing values in 1984 and 1985, and the sample is up to 2016 only. We used the ADF test with (1) breakpoint-intercept only with innovation and additive outliers; (2) breakpoint-intercept and trend with innovation outlier, and (3) breakpoint-intercept and trend with additive outlier.

Table 4.2 Trend of the CPI and the Money–Output Ratio Is Stochastic in Latin and South America: $\text{OLS} - \Delta \ln(y_t) = \alpha + \beta \, trend + \rho \ln(y_{t-1}) + \sum_{i=1}^{k} \delta_i \Delta \ln(y_{t-i}) + e_t$

	CPI			Broad Money – Real GDP Ratio		
	Sample	τ_ρ	*k*	*Sample*	τ_ρ	*k*
Bolivia	1962–2020	−1.91 (0.6340)	1	1962–2020	−1.74 (0.7183)	1
Chile	1977–2020	−2.82 (0.1963)	6	1963–2020	−1.25 (0.8907)	1
Colombia	1963–2020	−0.78 (0.9606)	2	1962–2020	−1.01 (0.9337)	1
Costa Rica	1963–2020	−0.89 (0.9495)	2	1961–2020	−1.11 (0.9185)	0
Dominican Republic	1962–2020	−1.50 (0.8160)	1	1963–2020	−1.86 (0.6577)	2
Ecuador	1962–2020	−1.66 (0.7559)	1	1962–2020	−2.41 (0.3683)	1
Guatemala	1966–2020	−2.14 (0.5093)	5	1961–2020	−1.76 (0.7107)	0
Honduras	1964–2020	−2.22 (0.4678)	3	1962–2020	−2.06 (0.5537)	1
Mexico	1968–2020	−1.82 (0.6802)	7	1965–2020	−2.48 (0.3355)	4
Paraguay	1966–2020	−2.59 (0.2828)	5	1963–2020	−2.27 (0.4409)	2
Uruguay	1969–2020	−0.59 (0.9756)	8	1965–2020	−1.53 (0.8078)	4

- τ_ρ is the ADF statistics. $H_0 : I(1)$.
- MacKinnon (1996) one-sided *P*-values are in parentheses.
- Lags are automatically determined by the AIC.

Testing the Relationship Between Money and Prices 39

Table 4.3 Trend of the CPI and the Money–Output Ratio Is Stochastic in the African Countries: OLS – $\Delta \ln(y_t) = \alpha + \beta\, trend + \rho \ln(y_{t-1}) + \sum_{i=1}^{k} \delta_i \Delta \ln(y_{t-i}) + e_t$

	CPI			*Broad Money – Real GDP Ratio*		
	Sample	τ_ρ	*k*	*Sample*	τ_ρ	*k*
Burkina Faso	1961–2020	−0.59 (0.9759)	0	1963–2020	−1.51 (0.8139)	0
Côte d'Ivoire	1962–2020	−0.50 (0.9805)	1	1963–2020	−1.90 (0.6377)	0
Gabon	1965–2020	−0.98 (0.9373)	2	1963–2020	−1.91 (0.6322)	2
Ghana	1965–2020	−1.72 (0.4156)	0	1970–2020	−1.33 (0.8665)	8
Nigeria	1966–2019	−2.32 (0.4151)	5	1962–2020	−2.68 (0.2472)	1
South Africa	1966–2020	−3.24 (0.0872)	5	1967–2020	−1.02 (0.9321)	1
Sudan	1963–2020	−2.94 (0.1575)	2	1962–2020	−2.06 (0.5535)	1

- τ_ρ is the ADF statistics. $H_0 : I(1)$
- MacKinnon (1996) one-sided *P*-values are in parentheses.
- Lags are automatically determined by the AIC.
- Gabon regression specification for the CPI includes only intercept, not trend in specification.

Table 4.4 Trend of the CPI and the Money–Output Ratio Is Stochastic in the Asian Countries: OLS – $\Delta \ln(y_t) = \alpha + \beta\, trend + \rho \ln(y_{t-1}) + \sum_{i=1}^{k} \delta_i \Delta \ln(y_{t-i}) + e_t$

	CPI			*Broad Money – Real GDP Ratio*		
	Sample	τ_ρ	*k*	*Sample*	τ_ρ	*k*
India	1962–2020	−2.82 (0.1949)	1	1961–2020	−0.58 (0.9763)	0
Japan	1962–2020	−1.61 (0.7767)	1	1961–2020	−2.34 (0.4056)	0
Korea	1963–2020	−1.66 (0.7566)	2	1962–2020	−1.55 (0.7985)	1
Malaysia	1968–2020	−1.80 (0.6905)	7	1961–2020	−1.13 (0.9150)	0
Nepal	1970–2020	−1.49 (0.8179)	5	1961–2020	−2.18 (0.4887)	0
Myanmar[i]	1965–2020	−1.86 (0.6574)	4	1964–2020	−3.36 (0.0658)	2
Philippines[ii]	1963–2020	−2.17 (0.2171)	2	1962–2020	−0.87 (0.7881)	1
Singapore	1965–2020	−1.03 (0.9301)	4	1964–2020	−1.59 (0.7813)	0
Sri Lanka[iii]	1976–2020	−2.32 (0.1692)	0	1976–2020	−2.26 (0.0231)	0

40 *Testing the Relationship Between Money and Prices*

	CPI			Broad Money – Real GDP Ratio		
	Sample	τ_ρ	k	Sample	τ_ρ	k
Thailand[iv]	1963–2020	−0.33 (0.9877)	2	1961–2020	−2.23 (0.1977)	0

- τ_ρ is the ADF statistics. $H_0 : I(1)$
- MacKinnon (1996) one-sided *P*-values are in parentheses.
- Lags are automatically determined by the AIC.

[i] Significant at the 10 percent level.
[ii] Only an intercept, no trend is in the specification.
[iii] Only an intercept, no trend is in the CPI specification, and broad money – real GDP ratio is significant.
[iv] Only an intercept, no trend in the broad money – real GDP ratio specification.

Table 4.5 Trend of the CPI and the Money–Output Ratio Is Stochastic in the Caribbean Countries: OLS $-\ \Delta\ln(y_t) = \alpha + \beta\ trend + \rho\ln(y_{t-1}) + \sum_{i=1}^{k}\delta_i\Delta\ln(y_{t-i}) + e_t$

	CPI			Broad Money – Real GDP Ratio		
	Sample	τ_ρ	k	Sample	τ_ρ	k
Haiti	1962–2020	−2.57 (0.2914)	1	1961–2020	−2.62 (0.2740)	0
Trinidad and Tobago	1962–2020	−0.97 (0.9400)	1	1961–2020	−0.59 (0.9754)	0

- τ_ρ is the ADF statistics. $H_0 : I(1)$
- MacKinnon (1996) one-sided *P*-values are in parentheses.
- Lags are automatically determined by the AIC.

Table 4.6 Trend of the CPI and the Money–Output Ratio Is Stochastic in the Inflation-Targeting Countries: OLS $-\ \Delta\ln(y_t) = \alpha + \beta\ trend + \rho\ln(y_{t-1}) + \sum_{i=1}^{k}\delta_i\Delta\ln(y_{t-i}) + e_t$

	CPI			Broad Money – Real GDP Ratio		
	Sample	τ_ρ	k	Sample	τ_ρ	k
Australia	1962–2020	−1.25 (0.8898)	1	1961–2020	−1.43 (0.8427)	0
Denmark	1971–2020	−2.12 (0.5215)	10	1961–2020	−0.69 (0.9687)	0
Norway	1971–2020	−2.65 (0.2612)	10	1964–2020	−2.07 (0.5477)	3
New Zealand	1966–2020	−3.20 (0.0944)	5	1978–2020	−1.67 (0.7411)	0
Sweden	1962–2020	−0.60 (0.9747)	1	1961–2020	−1.30 (0.8761)	0
UK	1968–2020	−1.52 (0.8080)	7	1966–2020	−0.40 (0.9850)	5
US	1964–2020	−1.16 (0.9073)	3	1962–2020	−1.74 (0.7202)	1
EU (15)	1998–2020	−2.22 (0.2039)	0	1998–2020	−0.05 (0.9441)	0

- τ_ρ is the ADF statistics. $H_0 : I(1)$
- MacKinnon (1996) one-sided *P*-values are in parentheses.
- Lags are automatically determined by the AIC.

Testing the Relationship Between Money and Prices   41

goodness of fit) is followed by the Durbin–Watson statistic. The reason we report these two statistics is that a very high R^2 (due to trend in the data) and a very low DW (serial correlation due to the trend in the data) indicate that the OLS regression's result is spurious (see Granger and NewBold [1974]) and that the log of the CPI and the log (broad money – real GDP ratio) are cointegrated. (Engle and Granger, 1987) identified six different tests for cointegration.[3] Then, under DOLS, we report the sample, which changes significantly because the regression involves leads and lags of Δlog (broad money – real GDP ratio) as regressors. We report the estimated intercept and the slope coefficients, and, in the last column of the table, we report the number of leads and lags needed to estimate the equation. We use heteroskedasticity- and autocorrelation-consistent (HAC) estimators of the variance–covariance matrix with the Newey–West method. The leads/lags are set according to the Akaike Information Criterion (AIC) via automatic search and Bartlett Kernel using the same automatic search for the optimal width. These are reported in table's footnotes. The residuals from the DOLS are tested for normality using the Jarque–Bera test, and the P-values are reported in the footnotes too. We have only a few cases that showed non-normality, while the majority of the countries have an excellent fit. The leads and lags of broad money in DOLS are very long and very variable across countries, thus the dynamic of the CPI varies across countries.

Next, we report the estimated intercept α_0 and the slope coefficient, α_1, which is the elasticity of the CPI with respect to broad money – real GDP ratio. The estimated coefficients of the MENA countries are presented in Table 4.7.[4] The slope coefficients have large magnitudes, and they are significantly different from zero; however, they are also significantly different from 1. The DOLS regressions have unusual short dynamics except for Algeria. The residuals are normal as indicated by the Jarque–Bera P-values, which is quite necessary. Pakistan's residuals are marginally significant, but, overall, these estimates are supportive of the QTM.

Table 4.8 reports the estimated QTM equation for 11 Latin and South American countries. The sample is the same, 1960 to 2020. The intercepts are significant and positive; however, Bolivia and Ecuador (DOLS) have negative signs, which could be interpreted as negative velocities. We could not reject the hypothesis that the intercepts are equal to 1 in Mexico with the Wald P-value of 0.2462.

---

3 Take the residuals from the OLS regression of the log of the CPI on the log of money–output ratio and test them for unit root using the ADF test, which we did. However, in 1999, I asked Clive Granger personally about his preferred test for cointegration among all six tests recommended for cointegration in the Engle–Granger paper. He said the Error-Correction regression test is his preferred test. Estimate: $\Delta lny_t = a + b\Delta lnx_t + \rho e_{t-1} + v_t$, where y is the log of the CPI, x is log money–output ratio, and e_{t-1} is the residuals from the OLS regression of lny on constant terms and lnx, and test $H_0 : \rho = 0$. The variables y and x are cointegrated if t_ρ is large (P-value is 0). Since this is an estimated coefficient with a non-normal distribution, the larger t_ρ, the more significant the test is. I would consider a value >3 to be indicative of cointegration.

4 The OLS regressions show that intercept is >1 for Algeria, Egypt, and Iran with the Wald statistics chi-squared P-values (0.0000), (0.0123), and (0.0000) in these countries, respectively. The hypothesis that the intercept of 1 in Pakistan and Turkey could not be rejected with P-values (0.2024) and (0.5113), respectively.

42   *Testing the Relationship Between Money and Prices*

Ecuador has a very large negative intercept. The slope coefficients are sizable, and significantly different from zero. The Ecuadorian data are very peculiar. The estimate of the intercept is negative and large. When we estimate the OLS and the DOLS regressions without intercepts, the slope coefficients are 0.63 and 0.67, respectively.

In Mexico and Paraguay, the slope coefficients are insignificantly different from 1. Hence, broad money per unit of real output has a one-to-one relationship with the CPI. The DOLS dynamics are very significant; that is, long lead and lag terms. All regressions have normal residuals as indicated by the Jarque–Bera P-values, except for Chile and only marginally for Guatemala.

The estimates show that all coefficients are significant; the magnitudes are large, albeit not equal to one, and significantly different from zero. However, the slope coefficients are insignificantly different from one in Côte d'Ivoire, Ghana, South Africa, and Sudan. There is only one insignificant intercept in the case of Sudan. All the residuals of DOLS are normal.

The OLS and DOLS estimates for the Asian countries, which are reported before show only three cases, where the residuals of the DOLS regressions are non-normal: Malaysia, the Philippines, and Thailand. However, we observe the same pattern here as in the other countries, where the coefficients are statistically significant, and for Myanmar and the Philippines the slope coefficients are insignificantly different from unity, thus a one-to-one relationship between money and prices exists. Nothing unusual so far, as the slopes are sizable in both countries and significant, and in Trinidad and Tobago, the slope is insignificantly different from 1.

Finally, Table 4.12 reports the estimates for the developed inflation-targeting countries. The slope coefficients are relatively smaller in magnitudes, but significant, and insignificantly different from unity in the case of Norway, Sweden, and the United States. Another important distinction in this table is that the slope coefficient α_1 is much smaller in magnitude in New Zealand compared with other countries, that is, 0.49. The only difference between New Zealand data and the rest of the countries is that they are quarterly, from March 1988. We used the RBNZ quarterly data because the World Development Indicators annual data have missing values for broad money. Note also that Australia and New Zealand also have significantly larger intercepts than all other countries.

To compare across countries, we report the average and the standard deviation of the intercept α_0 and the slope α_1 in Table 4.13. The overall average estimate of the intercept is 1.18. The MENA countries' and the Latin and South American countries' averages are below the overall average; while the averages of African, Asian, Caribbean, and the inflation-targeting countries are above the overall average. The MENA countries in our sample (excluding Iran) and the Latin and South American countries (excluding Guatemala) have, on average, a smaller intercept than the rest of the countries. The standard deviation is the highest in the Latin and South American countries and the lowest in the MENA countries. The rest of the countries have a very similar standard deviation. For all countries in our sample, a statistically different from 0 intercept means that even when the log of money per unit of real output is zero, there is something else, omitted

Table 4.7 OLS and Dynamic OLS for the MENA Countries: Relationship between Log (Broad Money – Real GDP Ratio) and Log CPI Is Consistent with the QTM

	OLS					DOLS			
	Sample	α_0	α_1	R^2	DW	Sample	α_0	α_1	Lead/Lag
Algeria	1969–2020	1.70 (0.0000)	0.77[i] (0.0000) [0.0007]	0.96	0.09	1970–2020	−0.35 (0.4898)	0.94[ii] (0.0000)	10/5
Egypt	1960–2020	1.26 (0.0000)	0.89[iii] (0.0000) [0.0004]	0.98	0.12	1966–2020	1.53 (0.0000)	0.92[iv] (0.0000)	0/5
Iran	1960–2020	1.62 (0.0000)	0.78[v] (0.0000) [0.0000]	0.98	0.09	-		-	-
Pakistan	1960–2020	0.85 (0.0000)	0.86[vi] (0.0000) [0.0178]	0.99	0.24	1962–2020	0.82 (0.0001)	0.86[vii] (0.0000)	1/1
Turkey	1960–2020	0.95 (0.0000)	0.93[viii] (0.0000) [0.0000]	0.99	0.52	1962–2020	0.93 (0.0000)	0.94[xi] (0.0000)	1/1

[i] HAC standard errors and covariance, pre-whitening with lag = 2, from AIC, with max lag = 3, Bartlett Kernel, Newey–West auto bandwidth 3.0778, with NW auto lag = 3.
[ii] HAC standard errors and covariance, Bartlett Kernel, NW, auto bandwidth 5.3624, NW auto lag = 3. The *P*-value of the Jarque–Bera test for normality of the residuals is (0.451790).
[iii] HAC standard errors and covariance, pre-whitening with lag = 2, from AIC, with max lag = 3, Bartlett Kernel, Newey–West auto bandwidth 1.4457, with NW auto lag = 3.
[iv] HAC standard errors and covariance, pre-whitening with lag = 2, from AIC, with max lag = 3, Bartlett Kernel, Newey–West auto bandwidth 3.1472, with NW auto lag = 3. The *P*-value of the Jarque–Bera test for normality of the residuals is (0.873197).
[v] Iran has two missing values in 1984 and 1985, and the DOLS regression could not be estimated.
[vi] HAC standard errors and covariance, pre-whitening with lag = 2, from AIC, with max lag = 3, Bartlett Kernel, Newey–West auto bandwidth 5.1731, with NW auto lag = 3.
[vii] HAC standard errors and covariance, pre-whitening with lag = 1, from AIC, with max lag = 3, Bartlett kernel, Newey–West auto bandwidth 4.8057, with NW auto lag = 3. The *P*-value of the Jarque–Bera test for normality of the residuals is (0.096656).
[viii] HAC standard errors and covariance, pre-whitening with lag = 1, from AIC, with max lag = 3, Bartlett kernel, Newey–West auto bandwidth 4.4103, with NW auto lag = 3.
[ix] HAC standard errors and covariance, pre-whitening with lag = 2, from AIC, with max lag = 3, Bartlett kernel, Newey–West auto bandwidth 4.5621, with NW auto lag = 3. The *P*-value of the Jarque–Bera test for normality of the residuals is (0.106781).
– OLS is a spurious regression with very high R^2 and very low *DW* statistic; therefore, there is cointegration between prices and real money/real GDP.
– *P*-values are in parentheses and adjusted for the degrees of freedom.
– *P*-values in square brackets are for the Wald Chi-Square test for the null hypothesis that the coefficient = 1.

from the QTM equation, explaining the variations, that is, the dynamic, of log of the CPI.

The average of the slope's estimates of the MENA countries is 0.92. Latin and South American's average is higher than any other group because of Ecuador, whose estimated slope is very large. The African, the Asian, and the

Table 4.8 OLS and Dynamic OLS for Latin and South American Countries: Relationship between Log (Broad Money − Real GDP Ratio) and Log CPI Is Consistent with the QTM

	OLS					DOLS			
	Sample	α_0	α_1	R^2	*DW*	*Sample*	α_0	α_1	*Lead/Lag*
Bolivia	1960–2020	−2.65 (0.5018)	0.90[i] (0.0000) [0.0014]	0.99	0.21	1971–2020	−0.42 (0.0000)	0.90[ii] (0.0000)	10/10
Chile	1970–2020	1.38 (0.0151)	0.81[iii] (0.0000) [0.0093]	0.98	0.24	1970–2022	2.13 (0.0000)	0.64[iv] (0.0000)	4/0
Colombia	1960–2020	1.60 (0.0000)	0.87[v] (0.0000) [0.0006]	0.99	0.16	[vi]	-	-	-
Costa Rica	1960–2020	1.63 (0.0000)	0.82 [vii] (0.0000) [0.0000]	0.98	0.31	1967–2020	1.75 (0.0000)	0.91[viii] (0.0000)	9/6
Dominican R	1960–2020	1.29 (0.0000)	0.89[ix] (0.0000) [0.0000]	0.99	0.70	1969–2020	1.06 (0.0000)	0.89[x] (0.0000)	4/8
Ecuador*	1960–2020	−6.51 (0.0000)	2.89[xi] (0.0000) [0.0000]	0.78	0.10	1970–2020	−10.8 (0.0000)	4.58[xii] (0.0000)	10/9
Guatemala	1960–2020	1.55 (0.0000)	0.84[xiii] (0.0000) [0.0016]	0.98	0.19	1961–2020	1.47 (0.0072)	0.87[xiv] (0.0000)	10/0
Honduras	1960–2020	0.88 (0.0000)	0.80[xv] (0.0000) [0.0000]	0.99	0.32	1968–2020	0.74 (0.0000)	0.84[xvi] (0.0000)	3/7

Table 4.8 (Continued)

	OLS					DOLS			
	Sample	α_0	α_1	R^2	*DW*	*Sample*	α_0	α_1	*Lead/Lag*
Mexico	1960–2020	1.52 (0.0013)	0.96[xvii] (0.0000) [0.8324]	0.99	0.38	1971–2020	1.46 (0.0000)	0.96[xviii] (0.0000)	6/10
Paraguay	1960–2020	1.99 (0.0000)	0.82[xix] (0.0000) [0.1196]	0.99	0.13	1971–2020	1.51 (0.0000)	0.87[xx] (0.0000)	4/10
Uruguay	1960–2020	1.35 (0.0000)	0.97[xxi] (0.0000) [0.0013]	0.99	0.32	1961–2020	1.50 (0.0000)	0.96[xxii] (0.0000)	9/0

[i] HAC standard errors and covariance, pre-whitening with lag = 1, from AIC, with max lag = 3, Bartlett kernel, Newey–West auto bandwidth 3.4989, with NW auto lag = 3.

[ii] HAC standard errors and covariance, Bartlett kernel, Newey–West auto bandwidth 1.7856, with NW auto lag = 3. The Jarque–Bera P-value is 0.333067.

[iii] HAC standard errors and covariance, pre-whitening with lag = 2, from AIC, with max lag = 3, Bartlett kernel, Newey–West auto bandwidth 2.3844, with NW auto lag = 3.

[iv] HAC standard errors and covariance, pre-whitening with lag = 3, from AIC, with max lag = 3, Bartlett kernel, Newey–West auto bandwidth 4.4575, with NW auto lag = 3. The Jarque–Bera P-value is 0.0150.

[v] HAC standard errors and covariance, pre-whitening with lag = 1, from AIC, with max lag = 3, Bartlett kernel, Newey–West auto bandwidth 4.4439, with NW auto lag = 3.

[vi] DOLS could not be used because of missing data in the sample.

[vii] HAC standard errors and covariance, pre-whitening with lag = 1, from AIC, with max lag = 3, Bartlett kernel, Newey–West auto bandwidth 3.8877, with NW auto lag = 3.

[viii] HAC standard errors and covariance, Bartlett kernel, Newey–West auto bandwidth 4.9046, with NW auto lag = 3. The Jarque–Bera P-value is 0.10448.

[ix] HAC standard errors and covariance, pre-whitening with lag = 1, from AIC, with max lag = 3, Bartlett kernel, Newey–West auto bandwidth 2.3487, with NW auto lag = 3.

[x] HAC standard errors and covariance, pre-whitening with lag = 3, from AIC, with max lag = 3, Bartlett kernel, Newey–West auto bandwidth 5.3537, with NW auto lag = 3. The Jarque–Bera P-value is 0.93365.

[xi] HAC standard errors and covariance, pre-whitening with lag = 1, from AIC, with max lag = 3, Bartlett kernel, Newey–West auto bandwidth 5.2241, with NW auto lag = 3.

(*Continued*)

(xii) HAC standard errors and covariance, Bartlett kernel, Newey–West auto bandwidth 6.0819, with NW auto lag = 3. The Jarque–Bera P-value is 0.51619.

(xiii) HAC standard errors and covariance, pre-whitening with lag = 1, from AIC, with max lag = 3, Bartlett kernel, Newey–West auto bandwidth 5.9193, with NW auto lag = 3.

(xiv) HAC standard errors and covariance, pre-whitening with lag = 3, from AIC, with max lag = 3, Bartlett kernel, Newey–West auto bandwidth 4.3083, with NW auto lag = 3. The Jarque–Bera P-value is 0.0784.

(xv) HAC standard errors and covariance, pre-whitening with lag = 1, from AIC, with max lag = 3, Bartlett kernel, Newey–West auto bandwidth 2.5560, with NW auto lag = 3.

(xvi) HAC standard errors and covariance, Bartlett kernel, Newey–West auto bandwidth 1.5670, with NW auto lag = 3.

(xvii) HAC standard errors and covariance, pre-whitening with lag = 1, from AIC, with max lag = 3, Bartlett kernel, Newey–West auto bandwidth 3.1865, with NW auto lag = 3. The Jarque–Bera P-value is 0.715549.

(xviii) HAC standard errors and covariance, Bartlett kernel, Newey–West auto bandwidth 5.5286, with NW auto lag = 3.

(xix) HAC standard errors and covariance, pre-whitening with lag = 1, from AIC, with max lag = 3, Bartlett kernel, Newey–West auto bandwidth 4.9509, with NW auto lag = 3. The Jarque–Bera P-value is 0.59763.

(xx) HAC standard errors and covariance, Bartlett kernel, Newey–West auto bandwidth 6.2513, with NW auto lag = 3 The Jarque–Bera P-value is 0.9622.

(xxi) HAC standard errors and covariance, pre-whitening with lag = 1, from AIC, with max lag = 3, Bartlett kernel, Newey–West auto bandwidth 10.7830, with NW auto lag = 3.

(xxii) HAC standard errors and covariance, pre-whitening with lag = 1, from AIC, with max lag = 3, Bartlett kernel, Newey–West auto bandwidth 4.6105, with NW auto lag = 3. The Jarque–Bera P-value is 0.3911.

– OLS is a spurious regression with very high R^2 and very low DW statistic; therefore, there is cointegration between prices and real money/real GDP.

– P-values are in parentheses and adjusted for the degrees of freedom.

– P-values in square brackets are for the Wald Chi-Square test for the null hypothesis that the coefficient = 1.

* Ecuadorian data are peculiar; hence, the slope estimates are inconceivably larger than 1 in magnitude.

Table 4.9 OLS and Dynamic OLS for the African Countries; Relationship between Log (Broad Money – Real GDP Ratio) and Log CPI Is Consistent with the QTM

	OLS					DOLS			
	Sample	α_0	α_1	R^2	DW	Sample	α_0	α_1	Lead/Lag
Burkina Faso	19622020	2.70 (0.000)	0.58[i] (0.0000) [0.0000]	0.96	0.30	1964–2020	2.77 (0.0000)	0.59[ii] (0.0000)	1/1
Côte d'Ivoire	1962–2020	1.85 (0.000)	0.94[iii] (0.0000) [0.5788]	0.95	0.18	1973–2020	2.40 (0.4940)	0.85[iv] (0.0000)	0/10
Gabon	1962–2019	2.46 (0.000)	0.66[v] (0.0000) [0.0000]	0.95	0.15	1962–2009	2.28 (0.0000)	0.77[vi] (0.0000)	10/1
Ghana	1971–2020	2.36 (0.000)	0.92[vii] (0.0000) [0.7701]	0.98	0.09	1971–2012	1.25 (0.0199)	0.86[viii] (0.0000)	8/9
Nigeria	1960–2019	2.03 (0.000)	0.88[ix] (0.0000) [0.0000]	0.98	0.20	1962–2016	2.02 (0.0000)	0.88[x] (0.0000)	4/0
South Africa	1965–2020	1.48 (0.000)	0.83[xi] (0.0000) [0.0664]	0.98	0.07	1974–2011	0.10 (0.7954)	0.94[xii] (0.0000)	9/8
Sudan	1960–2020	-0.39 (0.027)	1.03[xiii] (0.0000) [0.2731]	0.99	0.12	1968–2010	0.12 (0.2078)	1.04[xiv] (0.0000)	10/7

(*Continued*)

(i) HAC standard errors and covariance, pre-whitening with lag = 1, from AIC, with max lag = 3, Bartlett kernel, Newey–West auto bandwidth 5.5543, with NW auto lag = 3. Jarque–Bera P-value is 0.44313.

(ii) HAC standard errors and covariance, pre-whitening with lag = 1, from AIC, with max lag = 3, Bartlett kernel, Newey–West auto bandwidth 4.0138, Jarque–Bera P-value is 0.55166.

(iii) HAC standard errors and covariance, pre-whitening with lag = 1, from AIC, with max lag = 3, Bartlett kernel, Newey–West auto bandwidth 3.8015, with NW auto lag = 3. Jarque–Bera P-value is 0.51706.

(iv) HHAC standard errors and covariance, pre-whitening with lag = 1, from AIC, with max lag = 3, Bartlett kernel, Newey–West auto bandwidth 4.0138, Jarque–Bera P-value is 0.55166.

(v) HAC standard errors and covariance, pre-whitening with lag = 3, from AIC, with max lag = 3, Bartlett kernel, Newey–West auto bandwidth 2.3258, Jarque–Bera P-value is 0.26679.

(vi) HAC standard errors and covariance, Bartlett kernel, Newey–West auto bandwidth 6.1871, with NW auto lag = 3. Jarque–Bera P-value is 0.60882.

(vii) HAC standard errors and covariance, pre-whitening with lag = 1, from AIC, with max lag = 3, Bartlett kernel, Newey–West auto bandwidth 5.7805, with NW auto lag = 3. Jarque–Bera P-value is 0.32669.

(viii) HAC standard errors and covariance, Bartlett kernel, Newey–West auto bandwidth 4.3371, with NW auto lag = 3. Jarque–Bera P-value is 0.47890.

(ix) HAC standard errors and covariance, pre-whitening with lag = 2, from AIC, with max lag = 3, Bartlett kernel, Newey–West auto bandwidth 7.0778, with NW auto lag = 3. Jarque–Bera P-value is 0.36029.

(x) HAC standard errors and covariance, pre-whitening with lag = 1, from AIC, with max lag = 3, Bartlett kernel, Newey–-West auto bandwidth 5.1326, with NW auto lag = 3. Jarque–Bera P-value is 0.33569.

(xi) HAC standard errors and covariance, pre-whitening with lag = 2, from AIC, with max lag = 3, Bartlett kernel, Newey–West auto bandwidth 1.9755, with NW auto lag = 3. Jarque–Bera P-value is 0.09150.

(xii) HAC standard errors and covariance, Bartlett kernel, Newey–West auto bandwidth 6.0601, with NW auto lag = 3. Jarque–Bera P-value is 0.483522.

(xiii) HAC standard errors and covariance, pre-whitening with lag = 2, from AIC, with max lag = 3, Bartlett kernel, Newey–West auto bandwidth 3.1460, with NW auto lag = 3. Jarque–Bera P-value is 0.225345.

(xiv) HAC standard errors and covariance, Bartlett kernel, Newey–West auto bandwidth 11.9720, with NW auto lag = 3. Jarque–Bera P-value is 0.962155.

– OLS is a spurious regression with very high R^2 and very low *DW* statistic; therefore, there is cointegration between prices and real money/real GDP.

– P-values are in parentheses and adjusted for the degrees of freedom.

– P-values in square brackets are the Wald Chi-Square test for the null hypothesis that the coefficient = 1.

Table 4.10 OLS and Dynamic OLS for the Asian Countries; Relationship between Log (Broad Money – Real GDP Ratio) and Log CPI Is Consistent with the QTM

	OLS					DOLS			
	Sample	α_0	α_1	R^2	DW	Sample	α_0	α_1	Lead/Lag
India	1960–2020	1.48 (0.0000)	0.75[i] (0.0000) [0.0000]	0.99	0.32	1968–2010	0.96 (0.0000)	0.80[ii] (0.0000)	10/7
Japan	1960–2020	1.37 (0.0000)	0.60[iii] (0.0000) [0.0000]	0.98	0.49	1969–2012	0.44 (0.2974)	0.77[iv] (0.0000)	8/8
Korea	1960–2020	1.85 (0.0000)	0.60[v] (0.0000) [0.0000]	0.97	0.14	1971–2010	3.78 (0.0000)	0.35[vi] (0.0000)	10/10
Malaysia	1960–2020	2.24 (0.0000)	0.48[vii] (0.0000) [0.0000]	0.97	0.39	1971–2015	2.02 (0.0000)	0.55[viii] (0.0000)	5/10
Nepal	1960–2020	2.15 (0.0000)	0.61[ix] (0.0000) [0.0000]	0.99	0.50	1966–2010	3.43 (0.0000)	0.57[x] (0.0000)	10/5
Myanmar	1960–2020	1.28 (0.0000)	0.99[xi] (0.0000) [0.9215]	0.98	0.33	1968–2011	1.83 (0.0000)	1.09[xii] (0.0000)	9/6
Philippines	1960–2020	1.57 (0.0144)	0.78[xiii] (0.1168) [0.6664]	0.98	0.17	1963–2011	1.04 (0.0000)	0.85[xiv] (0.0000)	9/2
Singapore	1960–2020	1.81 (0.0000)	0.59[xv] (0.0000) [0.0000]	0.96	0.33	1971–2013	0.84 (0.0000)	0.74[xvi] (0.0000)	7/7
Sri Lanka	1960–2020	1.43 (0.0000)	0.84[xvii] (0.0000) [0.0000]	0.98	0.33	1985–2014	1.48 (0.0000)	0.87[xviii] (0.0000)	5/9
Thailand	1960–2020	1.56 (0.0000)	0.60[xix] (0.0000) [0.0000]	0.99	0.27	1961–2016	1.48 (0.0000)	0.61[xx] (0.0000)	3/0

(Continued)

(i) HAC standard errors and covariance, pre-whitening with lag = 2, from AIC, with max lag = 3, Bartlett kernel, Newey–West auto bandwidth 5.6054, with NW auto lag = 3.

(ii) HAC standard errors and covariance, Bartlett kernel, Newey–West auto bandwidth 4.7886, with NW auto lag = 3. The Jarque–Bera P-value is 0.363604.

(iii) HAC standard errors and covariance, pre-whitening with lag = 2, from AIC, with max lag = 3, Bartlett kernel, Newey–West auto bandwidth 1.9684, with NW auto lag = 3.

(iv) HAC standard errors and covariance, Bartlett kernel, Newey–West auto bandwidth 5.5848, with NW auto lag = 3. The Jarque–Bera P-value is 0.209690.

(v) HAC standard errors and covariance, pre-whitening with lag = 3, from AIC, with max lag = 3, Bartlett kernel, Newey–West auto bandwidth 3.2315, with NW auto lag = 3.

(vi) HAC standard errors and covariance, Bartlett kernel, Newey–West auto bandwidth 6.6408, with NW auto lag = 3. The Jarque–Bera P-value is 0.769946.

(vii) HAC standard errors and covariance, pre-whitening with lag = 1, from AIC, with max lag = 3, Bartlett kernel, Newey–West auto bandwidth 2.1491, with NW auto lag = 3.

(viii) HAC standard errors and covariance, Bartlett kernel, Newey–West auto bandwidth 2.3357, with NW auto lag = 3. The Jarque–Bera P-value is 0.028039.

(ix) HAC standard errors and covariance, pre whitening with lag= 1, from AIC, with max lag = 3, Bartlett kernel, Newey–West auto bandwidth 4.1020, with NW auto lag = 3.

(x) HAC standard errors and covariance, Bartlett kernel, Newey–West auto bandwidth 3.1472, with NW auto lag = 3. The Jarque–Bera P-value is 0.706677.

(xi) HAC standard errors and covariance, pre whitening with lag = 2, from AIC, with max lag = 3, Bartlett kernel, Newey–West auto bandwidth 7.2184, with NW auto lag = 3.

(xii) HAC standard errors and covariance, Bartlett kernel, Newey–West auto bandwidth 5.2467, with NW auto lag = 3. The Jarque–Bera P-value is 0.694513.

(xiii) HAC standard errors and covariance, pre-whitening with lag = 1, from AIC, with max lag = 3, Bartlett kernel, Newey–West auto bandwidth 3.1294, with NW auto lag = 3.

(xiv) HAC standard errors and covariance, pre-whitening with lag = 3, from AIC, with max lag = 3, Bartlett kernel, Newey–West auto bandwidth 5.2352, with NW auto lag = 3. The Jarque– Bera P-value is 0.002373.

(xv) HAC standard errors and covariance, pre-whitening with lag = 1, from AIC, with max lag = 3, Bartlett kernel, Newey–West auto bandwidth 2.8200, with NW auto lag = 3.

(xvi) HAC standard errors and covariance, Bartlett kernel, Newey–West auto bandwidth 3.4450, with NW auto lag = 3. The Jarque–Bera P-value is 0.947647.

(xvii) HAC standard errors and covariance, pre-whitening with lag = 3, from AIC, with max lag = 3, Bartlett kernel, Newey–West auto bandwidth 6.6950, with NW auto lag = 3.

(xviii) HAC standard errors and covariance, Bartlett kernel, Newey–West auto bandwidth 6.5787, with NW auto lag = 3. The Jarque–Bera P-value is 0.568337.

(xix) HAC standard errors and covariance, pre-whitening with lag = 3, from AIC, with max lag = 3, Bartlett kernel, Newey–West auto bandwidth 1.7625, with NW auto lag = 3.

(xx) HAC standard errors and covariance, pre whitening with lag = 2, from AIC, with max lag = 3, Bartlett kernel, Newey–West auto bandwidth 1.4041, with NW auto lag = 3. The Jarque–Bera P-value is 0.030516.

– OLS is a spurious regression with very high R^2 and very low DW statistic; therefore, there is cointegration between prices and real money/real GDP.

– P-values are in parentheses and adjusted for the degrees of freedom.

– P-values in square brackets are the Wald Chi-Square test for the null hypothesis that the coefficient = 1.

Table 4.11 OLS and Dynamic OLS for the Caribbean Countries: Relationship between Log (Broad Money – Real GDP Ratio) and Log CPI Is Consistent with the QTM

	OLS					DOLS			
	Sample	α_0	α_1	R^2	DW	Sample	α_0	α_1	Lead/Lag
Haiti	1960–2020	2.02 (0.0000)	0.79[i] (0.0000) [0.0000]	0.99	0.27	1961–2020	2.12 (0.0000)	0.80[ii] (0.0000)	0/0
Trinidad and Tobago	1960–2020	0.88 (0.0010)	0.92[iii] (0.0000) [0.2877]	0.97	0.11	1971–2012	0.58 (0.0000)	1.05[iv] (0.0000)	8/10

[i] HAC standard errors and covariance, pre-whitening with lag = 1, from AIC, with max lag = 3, Bartlett kernel, Newey–West auto bandwidth 2.4423, with NW auto lag = 3.

[ii] HAC standard errors and covariance, pre-whitening with lag = 2, from AIC, with max lag = 3, Bartlett kernel, Newey–West auto bandwidth 2.5822, with NW auto lag = 3. The Jarque–Bera *P*-value is 0.140949.

[iii] HAC standard errors and covariance, pre-whitening with lag = 1, from AIC, with max lag = 3, Bartlett kernel, Newey–West auto bandwidth 3.6687, with NW auto lag = 3.

[iv] HAC standard errors and covariance, Bartlett kernel, Newey–West auto bandwidth 2.5519, with NW auto lag = 3. The Jarque–Bera *P*-value is 0.500628.

– OLS is a spurious regression with very high R^2 and very low *DW* statistic; therefore, there is cointegration between prices and real money/real GDP.

– *P*-values are in parentheses and adjusted for the degrees of freedom.

– *P*-values in square brackets are the Wald Chi-Square test and the slope coefficient = 1.

52 *Testing the Relationship Between Money and Prices*

inflation-targeting countries have lower slopes on average. The MENA countries' and the Caribbean countries' average estimated slopes are equal to the overall average estimate of all countries. The variability of the estimated slopes is small; it is 0 in the MENA countries; the highest is in the Latin and South America countries because of Ecuador and almost equal in the rest of the countries. These results suggest that money has the same effect on prices, nearly one-to-one, on average across different countries. The DOLS-estimated long-run elasticities are consistent with the neutrality of money. New Zealand data are quarterly, hence different.

Figure 4.11 plots the slope estimates for all countries. The estimated responsiveness or the elasticity of the CPI with respect to money per unit of real output is close to 1 on average; however, it varies across countries.

Furthermore, the OLS regressions of all countries show very high R^2 statistics and very low DW statistics, which indicate spurious regressions (Granger and Newbold, 1974). This also indicates that the log of the CPI and the log of broad money per unit of real output are cointegrated (Engle and Granger, 1987). Most of the residuals are stationary. The ADF statistics for testing the null hypothesis of unit root in the residuals is rejected. Thus, prices and broad money share a long-term common trend. The data are consistent with the prediction of QTM, in general, in the sense that the CPI and broad money per unit of real output in every country in our sample share a common long-run trend, and the dynamic lag is long and variable across countries. Such evidence is widely accepted and confirmed in a voluminous empirical literature. The relationship between money and the CPI, however, is not exactly one-to-one in all 42 countries, however, but it is very close in many cases. The relationship between prices and money is one-to-one in many countries such as Mexico, Paraguay, Côte d'Ivoire, Ghana, Sudan, Philippines, Myanmar, Trinidad and Tobago, Sweden, and the United States. The relationship deteriorates, and the prediction of the QTM does not hold under successful inflation-targeting regimes. Next, we examine the more complex relationship between the inflation rate and the growth rate of broad money.

Table 4.12 OLS and Dynamic OLS for the Inflation-Targeting Countries: Relationship between Log (Broad Money – Real GDP Ratio) and Log CPI Is Consistent with the QTM

	OLS					DOLS			
	Sample	α_0	α_1	R^2	DW	Sample	α_0	α_1	Lead/Lag
Australia	1960–2020	4.88 (0.0000)	0.73[i] (0.0000) [0.0201]	0.96	0.04	1971–2014	4.33 (0.0000)	0.73[ii] (0.0000)	6/10
Denmark	1960–2020	1.05 (0.0000)	0.88[iii] (0.0000) [0.0001]	0.98	0.42	1971–2010	0.25 (0.0000)	1.07[iv] (0.0000)	10/10
Norway	1960–2020	1.23 (0.0001)	0.87[v] (0.0000) [0.3018]	0.97	0.09	1971–2010	1.92 (0.0000)	0.78[vi] (0.0000)	10/10
New Zealand	*88q1–21q4*	4.00 (0.0000)	0.47[vii] (0.0000) [0.0000]	0.98	0.16	88q2–18q4	3.90 (0.0000)	0.49[viii] (0.0000)	11/0
Sweden	1960–2020	1.05 (0.0000)	0.90[ix] (0.0000) [0.1752]	0.95	0.07	1971–2020	1.74 (0.0000)	0.76[x] (0.0000)	0/10
UK	1960–2020	1.77 (0.0000)	0.61[xi] (0.0000) [0.0000]	0.95	0.09	1971–2010	0.74 (0.0004)	0.71[xii] (0.0000)	10/10
US	1960–2020	0.30 (0.1264)	0.99[xiii] (0.0000) [0.9301]	0.97	0.15	1969–2010	0.43 (0.0266)	1.02[xiv] (0.0000)	10/8
EU (15)	1997–2020	1.01 (0.0000)	0.75[xv] (0.0000) [0.0000]	0.94	0.92	1999–2019	1.0 (0.0000)	0.76[xvi] (0.0000)	1/1

(i) HAC standard errors and covariance, pre-whitening with lag = 2, from AIC, with max lag = 3, Bartlett kernel, Newey–West auto bandwidth 2.40425, with NW auto lag = 3.

(ii) HAC standard errors and covariance, Bartlett kernel, Newey–West auto bandwidth 6.1658, with NW auto lag = 3. The Jarque–Bera P-value is 0.754072.

(iii) HAC standard errors and covariance, pre-whitening with lag = 1, from AIC, with max lag = 3, Bartlett kernel, Newey–West auto bandwidth 4.4003, with NW auto lag = 3.

(iv) HAC standard errors and covariance, pre-whitening with lag = 1, from AIC, with max lag = 3, Bartlett kernel, Newey–West auto bandwidth 3.4422, with NW auto lag = 3. The Jarque–Bera P-value is 0.657653.

(v) HAC standard errors and covariance, pre-whitening with lag = 1, from AIC, with max lag = 3, Bartlett kernel, Newey–West auto bandwidth 5.3225 with NW auto lag = 3.

(vi) HAC standard errors and covariance, Bartlett kernel, Newey–West auto bandwidth 4.49433, with NW auto lag = 3. The Jarque–Bera P-value is 0.398683.

(vii) New Zealand data are *quarterly*; source is the RBNZ because the WDI annual data for money have missing observations. HAC standard errors and covariance, pre-whitening with lag = 3, from AIC, with max lag = 5, Bartlett kernel, Newey–West auto bandwidth 6.5959 with NW auto lag = 4.

(viii) HAC standard errors and covariance, pre-whitening with lag = 4, from AIC, with max lag = 4, Bartlett kernel, Newey–West auto bandwidth 5.6321 with NW auto lag = 4.

(ix) HAC standard errors and covariance, pre-whitening with lag = 1, from AIC, with max lag = 3, Bartlett kernel, Newey–West auto bandwidth 4.2484 with NW auto lag = 3.

(x) HAC standard errors and covariance, pre-whitening with lag = 3, from AIC, with max lag = 3, Bartlett kernel, Newey–West auto bandwidth 35.0922 with NW auto lag = 3. The Jarque–Bera P-value is 0.111000.

(xi) HAC standard errors and covariance, pre-whitening with lag = 2, from AIC, with max lag = 3, Bartlett kernel, Newey–West auto bandwidth 2.4657 with NW auto lag = 3.

(xii) HAC standard errors and covariance, Bartlett kernel, Newey–West auto bandwidth 4.9589 with NW auto lag = 3. The Jarque–Bera P-value is 0.230042.

(xiii) HAC standard errors and covariance, pre-whitening with lag = 1, from AIC, with max lag = 3, Bartlett kernel, Newey–West auto bandwidth 4.1797 with NW auto lag = 3.

(xiv) HAC standard errors and covariance, Bartlett kernel, Newey–West auto bandwidth 5.0329 with NW auto lag = 3. The Jarque–Bera P-value is 0.936021.

(xv) HAC standard errors and covariance, pre-whitening with lag = 2, from AIC, with max lag = 2, Bartlett kernel, Newey–West auto bandwidth 1.6311 with NW auto lag = 2.

(xvi) HAC standard errors and covariance, pre-whitening with lag = 2, from AIC, with max lag 2, Bartlett kernel, Newey–West auto bandwidth 3.0457 with NW auto lag = 2.

– Italic values refer to quarterly values for New Zealand.

– OLS is a spurious regression with very high R^2 and very low DW statistic; therefore, there is cointegration between prices and real money/real GDP.

– P-values are in parentheses and adjusted for the degrees of freedom.

– P-values in square brackets are for the Wald Chi-Square test to test the slope coefficient = 1.

Table 4.13 Summary Statistics of the DOLS Estimates of the Intercepts and the Slopes

		MENA	South America	Africa	Asia	Caribbean	Inflation Targeting	Overall
Intercept	Mean	0.82	0.06	1.56	1.73	1.35	1.90	1.24
	STDEV	0.63	3.88	1.10	1.10	1.09	1.64	
Slope	Mean	0.92	1.24*	0.85	0.72	0.93	0.79	0.91
	STDEV	0.04	1.18	0.14	0.21	0.18	0.20	

We excluded Iran and Guatemala because DOLS was not estimated due to missing data.

* The average South American slope is greater than 1 because Ecuador has a very large slope estimate.

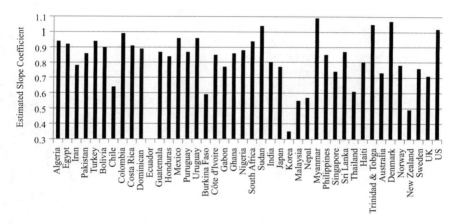

Figure 4.11 Estimated DOLS Slope Coefficients for all Countries, 1960–2020

Note: Ecuador is not included. Iran and Colombia are OLS Estimates.

Appendix 4.1
Dynamic OLS (DOLS)

The method is found in Phillips and Loreatn (1991), Saikkonen (1992), and Stock and Watson (1993) for the asymptotic theory. These are efficient estimators, which account for endogeneity and serial correlations. This literature on the issues surrounding this estimator is large, and we cannot cite all of it; however, some articles are necessary. See, for example (Kejriwal and Perron, 2008).

Assume the following model

$$y_t = \alpha' x_t + u_{ot},$$ (A4.1)

where y_t is the log of the CPI (lnP_t), and x_t is the log of broad money – real GDP ratio $ln\left(\dfrac{M_t}{Y_t}\right)$.

$$x_t = x_{t-1} + u_{xt}.$$ (A4.2)

Let $u_t = \left(u_{0t}, u_{xt}'\right)'$ and assume that u_t is stationary and Gaussian with zero mean and spectral density $f_{uu}(\lambda)$ with $f_{uu}(0) > 0$. The cointegration relation is efficiently estimated by an empirical leads and lags regression of the following type:

$$y_t = \alpha' x_t + \sum_{j=-k}^{k} \Delta x_{t+j} + u_{kt}$$ (A4.3)

The lag and lead truncation parameter k satisfies $k \to \infty$, and $k^3/n \to 0$ as the sample size. Phillips and Loretan (1991) note that, in practice, it is useful to augment regression formulation with lagged equilibrium relation regressors that help to whiten the error term u_{0t} in Eq. (A4.1) with respect to its own history. This leads to an empirical leads and lags and equilibrium lags regression equation:

$$y_t = \alpha' x_t + \sum_{j=-k}^{k} \rho_j' \Delta x_{t+j} + \sum_{s=1}^{r} \varphi_j (y_{t-s} - \alpha' x_{t-s}) + u_{krt}$$ (A4.4)

The DOLS is a very useful and efficient estimator in this case, because there is an important dynamic in the relationship between money and the CPI; that is, the lags are long and variable. DOLS jointly estimates the long-run cointegrating parameters, the dynamic, and a typical error correction term *a la* (Granger 1983), for example.

5 Money Growth and Inflation

Abstract

We provide time series and cross-sectional evidence that the growth rate of money is a significant explanatory variable of the inflation rates, whereby there is a one-to-one correspondence in many countries in our sample, especially in the United States. However, the correlation fizzles out under successful inflation-targeting.

In this chapter, we turn to testing the inflation rate (the log difference of the CPI) and the growth rate of broad money per unit of real output. (Lucas 1972a, 1980) stated that two central implications of the quantity theory of money that a given change in the rate of change in the quantity of money induces (1) an equal change in the rate of price inflation and (2) an equal change in nominal rates of interest. Then he stated (p. 1005) that these propositions possess a combination of theoretical coherence and empirical verification shared by no other propositions in monetary economics. Keep in mind that these views and the QTM itself have been seriously challenged by economists. For example, see (Wallace, 1981) and (Sargent and Smith, 1986, 1987) among others. They showed that the relationship depends on the effect on total liabilities on the consolidated balance sheet of the country. Today, no central bank in the developed countries cares much about the QTM.

The regression of the log-differenced data of money and the CPI is much more challenging to fit than fitting log-level regressions that we previously estimated because of many reasons. (1) Policy affects the time series properties of the data. If the central bank targets inflation *per se*, and succeeds, it would render it stationary. The explanation of the weakening correlation between money and inflation is that successful inflation-targeting reduces the variability of inflation significantly as compared with the variability of money or output. At the same time, money continues to grow untargeted and unconstrained by any policy. Perhaps the growth rate of money is driven by stochastic demand shocks, or it is deterministically driven by central banks. Thus, we have two time series, one with a high variance and the other one with low variance, which must result in low correlation between the two.

(Taylor, 2001) is an interview with Milton Friedman. He tells John Taylor a story of a positive correlation between the amounts of fuel used to heat a room and the temperature in that room. More fuel is associated with higher temperature

DOI: 10.4324/9781003382218-5

58   *Money Growth and Inflation*

and less fuel with lower temperature. Installing a thermostat in the room to cut the amount of fuel when temperature reaches a certain desired level breaks up the positive correlation between the amount of fuel and the temperature in the room. Thus, successful monetary policy intervention such as inflation targeting is akin to the thermostat – it breaks up the correlation between inflation and its determinants specified by the model used for policy. Eventually, the model fails. (2) Trend inflation has a much more complicated dynamic than trend CPI level. (3) In addition to the effects of country-specific shocks on inflation in every country, global shocks have different (asymmetrical) effects on inflation in different countries. We follow the same testing strategy by plotting the data and testing the inflation time series for unit root because some of the inflation data still have trends. Broad money per unit of real output has a unit root; therefore, the growth rate of broad money per unit of real GDP measured as $\Delta ln\left(\dfrac{M}{Y}\right)$ is stationary by construction. Then, we use DOLS to estimate the QTM equation in log-differenced form.

There are country-specific shocks that affect the inflation dynamic and some shocks with global implications for the inflation dynamic. For example, the effects of the first oil shock in 1973 and the second in 1979, which affected the inflation rate in many countries differently, are accounted for. Whether inflation is stationary or not is a concern. Secular inflation has dominated the world for a long time. The trend may be stochastic in some countries; inflation in some other countries does not have a stochastic trend, that is, no unit root. We have argued in Chapter 2 that inflation's time series could be a fractionally integrated series with $d > 0.5$. Therefore, it is not stationary. Or in some cases, although highly implausible, the CPI level is an I(2), an integrated series of order 2, which requires double differencing to render inflation I(0). Visually, there is a trend in the inflation data in many countries. As far as we are concerned, DOLS is a reasonably good and efficient estimator, which could handle regressing a unit root variable on a stationary variable, provided that the residuals of the regression are *independently and identically distributed* (*iid*). (McCallum, 1993) shows that the numbers of times the data are *differenced* do not affect the result when estimating a demand for real balances equation as long as the residuals are serially uncorrelated.

Visual inspection of the inflation time series appears to also show breaks. There are many reasons for a break in the inflation data. It could be a result of persistent shocks, that is, supply shocks in general, but another reason could be a monetary policy intervention such as targeting low and stable inflation *per se*, which renders inflation stationary. In such cases, policy then alters the time series properties of the data. Note also that the tests for unit root that we use fit a linear OLS regression, which quite probably confuses breaks in the data with a unit root. Therefore, before we proceed to examine the QTM in terms of log differences, that is, by estimating the equation: $\Delta ln P_t = \alpha \Delta ln\left(M_t / Y_t\right) + e_t$, we test the inflation rate $\Delta ln P_t$ for unit root using the ADF test with *breaks*.

We use four tests. The first minimizes the ADF t-stat, the second is intercept break min. ADF t-stat, the third is intercept break max ADF t-stat, and the fourth is intercept maximum absolute ADF t-stat. These tests are described in Appendix 5.1.

Money Growth and Inflation 59

The trend specifications are (1) with an intercept only and (2) with an intercept and trend. The break specifications are (1) an intercept only and (2) an intercept and trend. The break type is either an *innovation outlier* or an *additive outlier*. When we find that the results of the innovation outliers are the same as the additive outliers, we report only one of them. The results are sensitive to the modeling of the trend and the break. We use a number of commonly used Information Criteria to determine the lag specification, but we only report the AIC because the number of lags does not seem to change significantly with Information Criteria. The results of the unit root with a break are reported in Table A-5.1.[1]

For each country, we have four tests and two specifications. Therefore, we have 336 results. You could imagine how big the output would be if we use more tests; therefore, we only report these results. We found 171 cases, where the unit root hypothesis (with various breaks) is rejected. Thus, only 50 percent of the tests reject the unit root. Recall that the power of a weak test such as the ADF is irrelevant when it rejects the null of unit root; therefore, we take the rejection of the unit root as indicative of significant indication of stationarity. We are certain that there are breaks in the data, periods of policy changes, that is, before and after inflation targeting, and of supply shocks such as oil price shocks, natural disasters, wars, turbulent economic and political periods in the 1950s, 1960s, and early 1970s in the MENA, African, and Latin and South American countries, etc. Therefore, when testing the QTM in terms of growth rates of money and inflation, we argue that (1) the most efficient estimator is Dynamic OLS. (2) This estimator will account for the monetary lead/lag, and it could handle stationary and non-stationary mixed variables in the same equation, provided that the residuals are *iid*. (3) We control for oil price shocks. (4) We control for policy changes, such as adopting inflation-targeting regimes and exchange rate regimes; political, banking, and financial crisis (e.g., the Asian Financial Crisis 1997–1998 (AFC); and the Global Financial Crisis 2007–2008 (GFC)); draughts; earthquakes; harvest failure; etc. using dummy variables.[2]

There is one more important issue regarding the inflation-targeting countries and perhaps South Africa, Chile, Colombia, and Turkey. Under inflation targeting, the price level is indeterminate just as in the Keynesian system, and the central banks consider bygones-as-bygones, which means that central banks ignore shocks that affect the price level; the policy is only concerned with keeping the inflation rate at the target.

The MENA Countries

Before estimation, we plot the data for the MENA countries. Figure 5.1a is a 45° line scatter plot of the inflation rate and broad money – real GDP ratio growth.

---

1 We also used various panel unit root tests with common unit root (see Levin *et al.*, 2002; Breitung t-stat and with individual unit root, 2000) and individual unit roots (see (Im *et al.*, 2003); ADF – (Fisher, 1932) Chi-squared, and PP – Fisher Chi-squared). All panel unit root tests reject the unit root.
2 DOLS fits a large number of leads/lags of the explanatory variables. Searching for the optimal number of leads and lags using Information Criteria requires a very large sample. Our sample of the annual data from 1960 to 2020 or 2021 constrained the number of dummy variables we include in the regressions.

60 Money Growth and Inflation

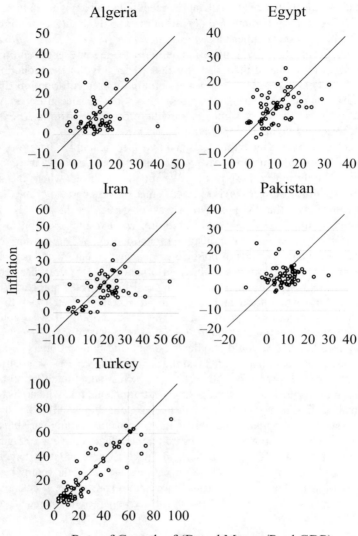

Figure 5.1a Significant Relationship between Money Per Unit of Output Growth Rate and Inflation in MENA Countries, 1961–2020

Data Source: World Development Indicators

These plots suggest that the correlation is strong and positive as predicted by the QTM. Turkey has a spectacular strong positive association between money growth and inflation. Figure 5.1b plots the time series of these two variables and shows they are positively correlated. Sometimes, the trend is steep as in the cases of Egypt and Turkey and sometimes is flatter as in the case of Pakistan. Volatility is visually apparent in the data. Table 5.1 reports the descriptive statistics.

Money Growth and Inflation 61

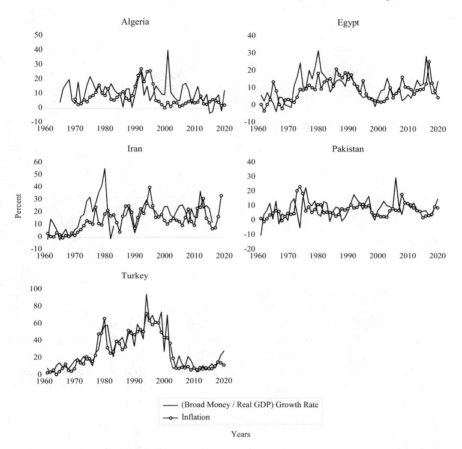

Figure 5.1b Money Per Unit of Output Growth Rate and Inflation Time Series in MENA Countries, 1961–2020
Data Source: World Development Indicators

Except for Pakistan, which has a positive yet flatter relationship between the inflation rate and the growth rate of broad money per unit of real output, all other MENA countries in our sample seem to have strong positive relationships. The obvious observations in the statistics in Table 5.1 are that the means of the two variables are very close, and the variances of money growth rates, however, are much greater than the variances of the inflation rates, which mean that broad money could account for the variations in inflation. On average, Turkey has a history of very high and variable inflation rate, declined because of inflation targeting, later in the sample, but it seems like Turkey's inflation targeting has been unable to stabilize the inflation rate again. Iran has a similar problem. Algeria, Egypt, and Pakistan have high average inflation rates, almost the same, and significantly lower than Iran and Turkey. The normality of the inflation time series is rejected in Algeria and Turkey. It is marginally rejected in Egypt and Pakistan. Iran's inflation time

62 *Money Growth and Inflation*

Table 5.1 Descriptive Statistics for Broad Money – Real GDP Ratio Growth and Inflation in MENA Countries, 1960–2020

	Broad Money – Real GDP Ratio Growth					Inflation				
	Mean	*STD*	*SKW*	*KURT*	*Jarque–Bera*	*Mean*	*STD*	*SKW*	*KURT*	*Jarque–Bera*
Algeria	11.2	7.4	0.87	5.9	(0.0012)	8.04	6.63	1.5	4.6	(0.0000)
Egypt	10.3	7.2	0.68	3.5	(0.0656)	9.20	6.01	0.3	2.8	(0.5922)
Iran	18.3	11.4	0.46	3.9	(0.1608)	14.0	8.94	0.5	3.0	(0.3185)
Pakistan	8.75	6.5	0.10	4.5	(0.0617)	7.61	4.68	1.2	5.0	(0.0000)
Turkey	28.2	22	0.95	2.9	(0.0099)	25.6	20.5	0.6	2.0	(0.0356)

STD – standard deviations (second moment); SKW – skewness (third moment) – S^2; KURT – kurtosis (fourth moment) – K. P-values of Jarque–Bera are in parentheses. The test value is $\frac{N}{6}\left(S^2 + \frac{K-3}{4}\right)^2$. It tests $H_0 : normal$

series is *iid*. For the growth rate of broad money per unit of real output, normality is rejected strongly in Algeria, Pakistan, and Turkey. The time series seems *iid* in Egypt and Iran only. We used more tests, which we do not report because the results are insignificantly different from the Jarque–Bera test.

Next, we test for the equality of the means and the variances of inflation and broad money per output growth rate. Table 5.2 reports the tests for the equality of means in the MENA group. The hypothesis of equality of the means is rejected in Algeria and Iran only.

Table 5.3 tests for the equality of the variances of inflation and broad money – real GDP ratio growth in the MENA countries.

The variance of inflation and broad money – real GDP ratio growth is equal in all countries, except Algeria and Pakistan. The F-test is a straightforward test.[3]

Table 5.4 reports the DOLS results. The samples represent the effective sample size after accounting for the lead/lag regressor. Algeria is an oil and gas producer; however, the effects of the 1973, 1979, and 2014 oil price shocks had an insignificant effect on inflation. In 1990, Algeria plunged into a civil war. This bloodshed crippled the economy for 6 years. We treat this as an adverse supply shock, which

---

3 This method is fully described in EViews. The Siegel–Tukey test assumes inflation and broad money – real GDP ratio growth to be independent and have equal medians. The median test is the Kruskal–Wallis one-way ANOVA with different assignments of ranks. The Kruskal–Wallis test is a generalization of the Mann–Whitney. The times series are ranked from the smallest value (rank 1) to the largest, and the sums of the ranks are compared for the two groups. The ranking alternates from the lowest to the highest value of every other rank. It first orders the observations from low to high and assigns rank 1 to the lowest, rank 2 to the highest, rank 3 to the second highest, rank 4 to second lowest, rank 5 to the third lowest, and so on. The values are corrected following (Sheskin, 1997, pp. 196–207). The Bartlett test compares the log-weighted-average variance with the weighted-sum of the logs of the variances. The Levene test is based on ANOVA of the absolute difference from the mean. This is an F-test (see Levene [1960]). The Brown–Forsyth is a modified Levene test. It uses absolute median difference instead of absolute mean difference. See (Conover *et al.*, 1981), (Brown and Forsyth, 1974a, 1974b), and (Neter *et al.*, 1996).

Money Growth and Inflation 63

Table 5.2 Are Mean Inflation and (Broad Money – Real GDP Ratio) Growth Equal in the MENA Countries in 1960–2020?

	t-test	Satterthwaite–Welch t-test	ANOVA F-test	Welch F-test	Equal
Algeria	(0.0009)	(0.0007)	(0.0009)	(0.0007)	NO
Egypt	(0.3456)	(0.3456)	(0.3456)	(0.3456)	YES
Iran	(0.0280)	(0.0302)	(0.0280)	(0.0302)	NO
Pakistan	(0.2754)	(0.2756)	(0.2754)	(0.2756)	YES
Turkey	(0.5064)	(0.5064)	(0.5064)	(0.5064)	YES

P-values are in parentheses.

Table 5.3 Are Variability of Inflation and (Broad Money – Real GDP Ratio) Growth Equal in the MENA Countries in 1960–2020?

	F-test	Siegel–Tukey	Bartlett	Levene	Brown–Forsyth	Equal
Algeria	(0.0000)	(0.0000)	(0.0000)	(0.0000)	(0.0000)	NO
Egypt	(0.1634)	(0.4934)	(0.1634)	(0.2123)	(0.2286)	YES
Iran	(0.0762)	(0.2232)	(0.0770)	(0.2009)	(0.1951)	YES
Pakistan	(0.0131)	(0.0188)	(0.0131)	(0.0282)	(0.0264)	NO
Turkey	(0.5885)	(0.1939)	(0.5885)	(0.8707)	(0.9846)	YES

P-values are in parentheses.

seems to have stagnated the country during this period. We use a dummy variable, which takes a value of 1 from 1990 to 1996 and 0 elsewhere. The war did not cause inflation, but it had a significant impact on inflation most probably because the fiscal and monetary policies were relatively loose. The regression slope coefficient *without the war dummy* variable is 0.77, which means a 1 percent increase in the broad money per unit of output growth rate increases inflation by 0.77 percent. Thus, money growth significantly affects inflation. The fit of this single-regressor equation measured by $\bar{R}^2$ is poor even though it has seven lead and zero lags of the rate of growth of money. Adding the war dummy variable improved the fit, $\bar{R}^2$ jumped to 0.69, and the magnitude of the slope coefficient was reduced to 0.50. Most importantly, the residuals are normal as shown by the Jarque–Bera *P*-value. These results are supportive of the QTM though the relationship between money growth and inflation is not one-to-one.

Egypt's slope coefficient is 0.91 and significant. There are 0 lead and 5 lags of the regressor. Egypt floated its exchange rate in 2016. A dummy variable that takes a value of 1 from 2016 to 2020 and zero elsewhere was found to be insignificant, hence not reported. The Egyptian Arab Spring dummy variable was also found to be insignificant. The residuals are normal as indicated by the Jarque–Bera *P*-value. The effect of the growth of broad money per unit of output on inflation is quite large in magnitudes, and much larger than the case of Algeria. We fit the equation with the growth of oil prices as an additional regressor, but the coefficient was insignificant, thus we do not report it. Money growth fuels inflation in Egypt.

64 Money Growth and Inflation

Iran is a major oil and gas producer. We could not estimate the DOLS regression for Iran for the same reason we could not do that earlier when we tested the levels of prices and money because of missing data in 1984, 1985, and 1986 (the period of the war with Iraq). An OLS regression instead, which skips over the missing data, however, gives an estimated slope coefficient of 0.30. Linear trend is also significant, as an additional regressor. The growth rate of oil prices was insignificant. The OLS residuals pass the normality test marginally with the Jarque–Bera P-value of 0.0842. So this result is unsupportive of the QTM although it is not the best way to estimate the equation. The scatter plots in Figure 5.1a nonetheless show a reasonably close association between money growth and inflation.

For Pakistan, the estimated DOLS slope coefficient is 0.81, which is highly significant. The residuals are normal. Money per unit of output growth increase by 1 percent increases inflation by 0.81 percent. The oil price shock 1973 dummy variable is very sizable and significant unlike the other three countries Algeria, Egypt, and Iran.

Turkey has had a history of very high, double-digit inflation. In 2002, Turkey adopted an inflation-targeting regime in 2002, which saw a significant decline in inflation over time. Consistent with the scatter plot, money per unit of output growth has a very large and significant effect on inflation. We estimated that a 1 percent increase in money/real GDP growth increases the inflation rate by almost 1 percent. The 1979 oil price shock dummy variable is large and significant, and the residuals are normal as indicated by the Jarque–Bera P-value. We also estimated the same equation over the sample from 2002 to 2020 – the inflation-targeting sample

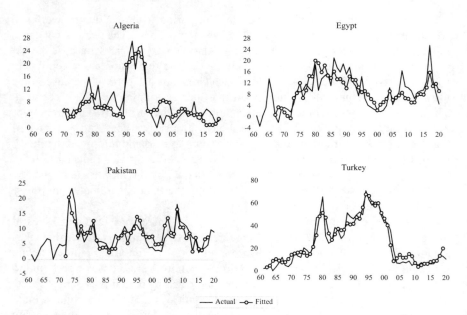

Figure 5.1c The Goodness of Fit of the Inflation and Broad Money Per Unit of Real Output Model in MENA Countries

period – separately and found that the slope coefficient got relatively smaller in magnitude, 0.72, as compared with 0.94 reported for the whole sample and statistically significantly different from zero. Thus, the coefficient got smaller in magnitude, and the fit deteriorated; the adjusted R^2 is 0.72 as compared with 0.90 in the full sample. These results are expected because inflation-targeting weakens the correlation between inflation and money growth. Successful inflation-targeting reduces the mean and the variance of inflation; therefore, the correlation between inflation and the more variable money growth must decline. We explain this more when we estimate the equation for the developed countries under inflation-targeting.

Note that DOLS is expected to have large $\bar{R}^2$ because of the large number of lead/lag of the growth rate of broad money per unit of real output regressors; however, these lead/lag regressors are important in the QTM. These lags and lead

Table 5.4 Dynamic OLS Estimated Broad Money – Real GDP Ratio Growth–Inflation Relationship in MENA Countries Dependent Variable is Inflation $\Delta lnCPI_t$

	Algeria (1970–2020)	Egypt (1967–2020)	Iran (1961–2020	Pakistan (1972–2020)	Turkey (1962–2020)
$\Delta ln\left(\dfrac{M}{Y}\right)_t$	0.50[i] (0.0016)	0.91[ii] (0.0000)	0.30[iii] (0.0008)	0.81[iv] (0.0000)	0.94[v] (0.0000)
d^{90-96}	15.4 (0.0000)	NA	NA	NA	NA
d^{73}	-	-	-	20.3 (0.0000)	-
d^{79}	3.6 (0.1416)	-	-	-	4.7 (0.1839)
d^e	NA	Insignificant	NA	NA	NA
$\bar{R}^2$	0.69	0.53	0.34	0.46	0.90
Jarque–Bera	(0.7928)	(0.9200)	(0.0842)	(0.3274)	(0.2475)

P-values are in parentheses.

d^{90-96} is a war dummy for the Algerian civil war from 1990 to 1996. It takes values of 1 during this period and zero elsewhere. d^{73} is the first oil shock dummy; d^{79} is the second oil shock dummy; and d^e is a dummy variable, which takes a value of 1 for the change of the exchange rate regime in Egypt from a fixed rate to a floating rate in 2016, and zero elsewhere. The independent variable $\dfrac{M}{Y}$ is the broad money – real GDP ratio. The Jarque–Bera is the *P*-value for testing the normality of the residuals.

[i] Auto lead/lag (0/2); based on AIC max = 10; HAC standard errors and covariance pre-whitening with lag = 3 from AIC max lag = 3; Bartlett kernel, Newey–West automatic bandwidth 3.0246, with auto lag = 3.

[ii] Auto leads/lags (0/5); based on AIC max = 10; HAC standard errors and covariance pre-whitening with lag = 2 from AIC max lag = 3; Bartlett kernel, Newey–West automatic bandwidth 5.6644, with auto lag = 3.

[iii] This is an OLS regression because of missing data in 1984–1986. HAC standard errors and covariance pre-whitening with lag = 1 from AIC max lag = 3; Bartlett kernel, Newey–West automatic bandwidth 4.2055, with auto lag = 3.

[iv] Auto leads/lags (2/10); based on AIC max = 10; HAC standard errors and covariance no pre-whitening; Bartlett kernel, Newey–West automatic bandwidth 4.2851, with auto lag = 3.

[v] Auto leads/lags (1/0); based on AIC max = 10; HAC standard errors and covariance pre-whitening with lag = 2 from AIC max lag = 3; Bartlett kernel, Newey–West automatic bandwidth 4.6211, with auto lag = 3.

66 *Money Growth and Inflation*

regressors are long indeed and may cause over-fitting. However, the $\bar{R}^2$ figures in Table 5.4 are not noticeably large in size. Figure 5.1c plots the actual inflation and the fitted values of the regressions given in Table 5.4. We will plot the actual and fitted values for all countries, too, but the goodness of fit is not an informative statistic here, because the QTM has only one explanatory variable, that is, money per unit of real output growth. The size of the slope coefficient is most important. Nonetheless, the MENA countries data fit the QTM model well. It makes sense that the MENA countries' inflation is probably attributed to printing money to finance government spending, wars, elections, etc., or to keep the exchange rate fixed at a desired level. Their central banks are not independent either.

The Latin and South American Countries

Next, we test the data of Latin and South American countries. The data are plotted in Figures 5.2a and 5.2b. Visually, the inflation–money growth relationships are quite different across the Latin and South American countries. The 45° lines scatter plots indicate that Bolivia, Honduras, Mexico, and Uruguay have a very strong relationship between money growth and inflation. Ecuador data are the most peculiar; the correlation is way off the 45° line. Ecuador experienced a political crisis for a very long time, which might explain this strange correlation. Recall from previous regressions in the levels of the CPI and money that the intercept was negative and significant, and the slope was very large in magnitude and greater than 1. On average, inflation is at least twice as high as money growth in Ecuador. Visually, there is a very large trough in money growth in 1998–2000, which refers to the political crisis. The 1998–1999 Ecuador economic crises were a period of economic instability that resulted from a combined inflationary-currency crisis, financial crisis, fiscal crisis, and sovereign debt crisis. The crisis resulted in a very high inflation and devaluation of the currency. On 9 January 2000, the US dollar was adopted as the national currency. Poor economic conditions and subsequent protests against the government resulted in the 2000 Ecuadorian coup d'état, which forced the president to resign.

Table 5.5 provides descriptive statistics for Latin and South American inflation and money growth. Except for Colombia and Uruguay, the data are not normal. Average inflation and money growth are very high, and the volatility is significant. Ecuador, which is the only country with inflation much larger than money growth on average, is the only country with a negative skewness statistic.

Table 5.6 provides tests for the equality of the means of broad money – real GDP ratio growth and the inflation rate. Seven out of the 11 countries in the sample have equal means.

Table 5.7 reports the test results of the hypothesis that the variances are equal.

These *P*-values indicate that we could not reject the null hypothesis that the variances of broad money – real GDP ratio growth and inflation are equal in all Latin and South American countries, except for Costa Rica. This is supportive of the QTM.

Money Growth and Inflation 67

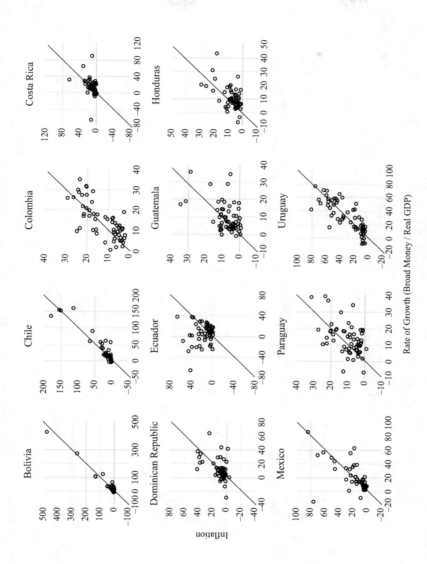

Figure 5.2a Significant Relationship between Money Per Unit of Output Growth Rate and Inflation in Latin and South American Countries, 1961–2020
Data Source: World Development Indicators

68 Money Growth and Inflation

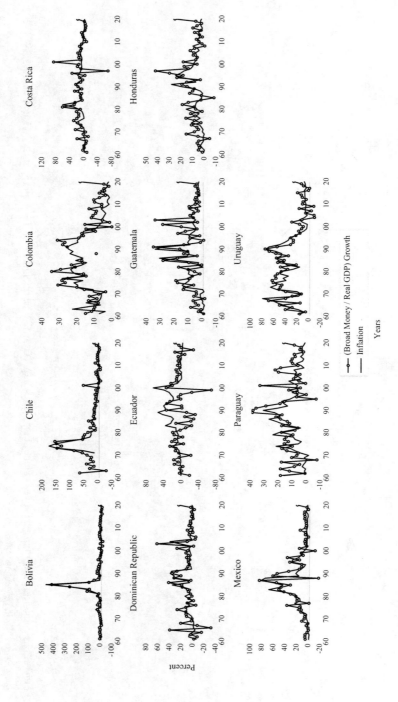

Figure 5.2b Money Per Unit of Output Growth Rate and Inflation Time Series in Latin and South American Countries, 1961–2020
Data Source: World Development Indicators

Money Growth and Inflation 69

Table 5.5 Descriptive Statistics for Broad Money – Real GDP Ratio Growth and Inflation in Latin and South American Countries in 1960–2020

	Broad Money – Real GDP Ratio Growth					Inflation				
	Mean	STD	SKW	KURT	J-B	Mean	STD	SKW	KURT	J-B
Bolivia	30.4	66.4	4.5	25.4	0.0000	26.2	72.0	4.9	28.7	0.000
Chile	29.2	39.0	2.0	7.0	0.0000	23.4	40.6	2.7	9.57	0.000
Colombia	18.5	8.98	0.5	2.5	0.2086	13.0	8.12	0.2	1.57	0.063
Costa Rica	13.2	19.0	0.2	10.7	0.0000	10.4	10.2	2.6	13.8	0.000
Dominican Republic	11.1	14.4	0.9	5.7	0.0000	9.52	10.7	1.8	5.59	0.000
Ecuador*	6.16	18.1	−1.2	5.9	0.0000	15.4	15.6	1.3	4.04	0.000
Guatemala	9.55	8.14	1.5	5.0	0.0000	7.38	7.06	1.9	7.82	0.000
Honduras	10.3	8.13	1.4	6.5	0.0000	7.66	6.08	1.7	5.63	0.000
Mexico	17.4	18.7	1.5	5.3	0.0000	15.5	19.3	2.0	6.55	0.000
Paraguay	13.4	9.48	0.7	4.1	0.0100	9.79	7.75	0.8	2.90	0.017
Uruguay	30.7	22.1	0.2	2.0	0.2411	29.8	22.5	0.5	1.90	0.069

- STD – standard deviations (second moment); SKW – skewness (third moment) – S^2; KURT – kurtosis (fourth moment) – K
- J-B denotes the *P*-values of Jarque–Bera. The test value is $\frac{N}{6}\left(S^2 + \frac{K-3}{4}\right)^2$. It tests $H_0 : normal$.
- Ecuador's average inflation is more than twice as large as average money growth.

Table 5.6 Are Mean Inflation and (Broad Money – Real GDP Ratio) Growth Equal in the Latin and South American Countries in 1960–2020?

	t-test	Satterthwaite–Welch t-test	ANOVA F-test	Welch F-test	Equal
Bolivia	(0.7392)	(0.7392)	(0.7392)	(0.7392)	YES
Chile	(0.4464)	(0.4480)	(0.4464)	(0.4480)	YES
Colombia	(0.0007)	(0.0008)	(0.0007)	(0.0008)	NO
Costa Rica	(0.3127)	(0.3223)	(0.3217)	(0.3223)	YES
Dominican Republic	(0.4850)	(0.4851)	(0.4850)	(0.4851)	YES
Ecuador	(0.0033)	(0.0033)	(0.0033)	(0.0033)	NO
Guatemala	(0.1222)	(0.1223)	(0.1222)	(0.1223)	YES
Honduras	(0.0425)	(0.0427)	(0.0425)	(0.0427)	NO
Mexico	(0.5947)	(0.4597)	(0.4957)	(0.4957)	YES
Paraguay	(0.0257)	(0.0258)	(0.0257)	(0.0258)	NO
Uruguay	(0.8312)	(0.8312)	(0.8312)	(0.8312)	YES

P-values are in parentheses.

Volatility of money and inflation in Latin and South African countries is relatively higher than in the MENA countries. For example, Bolivia had a huge one spike in 1985 (see Figure 5.2b). The commonly used unit root tests fail to reject the unit root because they fit a linear line through the data, which, most probably, confuses the spike with unit root. Inflation climbed from roughly 27 percent in 1981 to 80.5 in 1982, 132 in 1983, 262.5 in 1984, and 477.5 percent in 1985. Then

70　*Money Growth and Inflation*

Table 5.7 Are Variability of Inflation and (Broad Money – Real GDP Ratio) Growth Equal in Latin and South American Countries in 1960–2020?

	F-test	Siegel–Tukey	Bartlett	Levene	Brown–Forsyth	Equal
Bolivia	(0.5315)	(0.8031)	(0.5315)	(0.8806)	(0.8734)	YES
Chile	(0.7675)	(0.8864)	(0.7734)	(0.6710)	(0.6281)	YES
Colombia	(0.4437)	(0.1160)	(0.4456)	(0.7630)	(0.7057)	YES
Costa Rica	(0.0000)	(0.0120)	(0.0000)	(0.0228)	(0.0218)	NO
Dominican Republic	(0.0258)	(0.0470)	(0.0258)	(0.1342)	(0.0866)	NO
Ecuador	(0.2695)	(0.8811)	(0.2695)	(0.8724)	(0.6525)	YES
Guatemala	(0.2794)	(0.8811)	(0.2794)	(0.1935)	(0.3713)	YES
Honduras	(0.0280)	(0.9770)	(0.0280)	(0.1138)	(0.1485)	YES
Mexico	(0.8209)	(0.0374)	(0.8029)	(0.9344)	(0.8375)	YES
Paraguay	(0.1236)	(0.2902)	(0.1236)	(0.3800)	(0.3958)	YES
Uruguay	(0.9007)	(0.3199)	(0.9007)	(0.4950)	(0.6842)	YES

it began tumbling. It has been 3 percent since 2017, and less than 1 percent in 2020, but the minimum was −0.70. These trends appear in all countries in this region. Political, economical, banking, debt, and other financial crises and upheavals have dominated the period from 1960 to almost 2000 in this region.

Next, we fit the DOLS regressions. Table 5.8 reports the results. There are dummy variables for the period of political and economic instabilities in certain countries, for example, d^{80s} is a dummy variable that takes a value of 1 during the 1980s in Costa Rica. For Paraguay, d^{79-89} is the dummy variable to control for such problems during the period 1979–1989. In addition, we test dummy variables to control for the oil price shocks in 1973 and in 1979, with d^{73} and d^{79}, which take a value of 1 in these years only and 0 elsewhere. The inflation-targeting countries, Chile and Colombia, required dummy variables to control for the periods since the start of targeting, d^{π}.

Bolivia's data fit perfectly without a constant, trend, or any dummy variable. The residuals of the DOLS regression are normal as shown by the Jarque–Bera P-value. Chile is an inflation-targeting country. It started targeting price stability in 1990. Inflation was massive in the 1970s. It reached a peak of nearly 180 percent in 1974. That was also at the same time of the first oil price shock. It remained very high throughout the 1980s. Inflation then stabilized and became a single-digit in 1995. It fell steadily after implementing inflation targeting in 1999. We fit it with a dummy variable to capture the inflation-targeting period since 1999. It takes a value of 1 and 0 elsewhere. The increase of 1 percent in money per unit of output growth increases inflation by 0.72 percent. The inflation-targeting dummy variable is −2.75 as one might expect. Both oil price shocks have large positive coefficients 55 and 11. The residuals are normal as indicated by the Jarque–Bera P-value; however, we had to set the lags and the leads for DOLS because the automatic selection methods of the optimal number of lead/lag did not produce serially uncorrelated and *iid* residuals.

Table 5.8 Dynamic OLS Estimated Broad Money – Real GDP Ratio Growth–Inflation Relationship in Latin and South American Countries Dependent Variable is Inflation

Country/ Sample	Bolivia[i] (167–20)	Chile[ii] (71–17)	Colombia[iii] (61–20)	Costa Rica[iv] (65–15)	Dominican Republic[v] (62–20)	Ecuador[vi] (67–20)	Guatemala[vii] (68–20)	Honduras [viii]	Mexico[ix] (69–11)	Paraguay[x] (66–19)	Uruguay[xi] (71–10)
$\Delta ln\left(\dfrac{M}{Y}\right)_t$	0.92 (0.0000)	0.73 (0.0000)	0.68 (0.0000)	0.61 (0.000)	0.79 (0.0000)	-1.23 (0.1051)	0.81 (0.0000)	1.0 (0.0000)	0.95 (0.0000)	0.66 (0.0000)	0.56 (0.0000)
d^{79-89}	NA	NA	NA	NA	NA	NA	NA	-	NA	7.9 (0.0000)	NA
d^{73}		55.5 (0.0000)	1.57 (0.1194)	9.1 (0.0181)	2.9 (0.0485)	-	5.7 (0.0003)	-	-	-	23.0 (0.0005)
d^{79}		11.7 (0.0023)	6.4 (0.0000)	-	5.0 (0.0000)	-	6.4 (0.0000)	8.5 (0.0000)	-	-	-
$d^{\bar{\pi}}$	NA	−2.7 (0.0092)	−2.9 (0.0187)	NA	NA	NA	NA	NA	NA	NA	NA
d^{80s}	NA	NA	NA	18.8 (0.0000)	NA	NA	NA	NA	NA	NA	NA
$\bar{R}^2$	0.98	0.94	0.54	0.36	0.42	0.31	0.43	0.55	0.89	0.59	0.87
J-B	(0.5722)	(0.6715)	(0.1178)	(0.0758)	(0.2609)	(0.4647)	(0.0110)	(0.1885)	(0.7666)	(0.1266)	(0.8520)

P-values are in parentheses.

[i] Auto lead/lag (10/5) based on AIC with max lag; HAC standard errors and covariance, Bartlett kernel, Newey–West auto bandwidth 17.0628, NW auto lag length = 3.

[ii] Auto lead/lag (3/4) based on AIC with max lag; HAC standard errors and covariance; Bartlett kernel, Newey–West auto bandwidth 132.9394, NW auto lag length = 3.

[iii] Colombia has missing data. DOLS could not be estimated so we use OLS; HAC standard errors and covariance, pre-whitening with lag = 0 from AIC max lag = 3, Bartlett kernel, Newey–West auto bandwidth 2.6326, NW auto lag length = 3.

(Continued)

Table 5.8 (Continued)

(iv) Auto lead/lag (5/3) fixed; HAC standard errors and covariance, pre-whitening with lag = 3 from AIC with max lag = 3; Bartlett kernel, Newey–West auto bandwidth 1.6975, NW auto lag length = 3.

(v) Auto lead/lag (0/0) based on AIC with max lag; HAC standard errors and covariance, pre-whitening with lag = 0 from AIC with max lag = 3; Bartlett kernel, Newey–West auto bandwidth 4.5641, NW auto lag length = 3.

(vi) Auto lead/lag (0/5) based on AIC with max lag; HAC standard errors and covariance, pre-whitening with lag = 3 from AIC with max lag = 3; Bartlett kernel, Newey–West auto bandwidth 6.9489, NW auto lag length = 3.

(vii) Auto lead/lag (0/6) based on AIC with max lag; HAC standard errors and covariance, pre-whitening with lag = 3 from AIC with max lag = 3; Bartlett kernel, Newey–West auto bandwidth 2.9985, NW auto lag length = 3.

(viii) The regression includes a constant term. Lead/lag (6/4) are imposed on the data; HAC standard errors and covariance, pre-whitening with lag = 3 from AIC with max lag = 3; Bartlett kernel, Newey–West auto bandwidth 9.5488, NW auto lag length = 3.

(ix) Auto lead/lag (9/7) based on AIC with max lag; HAC standard errors and covariance; Bartlett kernel, Newey–West auto bandwidth 2.3868, NW auto lag length = 3.

(x) Auto lead/lag (1/4) based on AIC with max lag; HAC standard errors and covariance, pre-whitening with lag = 0 from AIC with max lag = 3; Bartlett kernel, Newey–West auto bandwidth 15.9385, NW auto lag length = 3.

(xi) Auto lead/lag (10/9) based on AIC with max lag; HAC standard errors and covariance, Bartlett kernel, Newey–West auto bandwidth 28.0272, NW auto lag length = 3.

Money Growth and Inflation 73

Colombia is also an inflation-targeting country. It started this monetary policy regime in 1999. The inflation time series looks completely different from that of Chile. DOLS is inapplicable because there are a few missing data in the sample. Nonetheless, we estimate an OLS, which is adjusted for missing data. The slope coefficient is 0.68, and both oil shock dummies in 1973 and in 1979 are positive and significant. Colombia is an oil producer itself. The magnitudes of these coefficients are significantly smaller than the case of Chile. The inflation-targeting dummy variable is significant, has a negative sign as expected, and is slightly larger than the case of Chile: -2.9 compared with -2.7 in Chile.

We also estimated the equation from 1999 to 2020 in the case of Chile, which is the period of inflation-targeting. Like the case of Turkey before, the slope coefficient gets smaller in magnitude, 0.42 as compared with 0.73 for the whole sample, and the fit deteriorates significantly as one might expect ($\bar{R}^2$ is negative). For Colombia, we fit the equation from 1999 to 2020. The slope coefficient is also smaller, 0.41 as compared to 0.68 in the full sample, and the adjusted R^2 is 0.55, which remains high relative to the full sample regression. The inflation rate is more volatile than in the case of Chile. The residuals are normal. The inflation-targeting subsample regressions results are not reported in Table 5.8.

The Dominican Republic estimated slope coefficient is 0.79, both oil price shocks are significant, and the regression fit is good. From the scatter plot, Ecuador data are expected to result in a negative slope coefficient, that is, the increase in money growth is associated with negative inflation. Most Latin and South American countries experienced banking, financial, debt, and political crises. Ecuador's inflation is volatile and increasing from 1980 to 2001. In 2000, it reached 67 percent. Fitting the data for the whole sample from 1961 to 2020 gives us a negative slope, which is consistent with the scatter plot shown earlier. This is the only case in 42 countries, where the inflation–money relationship is negative. However, when we fit the regression with a dummy variable to control for the period from 1980 to 2000, the slope coefficient turns positive with an estimated coefficient of 0.66 and statistically significantly different from zero.

Guatemala is another difficult case. This country had periods of high political and economical instability. When we fit DOLS and search for the dynamics, that is, the number of lead and lag-difference regressor, we find that the slope is 0.79, and both of the oil price shock dummy variables are positive and significant. The residuals though are non-normal. The Jarque–Bera P-value is small. We rerun the DOLS regression with fixed leads and lags to 6; the slope coefficient jumps to 0.85 and the residuals become normal with the Jarque–Bera P-value of 0.2600.

Honduras' regression also shows non-normal residuals. Honduras was a hard case to fit using automatic search methods for the lead/lag length so we imposed the number of lead/lag instead. We used 6 leads and 4 lags. The coefficient of the broad money per unit of output growth is 1. The residuals are normal as shown by the Jarque–Bera P-value.

Mexico, Paraguay, and Uruguay results are very supportive of the QTM, and the diagnostic statistics of the regressions are good. The only conclusion one should

74 Money Growth and Inflation

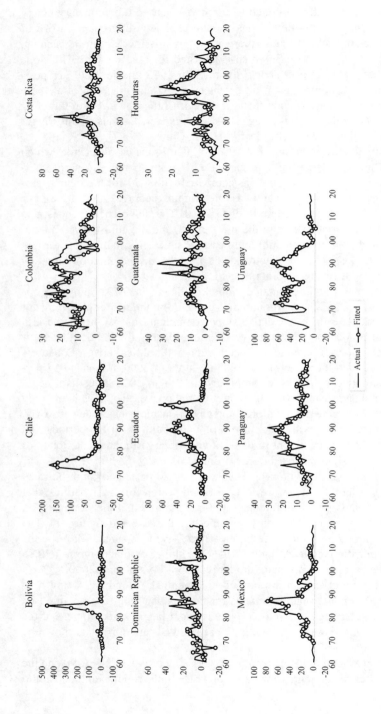

Figure 5.2c The Goodness of Fit of the Inflation and Broad Money Per Unit of Real Output Model of Latin and South American Countries

Money Growth and Inflation 75

arrive at from testing the Latin and American countries is that money growth causes inflation.

Figure 5.2c plots the actual inflation data and the fitted values from the dynamic regressions for the Latin and South American countries. Here too, just like the MENA countries, the dynamic fit is quite high. Inflation is largely accounted for by the variability of the rate of growth of broad money per unit of real output, given that we control for the various crises and oil shocks that hit the region during that period.

Regardless of the technical difficulties to fit the Latin and South American data, these results are largely consistent with the predictions of the QTM.

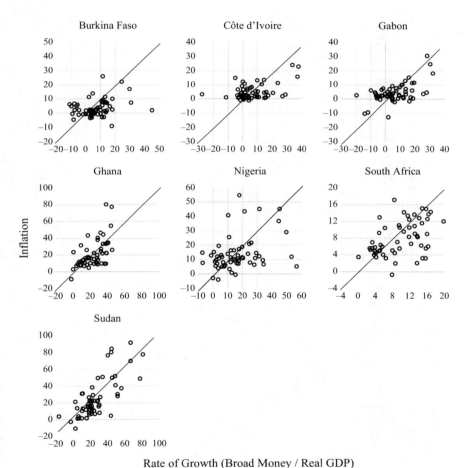

Figure 5.3a Significant Relationship between Money Per Unit of Output Growth Rate and Inflation in African Countries, 1961–2020

Data Source: World Development Indicators

76 *Money Growth and Inflation*

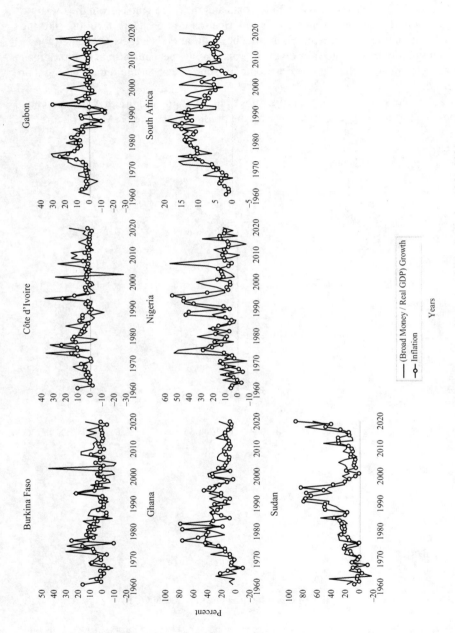

Figure 5.3b Money Per Unit of Output Growth Rate and Inflation Time Series in African Countries, 1961–2020
Data Source: World Development Indicators

Money Growth and Inflation   77

Table 5.9 Descriptive Statistics for Broad Money – Real GDP Ratio Growth and Inflation in African Countries, 1960–2020

	Broad Money – Real GDP Ratio Growth					Inflation				
	Mean	STD	SKW	KURT	J-B	Mean	STD	SKW	KURT	J-B
Burkina Faso	7.39	10.4	0.84	4.8	0.0000	3.88	6.27	1.35	5.5	0.000
Côte d'Ivoire	6.40	11.5	0.65	4.6	0.0055	5.04	5.51	1.60	5.5	0.000
Gabon	6.49	10.9	0.21	2.9	0.7965	4.46	6.95	1.12	6.8	0.000
Ghana	22.9	13.0	−0.03	1.9	0.2212	22.3	18.3	1.57	5.5	0.000
Nigeria	16.4	14.2	0.92	3.6	0.0083	14.0	12.0	1.64	5.4	0.000
South Africa	9.88	4.85	−0.05	1.8	0.2015	7.54	4.28	0.32	2.07	0.205
Sudan	26.2	19.1	0.86	3.8	0.0099	25.0	23.4	1.25	3.92	0.000

- STD – standard deviations (second moment); SKW – skewness (third moment) – S^2; KURT – kurtosis (fourth moment) – K.
- J-B denotes the P-values of Jarque–Bera. The test value is $\dfrac{N}{6}\left(S^2+\dfrac{K-3}{4}\right)^2$. Tests $H_0 : normal$

Table 5.10 Are Mean Inflation and (Broad Money – Real GDP Ratio) Growth Equal in the African Countries in 1960–2020?

	t-test	Satterthwaite–Welch t-test	ANOVA F-test	Welch F-test	Equal
Burkina Faso	(0.0281)	(0.0298)	(0.0281)	(0.0298)	NO
Côte d'Ivoire	(0.4083)	(0.4140)	(0.4083)	(0.4140)	YES
Gabon	(0.2354)	(0.2342)	(0.2354)	(0.2342)	YES
Ghana	(0.8466)	(0.8483)	(0.8466)	(0.8483	YES
Nigeria	(0.3480)	(0.3474)	(0.3480)	(0.3474)	YES
South Africa	(0.0072)	(0.0075)	(0.0072)	(0.0075)	NO
Sudan	(0.7521)	(0.7521)	(0.7521)	(0.7521)	YES

P-values are in parentheses.

The African Countries

African countries have had all sorts of crises. There were foreign military interventions in the 1960s and the Cold War political issues, military coups, civil unrests, economic and financial problems, draughts, and oil shocks. These shocks must have affected the money growth–inflation relationship in the short run and could have had a longer effect. We plot the data in Figures 5.3a and 5.3b, and Table 5.9

78 Money Growth and Inflation

Table 5.11 Is Variability of Inflation and (Broad Money – Real GDP Ratio) Growth Equal in the African Countries in 1960–2020?

	F-test	Siegel–Tukey	Bartlett	Levene	Brown–Forsyth	Equal
Burkina Faso	(0.0002)	(0.0770)	(0.0002)	(0.0032)	(0.0023)	NO
Côte d'Ivoire	(0.0000)	(0.0000)	(0.0000)	(0.0001)	(0.0010)	NO
Gabon	(0.0007)	(0.0004)	(0.0007)	(0.0004)	(0.0006)	NO
Ghana	(0.0124)	(0.9449)	(0.0125)	(0.2711)	(0.5753)	YES
Nigeria	(0.2074)	(0.0244)	(0.2072)	(0.1140)	(0.0855)	YES
South Africa	(0.3470)	(0.3122)	(0.3490)	(0.1916)	(0.1691)	YES
Sudan	(0.1278)	(0.0651)	(0.1277)	(0.2036)	(0.2960)	YES

Table 5.12 Dynamic OLS Estimated Broad Money – Real GDP Ratio Growth–Inflation Relationship in African Countries Dependent Variable is Inflation

Country/ Sample	Burkina Faso[i] (73–2011)	Côte d'Ivoire [ii] (72–20)	Gabon[iii] (63–18)	Ghana[iv] (72–13)	Nigeria[v] (62–15)	South Africa[vi] (76–20)	Sudan[vii] (72–11)
$\Delta ln\left(\dfrac{M}{Y}\right)_t$	0.63 (0.0001)	0.73 (0.0001)	0.59 (0.0000)	0.88 (0.0000)	0.88 (0.0000)	0.90 (0.0000)	1.0 (0.0000)
d^{73} Oil shock	-	-	-	-	-	-s	-
d^{79} Oil shock	7.5 (0.0288)	13.2 (0.0000)	-	-	-	-	-
$d^{\bar{\pi}}$	NA	NA	NA	NA	NA	-2.6 (0.1057)	-
$\bar{R}^2$	0.43	0.40	0.36	0.66	0.39	0.46	0.81
Jarque–Bera	(0.8079)	(0.7528)	(0.000)	(0.5785)	(0.0002)	(0.5121)	(0.8752)

P-values are in parentheses.

[i] Auto lead/lag (9/9) based on AIC max lag; HAC standard errors and covariance, Bartlett kernel with Newey–West auto bandwidth 3.1492, NW lag length = 3.

[ii] Auto lead/lag (0/8) based on AIC max lag; HAC standard errors and covariance, Bartlett, pre-whitening with lag = 3, from AIC with max lag = 3, kernel with Newey–West auto bandwidth 2.7912, NW lag length = 3.

[iii] Auto lead/lag (1/0) based on AIC max lag; HAC standard errors and covariance, Bartlett, pre-whitening with lag = 1, from AIC with max lag = 3, kernel with Newey–West auto bandwidth 2.9227, NW lag length = 3.

[iv] Auto lead/lag (7/10) based on AIC max lag; HAC standard errors and covariance, Bartlett kernel with Newey–West auto bandwidth 7.3848, NW lag length = 3.

[v] Auto lead/lag (5/0) based on AIC max lag; HAC standard errors and covariance, Bartlett kernel with Newey–West auto bandwidth 3.9881, NW lag length = 3.

[vi] Auto lead/lag (0/9) based on AIC max lag; HAC standard errors and covariance, Bartlett kernel with Newey–West auto bandwidth 5.3333, NW lag length = 3.

[vii] Auto lead/lag (9/10) based on AIC max lag; HAC standard errors and covariance, Bartlett kernel with Newey–West auto bandwidth 5.2838, NW lag length = 3.

Money Growth and Inflation 79

reports the mean, the standard deviation, the skewness and the kurtosis statistics, and the *P*-value of the Jarque–Bera statistics for normality.

There is a significant association between money growth and inflation in African countries. South Africa adopted inflation targeting in 2000, hence the weaker association between money growth and inflation compared with the rest of the countries.

The statistics show that the magnitudes of money growth and inflation rates are smaller than Latin and South American countries; nonetheless, there is inflation everywhere. There is more variation in money per unit of output than inflation, which suggests that money growth could explain some of the inflation rate. Table 5.10 tests the equality of the means.

With the exception of Burkina Faso and South Africa, broad money per unit of output growth rate and the inflation rate are equal on average. Table 5.11 reports the test results of the hypothesis that the variances are equal.

These statistics show that the variances of money per unit of output growth and inflation are unequal in Burkina Faso, Côte d'Ivoire, and Gabon; they are equal in Ghana, Nigeria, South Africa, and Sudan as well.

The regression results are reported in Table 5.12. The estimated slope coefficients α_1 are quite large, close to 1 in many countries, and 1 in the case of Sudan, except Gabon. Gabon and Nigeria have non-normal residuals as indicated by the *P*-value of the Jarque–Bera statistic. The 1979 second oil price shock dummy variable is significant in Burkina Faso and Côte d'Ivoire only.

South Africa adopted an inflation-targeting regime in 2000. The dummy variable is significant and has the negative expected sign. Thus, inflation targeting was successful in targeting a lower and stable inflation. The magnitude of the dummy variable is large as expected. The fit is relatively high. DOLS fits long lags and leads in most countries. Thus, the dynamics are rich. These results are supportive of the QTM. We run the same regression for the inflation-targeting sample from 2000 to 2020. The slope coefficient is smaller, 0.53, as compared with 0.90 as one would expect, and the fit deteriorates markedly. Inflation-targeting reduces the correlation between inflation and other non-targeted variables because it changes the time series properties of inflation; it becomes I(0) under successful targeting. These results are just like the previous cases of Turkey and Chile, where the relationship between money growth and successful inflation-targeting expected to deteriorate.

Figure 5.3c plots the actual inflation data and the fitted values of the dynamic regressions reported earlier for the African countries. Given the poor quality of the data, we are still able to trace out the correlation between the inflation rate and the growth rate of the broad money per unit of real output in this region.

80 Money Growth and Inflation

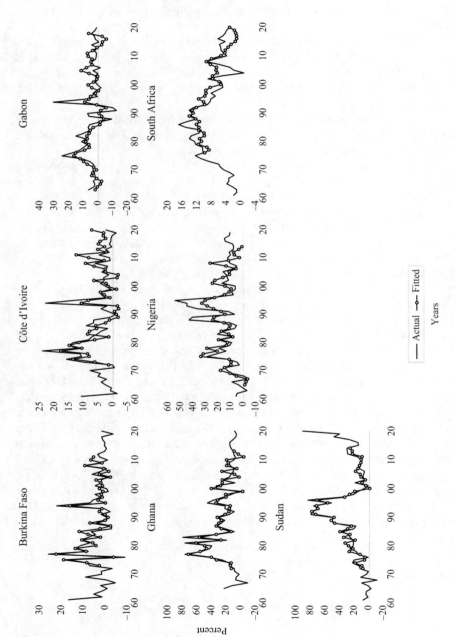

Figure 5.3c The Goodness of Fit of the Inflation and Broad Money Per Unit of Real Output Model in African Countries

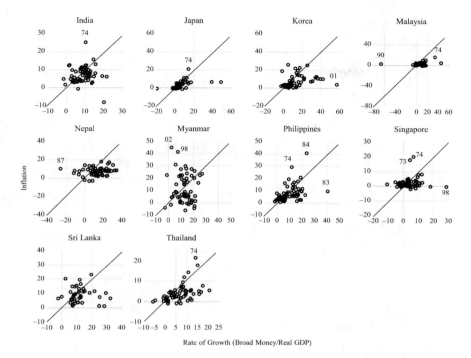

Figure 5.4a Significant Relationship between Money Per Unit of Output Growth Rate and Inflation in Asian Countries, 1961–2020

Data Source: World Development Indicators

The Asian Countries

The data of the ten Asian countries are plotted in Figures 5.4a and 5.4b. The relationship between inflation and money growth seems relatively weaker in the Asian countries. Myanmar, Singapore, and Sri Lanka appear to have relatively weaker associations between money growth and inflation. Tables 5.13, 5.14, and 5.15 report the descriptive statistics, test of the equality of the means of broad money per unit of real output and the inflation rate, and test of the equality of the variances.

The aforementioned results suggest that the mean inflation and mean money growth are unequal. Money growth means are significantly high except in the cases of Malaysia, Myanmar, and the Philippines.

Table 5.15 reports the test results of the hypothesis that the variances are equal.

Statistically, except for India, Myanmar, the Philippines, and Sri Lanka, the variance of money growth is larger than the variance of inflation. The graphs clearly show that some countries have a very poor correlation between inflation and the

82 Money Growth and Inflation

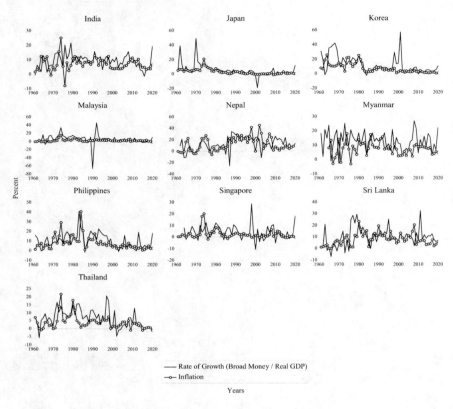

Figure 5.4b Money Per Unit of Output Growth Rate and Inflation Time Series in Asian Countries, 1961–2020
Data Source: World Development Indicators

Table 5.13 Descriptive Statistics for Broad Money – Real GDP Ratio Growth and Inflation in Asian Countries in 1960–2020

	Broad Money – Real GDP Ratio Growth					Inflation				
	Mean	STD	SKW	KURT	J-B	Mean	STD	SKW	KURT	J-B
India	9.16	4.75	0.19	3.17	0.8022	7.15	4.52	0.52	7.19	0.000
Japan	5.36	9.03	2.50	13.8	0.0000	2.85	3.85	2.08	9.39	0.000
Korea	12.5	12.2	1.50	5.09	0.0000	7.26	6.51	1.27	3.82	0.000
Malaysia	5.90	12.6	−2.42	20.2	0.0000	2.88	2.74	2.18	16.0	0.000
Nepal	12.9	6.42	−0.11	2.79	0.8960	7.50	4.51	−0.06	3.26	0.902
Myanmar	12.6	12.0	−0.71	3.56	0.0570	12.0	11.3	0.65	2.80	0.119
Philippines	10.4	7.70	0.98	5.12	0.0003	7.95	7.03	2.37	10.3	0.000
Singapore	4.22	6.12	0.98	6.31	0.0000	2.44	3.78	3.12	14.2	0.000

	Broad Money – Real GDP Ratio Growth					Inflation				
	Mean	STD	SKW	KURT	J-B	Mean	STD	SKW	KURT	J-B
Sri Lanka	12.1	7.29	0.96	3.99	0.0122	9.03	5.09	0.69	3.28	0.154
Thailand	6.72	5.56	0.19	2.73	0.7566	4.07	4.23	2.09	8.51	0.000

- STD – standard deviations (second moment); SKW – skewness (third moment) – S^2 ; KURT – kurtosis (fourth moment) – K.
- J-B denotes the P-values of Jarque–Bera. The test value is $\dfrac{N}{6}\left(S^2 + \dfrac{K-3}{4}\right)^2$. Tests H_0 : *normal*

Table 5.14 Are Mean Inflation and (Broad Money – Real GDP Ratio) Growth Equal in the Asian Countries in 1960–2020?

	t-test	Satterthwaite–Welch t-test	ANOVA F-test	Welch F-test	Equal
India	(0.0192)	(0.0192)	(0.0192)	(0.0192)	NO
Japan	(0.0502)	(0.0513)	(0.0502)	(0.0513)	NO
Korea	(0.0042)	(0.0044)	(0.0042)	(0.0044)	NO
Malaysia	(0.0737)	(0.0758)	(0.0737)	(0.0758)	YES
Nepal	(0.0000)	(0.0000)	(0.0000)	(0.0000)	NO
Myanmar	(0.8129)	(0.8129)	(0.8129)	(0.8129)	YES
Philippines	(0.0679)	(0.0679)	(0.0679)	(0.0679)	YES
Singapore	(0.0487)	(0.0520)	(0.0487)	(0.0520)	NO
Sri Lanka	(0.0183)	(0.0190)	(0.0183)	(0.0190)	NO
Thailand	(0.0032)	(0.0034)	(0.0032)	(0.0034)	NO

P-values are in parentheses.

Table 5.15 Are Variability of Inflation and (Broad Money – Real GDP Ratio) Growth Equal in the Asian Countries in 1960–2020?

	F-test	Siegel–Tukey	Bartlett	Levene	Brown–Forsyth	Equal
India	(0.7011)	(0.3024)	(0.7011)	(0.4625)	(0.4484)	YES
Japan	(0.0000)	(0.8894)	(0.0000)	(0.0215)	(0.0504)	NO
Korea	(0.0000)	(0.6423)	(0.0000)	(0.0006)	(0.0106)	NO
Malaysia	(0.0000)	(0.0000)	(0.0000)	(0.0002)	(0.0003)	NO
Nepal	(0.0075)	(0.0622)	(0.0074)	(0.0078)	(0.0074)	NO
Myanmar	(0.9198)	(0.1291)	(0.9198)	(0.4654)	(0.7588)	YES
Philippines	(0.4843)	(0.1286)	(0.4843)	(0.0890)	(0.0691)	YES
Singapore	(0.0002)	(0.0001)	(0.0002)	(0.0008)	(0.0008)	NO
Sri Lanka	(0.0159)	(0.8149)	(0.0160)	(0.1603)	(0.2073)	YES
Thailand	(0.0403)	(0.0166)	(0.0404)	(0.0071)	(0.0069)	NO

P-values are in parentheses.

growth rate of broad money per unit of real output. India is visually clear, and so is Myanmar and, to some extent, Singapore. Japan, Korea, and the Philippines have a visual high correlation and, to some extent, Thailand too. A few countries have been affected directly by the Asian Financial Crisis in 1997–1998 such as Korea,

84 *Money Growth and Inflation*

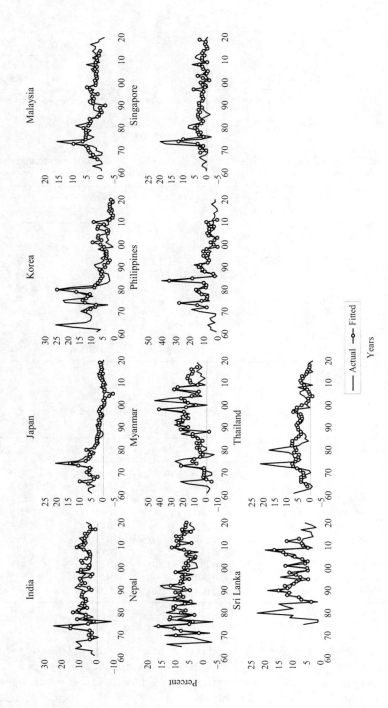

Figure 5.4c The Goodness of Fit of the Inflation and Broad Money Per Unit of Real Output Model in Asian Countries

Table 5.16 Dynamic OLS Estimated Broad Money – Real GDP Ratio Growth–Inflation Relationship in Asian Countries Dependent Variable is Inflation.

Country/ Sample	India[i] (69–18)	Japan [ii] (65–19)	Korea [iii] (70–20)	Malaysia [iv] (62–15)	Nepal [v] (70–20)	Myanmar[vi] (66–17)	Philippines [vii] (72–11)	Singapore[viii] (69–19)	Sri Lanka[ix] (85–13)	Thailand[x] (64–18)
$\Delta ln\left(\dfrac{M}{Y}\right)_t$	0.43 (0.0305)	0.54 (0.0000)	0.49 (0.0000)	0.22 (0.0001)	0.60 (0.0000)	0.83 (0.0000)	0.86 (0.0000)	0.56 (0.0001)	0.85 (0.0000)	0.58 (0.0000)
d^{73} Oil shock	6.15 (0.0000)	1.83 (0.0054)	-	4.61 (0.0000)	4.19 (0.0146)	14.5 (0.0001)	-	8.01 (0.0051)	-	-
d^{79} Oil shock	-	-	8.30 (0.0000)	-	-3.60 (0.0000)	-	-	-	-	1.74 (0.0000)
d^{80}	-	2.91 (0.0000)	16.85 (0.0000)	2.37 (0.0000)	-	-	-	-	-	-
d^{97-98}	-	-	-	2.40 (0.0000)	-	22.75 (0.0000)	5.47 (0.1897)	-	-	−1.01 (0.1482)
d^{Bank}	-	-	-	-	-	10.35 (0.0359)	-	-	-	-
$d^{Political}$	-	-	-	-	-	13.99 (0.0001)	-	-	-	-
$\overline{R}^2$	0.33	0.76	0.56	0.19	0.31	0.32	0.67	0.25	0.24	0.44
Jarque–Bera	(0.0382)	(0.0000)	(0.0171)	(0.0000)	(0.8318)	(0.0014)	(0.8034)	(0.0000)	(0.1714)	(0.2628)

P-values are in parentheses.

[i] Fixed lead/lag (2/6) based on AIC max lag; HAC standard errors and covariance, Bartlett, pre-whitening with lag = 3, from AIC with max lag = 3, kernel with Newey–West auto bandwidth 3.6458, NW lag length = 3.

[ii] Auto lead/lag (1/3) based on AIC max lag; HAC standard errors and covariance, Bartlett, pre-whitening with lag = 1, from AIC with max lag = 3, kernel with Newey–West auto bandwidth 3.1874, NW lag length = 3.

[iii] Auto lead/lag (0/8) based on AIC max lag; HAC standard errors and covariance, Bartlett kernel with Newey–West auto bandwidth 2.6534, NW lag length = 3.

[iv] Auto lead/lag (6/4) based on AIC max lag; HAC standard errors and covariance, Bartlett, pre-whitening with lag = 1, from AIC with max lag = 3, kernel with Newey–West auto bandwidth 2.1366, NW lag length = 3.

[v] Auto lead/lag (0/8) based on AIC max lag; HAC standard errors and covariance, Bartlett, pre-whitening with lag = 1, from AIC with max lag = 3, kernel with Newey–West auto bandwidth 4.2056, NW lag length = 3.

[vi] Fixed lead/lag (3/3) based on AIC max lag; HAC standard errors and covariance, Bartlett, pre-whitening with lag = 3, from AIC with max lag = 3, kernel with Newey–West auto bandwidth 5.2585, NW lag length = 3.

[vii] Auto lead/lag (9/10) based on AIC max lag; HAC standard errors and covariance, Bartlett, pre-whitening with lag = 1, from AIC with max lag = 3, kernel with Newey–West auto bandwidth 3.8462, NW lag length = 3.

[viii] Auto lead/lag (1/4) based on AIC max lag; HAC standard errors and covariance, Bartlett kernel with Newey–West auto bandwidth 5.3618, NW lag length = 3.

[ix] Auto lead/lag (6/9) based on AIC max lag; HAC standard errors and covariance, Bartlett kernel with Newey–West auto bandwidth 2.1276, NW lag length = 3.

[x] Auto lead/lag (1/1) based on AIC max lag; HAC standard errors and covariance, Bartlett kernel with Newey–West auto bandwidth 2.2165, NW lag length = 3.

Malaysia, Myanmar, and the Philippines; thus, we fit a dummy variable to account for this crisis. The data do not show a significant spike or trough in inflation during the crisis in every country. Therefore, we test a dummy variable country by country. We will not report the estimated coefficient if it is insignificant. Myanmar, in particular, had a severe banking crisis in 2003 and a political crisis in 2007. Interestingly, inflation fell in Thailand during the Asian Financial Crisis. Korea had an uprising in 1980. We will fit an appropriate dummy variable for each of these turbulent events.

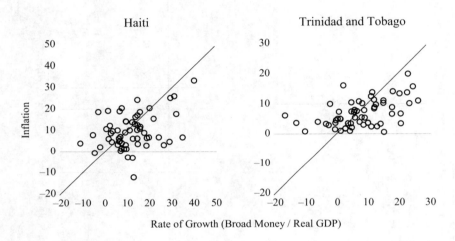

Figure 5.5a Reasonably Significant Relationship between Money Per Unit of Output Growth Rate and Inflation in Caribbean Countries, 1961–2020

Data Source: World Development Indicators

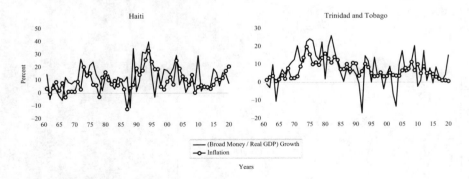

Figure 5.5b Money Per Unit of Output Growth Rate and Inflation Time Series in Caribbean Countries, 1961–2020

Data Source: World Development Indicators

Money Growth and Inflation 87

Asian countries suffered some serious political, financial, and banking crises. In addition, their dependency on oil imports also affects the fit of the QTM. Thus, isolating the effect of money growth required a lot more work. Figure 5.4c plots the actual inflation data and the fitted values of the regressions reported in Table 5.16.

The fit is relatively weaker in Asia than the cases of Latin and South America, Africa, and the MENA countries regardless of the lead/lag dynamics we had in DOLS. The adjusted R^2 statistics are relatively low, and peculiarly so for Dynamic OLS regressions like these. Generally speaking, the Asian data are the least supportive of the QTM so far.

Table 5.17 Descriptive Statistics for Broad Money – Real GDP Ratio Growth and Inflation in Caribbean Countries, 1960–2020

	Broad Money – Real GDP Ratio Growth					Inflation				
	Mean	STD	SKW	KURT	J-B	Mean	STD	SKW	KURT	J-B
Haiti	11.9	10.1	0.52	3.42	0.1993	9.54	8.07	0.40	3.57	0.284
Trinidad and Tobago	7.76	9.13	-0.19	3.02	0.8328	6.68	4.43	0.69	2.87	0.087

- STD – standard deviations (second moment); SKW – skewness (third moment) – S^2 ; KURT – kurtosis (fourth moment) – K.
- J-B denotes the P-values of Jarque–Bera. The test value is $\dfrac{N}{6}\left(S^2 + \dfrac{K-3}{4}\right)^2$. Tests H_0 : *normal*

Table 5.18 Are Mean Inflation and (Broad Money – Real GDP Ratio) Growth Equal in the Caribbean Countries in 1960–2020?

	t-test	Satterthwaite– Welch t-test	ANOVA F-test	Welch F-test	Equal
Haiti	(0.1580)	(0.1581)	(0.1580)	(0.1581)	YES
Trinidad and Tobago	(0.5105)	(0.5110)	(0.5105)	(0.5110)	YES

P-values are in parentheses.

Table 5.19 Are Variability of Inflation and (Broad Money – Real GDP Ratio) Growth Equal in Caribbean Countries in 1960–2020?

	F-test	Siegel–Tukey	Bartlett	Levene	Brown–Forsyth	Equal
Haiti	(0.0854)	(0.7588)	(0.0854)	(0.1190)	(0.2017)	YES
Trinidad and Tobago	(0.0000)	(0.0005)	(0.0000)	(0.0000)	(0.0000)	NO

P-values are in parentheses.

88 Money Growth and Inflation

Table 5.20 Dynamic OLS Estimated Broad Money – Real GDP Ratio Growth–Inflation Relationship in Caribbean Countries. Dependent Variable is Inflation

Country/ Sample	Haiti[i] (64–20)	Trinidad and Tobago[iii] (66–19)
$\Delta ln\left(\dfrac{M}{Y}\right)_t$	0.73 (0.0000)	0.56 (0.0000)
d^{73} Oil shock	7.60 (0.0002)	3.61 (0.0000)
d^{79} Oil shock	–	1.20 (0.0000)
d^{91-94}	10.52 (0.0000)	—
$\bar{R}^2$	0.45	0.48
J-B	(0.0000)	(0.7979)

P-values are in parentheses.

[i] Auto lead/lag (0/2) based on AIC max lag; HAC standard errors and covariance, Bartlett, pre-whitening with lag = 2, from AIC with max lag = 3, kernel with Newey–West auto bandwidth 2.4848, NW lag length = 3.

[ii] Auto lead/lag (1/4) based on AIC max lag; HAC standard errors and covariance, Bartlett, pre-whitening with lag = 3, from AIC with max lag = 3, kernel with Newey–West auto bandwidth 6.4610, NW lag length = 3.

[iii] The dummy variable in Haiti covers the period 1991 to 1994 with a value of 1, and 0 elsewhere. In 1991, Haiti had a coup d'état, political crisis, and US intervention in 1994.

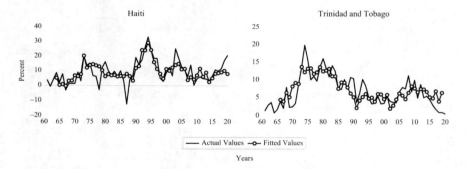

Figure 5.5c The Goodness of Fit of the Inflation and Broad Money Per Unit of Real Output Model in Caribbean Countries

The fit is not very high as indicated by the adjusted R^2 statistic. Figure 5.5c plots the actual inflation date and the fitted values of the regression. One cannot easily dismiss money growth as the main driver of inflation in these two Caribbean countries.

The Caribbean Countries

Figure 5.5a and Figure 5.5b plot the data for the two Caribbean countries in the sample, Haiti and Trinidad and Tobago. Haiti is an unstable country with natural disasters, political unrests, and more. The data, however, show a reasonable positive relationship between money growth and inflation.

Tables 5.17, 5.18, and 5.19 report the descriptive statistics, the testing of the equality of the mean, and the variance for inflation and the growth rate of money per unit of real output.

The aforementioned results suggest that mean inflation and mean money growth are equal. Table 5.19 reports the test results of the hypothesis that the variances are equal.

The variability of the growth rate of broad money growth per unit of real output exceeds that of the inflation rate in Trinidad and Tobago, but not in Haiti. Table 5.20 reports the estimates of the QTM equation, which shows that money growth explains a lot of the variations in inflation.

The Developed Inflation-Targeting Countries

Finally, we analyze the advanced inflation-targeting regimes of Australia, Denmark, Norway, New Zealand, Sweden, the United Kingdom and United States. These countries are harder to fit than all others because monetary policy, from 1990s until 2020, successfully stabilized inflation around a low average target and reduced its variability significantly.

New Zealand was the first developed country to adopt inflation-targeting regime. The Reserve Bank of New Zealand embarked on a disinflation process, which began at least 2 years before the 1990 Price Stability ACT; whereby they experimented with various instruments.[4] Their approach was *atheoretical*. However, it succeeded in bringing inflation to the target of 0 to 2 a year earlier than the stipulated date in the ACT by having something called *Exchange Rate Comfort Zone*. This is a zone, where they "felt" that the currency fluctuates within, which might be consistent with price stability. There is no theoretical basis for that approach. I interviewed Governor Don Brash (1988–2002) on 27 March 2002, just before he left the Governorship of the RBNZ. I asked him,

> You started your job here in September 1988. Inflation was no longer in the double digits, but was still reasonably high (inflation stood at 7.8 %). We then saw a large disinflation with inflation falling to 4.8% in September 1990 (two years after you started), and falling further to below 3% in 1992. How did you do it? Back then there was no output gap in the Bank's literature, you did not control the interest rate (cash rate) directly, and the exchange rate was floating. So how did you do it? Describe how you think the process worked.

Brash said, when I came on 1 September 1988, I did not think that either the Bank or I had a very clear understanding of the monetary policy transmission mechanism. I do not recall anyone talking about money growth.[5] There was no mention of the Phillips curve either.

---

4 See (Walsh, 1995) for his modeling of the Reserve Bank of New Zealand's price stability act.
5 The New Zealand Association of Economists published parts of this interview in the Asymmetric Information Publication online.

90 *Money Growth and Inflation*

Then the RBNZ followed a unique monetary policy framework from 1989 to 1999. It was called *Open Mouth Operation*. (Guthrie and Wright, 2000) explained, and I was a witness during that period. The RBNZ would make statements and talk to the local commercial banks directly to say something like the lending rates seem higher/lower than what the RBNZ would like to see. The RBNZ would make noise when it felt that inflation is drifting away from the target, and that action is required to keep inflation on target. The RBNZ statements, rather than open market operations, were used to implement monetary policy. Interestingly, the bankers oblige. Some of them get on the phone with the RBNZ seniors or the Governor and discuss the matter further. In the extreme, policy instruments can be held constant, and yet interest rates will evolve along the path desired by the RBNZ. (Guthrie and Wright, 2000) show how the recent implementation of monetary policy in New Zealand works in this way. Using announcement data from New Zealand, they reported that *open mouth operations* lead to large changes in interest rates across all maturities, and these changes cannot be explained by open market operations.

In March 1999, the RBNZ began actively using the overnight short interest rate as a policy instrument (the OCR – Official Cash Rate), and *Open Mouth Operation* ceased to operate. The Reserve Bank of New Zealand's Exchange Settlement Account System (ESAS) is used by banks and other approved financial institutions

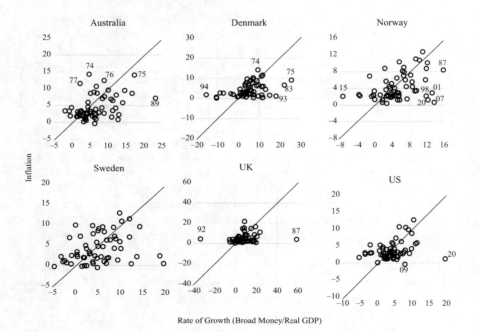

Figure 5.6a Significant Relationship between Money Per Unit of Output Growth Rate and Inflation in Inflation-Targeting Countries, 1961–2020

Data Source: World Development Indicators

to settle their obligations on a Real-Time Gross Settlement (RTGS) basis. ESAS came into live operation in March 1998 as part of the implementation of RTGS in New Zealand. The settlement amount of money available for banks to borrow is somewhere from six to nine billion NZD. The RBNZ determines the corridor of interest rate at which banks could borrow from and deposit at, overnight, to make the settlements. The RBNZ could also reduce that amount of cash for settlements below 6 if needed to tighten monetary conditions.

Australia followed New Zealand with inflation-targeting in 1992, Denmark in 1992, the United Kingdom in 1993, Sweden in 1994, Norway in 2001, and the United States very recently in 2012. Every country has a different inflation target. Some have a specific target, for example, 2 percent; others have a range like New Zealand. It is very important to understand that these central banks share the emphasis on the short-to medium-term inflation outcome. No one seems to think seriously about the long run. Some central banks suggest the business cycle as the targeting horizon of inflation, as if they know what the length of the business cycle is. There is a huge literature on inflation targeting, and interested readers should begin with discussion papers produced by the central banks, which are posted on their websites. Central banks in the developed inflation-targeting countries produced some significant research and made a tremendous contribution to this literature.

William Poole (President of the Federal Reserve Bank of St. Louis, 1994, pp. 109–110) said that the Fed has been quite successful in recent years in aggressively adjusting the Fed funds rate (the policy interest rate) and has come to the point of essentially ignoring information from the monetary aggregates. Ignoring the aggregates is a mistake. Evidence is overwhelming across the ages of the important role of money growth in causing inflation.

So policy affects the time series properties of the inflation data and reduces the correlation with broad money per unit of real output over the periods of inflation-targeting. Figures 5.6a and 5.6b plot the data, except for New Zealand, which we plot separately because the data are quarterly from March 1988 to June 2022. At least visually, it is quite clear that the data do not fit as well as the rest of the countries in our sample.

Note that the growth rates of money increased significantly by 2020. This was the period of COVID-19 – high spending financed by fresh money from central banks. For New Zealand, Figures 5.7a and 5.7b plot the data.

In New Zealand, the inflation rate and broad money per unit of real output growth have no correlation over the sample. Keep in mind that this sample covers the period of inflation-targeting. The Reserve Bank of New Zealand successfully stabilized the inflation rate around the target and reduced its variability significantly; however, money was kept to grow freely; thus the breakdown in the relationship. Also note that at the end of the sample, in 2022, the growth rate of money/ real GDP increased, dipped, and then increased again very significantly as real GDP plummeted during the COVID-19 shutdown, and inflation began to climb but significantly lower than money growth. The COVID-19 public spending was financed by huge new money (50 to 100 billion dollars).

Tables 5.21, 5.22, and 5.23 report the descriptive statistics using annual data, the testing of the equality of the mean, and the variance for inflation and the growth

92 Money Growth and Inflation

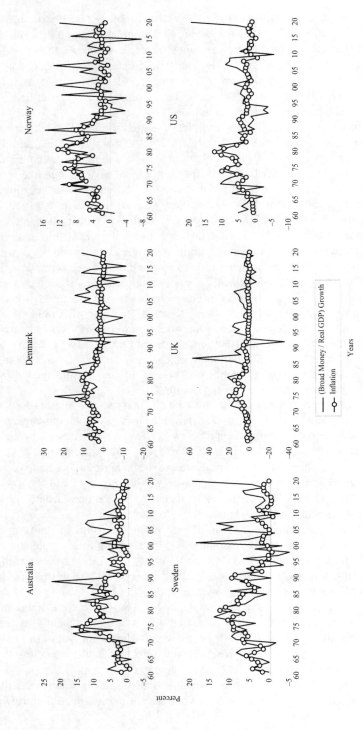

Figure 5.6b Money Per Unit of Output Growth Rate and Inflation in the Inflation Time Series in Inflation-Targeting Countries, 1961–2020
Data Source: World Development Indicators

Money Growth and Inflation   93

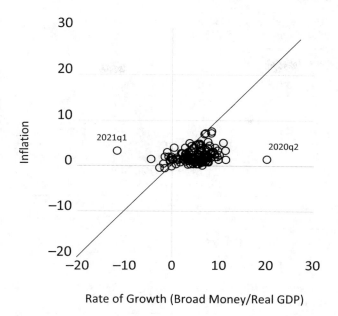

Figure 5.7a Scatter Plots of New Zealand Year-on-Year *Quarterly* Data from March 1988 to June 2022

Data Source: RBNZ

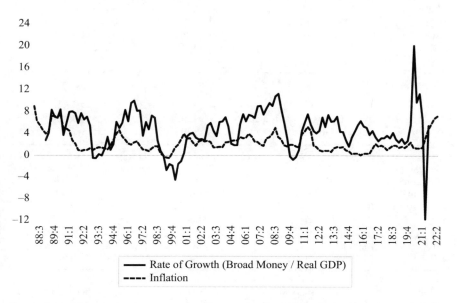

Figure 5.7b New Zealand Year-on-Year *Quarterly* Time Series Data from March 1988 to June 2022

Data Source: World Development Indicators

94 *Money Growth and Inflation*

Table 5.21 Descriptive Statistics for Broad Money – Real GDP Ratio Growth and Inflation in Inflation-Targeting Countries (*Annual* Data 1960–2020)

	(Broad Money – Real GDP Ratio) Growth					Inflation				
	Mean	STD	SKW	KURT	J-B	Mean	STD	SKW	KURT	J-B
Australia	6.53	4.88	0.95	4.06	0.0025	4.53	3.57	1.08	3.31	0.002
Denmark	4.94	7.19	−0.17	4.43	0.0658	4.33	3.36	0.92	2.97	0.013
Norway	5.24	4.60	−0.07	3.07	0.9686	4.34	3.05	0.96	2.92	0.009
NZ*	8.46	12.4	3.83	20.5	0.0000	4.84	4.86	1.21	2.94	0.007
Sweden	5.22	5.10	0.54	3.35	0.1969	4.15	3.51	0.64	2.29	0.069
UK	7.49	10.8	0.87	12.4	0.0000	4.92	4.44	1.81	6.00	0.000
US	4.25	4.14	0.59	5.06	0.0085	3.16	2.63	1.55	5.36	0.000

* New Zealand annual data for (money/real GDP) growth starts in 1978.
• STD – standard deviations (second moment); SKW – skewness (third moment) – S^2; KURT – kurtosis (fourth moment) – K.
• J-B is the *P*-values of Jarque–Bera. The test value is $\frac{N}{6}\left(S^2+\frac{K-3}{4}\right)^2$. Tests $H_0 : normal$.

Table 5.22 Are Mean Inflation and (Broad Money – Real GDP Ratio) Growth Equal in Inflation-Targeting Countries in 1960–2020?

	t-Test	Satterthwaite–Welch t-test	ANOVA F-test	Welch F-test	Equal
Australia	(0.0116)	(0.0117)	(0.0116)	(0.0117)	NO
Denmark	(0.5556)	(0.5561)	(0.5556)	(0.5561)	YES
Norway	(0.2072)	(0.2075)	(0.2072)	(0.2075)	YES
NZ	(0.0695)	(0.1219)	(0.0695)	(0.1219)	YES
Sweden	(0.1811)	(0.1815)	(0.1811)	(0.1815)	YES
UK	(0.0939)	(0.0952)	(0.0939)	(0.0952)	NO
US	(0.3163)	(0.3167)	(0.3163)	(0.3167)	YES

The null hypothesis is that the means are equal. The *P*-values are in parentheses.

Table 5.23 Are Variability of Inflation and (Broad Money – Real GDP Ratio) Growth Equal in the Inflation-Targeting Countries in 1960–2020?

	F-test	Siegel–Tukey*	Bartlett	Levene	Brown–Forsyth
Australia	(0.0173)	(0.9477)	(0.0173)	(0.0727)	(0.0568)
Denmark	(0.0000)	(0.1765)	(0.0000)	(0.0018)	(0.0013)
Norway	(0.0019)	(0.3355)	(0.0019)	(0.0189)	(0.0134)
NZ	(0.0000)	(0.8798)	(0.0000)	(0.0293)	(0.0582)
Sweden	(0.0048)	(0.2738)	(0.0048)	(0.0423)	(0.0442)
UK	(0.0000)	(0.0015)	(0.0000)	(0.0026)	(0.0019)
US	(0.0005)	(0.0230)	(0.0005)	(0.0099)	(0.0070)

The null hypothesis is that the variances are equal. *P*-values are in parentheses.
* Unlike all other tests, the *P*-values of the Siegle–Tukey test statistic are high, which means we cannot reject the null hypothesis that the variance of money/real GDP growth and inflation are equal. It is highly likely that this test has a low power. The other four tests suggest a rejection of the null; hence the variance of (money/real GDP) growth (see Table 5.21) is > variance of inflation.

rate of money per unit of real output. The World Development Indicators annual data for 2021 onward are available for inflation but unavailable for broad money – real GDP ratio because real GDP data are usually published with at least a year lag.

Clearly, the aforementioned statistics show that the developed inflation-targeting countries have lower inflation rates than the rest of the world, on average, but not as low as Japan, Malaysia, and Singapore. Money growth, however, is relatively high on average.

The aforementioned results suggest that the mean inflation and mean money growth are unequal in Australia, and perhaps in the United Kingdom at the 10 percent level.

Table 5.23 reports the test results of the hypothesis that the variances are equal.

Under successful inflation-targeting, the variance of inflation is much smaller than the variance of money growth. Next, we fit the QTM equation to the inflation-targeting countries using DOLS. We will fit three samples: the full sample, before inflation-targeting, and under inflation-targeting. We expect to find deterioration in the fit under inflation targeting and smaller estimated slope coefficient. At the end of the sample, and in all countries, the growth rate of broad money per unit of real output is literally divorced from inflation. Inflation-targeting, when successful, brings anticipated inflation down, however, most importantly reduces the variability of inflation. The correlation between inflation and money growth is low when the variance of inflation is small (due to targeting) and the variance of money growth is high. Recall that inflation-targeting countries do not consider money growth when formulating monetary policy.

Tables 5.24(a to g) report the Dynamic OLS regression estimates of the slope coefficients for each country, the full sample, the period before inflation targeting, and the period under inflation targeting. New Zealand has quarterly data, which cover the inflation-targeting period only; hence, we report only one regression. The United States started inflation targeting very late in the sample (2012); therefore, we only use the full sample regression. The results of the rest of the countries are very self-explanatory; the magnitude of the estimated slope coefficients falls significantly under inflation-targeting; the correlation between money growth and inflation is curtailed.

For Australia, the slope coefficient is 0.77 and highly significant. It is different from 1, but remains sizable. We fit two dummy variables. The first is for the Asian Financial Crisis (AFC) in 1997/1998. The coefficient is negative 4.7 and significant. Inflation has fallen during the AFC. The dummy variable for the GFC in 2007/2008 turned out to be insignificant. We also tested the first and second oil price shocks in 1973 and 1979, but they were insignificant. When we estimate the regression for the periods before and during inflation targeting, the slope coefficient for the period before inflation targeting is 0.94, which then fell to 0.42 under inflation-targeting. Inflation-targeting breaks the link with money growth as we explained earlier. Figure 5.8a plots actual inflation, the fitted values, and the residuals.

For Denmark, the slope coefficient is 1 in the full sample, which shows the strength of the relationship between money growth and inflation. Over the periods before and during inflation-targeting, the slope magnitudes fall from 0.93 to 0.57, as expected. The GFC has a negative impact on inflation. Figure 5.8b plots the actual, fitted values and the residuals.

96 Money Growth and Inflation

Table 5.24a Dynamic OLS Estimated (Broad Money – Real GDP Ratio) Growth–Inflation Relationship in the Inflation-Targeting Countries: Australia

Sample	Full Sample	Before Inflation-Targeting	Inflation-Targeting
	(1971–2010) [i]	(1967–2015) [ii]	
α	0.77	-	-
	(0.0000)		
α_1	-	0.94	-
		(0.0000)	-
α_2	-	-	0.42
			(0.0000)
d_{AFC}	−4.70	-	-
	(0.0008)	-	-
d_{GFC}	1.30	-	-
	(0.6615)	-	-
$\bar{R}^2$	0.57	0.45	
J-B	(0.3393)	(0.6609)	

P-values are in parentheses.

[i] We use DOLS to estimate $\pi_t = \alpha \Delta ln\left(\frac{M}{Y}\right)_t + \varepsilon_t$, auto lead/lag (10/9) based on AIC max lag = 10; HAC standard errors and covariance, Bartlett kernel with Newey–West auto bandwidth 4.3090, NW lag length = 3. The dummy variable d_{GFC} has a value of 1 during the GFC in 2007/2008, and 0 elsewhere. The dummy variable d_{AFC} has a value of 1 during the Asian Financial Crisis 1997/1998, and 0 elsewhere.

[ii] We use DOLS to estimate $\pi_t = \alpha_1 \Delta ln\left(\frac{M}{Y}\right)_t \times d_1 + \alpha_2 \Delta ln\left(\frac{M}{Y}\right)_t \times d_2 + \varepsilon_t$, where d_1 is a dummy variable that takes a value of 1 during the period before inflation targeting and 0 elsewhere, and d_2 is a dummy variable, which takes a value of 1 during the period of inflation targeting and 0 elsewhere. We use fixed lead/lag (5/5) because the sample gets smaller and unable to search for optimal lead/lag structure. HAC standard errors and covariance (Bartlett kernel, Newey–West automatic bandwidth 4.1324, NW automatic lag length = 3.

J-B is the Jarque–Bera test for normality of the residuals.

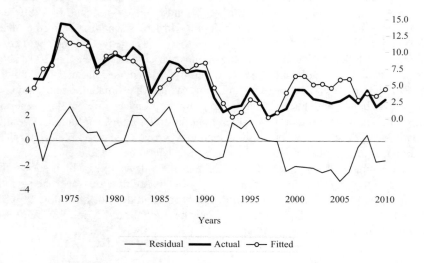

Figure 5.8a Australia's Actual, Fitted Values and the Residuals

Money Growth and Inflation 97

Table 5.24b Dynamic OLS Estimated (Broad Money – Real GDP Ratio) Growth–Inflation Relationship in the Inflation-Targeting Countries: Denmark

Sample	Full Sample	Before Inflation-Targeting	Inflation-Targeting
	(1967–2010) [i]	(1967–2015) [ii]	
α	1.02	-	-
	(0.0000)	-	-
α_1	-	0.93	-
	-	(0.0000)	-
α_2	-	-	0.57
	-	-	(0.0000)
d_{GFC}	−2.2	-	-
	(0.0440)	-	-
$\bar{R}^2$	0.82	0.70	
J-B	(0.8743)	(0.5042)	

P-values are in parentheses.

[i] We use DOLS to estimate $\pi_t = \alpha \Delta ln\left(\frac{M}{Y}\right)_t + \varepsilon_t$, auto lead/lag (10/5) based on AIC max lag; HAC standard errors and covariance, Bartlett kernel with Newey–West auto bandwidth 3.2478, NW lag length = 3. The dummy variable d_{GFC} has a value of 1 during the GFC and 0 elsewhere.

[ii] We use DOLS to estimate $\pi_t = \alpha_1 \Delta ln\left(\frac{M}{Y}\right)_t \times d_1 + \alpha_2 \Delta ln\left(\frac{M}{Y}\right)_t \times d_2 + \varepsilon_t$, where d_1 is a dummy variable that takes a value of 1 during the period before inflation targeting and 0 elsewhere, and d_2 is a dummy variable, which takes a value of 1 during the period of inflation targeting and 0 elsewhere. We use fixed lead/lag (5/5) because the sample gets smaller and unable to search for optimal lead/lag structure. HAC standard errors and covariance (Bartlett kernel), Newey–West automatic bandwidth 2.6599, NW automatic lag length = 3.

J-B is the Jarque–Bera test for normality of the residuals.

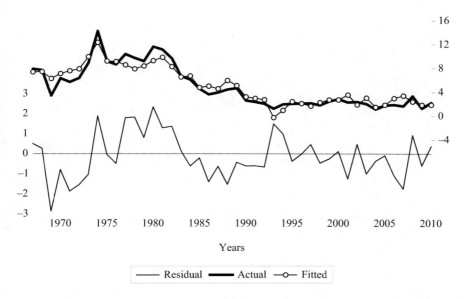

Figure 5.8b Denmark's Actual, Fitted Values and the Residuals

98 Money Growth and Inflation

Table 5.24c Dynamic OLS Estimated (Broad Money – Real GDP Ratio) Growth–Inflation Relationship in the Inflation-Targeting Countries: Norway

Sample	Full Sample (1966–2019)[i]	Before Inflation-Targeting (1967–2015)[ii]	Inflation-Targeting
α	0.85 (0.0000)	- -	- -
α_1	- -	1.0 (0.0000)	- -
α_2	- -	- -	0.35 (0.0000)
d_{GFC}	0.88 (0.1475)	- -	
$\bar{R}^2$	0.45	0.59	
J-B	(0.4902)	(0.2179)	

P-values are in parentheses.

(i) We use DOLS to estimate $\pi_t = \alpha \Delta ln\left(\frac{M}{Y}\right)_t + \varepsilon_t$, auto lead/lag (1/4) based on AIC max lag; HAC standard errors and covariance (pre-whitening with lag = 2 from AIC with max lag = 3, Bartlett kernel with Newey–West auto bandwidth 2.5167, NW lag length = 3. The dummy variable d_{GFC} has a value of 1 during the GFC and 0 elsewhere.

(ii) We use DOLS to estimate $\pi_t = \alpha_1 \Delta ln\left(\frac{M}{Y}\right)_t \times d_1 + \alpha_2 \Delta ln\left(\frac{M}{Y}\right)_t \times d_2 + \varepsilon_t$, where d_1 is a dummy variable that takes a value of 1 during the period before inflation targeting and 0 elsewhere, and d_2 is a dummy variable which takes a value of 1 during the period of inflation targeting and 0 elsewhere. We use fixed lead/lag (5/5) because when the sample gets smaller, the automatic search for the optimal lead/lag structure becomes impossible. HAC standard errors and covariance (Bartlett kernel), Newey–West automatic bandwidth 56.2861, NW automatic lag length = 3.

J-B is the Jarque–Bera test for normality of the residuals.

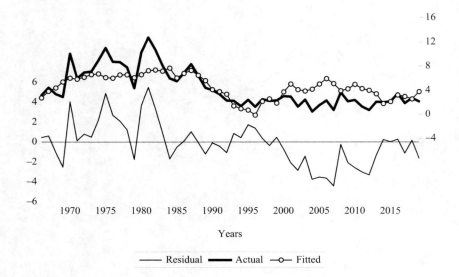

Figure 5.8c Norway's Actual, Fitted Values and the Residuals

Table 5.24d Dynamic OLS Estimated (Broad Money – Real GDP Ratio) Growth–Inflation Relationship in the Inflation-Targeting Countries: New Zealand (Quarterly Data)

Sample	Full Sample Under Inflation Targeting
	(Mar 88–Jun 21)
$\Delta ln\left(\dfrac{M}{Y}\right)_t$	0.38 (0.0000)
d_{AFC}	−0.77 (0.0013)
d_{GFC}	1.05 (0.0017)
$\bar{R}^2$	−0.17
J-B	(0.0099)

P-values are in parentheses.

Auto lead/lag (1/1) based on AIC max lag; HAC standard errors and covariance, pre-whitening with lag = 4 from AIC with max lag = 5, Bartlett kernel with Newey–West auto bandwidth 5.0164, NW lag length = 4. d_{AFC} is a dummy variable that takes a value of 1 during the Asian Financial Crisis in 1997/1998. d_{GFC} is a dummy variable that takes a value of 1 during the GFC in 2007/2008. J-B is the Jarque–Bera test for normality of the residuals.

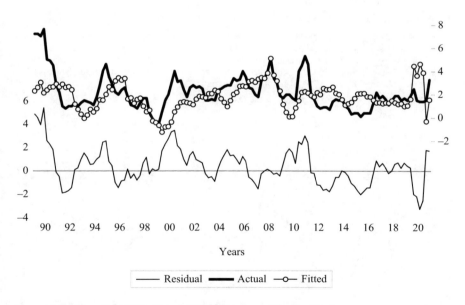

Figure 5.8d New Zealand's Actual, Fitted Values and the Residuals

Table 5.24e Dynamic OLS Estimated (Broad Money – Real GDP Ratio) Growth–Inflation Relationship in the Inflation-Targeting Countries: Sweden

Sample	Full Sample (1964–2019) [i]	Before Inflation-Targeting (1967–2015) [ii]	Inflation-Targeting
α	0.88 (0.0000)	- -	- -
α_1	- -	1.09 (0.0000)	- -
α_2	- -	- -	0.24 (0.0023)
d_{GFC}	−1.47 (0.0269)	- -	- -
$\overline{R}^2$	0.37	0.76	
J-B	(0.2988)	(0.0074)	

P-values are in parentheses.

[i] We use DOLS to estimate $\pi_t = \alpha \Delta ln\left(\dfrac{M}{Y}\right)_t + \varepsilon_t$, auto lead/lag (1/2) based on AIC max lag; HAC standard errors and covariance (pre-whitening with lag = 1 from AIC with max lag = 3, Bartlett kernel with Newey–West auto bandwidth 4.6623, NW lag length = 3. The dummy variable d_{GFC} has a value of 1 during the GFC and 0 elsewhere.

[ii] We use DOLS to estimate $\pi_t = \alpha_1 \Delta ln\left(\dfrac{M}{Y}\right)_t \times d_1 + \alpha_2 \Delta ln\left(\dfrac{M}{Y}\right)_t \times d_2 + \varepsilon_t$, where d_1 is a dummy variable that takes a value of 1 during the period before inflation targeting and 0 elsewhere, and d_2 is a dummy variable, which takes a value of 1 during the period of inflation targeting and 0 elsewhere. We use fixed lead/lag (5/5) because the sample gets smaller, and searching for optimal lead/lag structure becomes impossible. HAC standard errors and covariance (Bartlett kernel, Newey–West automatic bandwidth 3.0630, NW automatic lag length = 3).

J-B is the Jarque–Bera test for normality of the residuals.

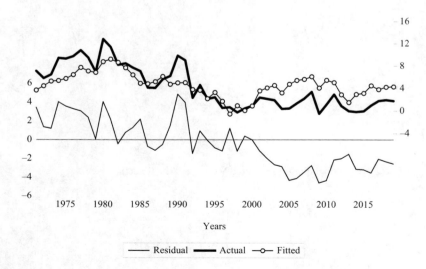

Figure 5.8e Sweden's Actual, Fitted Values and the Residuals

Money Growth and Inflation 101

Table 5.24f Dynamic OLS Estimated (Broad Money – Real GDP Ratio) Growth–Inflation Relationship in the Inflation-Targeting Countries: The United Kingdom

Sample	Full Sample	Before Inflation-Targeting	Inflation-Targeting
	(1962–2010)[i]	(1968–2014)[ii]	
α	0.71	-	-
	(0.0000)	-	-
α_1	-	0.81	-
	-	(0.0022)	-
α_2	-	-	0.31
	-	-	(0.0108)
d_{73}	2.27		
	(0.0289)		
d_{79}	10.1		
	(0.0013)		
d_{GFC}	−4.75	-	-
	(0.0000)	-	-
$\bar{R}^2$	0.44	0.57	
J-B	(0.0000)	(0.0541)	

P-values are in parentheses.

(i) We use DOLS to estimate $\pi_t = \alpha \Delta ln\left(\dfrac{M}{Y}\right)_t + \varepsilon_t$, auto lead/lag (10/0) based on AIC max lag; HAC standard errors and covariance (Bartlett kernel with Newey–West auto bandwidth 4.8002, NW lag length = 3). The dummy variable d_{73} takes a value of 1 in 1973 oil price shock and 0 elsewhere. The dummy variable d_{79} takes a value of 1 in 1979 second oil price shock and 0 elsewhere. The dummy variable d_{GFC} has a value of 1 during the GFC and 0 elsewhere.

(ii) We use DOLS to estimate $\pi_t = \alpha_1 \Delta ln\left(\dfrac{M}{Y}\right)_t \times d_1 + \alpha_2 \Delta ln\left(\dfrac{M}{Y}\right)_t \times d_2 + \varepsilon_t$, where d_1 is a dummy variable that takes a value of 1 during the period before inflation targeting and 0 elsewhere, and d_2 is a dummy variable, which takes a value of 1 during the period of inflation targeting and 0 elsewhere. We use fixed lead/lag (6/6) because the sample gets smaller, and searching for optimal lead/lag structure becomes impossible. HAC standard errors and covariance (Bartlett kernel, Newey–West automatic bandwidth 4.6313, NW automatic lag length = 3). Adjusted R^2 could not be calculated so I report R^2.

J-B is the Jarque–Bera test for normality of the residuals.

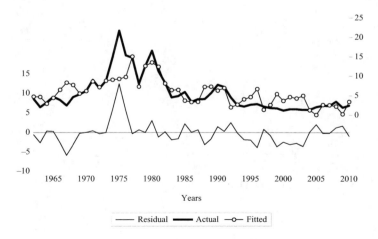

Figure 5.8f The UK's Actual, Fitted Values and the Residuals

Money Growth and Inflation

Table 5.24g Dynamic OLS Estimated (Broad Money – Real GDP Ratio) Growth–Inflation Relationship in the Inflation-Targeting Countries: The United States

Sample	Full Sample (1972–2012)
$\Delta ln\left(\dfrac{M}{Y}\right)_t$	1.1 (0.0000)
d_{73}	1.09 (0.6441)
d_{79}	4.34 (0.0140)
d_{GFC}	−0.51 (0.6762)
$\bar{R}^2$	0.51
J-B	(0.0190)

P-values are in parentheses.

Auto lead/lag (8/10) based on AIC max lag; HAC standard errors and covariance, Bartlett kernel with Newey–West auto bandwidth 2.4397, NW lag length = 3. J-B is the Jarque–Bera test for normality of the residuals. The dummy variable d_{73} takes a value of 1 in 1973 oil price shock and zer0 elsewhere. The dummy variable d_{79} takes a value of 1 in 1979 second oil price shock and 0 elsewhere. The dummy variable d_{GFC} has a value of 1 during the GFC and 0 elsewhere.

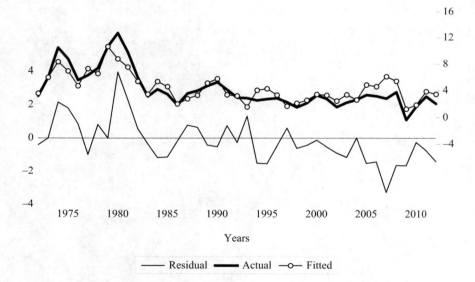

Figure 5.8g The US Actual, Fitted Values and the Residuals

These results suggest that there is a significant correlation between money growth and inflation. In the United States and Denmark, the slope coefficient is 1, and it is just as high in Sweden, Norway, and the United Kingdom.[6] Australia has a relatively smaller slope coefficient, nonetheless money growth explains inflation. The dynamic is quite complex. There are long and variable lead/lag relationships. The New Zealand data, which are quarterly and cover the inflation-targeting period only, explain the point we made many times earlier that the correlation between money and inflation fizzles out when inflation is successfully targeted at a low and stable level. The slope coefficient in the case of New Zealand is relatively small. The same is true for the slope coefficients in the other countries for the period of inflation targeting. The magnitudes are reduced significantly. Our tests suggest that the correlation between money growth and inflation weakened during the periods of successful inflation targeting in the seven developed countries in the sample. That probably suggests (1) inflation has become more stationary and low variance, while money kept trending up and more variable. (2) Policymakers may have viewed money to

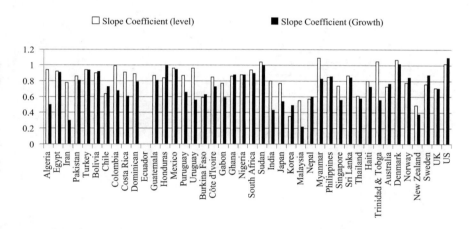

Figure 5.9 DOLS-Estimated Slope Coefficients: 1960–2020

6 The UK sample is for 1960–2020. The United Kingdom exited the European Union at the end of January 2020, that is, Brexit. It is hard to estimate the effect of Brexit on inflation with one observation only. Nonetheless, we fit the DOLS equation with an additional dummy variable, which takes a value of 1 in 2020 and 0 elsewhere. Estimating one additional parameter made it impossible to auto-search for the lead/lag regression. We estimated the regression with 1, 2, and up to 3 lags and no lead. The Brexit dummy variable has a coefficient of −2.3 with a P-value (0.0598). Thus, the effect is negative. Adding more lags up to 6 rendered the coefficient estimates insignificant. The equation could not be estimated with more than 6 lags. Future research should examine the effect of Brexit in more detail because the output gap exhibited a significant dip in 2020.

have no effect on inflation, when inflation expectations are anchored. (3) The public has no fear of inflation when inflation targeting is successful for a sufficiently long period – that is, the reputation and credibility of the central bank are strong.

Let's plot the estimated slope coefficients for all countries from the DOLS regressions of inflation on the growth rate of broad money per unit of real output, alongside the estimated coefficients of the log CPI on log money per unit of real output, which we estimated in the previous chapter for comparison. Figure 5.9 shows that these estimates of the responsiveness or the elasticity of inflation to the growth rate of money per unit of real output are close to 1 on average, but, however, vary across countries. We consider these estimates to be reasonable evidence for the predictions of the QTM.

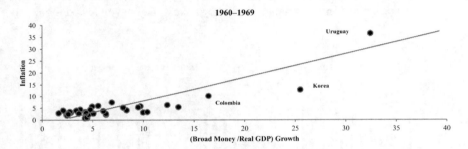

Figure 5.10a 45° Scatter Plots of All Countries' Ten-Year Averages of Growth Rate of Broad Money Per Unit of Real Output and Inflation, 1960–1969

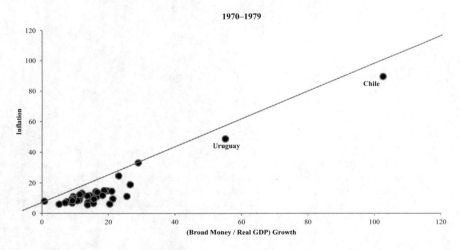

Figure 5.10b Ten-Year Averages of Growth Rate of Broad Money Per Unit of Real Output and Inflation, 1970–1979

Money Growth and Inflation   105

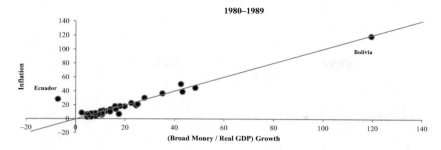

Figure 5.10c Ten-Year Averages of Growth Rate of Broad Money Per Unit of Real Output and Inflation, 1980–1989

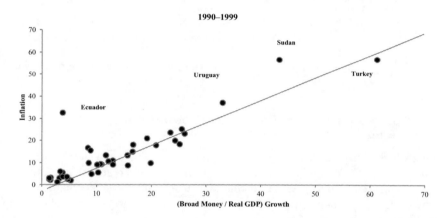

Figure 5.10d Ten-Year Averages of Growth Rate of Broad Money Per Unit of Real Output and Inflation, 1990–1999

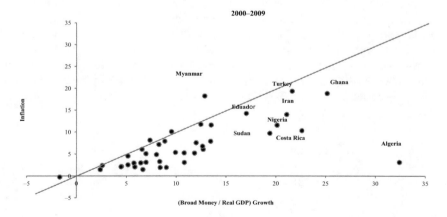

Figure 5.10e Ten-Year Averages of Growth Rate of Broad Money Per Unit of Real Output and Inflation, 2000–2009

106 *Money Growth and Inflation*

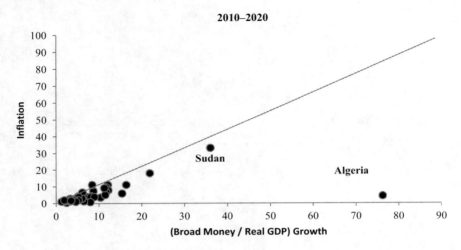

Figure 5.10f Ten-Year Averages of Growth Rate of Broad Money Per Unit of Real Output and Inflation, 2010–2022

The Cross-Sectional Evidence for Money Growth–Inflation Relationship

Finally in this chapter, we examine the long-run relationship between money growth and the CPI inflation rate. We take a 10-year average of the growth rate of broad money and the inflation rates for all countries, that is, from 1960 to 2020. We then provide 45° scatter plots. Figures 5.10a to 5.10f show that the long-run relationship between the growth rate of broad money and inflation are consistent with the QTM. There are differences in the fit over time, whereby the fit is not one-to-one, for example, 1970–1979 and 2000–2009, but in general the cross-sectional data fit the theory almost perfectly. The period 2000 onward includes much inflation-targeting experiences, where the relationship between money growth and inflation deteriorated (the thermostat story). There are a few outliers: Uruguay, Korea, and Colombia in the 1960s; Chile and Uruguay in the 1970s; Bolivia and Ecuador in the 1980s; Algeria, Turkey, Iran, Nigeria, Ghana, Sudan, Ecuador, Costa Rica, and Myanmar in the 2000s; Turkey, Sudan and Uruguay in the 1990s; and only Algeria and Sudan during the period 2010 to 2020. All the outliers represent more money growth.

Appendix 5.1

Unit Root Tests with Break

Following (Perron, 1989), consider four basic models for data with a one-time break. For trending data, we have models with (1) a change in level, (2) a change in both level and trend, and (3) a change in trend. In addition, consider two versions of the four models, which differ in their treatment of the break dynamics. First is the innovational outlier model, which assumes that the break occurs gradually, with the breaks following the same dynamic path as the innovations. The second is the additive outlier (AO) model that assumes that the breaks occur suddenly. The tests considered here evaluate the null hypothesis that the data follow a unit root process, possibly, with a break against a trend stationary with break alternative.

There are a variety of specifications for the null and alternative hypotheses, depending on the assumptions one wants to make about the break dynamics, trend behavior, and whether the break date is known, or endogenously determined. It seems to me that the additive outlier model may be more suitable for modeling the oil price shocks.

Innovation outlier test is given by:

$$y_t = y_{t-1} + \beta + \theta(L)(\gamma D_t(T_b) + \delta DU_t(T_b)) + \varepsilon_t, \tag{A5.1}$$

where ε_t is an *iid* error and $\theta(L)$ is a lag polynomial, which represents the dynamics of the I(0) and invertible ARMA errors. The break variables have the same dynamics of the errors. The alternative hypothesis assumes a trend-stationary model with breaks in the intercept and the slope. The break dynamics is like the innovation's dynamics.

$$y_t = \mu + \beta t + \theta(L)(\gamma D_t(T_b) + \delta DU_t(T_b)) + v_t \tag{A5.2}$$

The ADF test specification is:

$$y_t = \alpha_0 + \alpha_1 t + \alpha_2 DU_t(T_b) + \alpha_3 DT_t(T_b) + \alpha_4 D_t(T_b) + \rho y_{t-1} + \sum_{i=1}^{k} \eta_i \Delta y_{t-i} + \epsilon \tag{A5.3}$$

Table A-5.1 ADF Tests of Unit Root with a Break

Break Type: Innovation Outlier

Country (Sample)	Min. t				Intercept Break Min. t				Intercept Break Max. t				Intercept Break Absolute Max. t			
	Trend and Break Specifications				Trend and Break Specifications				Trend and Break Specifications				Trend and Break Specifications			
	Lag	Intercept	Lag	Intercept and Trend	Lag	Intercept	Lag	Intercept and Trend	Lag	Intercept	Lag	Intercept and Trend	Lag	Intercept	Lag	Intercept and Trend
Algeria (70–20)	1	(0.0545) /1994	0	(0.1575) /1995	0	(0.1761) /1995	0	(0.1575) /1995	0	(0.5912) /1976	0	(0.7461) /2012	0	(0.3421) /1995	0	(0.1575) /1995
Egypt (61–20)	0	(0.1379) /1972	0	(0.4668) /1973	9	(0.5343) /1992	9	(0.7588) /2013	0	(0.0672) /1972	0	(0.3293) /1969	0	(0.1328) /1972	9	(0.8921) /2013
Iran (61–20)	1	(0.0001) /1973	1	(0.0001) /1998	1	(0.1711) /2013	1	(0.0138) /1973	1	(0.0001) /1973	1	(0.3041) /2012	1	(0.0001) /1973	1	(0.0260) /1990
Pakistan (61–20)	10	(0.0001) /1987	4	(0.0468) /1981	10	(0.0001) /1987	0	(0.1630) /1975	0	(0.1255) /1969	8	(0.2679) /2013	10	(0.0001) /1987	0	(0.2831) /1975
Turkey (61–20)	0	(0.8803) /2001	9	(0.2765) /1986	0	(0.4970) /1998	4	(0.7649) /1981	0	(0.6383) /1970	0	(0.9525) /2008	0	(0.8226) /1998	4	(0.8967) /1981
Bolivia (61–20)	0	(0.0001) /1985	0	(0.0001) /1985	0	(0.0001) /1985	0	(0.0001) /1985	1	(0.1142) /1979	1	(0.2296) /2008	0	(0.0001) /1985	0	(0.0001) /1985
Chile (71–20)	0	(0.0001) /1976	0	(0.0001) /1975	0	(0.0001) /1977	9	(0.7140) /1992	4	(0.6979) /1983	0	(0.4170) /1979	0	(0.0001) /1977	0	(0.6140) /1979
Colombia (61–20)	1	(0.2364) /1998	0	(0.0592) /1972	1	(0.1130) /1998	0	(0.1867) /1978	0	(0.5786) /1971	0	(0.1778) /1969	1	(0.2241) /1998	0	(0.3176) /1978
Costa Rica (61–20)	1	(0.0980) /2008	10	(0.0001) /1981	8	(0.9046) /1982	3	(0.0001) /1982	1	(0.0821) /1973	1	(0.1689) /2013	8	(0.9999) /1982	3	(0.0001) /1982
Dominican Republic (61–20)	0	(0.0001) /2004	1	(0.0001) /1991	0	(0.0001) /2004	10	(0.0185) /1989	0	(0.0371) /1972	0	(0.0649) /1969	0	(0.0001) /2004	10	(0.0354) /1989
Ecuador (61–20)	0	(0.0323) /2000	1	(0.0001) /2000	0	(0.0159) /2000	3	(0.0161) /1987	0	(0.5514) /1971	0	(0.7513) /2012	0	(0.0314) /2000	3	(0.0298) /1987

Country																
Nigeria (61–20)	1	(0.0399)/1974	1	(0.0001)/1995	5	(0.2861)/1995	10	(0.0408)/1990	1	(0.0195)/1974	2	(0.5466)/2012	1	(0.0389)/1974	10	(0.0792)/1990
S Africa (61–20)	10	(0.2065)/1995	0	(0.6341)/1972	4	(0.4550)/1991	10	(0.6322)/1987	0	(0.6014)/1969	4	(0.9999)/2002	4	(0.7786)/1991	10	(0.8029)/1987
Sudan (61–20)	0	(0.9461)/2019	0	(0.8323)/1999	1	(0.8470)/1993	3	(0.8702)/1986	1	(0.7621)/2011	1	(0.9160)/2013	1	(0.9712)/2011	1	(0.9775)/2013
India (61–20)	1	(0.0001)/1978	1	(0.0001)/1974	4	(0.0001)/1998	3	(0.2645)/1975	5	(0.2985)/1977	5	(0.4307)/1977	4	(0.0001)/1998	0	(0.3152)/1975
Japan (61–20)	10	(0.0001)/1981	1	(0.2403)/1980	8	(0.0001)/1976	6	(0.8895)/1975	0	(0.4862)/2013	8	(0.1946)/1997	8	(0.0128)/1976	6	(0.9175)/1975
Korea (61–20)	1	(0.0001)/1986	1	(0.0001)/1980	9	(0.0140)/1981	10	(0.0001)/1984	7	(0.6414)/1974	1	(0.0001)/1974	9	(0.0282)/1981	10	(0.0001)/1984
Malaysia (61–20)	0	(0.0330)/1973	0	(0.0000)/1974	6	(0.9596)/1975	4	(0.0001)/1982	0	(0.0381)/1970	6	(0.9657)/1991	6	(0.9999)/1975	4	(0.0001)/1982
Nepal (65–20)	0	(0.0001)/1974	0	(0.0001)/1976	4	(0.2597)/1994	10	(0.1747)/1984	0	(0.0001)/1972	10	(0.2224)/1980	4	(0.4832)/1994	10	(0.3005)/1984
Myanmar (61–20)	0	(0.0491)/2002	1	(0.0001)/1988	3	(0.4138)/2008	1	(0.0001)/1996	0	(0.0559)/1971	3	(0.7199)/1981	3	(0.7268)/2008	1	(0.0001)/1996
Guatemala (61–20)	0	(0.0715)/1972	1	(0.0001)/1993	3	(0.4771)/1993	1	(0.0001)/1993	0	(0.0358)/1972	1	(0.1492)/2008	3	(0.8021)/1993	1	(0.0001)/1993
Honduras (61–20)	0	(0.4852)/1971	1	(0.0001)/1989	2	(0.5603)/1997	6	(0.0219)/1992	0	(0.2388)/1972	0	(0.3724)/1970	2	(0.8796)/1997	6	(0.0241)/1992
Mexico (61–20)	5	(0.7637)/1995	5	(0.0505)/1981	6	(0.6223)/1988	7	(0.1581)/1996	0	(0.5530)/1972	6	(0.9635)/2001	6	(0.9216)/1988	7	(0.2763)/1996
Paraguay (61–20)	0	(0.3299)/1970	2	(0.0001)/1993	4	(0.8512)/1991	2	(0.0001)/1993	0	(0.2031)/1971	4	(0.9744)/2011	4	(0.9744)/2011	2	(0.0001)/1993
Uruguay (61–20)	7	(0.0471)/1995	7	(0.3715)/1996	7	(0.0240)/1995	7	(0.2811)/1974	7	(0.8102)/1982	10	(0.6825)/1980	7	(0.0458)/1995	7	(0.4585)/1974
Burkina Faso (61–20)	0	(0.0001)/1985	0	(0.0001)/1983	0	(0.0001)/1985	0	(0.0001)/1981	0	(0.0001)/1969	0	(0.0001)/1969	0	(0.0001)/1985	0	(0.0001)/1981

(Continued)

Table A-5.1 – Continued

Break Type: Innovation Outlier

Country (Sample)	Min. t				Intercept Break Min. t				Intercept Break Max. t				Intercept Break Absolute Max. t			
	Trend and Break Specifications				*Trend and Break Specifications*				*Trend and Break Specifications*				*Trend and Break Specifications*			
	Lag	Intercept	Lag	Intercept and Trend	Lag	Intercept	Lag	Intercept and Trend	Lag	Intercept	Lag	Intercept and Trend	Lag	Intercept	Lag	Intercept and Trend
Côte d' Ivoire	0	(0.0001) /1977	0	(0.0001) /1977	0	(0.0321) /1995	0	(0.0001) /1978	0	(0.0341) /1968	2	(0.6405) /1994	0	(0.0597) /1995	0	(0.0101) /1978
Gabon (63–20)	1	(0.0001) /1982	1	(0.0001) /1983	7	(0.0531) /1986	1	(0.0001) /1978	0	(0.0235) /1970	7	(0.4221) /2000	7	(0.1029) /1986	1	(0.0001) /1978
Ghana (65–20)	0	(0.0001) /1983	0	(0.0001) /1977	10	(0.0001) /1998	2	(0.0001) /1984	0	(0.0596) /1976	10	(0.0001) /2006	10	(0.0001) /1998	2	(0.0184) /1984
Philippines (61–20)	1	(0.0001) /1995	1	(0.0001) /1987	9	(0.0348) /1993	1	(0.0001) /1985	0	(0.0001) /1970	0	(0.0001) /1970	9	(0.0666) /1993	1	(0.0001) /1985
Singapore (61–20)	3	(0.0391) /1984	0	(0.0298) /1973	3	(0.0191) /1984	5	(0.9254) /1975	0	(0.0423) /1971	3	(0.1476) /1997	3	(0.0318) /1984	5	(0.9809) /1975
Sri Lanka (75–20)	0	(0.0001) /2008	4	(0.0001) /2005	4	(0.0001) /2013	7	(0.0177) /2007	0	(0.0512) /1986	4	(0.0001) /2013	4	(0.0101) /2013	7	(0.0335) /2007
Thailand (61–20)	1	(0.0001) /1980	1	(0.0001) /1980	1	(0.0155) /1998	8	(0.3401) /1975	0	(0.0985) /1971	6	(0.9999) /1988	1	(0.0305) /1998	8	(0.5278) /1975
Haiti (61–20)	0	(0.0158) /1987	0	(0.0661) /1987	0	(0.1466) /2004	5	(0.0733) /1992	0	(0.1193) /1988	0	(0.0746) /2008	0	(0.1193) /1988	5	(0.1371) /1992
Trinidad and Tobago (61–20)	9	(0.0994) /1994	0	(0.0459) /1971	9	(0.0497) /1994	0	(0.3140) /1975	0	(0.3719) /1971	0	(0.4604) /2012	9	(0.0964) /1994	0	(0.4982) /1975
Australia (61–20)	1	(0.2391) /1990	1	(0.4381) /1983	4	(0.7726) /1977	0	(0.3866) /1975	0	(0.6237) /1969	0	(0.8156) /1995	4	(0.9731) /1977	0	(0.5821) /1975
Denmark (61–20)	10	(0.0466) /1984	9	(0.0285) /2004	5	(0.0752) /1982	8	(0.4074)	10	(0.8147) /2014	10	(0.0512) /1999	5	(0.1500) /1982	10	(0.0969) /1999

Country (period)								
Norway (61–20)	0 (0.0176) /1989	0 (0.0712) /1969	4 (0.3920) /1982	0 (0.2422) /1971	0 (0.4640) /1969	9 (0.9999) /1994	4 (0.6922) /1982	9 (0.9999) /1994
NZ 88q1–21q4	0 (0.0217) /90q2	0 (0.2653) /90q2	9 (0.0765) 11q2	9 (0.9074) /95q2	9 (0.1402) /18q2	12 (0.1033) /14q3	9 (0.2765) /18q2	12 (0.1871) /14q3
Sweden (61–20)	0 (0.0211) /1991	0 (0.0966) /1991	0 (0.0001) /1991	0 (0.0631) /1981	0 (0.5808) /1969	0 (0.4108) /2008	0 (0.0210) /1991	0 (0.1187) /1981
UK (61–20)	9 (0.0107) /1992	1 (0.1374) /1982	9 (0.0001) /1992	7 (0.8995) /1976	0 (0.6127) /1968	9 (0.9861) /1987	9 (0.0106) /1992	7 (0.9715) /1976
US (61–20)	1 (0.1799) /1990	1 (0.0001) /1982	4 (0.2955) /1981	1 (0.0001) /1982	0 (0.5382) /1968	4 (0.9999) /1987	4 (0.5467) /1981	1 (0.0001) /1982

[i] The lag structure is determined by automatic AIC.

[ii] P-values are in parentheses; the Vogelsang (1993) asymptotic one-sided P-value.

[iii] "/" denotes the break date.

[iv] NZ – New Zealand is quarterly data.

112 *Money Growth and Inflation*

We estimate this equation with an intercept, and with an intercept and trend.
The additive outlier model is:

$$y_t = y_{t-1} + \beta + \theta D_t(T_b) + \delta DU_t(T_b) + + \psi(L)\varepsilon_t \qquad (A5.4)$$

The errors are *iid*; $\psi(L)$ are polynomials, which capture the dynamics of the I(0) and invertible ARMA error process; β is a drift parameter, where the full impact of the break occurs immediately.

6 The Neutrality of Money

Abstract

Although money growth in all 42 countries in our sample has been very high, especially in developing countries and during periods before inflation-targeting in developed countries, increasing the quantity of money – money growth – is unrelated to real GDP growth in all 42 countries in our sample. This is the expected super-neutrality result. Further, and most importantly, money growth has not stimulated real GDP in the short run either, except in a few countries in our sample from 1960 to 2020, namely Singapore, Gabon, South Africa, Trinidad and Tobago, New Zealand, and the United States between 1960 and 1985 only. These latest test results beg the question: why do countries, and especially the developed inflation-targeting countries, continue to print money at high rates? What purpose does a high growth rate of money serve if it does not stimulate the real economy?

So far, we have a reasonably significant evidence of positive relationship between money and the general CPI level, and money growth and the inflation rate in 42 countries. The second important prediction of the theory is that the increase in the quantity of money does not have any effect on real variables such as real output or unemployment, for example. In another word, pouring more money in the economy does not increase real GDP or reduce unemployment. Thus, money is neutral. To be precise, neutrality means that in the *long run*, where growth of the real variables ceases, and all other variables are at their natural levels, printing more money has no effect on any of these real variables but only increases inflation. This subject will be studied in more details when we analyze the Phillips curve later in this book.

Monetary theories are contentious. There are strong differences of opinions between economists. Most central banks and policymakers hold non-Monetarists' views for good reasons. We will have to say something about the meaning of the long run because many economists seem to understand it as a calendar time. Keynes is widely quoted to have said, "*We are all dead in the long run*;" therefore, people who believe in this statement suggest that we should not care about the long run. I think that this statement, however, is a very disturbing suggestion because there have been times of very high inflation and hyperinflation, and people were very much alive and suffering from it. Soon, people will be suffering from high inflation and unemployment. The long run in the context of modern economic theory, which

DOI: 10.4324/9781003382218-6

114   *The Neutrality of Money*

involves expectations about the future, means that there is no change in all economic variables in the long run; that is, no growth, and furthermore, the expected values are equal to the actual values.

What about the *short run*? Keynesian economics predicts *sticky prices* in the short run. It means that when money is poured into the economy, the aggregate demand curve shifts up and real output increases before prices catch up. There will be a period of high real output. This is the point most interesting to politicians. Governments would be happiest if real output increases and unemployment falls just before elections and for, say, 3 or 4 years. We often hear people talking about monetary policy and economic growth. There is no such a thing in economic theory. Monetary policy cannot reduce unemployment below its natural rate and cannot increase real GDP above its potential level. There are theories to explain why prices are sticky in the short run, and there is a significant amount of empirical research to support and not so support this prediction. The general consensus, however, is that, prices do take longer time than output to change. We will go through this proposition in more detail later.

Accepting that prices are sticky in the short run, therefore, the central bank *might* think it is able to simulate the *real* economy in the *short run* only although it is difficult to show robust statistical evidence for it using our data. In the long run, the theory predicts only higher inflation and no change in real output or unemployment. The neutrality of money doctrine is of no use for New Keynesian, and it appears to be ignored by central banks in the developed countries *per se* because the data show a continuously increasing quantity of money. So if printing money does not stimulate the economy in the short run and generates inflation in the long run (although non-inflationary under a successful inflation-targeting policies), why do we observe a significant increase in the quantity of money in all the 42 countries in the sample? We will answer this question in the next chapter.

A Formal Representation of Money Neutrality

Here is a formal representation of money neutrality. Suppose that we have a macroeconomic model, which is a set of equations. It could be an aggregate demand, aggregate supply, a labor demand, a labor supply, a money demand, and money supply equations among m structural equations. Thus, we could have m *endogenous* variables measured in dollars, for example. Suppose that there $m - m_1$ endogenous variables not measured in dollars. These are measured in real units, for example, unemployment. Similarly, assume that there are n exogenous variables measured in dollars, and $n - n_1$ remaining exogenous variables measured not in dollars. The system looks like this:

$$F[Y, X] = 0$$

where $F' = [f_1, f_{2,\ldots} f_m]$; $Y' = [y_1, y_2, \cdots y_m]$; and $X' = [x_1, x_2, \cdots x_n]$, or

$$f_1(y_1 \quad \cdots \quad y_m, x_1 \quad \cdots \quad x_n) = 0$$

$$f_2(y_1 \quad \cdots \quad y_m, x_1 \quad \cdots \quad x_n) = 0$$

$$\vdots \tag{6.1}$$

$$f_m\left(y_1 \quad \cdots \quad y_m, x_1 \quad \cdots \quad x_n\right) = 0$$

Assume that for some values of the exogenous variables $x_1^0, \cdots x_n^0$, the afore-mentioned system is in equilibrium, given the endogenous variables have the following values, $y_1^0 \cdots y_m^0$. In other words, these values of the exogenous and endogenous variables satisfy the aforementioned system. The system is *neutral*, if some specific values $\gamma y_1^0, \cdots \gamma y_{m1}^0, y_{m+1}^0, \cdots y_m^0$ and $\gamma x_1^0, \cdots \gamma x_n^0, x_{n+1}^0, \cdots x_n^0$ for any scalar $\gamma > 0$ satisfy the equilibrium condition in Eq. (6.1). The system is *neutral* if, starting from an initial position of equilibrium, multiplying all the endogenous and the exogenous variables that are measured in the monetary unit by a positive scalar leaves the system in equilibrium. The economic model made of a number of equations would be neutral if we could rewrite it such that each equation has only *real* variables. Essentially, nominal variables in the system, such as money and wages, could be divided by another nominal variable such as the price level; hence we end up with a system written in real units. Therefore, doubling the nominal quantities would not have any effect on the equilibrium values of these variables.

The quantity of money and the growth rate of money never factored in policy discussions in central banks in the developed countries. This is especially true when the Reserve Bank of New Zealand adopted the interest rate (the Official Cash Rate, OCR) as a policy instrument in 1999. Most central banks in the advanced world adopted inflation-targeting regimes, where short-term interest rate is the policy instrument and forgot about money.

Next, we provide tests for neutrality.

Does the Increase in the Quantity of Money Increase Real GDP in the Long Run?

It must be very well understood by economists, policymakers, and politicians in the developed countries that the growth rate of money cannot induce economic growth. There is strong evidence for neutrality and superneutrality in the data for the 42 countries in the sample. One cannot know for sure the views of economists, policymakers, and especially politicians about money growth in developing coun-tries, because the growth rates of money in our sample are incredibly high. One might wonder why. Here we show that there is no relationship between money growth and real GDP growth.

Tables 6.1 to 6.6 report the 10-year averages of broad money growth rates and real GDP. The growth rates of money are very high all over the world through the entire sample, except for a few years of inflation-targeting in the six developed countries in the sample.

Figure 6.1 is a 45° line scatter plot of the full-sample cross-sectional 10-year average money growth and real GDP of 42 countries. Money growth is not associ-ated with real GDP growth. The scatter points are on one side of the 45° line.

Figures 6.2 to 6.7 are the scatter plots of the country's 10-year average money growth and real GDP growth.

Table 6.1 Ten-Year Averages of Broad Money and Real GDP Growth Rates in the MENA Countries

	1960–1969		1970–1979		1980–1989		1990–1999		2000–2009		2010–2020	
	Money	*GDP*	*Money*	*GDP*	*Money*	*GDP*	*Money*	*GDP*	*Money*	*GDP*	*Money*	*GDP*
Algeria	17.82	3.01	19.25	6.58	13.52	2.73	14.90	1.53	16.74	3.80	8.08	1.92
Egypt	8.03	4.86	19.25	5.98	22.37	6.45	12.95	4.38	13.10	4.85	15.79	3.70
Iran	15.58	11.26	27.12	3.54	19.24	−2.20	23.00	3.79	25.41	4.33	24.18	0.89
Pakistan	10.45	6.55	15.10	4.68	12.72	6.63	14.79	3.88	16.44	4.43	12.15	3.45
Turkey	14.39	5.46	26.97	4.55	47.23	3.97	65.08	3.82	25.45	3.81	17.07	5.31

Data Source: World Development Indicators

Table 6.2 Ten-Year Averages of Broad Money and Real GDP Growth Rates in the Latin and South American Countries

	1960–1969		1970–1979		1980–1989		1990–1999		2000–2009		2010–2020	
	Money	*GDP*	*Money*	*GDP*	*Money*	*GDP*	*Money*	*GDP*	*Money*	*GDP*	*Money*	*GDP*
Bolivia	14.94	5.37	23.00	4.48	119.09	−0.47	23.79	3.90	11.63	3.61	10.42	3.28
Chile	32.67	4.42	98.92	2.24	27.82	3.32	18.84	5.88	12.42	4.09	9.10	2.39
Colombia	16.65	4.87	25.30	5.57	25.12	3.33	24.37	2.78	12.71	3.82	10.41	2.67
Costa Rica	8.39	5.67	25.26	6.14	24.64	2.11	13.65	4.76	26.78	4.18	6.29	2.97
Dominican Republic	6.72	4.38	18.31	7.79	21.53	3.67	20.41	4.78	17.68	4.16	10.93	4.34
Ecuador	9.91	3.65	18.02	6.97	−4.55	2.57	6.04	2.26	20.85	3.80	7.72	1.77
Guatemala	9.46	5.34	16.05	5.69	13.37	0.93	15.69	3.98	16.01	3.35	8.86	3.00
Honduras	10.71	4.77	14.41	5.26	11.44	2.58	23.56	2.69	13.24	4.38	10.66	2.41
Mexico	12.56	6.59	21.72	6.22	44.84	2.23	28.58	3.38	8.39	1.43	9.64	1.60
Paraguay	15.16	4.93	21.07	7.96	22.74	4.72	19.58	3.02	15.76	2.31	12.69	3.74
Uruguay	35.68	1.26	53.68	2.63	48.93	0.51	36.59	3.57	9.40	2.04	14.20	2.02

Data Source: World Development Indicators

Table 6.3 Ten-Year Averages of Broad Money and Real GDP Growth Rates in the African Countries

	1960–1969		1970–1979		1980–1989		1990–1999		2000–2009		2010–2020	
	Money	GDP	Money	GDP	Money	GDP	Money	GDP	Money	GDP	Money	GDP
Burkina Faso	6.51	3.18	16.70	3.18	12.05	3.60	8.62	4.93	10.90	5.14	13.46	5.47
Côte d'Ivoire	15.17	8.19	18.18	7.29	4.27	-0.34	6.58	2.82	7.06	0.62	12.23	5.75
Gabon	9.48	6.45	22.71	7.94	7.32	1.53	5.57	2.34	9.55	0.53	6.72	3.43
Ghana	9.86	2.24	27.28	1.23	36.98	1.85	30.29	4.18	30.37	5.22	22.35	5.95
Nigeria	9.73	2.33	26.99	6.45	14.82	−1.18	27.81	2.22	27.48	7.36	11.48	3.06
South Africa	9.84	5.60	13.55	3.19	16.27	2.17	12.05	1.36	14.32	3.52	6.81	0.95
Sudan	11.98	1.15	21.38	3.90	31.01	3.17	47.59	4.24	24.17	4.78	34.73	−1.29

Data Source: World Development Indicators

Table 6.4 Ten-Year Averages of Broad Money and Real GDP Growth Rates in the Asian Countries

	1960–1969		1970–1979		1980–1989		1990–1999		2000–2009		2010–2020	
	Money	GDP	Money	GDP	Money	GDP	Money	GDP	Money	GDP	Money	GDP
India	9.23	3.78	15.89	2.81	15.75	5.52	15.70	5.59	16.01	6.08	11.28	5.17
Japan	19.42	9.92	19.30	4.34	9.02	4.23	4.29	1.45	−1.23	0.44	3.17	0.71
Korea	35.74	9.03	26.40	9.99	17.81	8.43	17.26	6.95	15.60	4.78	6.49	2.90
Malaysia	10.59	6.33	20.79	7.80	13.79	5.66	10.70	6.88	9.15	4.64	6.14	4.21
Nepal	16.46	2.44	16.20	2.54	17.88	3.94	17.71	4.72	15.82	3.97	15.89	4.21
Myanmar	4.38	2.85	12.66	4.18	12.87	1.83	29.08	5.57	24.57	11.70	22.08	6.66
Philippines	12.92	4.95	17.20	5.56	18.26	1.97	18.46	2.75	9.59	4.43	10.73	4.73
Singapore	13.48	8.47	13.54	8.76	13.85	7.47	12.19	6.91	7.55	5.16	5.97	3.87
Sri Lanka	#N/A	#N/A	31.10	4.99	15.22	4.05	17.31	5.12	14.39	4.85	16.56	4.30
Thailand	12.44	7.52	16.94	7.21	17.62	7.00	14.00	4.92	6.81	4.20	6.74	2.66

Data Source: World Development Indicators

Table 6.5 Ten-Year Averages of Broad Money and Real GDP Growth Rates in the Caribbean Countries

	1960–1969		1970–1979		1980–1989		1990–1999		2000–2009		2010–2020	
	Money	*GDP*	*Money*	*GDP*	*Money*	*GDP*	*Money*	*GDP*	*Money*	*GDP*	*Money*	*GDP*
Haiti	5.37	0.82	19.48	4.43	10.63	−0.17	16.68	0.01	14.62	2.14	12.09	0.81
Trinidad & Tobago	8.17	4.79	22.18	4.50	8.68	−1.57	8.42	5.04	12.72	6.15	4.11	−1.02

Data Source: World Development Indicators

Table 6.6 Ten-Year Averages of Broad Money and Real GDP Growth Rates in the Developed Inflation-Targeting Countries

	1960–1969		1970–1979		1980–1989		1990–1999		2000–2009		2010–2020	
	Money	*GDP*	*Money*	*GDP*	*Money*	*GDP*	*Money*	*GDP*	*Money*	*GDP*	*Money*	*GDP*
Australia	7.80	4.73	11.63	3.36	14.01	3.28	7.99	3.21	10.15	3.18	7.52	2.32
Denmark	10.19	5.05	10.64	2.34	11.11	1.87	3.98	2.41	5.42	0.95	2.76	1.47
Norway	8.28	4.34	12.31	4.36	10.82	2.79	4.86	3.49	7.66	1.81	5.53	1.26
NZ	#N/A	#N/A	16.95	1.24	21.14	1.99	6.57	2.76	6.25	2.71	7.58	2.71
Sweden	8.22	4.34	10.62	2.47	8.64	2.26	3.32	1.70	8.72	2.07	6.61	2.00
UK	5.04	3.06	13.48	2.92	20.15	2.60	6.79	2.20	9.97	1.58	2.82	0.90
USA	7.34	4.54	10.45	3.10	8.35	3.05	4.51	3.16	7.04	1.87	5.21	1.73

Data Source: World Development Indicators

The Neutrality of Money 119

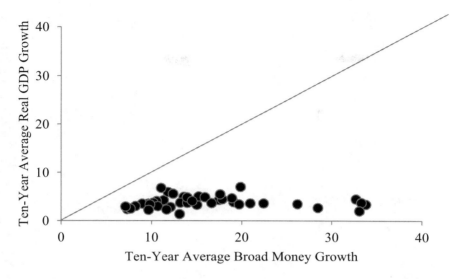

Figure 6.1 45° Line Scatter Plot of the Full-Sample 10-Year Average Money Growth and Real GDP for all 42 Countries

Algeria and Turkey reduced money growth in the last decade significantly. However, money grew significantly faster than real GDP over the whole sample.

Most of the growth of money was in the 1960s, 1970s, 1980s, and 1990s. Recently, the Latin and South American countries reduced money growth significantly.

Many African countries tried hard to reduce the growth rate of money. Relatively, Africa still has high growth rates of money.

The Asian countries reduced money growth rates in the past decade significantly. The Asian countries understood that money cannot cause real growth.

The two Caribbean countries in our sample have different and volatile growth patterns than the other countries in our sample. They growth rate of money was very low in the 1960s, and then jumped significantly to a very high rate in the 1970s, followed by low rates in the 1980s. Today's growth rates are similar to that in between the 1960s and 1980s on one hand and between the 1970s and 2000s on the other. Nonetheless, there is no correlation between money and GDP growth.

The inflation-targeting countries in our sample started explicit inflation-targeting in the 1990s; the United States started in 2012. There is no association between money and real GDP growth on average along the 45° line. The data suggest that that money is super-neutral. There is a wide agreement among people that this is what we ought to expect to see in the data. There is also a wide agreement that money might have real effects in the short run mainly because of price rigidity.[1]

---

1 Readers might be interested in other views about the relationship between inflation and economic growth. See for example, (Fischer, 1983) who explains why inflation and growth are negatively correlated, and (Dornbusch and Frenkel, 1973) explain an interesting approach to understanding inflation and growth.

120 *The Neutrality of Money*

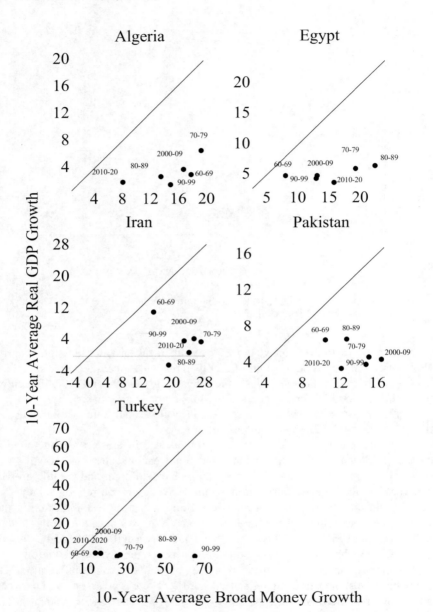

Figure 6.2 Ten-Year Average Money and Real GDP Growth Rates: The MENA Countries

Does the Increase in the Quantity of Money Increase Real GDP in the Short Run?

The theory predicts that printing more money causes *only* more inflation and no real growth in the long run. The cross-sectional scatter plots shown before

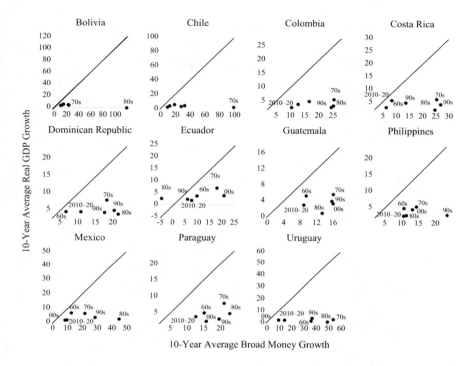

Figure 6.3 Ten-Year Average Money and Real GDP Growth Rates: The Latin and South American Countries

are supportive of such prediction. However, the theory also predicts that the increase in the quantity of money might increase real GDP in the short run if prices are sticky and the adjustment takes time. There seems to be evidence for price stickiness, which we do not cite; however, see, for example, (Calvo, 1983), (Rotemberg, 1982), Bils and (Klenow, 2004), (Eichenbaum and Fisher, 2004), (Barsky *et al.*, 2007), (Boivin *et al.*, 2009), and (Alvarez *et al.*, 2022a). This stickiness may motivate governments and central banks to print more money in order to stimulate, fine-tune, or stabilize the economy whatever the appropriate word is.

Price stickiness is widely accepted by economists as an explanation of an upward sloping short-run aggregate supply. The idea is that firms do not instantly change prices when demand changes. In some cases, prices are set by long-term contracts, hence do not change instantly. There are stories about firms holding on to old prices for some time to keep their customers. The magnitudes of the price and income elasticity of demand have significant effects too. Menu Cost is another theoretical explanation, whereby it costs firms to change posted prices. On the contrary, one cannot help watching petrol and gas prices at the pump change more than once a day in many parts of the world, especially in New Zealand and Australia,

122 *The Neutrality of Money*

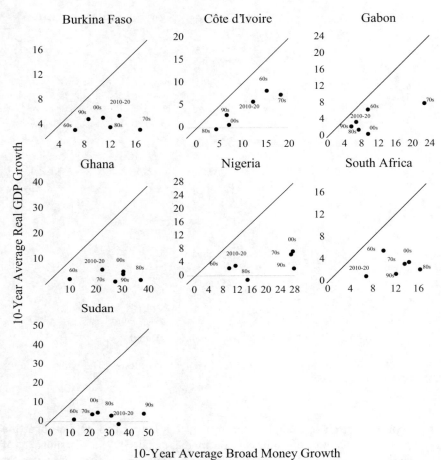

Figure 6.4 Ten-Year Average Money and Real GDP Growth Rates: The African Countries

where I observe these changes all the time. Customers may not like that but they could do nothing about it. There is almost no stickiness in this case. In the world today, where people trade freely on the Internet, prices are significantly less sticky that people think.

The prices changes much faster and much frequently today than before. Recently, many US companies contacted their customers all over the world by email telling them that they dropped prices because they recognize the significant appreciation of the US dollar (October 2022). This reaction was unimaginable a few years ago.

At the firm level, the desired price depends on the aggregate price level in the economy. Higher price level indicates higher costs. Thus, the higher the aggregate price level the more the firm wants to change its price. Aggregate income matters

The Neutrality of Money 123

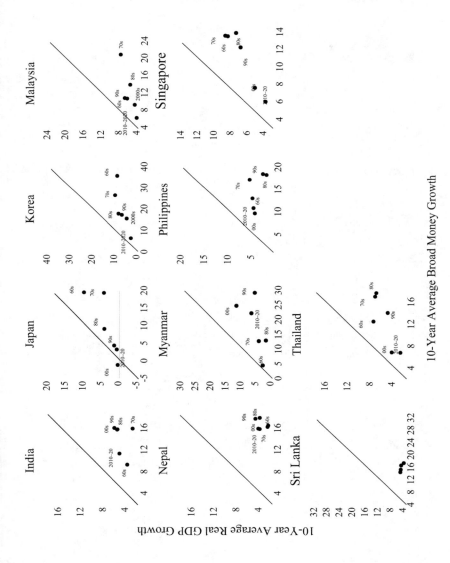

Figure 6.5 Ten-Year Average Money and Real GDP Growth Rates: The Asian Countries

124   *The Neutrality of Money*

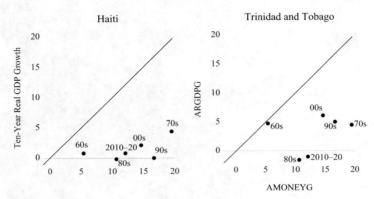

Figure 6.6 Ten-Year Average Money and Real GDP Growth Rates: The Caribbean Countries

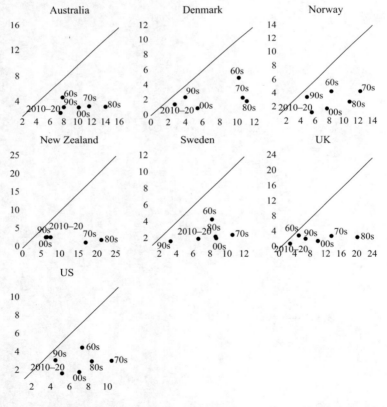

Figure 6.7 Ten-Year Average Money and Real GDP Growth Rates: The Inflation-Targeting Countries

The Neutrality of Money   125

too. Marginal cost increases at higher levels of production, thus the higher the demand the higher the firm's price is. Firms that set prices in accordance with the sticky-price theory have to make expectations about the future-expected general price and output. When output is equal to expected output, the price of the firm is equal to the expected general price level. It means that firms with sticky prices set their own prices on the basis of their expectations of the other firms' prices.

Therefore, the QTM would be consistent with money stimulating the economy when prices are sticky. Recall that (Fisher, 1911) assumed, as we said earlier, that velocity changes are small in the short run. This may or may not be the case in different countries of course, and it is pretty much an empirical question.

We should be more willing to accept the prediction of the theory if we observe a positive correlation between money and output in the short run; that is, the deviations of broad money from trend and the output gap. To account for the short run, we measure the deviations of broad money from trend and the output gap of real GDP using the (Hodrick and Prescott, 1997) filter. It is equally appropriate to use the Band-Pass filter (Baxter and King, 1999) or frequency filters such as the full sample asymmetric (Christiano and Fitzgerald, 2003), (Beveridge and Charles Nelson filter, 1981), or even the first difference operator.

Then we test the correlation using a 95 percent Chi–Squared Confidence Ellipse test with 45° line. Figure 6.8 plots the MENA countries' data. Iran is not included because it has a couple of missing values in the broad money data as we mentioned earlier. The relationships are statistically insignificant. The deviations of broad money from trend have much larger variance than the output gap. Money has not increased real GDP in the short run. For Turkey, the correlation is negative.

Figure 6.9 shows the 45° scatter plot with Chi-Squared Confidence Ellipse test for the Latin and South American countries.

The relationships are also statistically insignificant between the deviations of broad money from trend and the output gap in Latin and South American countries and show larger variance in broad money than in the real output gap.

Figure 6.10 is the scatter plot Chi-Squared test for the short-run money–output relationship in Africa. Most African countries have insignificant relationships between money and output in the short run, similar to the MENA countries and Latin and South America, except for Gabon and South Africa, which seem to show some positive correlation and tighter concentration of scatter points around the 45° line.

Figures 6.10a and 6.10b are line plots of the cyclical fluctuations of money and real output gap for Gabon and South Africa. There is some positive correlation in the data, however, but not in every period. Would that mean prices were stickier in some periods, but not others? We do not have detailed and finer data for these two countries to answer this question. However, the data seem to suggest that money has had positive real effects at some points in time in these two countries, and they are the two cases we have so far.

Figure 6.11 plots the data of Asian countries. The data of all the Asian countries in the sample exhibit no significant short-run relationship between money and real output with varying significance, except in Singapore. Figure 6.11a focuses on Singapore. The correlation between broad money fluctuations and the

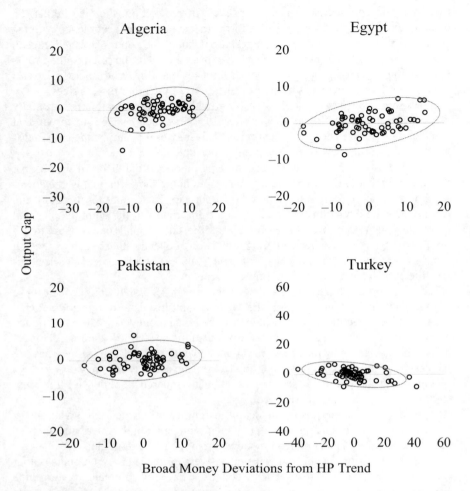

Figure 6.8 45° Scatter Plot with 95 Percent Chi-Squared Confidence Ellipse Test of Money and Real Output in MENA Countries, 1960–2020

Note: Iran is removed because of missing data.

real output gap is visible and strong. Again, we cannot speculate beyond price stickiness as a reason for such correlation. However, Singapore is a country, where the monetary authority keeps a watchful eye on the exchange rate, that is, some type of managed float. It does that, we speculate for lack of information about how it does that, by keeping the ratio of domestic money (most likely the base) to foreign reserves at a level consistent with its desired exchange rate. Thus, the quantity of money manipulation is an issue here. Therefore, we have three cases of close associations between money and real output in our sample of 42 countries.

The Neutrality of Money 127

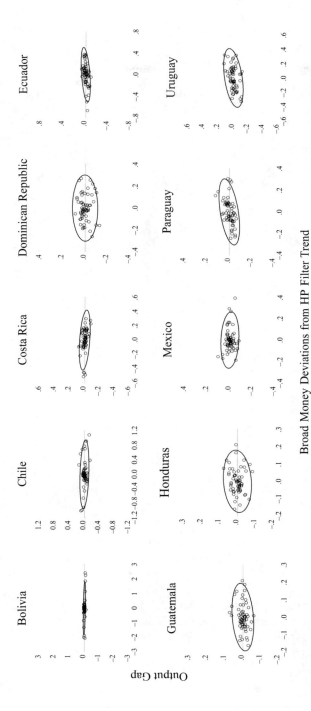

Figure 6.9 45° Scatter Plot with 95 Percent Chi-Squared Confidence Ellipse Test of Money and Real Output in Latin and South America, 1960–2020

Note: Colombia is removed because of missing values.

128   *The Neutrality of Money*

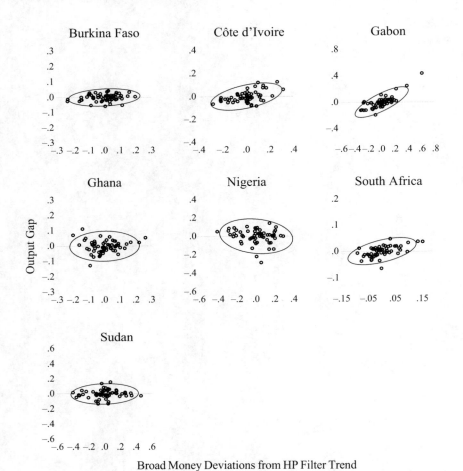

Figure 6.10 45° Scatter Plot with 95 Percent Chi-Squared Confidence Ellipse Test of Money and Real Output in Africa, 1960–2020

Next, we plot the two Caribbean countries in Figure 6.12.

Figure 6.12a focuses on Trinidad and Tobago's short-run fluctuations of broad money and the output gap. There is a significant association between money and output.

The last scatter plot is for the developed inflation-targeting countries. Figure 6.13 shows that the correlation between broad money deviations from trend and the real output gap is statistically insignificant in all countries; it is negative in the United States.

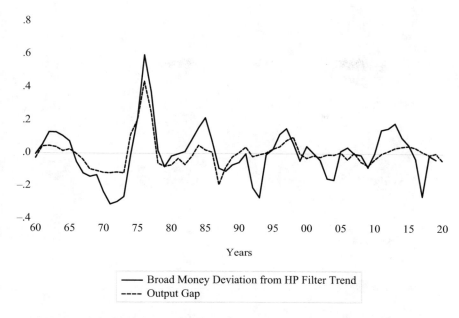

Figure 6.10a Gabon's Cyclical Broad Money Fluctuations and the Real Output Gap

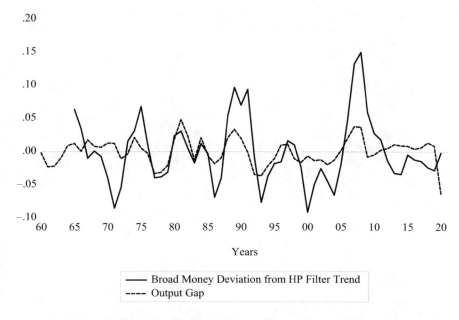

Figure 6.10b South Africa's Cyclical Broad Money Fluctuations and the Real Output Gap

130 The Neutrality of Money

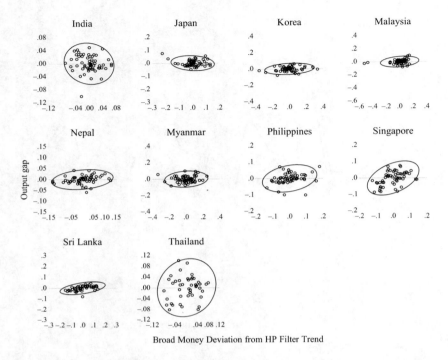

Figure 6.11 45° Scatter Plot with 95 Percent Chi-Squared Confidence Ellipse Test of Money and Real Output in Asia, 1960–2020

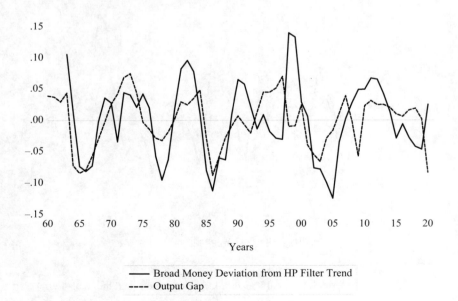

Figure 6.11a Singapore's Broad Money Fluctuations and Real Output Gap

The Neutrality of Money 131

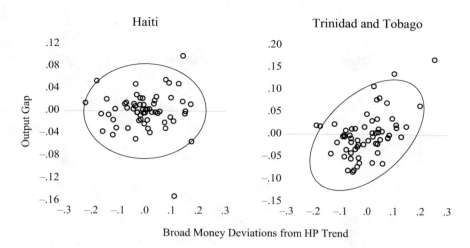

Figure 6.12 45° Scatter Plot with 95 Percent Chi-Squared Confidence Ellipse Test of Money and Real Output in the Caribbean Countries, 1960–2020

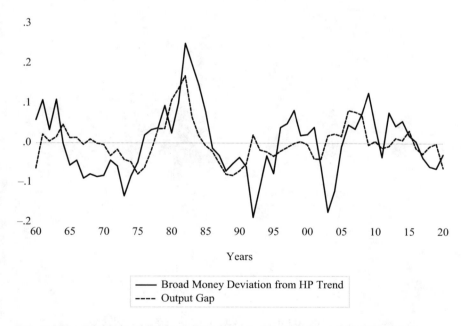

Figure 6.12a Trinidad and Tobago's Broad Money Fluctuations and Real Output Gap

132   *The Neutrality of Money*

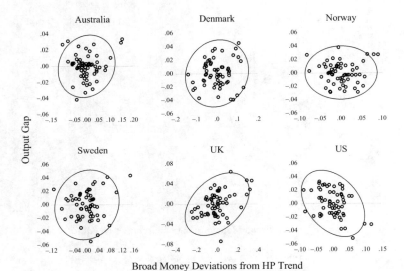

Figure 6.13   45° Scatter Plot with 95 Percent Chi-Squared Confidence Ellipse Test of Money and Real Output in the Developed Inflation-Targeting Countries, 1960–2020

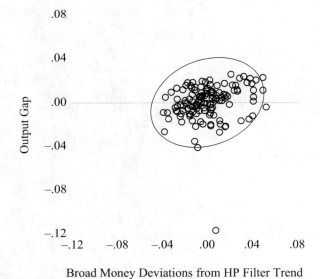

Figure 6.14   45° Scatter Plot with 95 Percent Chi-Squared Confidence Ellipse Test of New Zealand *Quarterly* Money and Real Output, March 1988 to December 2021*

Data Source: RBNZ. *Broad money data are from March 88 to December 2021 only.

The Neutrality of Money 133

New Zealand data are quarterly. Figure 6.14 plots the Chi-Squared tests for the correlations between money and real output. It has become very difficult to find the data for broad money on the RBNZ website.

The correlation in New Zealand is more positive than in every other inflation-targeting country.

We redo the Chi-Squared tests for the correlation between money and real output for five of the inflation-targeting countries, which are Australia, Denmark, Norway,

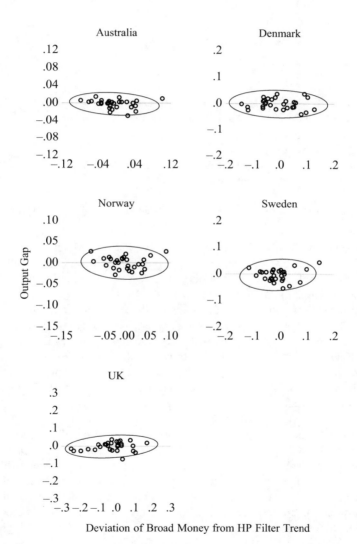

Figure 6.15 45° Scatter Plot with 95 Percent Chi-Squared Confidence Ellipse Test of Money and Output Gap in Inflation-Targeting Countries, 1992–2020

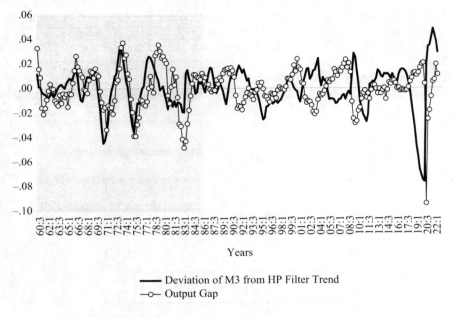

Figure 6.16 The US *Quarterly* Fluctuations of Broad Money and the Real Output Gap

Sweden, and the United Kingdom from 1992 to 2020, which is approximately the period of inflation-targeting in these countries. We exclude the United States because the sample for the inflation-targeting period is too small (2012–2020), see Figure 6.15. The correlation remains insignificant. Clearly, there is no significant correlation between money and real output in the short run, under inflation targeting. The highest correlation is in the New Zealand data, but these data are quarterly which might have something to do with temporal aggregation. Figure 6.16 plots the US M3 deviations from the HP-filter's trend and the output gap.

There is more positive correlation between broad money and real output over the business cycle early in the sample from the 1960s to mid-1980s, and weaker correlation thereafter.

We have shown the evidence of no correlation between money growth and real GDP growth in the long run and in the short run. We showed that increasing the quantity of money has not stimulated real GDP in the short run, except in a few countries in our sample, which are Singapore, Gabon, South Africa, Trinidad and Tobago, New Zealand, and the United States between 1960 and 1985 only. These latest test results beg the question: why do countries, and especially the developed inflation-targeting countries, continue to print money at high rates if money does not stimulate the real economy in the short run? What purpose does a high growth rate of money serve if it does not stimulate the real economy? The next chapter attempts to shed more light on this issue.

7 Why Do Central Banks Print More Money?

Abstract

Our evidence suggests that money is not associated with real GDP in both the long and the short runs. It is well understood that central banks use liquidity to manage aggregate demand and financial crises. But how do we explain the continuously accelerating money creation? We examine three potential explanations for the significant increases in money creations over the sample from 1960 to 2020. These explanations may include (1) seigniorage revenues; (2) continuous deficit spending financed by fiat money creations, and (3) the propping up of asset prices such as stock and housing, which might have been considered real wealth. We find that these variables are highly associated with money growth.

The evidence we presented earlier include a statistically significant long-run correlation between broad money and the CPI. The two levels share a common trend; and there is a significant long-run correlation between the growth rate of broad money and the inflation rate although the correlation deteriorates under successful inflation targeting regimes in developed countries. Central banks in developed inflation-targeting countries, nonetheless, continue to create new money and at higher rates. These central banks must have believed that the increase in the quantity of money does not lead to inflation and inflation expectations. Then we showed that the increase in the quantity of money failed to stimulate the real economy, that is, real GDP, in both the long and short runs except in few countries. Yet, all the central banks continue to print money at high rates. So why is that?

There could be a number of reasons. Since testing requires time series data, which are hard to find, we consider three hypotheses to test and in a fewer countries out of our sample. First, governments enjoy having seigniorage revenues from issuing new money. Second, government spending is a good reason for printing more money in order to finance its programs. A recent example is the COVID-19, which triggered massive government spending. Other examples include wars and social welfare programs. Third, a possible explanation for the ever increase in the creation of money is that an increase in the quantity of money, or the growth rate of money, induces higher demand for assets (land, real-estate, precious metals such as gold, and durables, etc.) which may be viewed by some politicians

DOI: 10.4324/9781003382218-7

136 *Why Do Central Banks Print More Money?*

and policymakers as an increase in wealth. Adam Smith wrote a chapter on this in *The Theory of Moral Sentiments*, where he argued that it is human nature (a disposition) to *admire the rich*. Capital gains are a welcome measure of prosperity by politicians. Governments may even like to tax capital gains. Since money must be held willingly, excess money must motivate purchasing assets. The buying of assets does not necessarily imply hedging against anticipated inflation because agents don't anticipate inflation in inflation-targeting countries. People spend the extra cash on assets anyway, and asset price inflation is evident in the data of many developed countries that have successfully targeted low and stable inflation rates.

Seigniorage Revenues

The question is whether, or not, the continuous increase in money growth is strongly associated with increasing seigniorage. We need a simple theoretical model to motivate the test of such hypotheses. The framework we use to shed light on this difficult question is based on (Sargent and Wallace's, 1974) – "Some Unpleasant Monetarist Arithmetic." In their story, if monetary policy is taken to be an *open market operation,* then it is arguable that monetary policy may be unable to control inflation in the long run.

We will use very simplistic formal representation here, but we will elaborate on this matter in the last chapter of this book when we discuss fiscal authority–monetary authority, dynamic policy interactions, the Fiscal Theory of Inflation, the Fiscal Theory of the Price Level, and Modern Monetary Theory. For now, let the government *real* debt is $\dfrac{D}{P}$, where D is nominal debt and P is the market price level, and it is committed to pay interest for. The government borrows to finance its deficit, where spending G exceeds the tax revenues, T. The government also receives seigniorage revenues from the central bank's money, $\dfrac{\Delta M}{P}$, where M is the money base, which we showed that it is small in developed countries and large in developing countries. In such a case, the treasury has to decide how much of the quantity of the combination of bonds and seigniorage required to financing its deficit.

Sargent and Wallace argued that in a system, where fiscal policy dominates, the treasury independently chooses its current and future budget deficits and the revenues required from both the bond it sells and seigniorage to finance them. Here, the central bank faces a constraint imposed by government bonds for it must finance with seigniorage and the difference between the revenues demanded by the treasury and the amount of bonds to be sold. Therefore, when there is *real* deficit, the government borrows by selling bonds and also by increasing seigniorage. If the government commits itself to these two revenues, the budget constraint remains unchanged, that is, the real debt $\dfrac{D}{P}$ is unchanged. Thus, the increase in G and the increase in M and D are the same size in theory. Formally, the budget constraint is given by a simple equation:

$$\frac{D}{P} = FB + S, \tag{7.1}$$

The left hand side represents real debt. The right hand side represents the real Fiscal Balance FB plus seigniorage.

Note that this article was written before any government thought about explicit inflation targeting. Today's inflation-targeting central banks do not target the quantity of the money base. The data show that the quantity of money has been growing and freely fluctuating without much of an effect on the CPI inflation target presumably because inflation expectations have been stable (anchored). Most central banks, especially in developed countries, use the short-term interest rate as an instrument to stabilize inflation, conditional on expected inflations. Under inflation targeting, *bygones are bygones*, which means when shocks increase the price level P today, the central bank does not reduce it in the next period. The price keeps rising. What matters for the central bank is that the ΔP remains at target. Thus, under such a scenario, Eq. (7.1) is probably not a determinant of the price level.

For the noninflation-targeting countries, we expect the correlation between the growth of government consumption expenditures ΔlnG_t and the growth rate of the monetary base ΔlnM_t^B to be greater than 0. It reflects the proposition that when spending exceeds revenues, that is, $G - T > 0$ (deficit), the government borrows by increasing D and seigniorage S to keep the ratio $\dfrac{D}{P}$ unchanged in the government budget constraint above. That is one possible answer to the question: why governments print more money? We also expect the correlation between money growth and government expenditures to be positive in inflation-targeting countries too because those central banks do not target the money base to achieve its target as explained earlier.

Haslag's (1998) Federal Reserve Bank of Dallas article, among a stack of papers that explain and calculate seigniorage revenues, provides very preliminary yet informative information about the subject. The main finding of the article is that there is a systematic, positive relationship between a country's monetary policy settings and its reliance on seigniorage revenue. Thus, countries that rely most heavily on seigniorage revenue tend to have the highest values of the monetary policy measure. There is some additional evidence that the relationship between the monetary policy variable and the seigniorage rate is nonlinear for OECD countries, which are relatively rich and financially sophisticated.

The evidence suggests that OECD countries rely on seigniorage revenue at an increasing rate for given changes in the monetary policy variable. He estimated seigniorage to be about 2 percent of GDP, maybe a little more or a little less. That is still a substantial sum, for example, for the United States, it is 380 billion USD. It is expected to be higher in politically less stable countries and developing countries.

We calculate seigniorage as the change in the monetary base/CPI ratio, then as a percent of nominal Gross Domestic Product (NGDP) or Nominal Gross Domestic Expenditures (NGDE) for some countries. The money base is total balances maintained plus currency in circulation. Figure 7.1 plots the US data. Seigniorage revenues have been stable and below 1 percent on average. The average of the seigniorage/NGDE ratio from 1960 to 2020 is 0.0006 percent; however, as the base significantly increased because of COVID-19 federal spending, seigniorage/NGDE percent increased to 0.015 percent. Not only that, but volatility increased significantly lately as well.

138 *Why Do Central Banks Print More Money?*

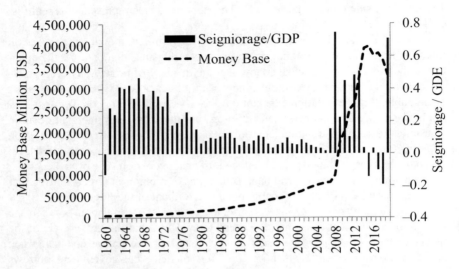

Figure 7.1 US Money Base Increasing and (Seigniorage/GDE)
Money Base Data Source: Federal Reserve Bank of St Louis (FRED)
Note: GDE is Nominal Gross Domestic Expenditures.

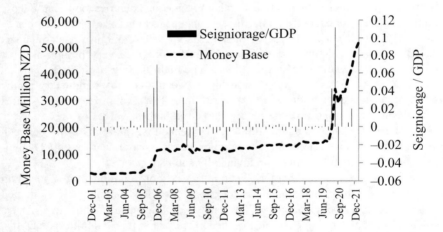

Figure 7.2 New Zealand Quarterly Money Base and (Seigniorage/Nominal GDP)
Money Base Data Source: Reserve Bank of New Zealand

We do not examine the seigniorage revenues for all *developing coun*tries in our sample, because the data of the monetary base are not readily available for most developing countries. Many of the central banks in developing countries report monetary data, but they have missing values, incomplete time series, or are not electronically available in time series format. Other data are cramped in tables published in pdf formats, which are difficult to download and use. The International

Monetary Fund – International Financial Statistics (IMF-IFS) report data for all developing countries, but they also have missing observations. We were able to retrieve some data for Korea, Malaysia, Turkey, and Gabon.

New Zealand's monetary base has exploded recently. Figure 7.2 shows the Reserve Bank of New Zealand data and their calculated seigniorage revenues–nominal GDP ratio. The monetary bases defined as total money base by the RBNZ, include more liabilities. The money base exploded in 2020–2022 period mostly due to financing the government spending on COVID-19.

Figure 7.3 plots the UK data, which are a little different from both the United States and New Zealand. Seigniorage-NGDE ratio has an average of 0.12 percent, and volatility is higher.

Figure 7.4 plots the money base and calculated seigniorage revenues using data from the IMF-IFS for Korea. The data ends in 2016. Declining seigniorage/NGDE ratio is quite remarkable.

Malaysia has data from 2000 onwards only. Figure 7.5 plots the same variables, and the picture is not significantly different from the Korean and the American. Average seigniorage/NGDE ratio is 0.6 percent of GNE in 2020, which is significantly larger than the United States, New Zealand, the U.K, and Korea.

I will plot two more countries whose data are available from 2001, which are Turkey and Gabon. Figure 7.6 plots the Turkish data, and Figure 7.7 plots Gabon's. Seigniorage revenues are not particularly different from the other countries.

Turkey's seigniorage-GDE ratio is relatively high over the sample but declined significantly over time and as the central bank began targeting inflation.

Although our sample of seigniorage is small, the developed inflation-targeting countries (the United States became an inflation-targeting country only in 2012) including Turkey (an inflation-targeting country) have relatively smaller

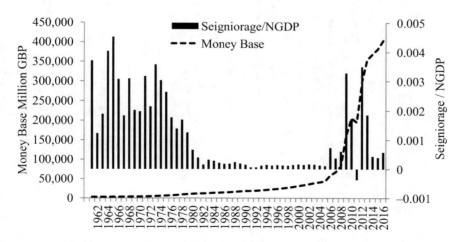

Figure 7.3 UK Money Base and (Seigniorage/GDE)

Money Base Data Source: FRED

Note: GDE is Nominal Gross Domestic Expenditures.

140 *Why Do Central Banks Print More Money?*

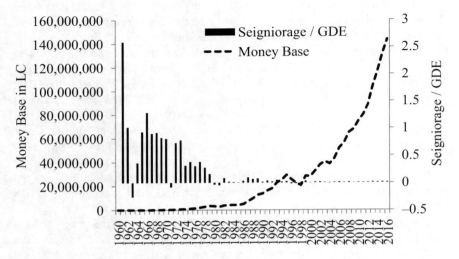

Figure 7.4 Korea's Money Base and (Seigniorage/NGDE)
Money Base Data Source: IMF-IFS
Note: GDE is Nominal Gross Domestic Expenditures.

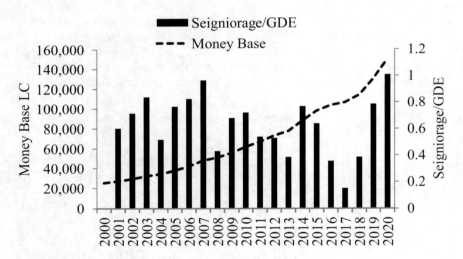

Figure 7.5 Malaysia's Money Base and (Seigniorage/NGDE)
Money Base Data Source: IMF-IFS
Note: GDE is Nominal Gross Domestic Expenditures.

seigniorage–Gross Domestic Expenditure ratios. Table 7.1 reports descriptive statistics. New Zealand which has had a low and stable inflation for a long time since 1989 has a very insignificant and stable seigniorage, followed by the United Kingdom, which also has a stable inflation since the early 1990s. The US mean

Why Do Central Banks Print More Money? 141

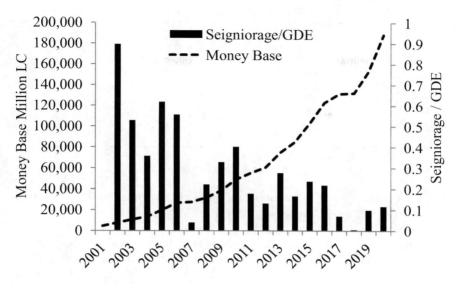

Figure 7.6 Turkey's Money Base and (Seigniorage/GDE)
Money Base Data Source: IMF-IFS
Note: GDE is Nominal Gross Domestic Expenditures.

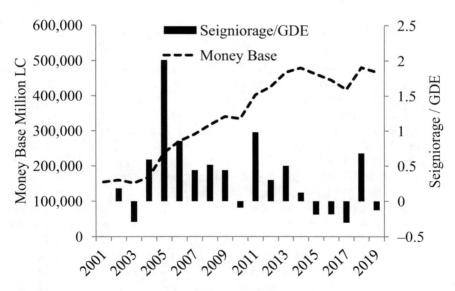

Figure 7.7 Gabon's Money Base and (Seigniorage/GDE)
Money Base Data Source: IMF-IFS
Note: GDE is Nominal Gross Domestic Expenditures.

142 *Why Do Central Banks Print More Money?*

Table 7.1 Descriptive Statistics of (Seigniorage/NGDE) in Selected Countries

Country	Sample	Mean	Standard Deviation
US	1960–2019	0.18	0.19
UK	1960–2016	0.12	0.13
New Zealand*	Mar 02–Dec 20	0.02	0.004
Turkey	2002–2021	0.28	0.23
Korea	1960–2016	0.23	0.47
Malaysia	2000–2020	0.61	0.22
Gabon	2002–2019	0.35	0.57

* New Zealand has *quarterly* data, and the ratio of (Seigniorage/NGDP) instead of NGDE, so the figure must be multiplied by 4 to compare it with the rest of the annual data.

seigniorage and standard deviation is not significantly different from the United Kingdom. The noninflation-targeting countries Malaysia, Gabon, and Korea have much higher and more volatile seigniorage on average. Turkey which adopted inflation targeting has a higher seigniorage than Korea, but is much less volatile. There are clearly significant differences between developed and developing countries as their financial markets and central banking frameworks differ significantly. The evidence taken from a few countries may suggest that developing countries rely more on seigniorage revenues than developed countries. This might explain why developing countries print money at relatively higher rates, but surely does not explain why a country like New Zealand does. Money growth is relatively high in all countries, and the trend and the relationships with CPI and inflation are evident in the data.

Government Consumption Expenditures

To test the hypothesis that government expenditures growth is financed by fiat money growth, we use general government final consumption expenditure, which includes all government current expenditures for purchases of goods from the World Development Indicators – World Bank, as a measure of G for all countries, and use the 95 Percent Chi-Squared Confidence Ellipse test scatter plots.

We start with the United Kingdom. The UK government had run a budget deficit since 1960. Figure 7.8a plots real surplus, that is, real taxes less real government expenditures, from 1972 to 2019. We do not have more data. Figure 7.8b plots nominal and real government consumption and the CPI. The trend is stochastic, that is, unit root. We tested the data using the same commonly used tests for unit root in the literature, which we used earlier, and we failed to reject the unit root in log government consumption expenditures. We do not report the results in tables because they take space, and they are similar to the tables we reported earlier for the CPI. The caveat, which we discussed earlier, is that these tests have weak powers against stationary alternatives. That said, the log-difference is I(0), which is what we use to test for the correlation. We apply the same tests to every country. Figure 7.8c plots the 45° line/95 Percent Chi-Squared Confidence Ellipse test for the UK data from 1960 to 1992, that is, before inflation-targeting, and Figure 7.8d plots the data from 1993 to 2016, that is, under inflation-targeting (remember that the money base data are from 1960 to 2016 only).

Why Do Central Banks Print More Money? 143

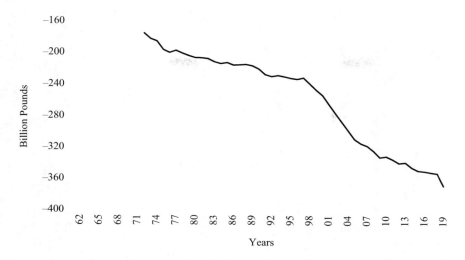

Figure 7.8a UK Real Budget Surplus (Real Tax Revenues Less Real Government Expenditures)

Data Source: World Development Indicators

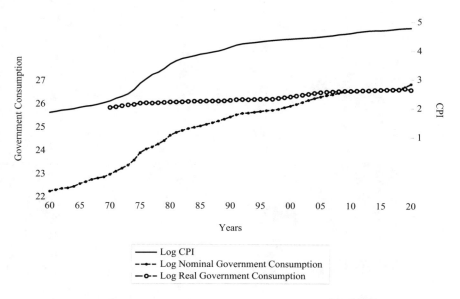

Figure 7.8b UK Nominal and Real Government Consumption and the CPI

Data Source: World Development Indicators

144 *Why Do Central Banks Print More Money?*

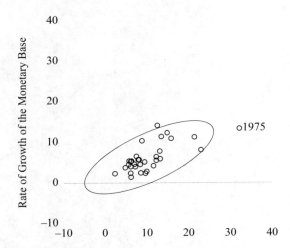

Figure 7.8c 45° Line Scatter Plots and 95 Percent Chi-Squared Confidence Ellipse Test for UK Data Before Inflation-Targeting, 1960–1992

Data Source: World Development Indicators and IMF-IFS

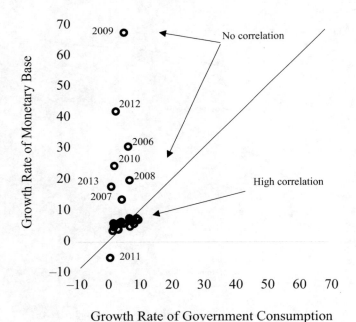

Figure 7.8d 45° Line Scatter Plot of UK Inflation-Targeting, 1993–2016

Data Source: World Development Indicators and IMF-IFS

Why Do Central Banks Print More Money? 145

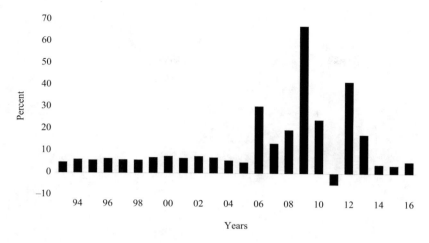

Figure 7.8e Growth Rates of the Monetary Base in the United Kingdom During Inflation-Targeting, 1993–2016
Data Source: FRED

Before inflation-targeting, the 95 Percent Chi-Squared Confidence Ellipse test indicates that the correlation between the growth rate of government consumption expenditures and the growth rate of the money base is statistically significant.

For the inflation-- targeting period, we use the 45° line scatter plot instead of a formal test statistic because the sample is small, 1993–2016. There are noticeable outliers in the monetary base growth rate during the GFC (2007–2008), the Great Recession (2009) up to 2013; however, except for a dip in 2011, the growth rate of the monetary base and government expenditures growth increased significantly. Figure 7.8e plots the growth rates of the monetary base for the United Kingdom during the period of inflation targeting.

We test New Zealand's growth rates of government consumption expenditures and the monetary base next. The data are *quarterly* and cover the period of inflation-targeting *only*. Figure 7.9a plots the test. There are many outliers in the monetary base, especially in 2006, 2011–2012, and 2020 for COVID-19 government's relief programs. Otherwise, most of the data are fluctuating around the 45° line. We also show the scatter plot for government consumption expenditures and broad money in Figure 7.9b, where the correlation is significantly stronger than in the case of the monetary base.

It is not unreasonable to assume that the newly printed money, that is, the growth of the monetary base, to cover the government's borrowing for the relief programs of COVID-19, up to 100 billion dollars, may have found its way to households, workers, and firm bank accounts and showed up in higher money aggregates, M1 and M2, among other possibilities. We test broad money in Figure 7.9b. The correlation is significant around the 45° line.

Table 7.2 reports the descriptive statistics and shows that, on average, the monetary base growth rate is significantly higher than that of broad money and government consumption expenditures. It is also significantly more volatile.

146 *Why Do Central Banks Print More Money?*

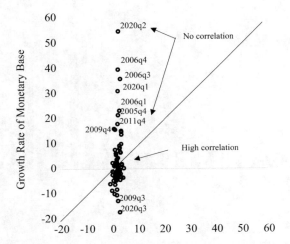

Figure 7.9a 45° Line Scatter Plot of Government Consumption Expenditures and the Monetary Base of New Zealand, March 2002 to December 2020

Data Source: Reserve Bank of New Zealand

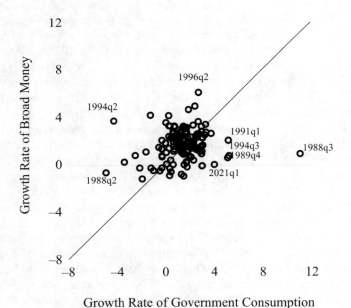

Figure 7.9b 45° Line Scatter Plot of New Zealand *Broad Money* and Government Consumption Expenditures, March 2002 to December 2020

Data Source: Reserve Bank of New Zealand

Table 7.2 Descriptive Statistics: New Zealand Government Growth Rates of Consumption Expenditures, Broad Money, and the Monetary Base in March 2002 to September 2021

	Average	Standard Deviation	Skewness	Kurtosis	J-B P-value
Government Consumption	1.56	1.03	−0.17	2.87	(0.8041)
Broad Money	1.89	1.06	−0.16	3.85	(0.2578)
Monetary Base	3.29	11.4	2.06	8.61	(0.0000)

J-B is Jarque–Bera test for normality.

It is broad money that, on average, is almost identical to government consumption expenditures. The monetary base has a significantly greater growth rate and is more volatile.

Next, we examine the US data, which should be an interesting case because the US government spending is massive on the scale compared with other countries, and because the US government borrows continuously to finance its huge spending, and also because the Fed became an explicit inflation targeting country in 2012. Figure 7.10a plots the real surplus (deficit) measured by real tax revenues less real government expenditures. It is similar to the United Kingdom which depicts continuously increasing deficits in real terms.

Figure 7.10b shows the trend in nominal and real government consumption expenditures. Figure 7.10c is a 45° line scatter plot.

With the exception of the outliers during the GFC in 2007/2008, the Great Recession in 2009 and 2019–2020, where a spending increase of five trillion dollars to finance several COVID-19 different spending packages, the correlation between the monetary base and government consumption is very significant. Figure 7.10d is a scatter plot of the broad money and government consumption expenditures growth rates. The 95 Percent Chi-Squared Confidence Ellipse test shows positive but marginally significant correlation.

The remaining countries, which we have data for the monetary base, are Turkey, Korea, Malaysia, and Gabon. We expect stronger correlation between the money base and government spending in developing noninflation-targeting countries. Figure 7.11a plots the 95 Percent Chi-Squared Confidence Ellipse test to test the correlation between government consumption expenditures and the monetary base for Turkey. Recall that the monetary base data are only available since 2001, and Turkey started targeting inflation in 2002. Therefore, the test is for the correlation during the inflation-targeting period. Figure 7.11b is the test using broad money instead of the monetary base. The correlation is positive and much more significant than with the monetary base.

Figure 7.12a plots the Korean data. Figure 7.12b plots the 95 Percent Chi-Squared Confidence Ellipse test of the correlation between the monetary base and nominal government consumption expenditures during the period of inflation targeting, which is positive but only marginally significant. Figure 12.7c shows the test for the full sample. The correlation is more significant. Figure 12.7d shows the test using broad money instead. The correlation with government consumption expenditures is even more significant.

148 Why Do Central Banks Print More Money?

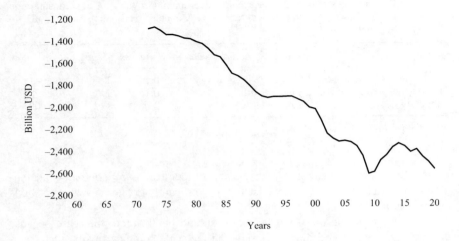

Figure 7.10a US Real Surplus (Deficit)
Data Source: World Development Indicators

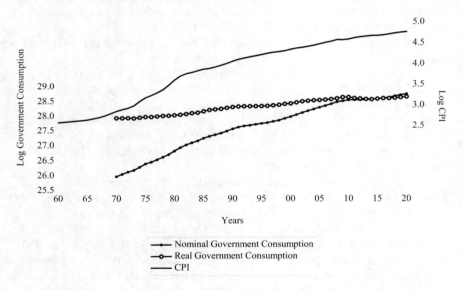

Figure 7.10b US CPI, Nominal, and Real Government Consumption Expenditures
Data Source: World Development Indicators

Figure 7.13a displays the log of nominal and real government consumption expenditures and the log of the CPI for Malaysia. The trend is similar to the trends we have seen before for the other developed and developing countries. Figure 7.13b tests Malaysia's growth rate of money base and the growth rate of government consumption expenditures.

Why Do Central Banks Print More Money? 149

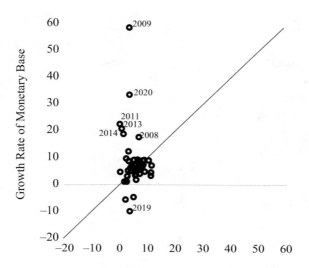

Figure 7.10c 45° Line Scatter Plot of US Monetary Base and Government Consumption Expenditures, 1970–2020

Data Source: FRED and World Development Indicators and IMF-IFS

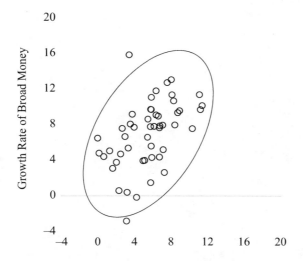

Figure 7.10d 45° Line Scatter Plot and 95 Percent Chi-Squared Confidence Ellipse Test of US Broad Money and Government Consumption Expenditures, 1971–2020

Data Source: World Development Indicators

150 *Why Do Central Banks Print More Money?*

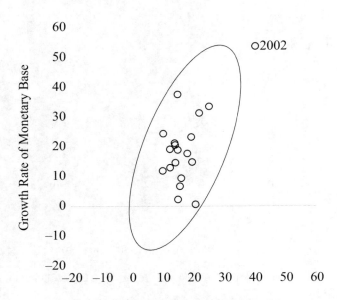

Figure 7.11a 95 Percent Chi-Squared Confidence Ellipse Test for Turkey Monetary Base and Government Consumption Expenditures, 2002–2020

Data Source: Word Development Indicators and IMF-IFS

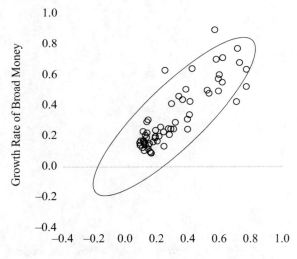

Figure 7.11b 95 Percent Chi-Squared Confidence Ellipse Test for Turkey Broad Money and Government Consumption Expenditures, 1960–2020

Data Source: Word Development Indicators

Why Do Central Banks Print More Money? 151

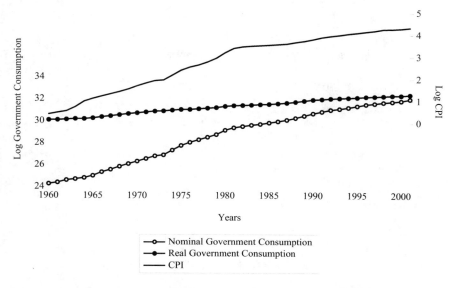

Figure 7.12a Korea CPI and Nominal and Real Government Consumption Expenditures
Data Source: World Development Indicators

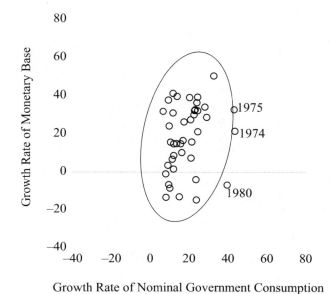

Figure 7.12b 95 Percent Chi-Squared Confidence Ellipse Test for Korea Monetary Base and Government Consumption Expenditures Before Inflation-Targeting, 1961–2002

Data Source: World Development Indicators and IMF-IFS

152 *Why Do Central Banks Print More Money?*

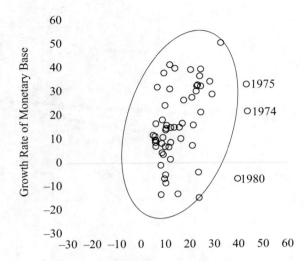

Figure 7.12c 95 Percent Chi-Squared Confidence Ellipse Test for Korea Broad Money and Government Consumption Expenditures, Full Sample, 1961–2016

Data Source: World Development Indicators and IMF-IFS

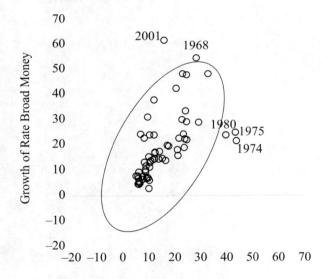

Figure 7.12d 95 Percent Chi-Squared Confidence Ellipse Test for Korea Broad Money and Government Consumption Expenditures, Full Sample, 1961–2020

Data Source: World Development Indicators

Why Do Central Banks Print More Money? 153

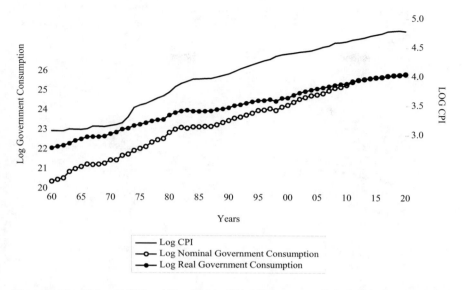

Figure 7.13a Malaysia CPI and Nominal and Real Government Consumption Expenditures
Data Source: World Development Indicators

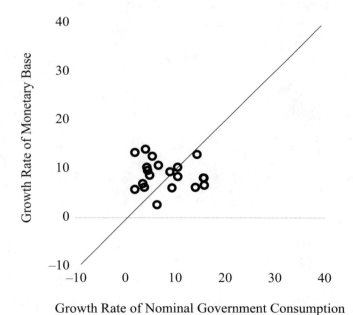

Figure 7.13b 45° Line Scatter Plot of Malaysia Monetary Base and Government Consumption Expenditures in Inflation-Targeting Period, 2000–2020
Data Source: World Development Indicators

154 *Why Do Central Banks Print More Money?*

The sample is small for using a statistical test; however, there is a rather clear positive association between the monetary base and nominal government expenditures.

Figure 7.14a plots the data for Gabon.

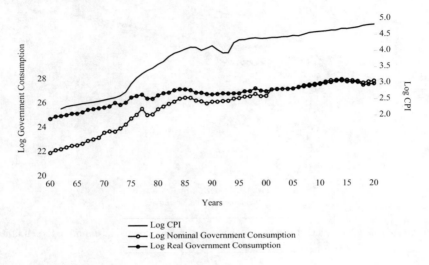

Figure 7.14a Gabon CPI and Nominal and Real Government Consumption Expenditures
Data Source: World Development Indicators

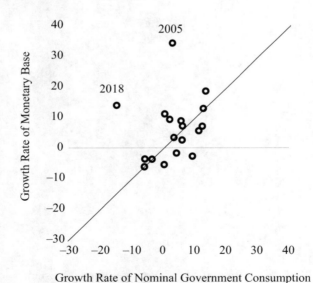

Figure 7.14b 45° Line Scatter Plot of Gabon Monetary Base and Government Consumption Expenditures, 2002–2019
Data Source: World Development Indicators

Why Do Central Banks Print More Money? 155

The sample is too small to test for the correlation statistically; however, it is quite evident from Figure 7.14b that there is rather a close association between the growth rate of the monetary base and government consumption expenditures along the 45° line.

We could safely conclude that there is a close positive association between money (monetary base and broad money) and nominal government expenditures growth rates in the small sample of countries we have data for, which are the United Kingdom, New Zealand, the United States, Korea, Malaysia, Turkey, and Gabon. The relationship holds under inflation targeting too. There is strong evidence that governments run fiscal deficits, which are financed by central bank money. COVID-19 spending programs in many countries were financed by central banks exchanging government bonds for cash. The government also wrote checks to households, workers, firms, businesses, etc., and some of this money found their way into the money supply as M1, M2, or broader aggregates. In the developed countries, different governments have different views on social welfare programs. Spending on such programs increases and decreases depending on which government is in office, but the differences are small in magnitude. In many developing countries, spending on such programs is expected to increase with population and regardless of which government is in office. Next, we test for the correlation between *broad money* and nominal government expenditures' growth rates in the remaining countries.

Figure 7.15 is both a 95 Percent Chi-Squared Confidence Ellipse test and a 45° line for the growth rates of broad money and nominal government consumption expenditures for the remaining MENA countries, Algeria, Egypt, Iran, and Pakistan. There is a significant positive correlation.

Figure 7.16 plots the Latin and South American data. The correlation between government expenditures and broad money is positive and statistically more significant than all other countries. Most of these correlations are incredibly significant. Figure 7.17 is the 95 Percent Chi-Squared Confidence Ellipse test, for the African data, excluding Gabon which is presented earlier. The correlation is positive and statistically significant. Nigeria, like Iran, has a smaller correlation. It is a major oil producer too, which would use petrodollars to finance its spending. Sudan has a very strong positive correlation.

The 95 Percent Chi-Squared Confidence Ellipse test and 45° line scatter plots for the Asian countries are shown in Figure 7.18. The correlation between the growth rates of government spending and broad money in India, Nepal, the Philippines, and Singapore is insignificant. All other countries have statistically significant correlation between the growth rates of broad money and nominal government consumption expenditures. Japan, Korea, Malaysia, Sri Lanka, and Thailand have significant positive correlation. Japan, Malaysia, and Sri Lanka have a one-to-one association between government spending and money.

The Caribbean countries, Haiti and Trinidad and Tobago, do not have data. Figure 7.19 tests the Australian data.

The correlation is positive and marginally significant. Figure 7.20 plots the test statistics for Denmark. The correlation is significant.

Figure 7.21 tests the Norwegian growth rates of nominal government consumption expenditures and broad money and indicates that the correlation is stronger

156 *Why Do Central Banks Print More Money?*

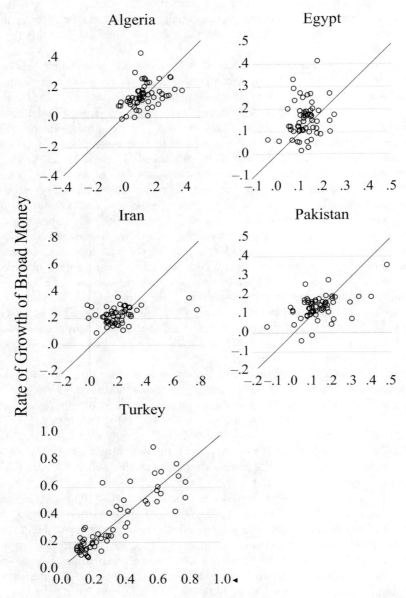

Figure 7.15 95 Percent Chi-Squared Confidence Ellipse Test and 45° Line Scatter Plot of MENA Countries' Broad Money and Nominal Government Consumption Expenditures, 1961–2020

Data Source: World Development Indicators

Why Do Central Banks Print More Money? 157

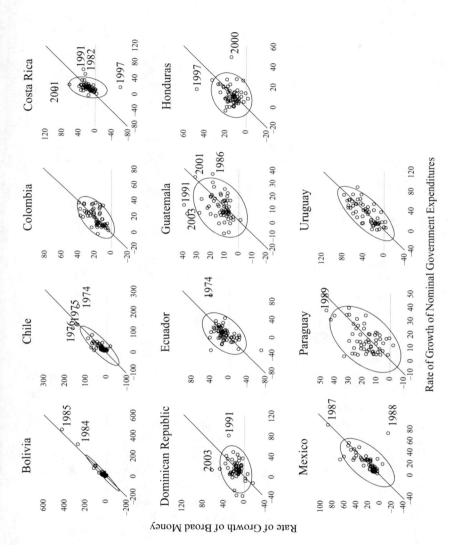

Figure 7.16 95 Percent Chi-Squared Confidence Ellipse Test and 45° Line Scatter Plot of Latin and South America's Broad Money and Nominal Government Consumption Expenditures, 1961–2020

Data Source: World Development Indicators

158 *Why Do Central Banks Print More Money?*

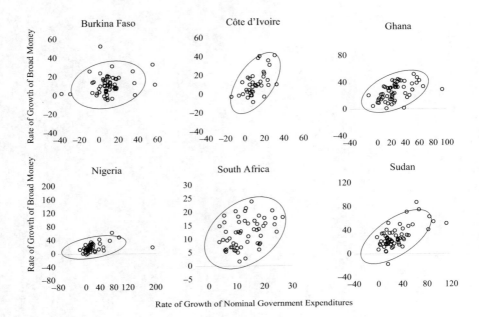

Figure 7.17 95 Percent Chi-Squared Confidence Ellipse test for African Countries' Broad Money and Nominal Government Consumption Expenditures, 1961–2020

Data Source: World Development Indicators

Note: Gabon not included; Côte d'Ivoire and Nigeria have many missing values.

than in Denmark. Norway is an oil producer with a small population and large social welfare programs. It is rather expected to see a high correlation between government spending and money creation.

Figure 7.22 tests the Swedish data. The correlation is relatively insignificant and smaller than in Denmark and Norway; nonetheless, it is positive.

To sum up, all the countries in our sample, the developing and the developed inflation-targeting countries, display positive correlation between the nominal government consumption expenditures and broad money growth rates. Generally speaking, the hypothesis that government consumption expenditure probably induces central banks to issue new money to finance the budget deficits is supported by the data. Central banks could hold the government bonds and pay the government a check or they could sell the bonds to the public. The governments write checks to economic agents for their purchases. Some of this money finds its way to broader aggregates in the banking system in various forms of deposits and bank accounts.

We test this hypothesis that money growth and asset prices are highly correlated.

Why Do Central Banks Print More Money? 159

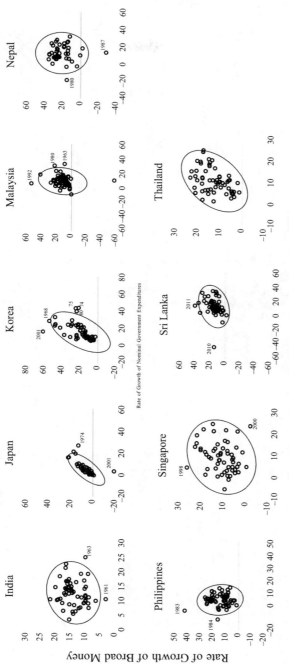

Figure 7.18 95 Percent Chi-Squared Confidence Ellipse Test for Asian Countries' Broad Money and Nominal Government Consumption Expenditures, 1961–2020

Data Source: World Development Indicators

Note: Myanmar does not report data, Japan's data start in 1971, and Nepal starts in 1976.

160 *Why Do Central Banks Print More Money?*

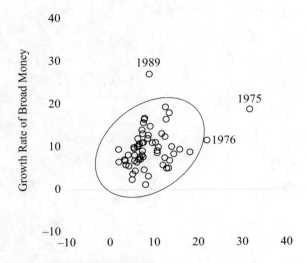

Figure 7.19 95 Percent Chi-Squared Confidence Ellipse Test and 45° Line Scatter Plots for Australia's Broad Money and Nominal Government Consumption Expenditures, 1961–2020

Data Source: World Development Indicators

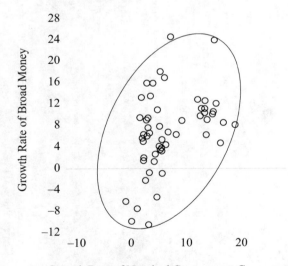

Figure 7.20 95 Percent Chi-Squared Confidence Ellipse Test and 45° Line Scatter Plots for Denmark's Broad Money and Nominal Government Consumption Expenditures, 1967–2020

Data Source: World Development Indicators

Why Do Central Banks Print More Money? 161

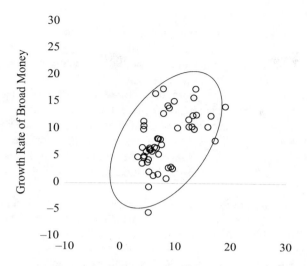

Figure 7.21 95 Percent Chi-Squared Confidence Ellipse Test and 45° Line Scatter Plots for Norway's Broad Money and Nominal Government Consumption Expenditures, 1971–2020

Data Source: World Development Indicators

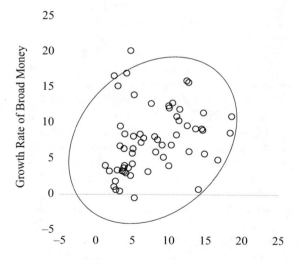

Figure 7.22 95 Percent Chi-Squared Confidence Ellipse Test and 45° Line Scatter Plots for Sweden's Broad Money and Nominal Government Consumption Expenditures, 1961–2020

Data Source: World Development Indicators

162   *Why Do Central Banks Print More Money?*

Excess Money and Asset Prices

Friedman (1988) shows that the real quantity of broad money per unit of real output is positively related to the deflated price of equities at some lag. Quarterly data for the period from 1961 to 1986 suggest that the real quantity of money (defined as M2) demanded relative to income is positively related to the deflated price of equities (Standard and Poor's composite) three quarters earlier and negatively related to the contemporaneous real stock price. He suggested that annual data for a century indicate that the apparent dominance of the wealth effect is the exception, not the rule – that is, money could not possibly induce real wealth. There are some economists and policymakers who do believe that the Fed, at some point in time, intentionally inflated asset prices because they believed that they constitute wealth.

In theory, monetary policy (interest rate and money) affects asset price inflation (inflation in house price, stock price, government securities, etc.). The relationship among asset prices, bond prices, and monetary policy is a large literature in financial economics, macroeconomics, and monetary policy, so I will only reference a small number of papers then test the association of asset prices and monetary policy.

Razzak and Moosa (2018) use portfolio theory in a model with three asset prices to show that the effects of monetary policy shocks measured either with the quantity of money or interest rates significantly affect housing prices in the United States. Loose monetary policy (low interest rate or higher money growth) prop up housing, asset, and bond prices.

Mishkin (2001), for example, examined the role of asset prices in the transmission mechanism of monetary policy shocks and argued that central banks have been often tempted to use them as targets of monetary policy. He showed that despite the significance of asset prices in the conduct of monetary policy, targeting asset prices by central banks is likely to lead to worse economic outcomes and might even erode the support for their independence.

The stock market reacts to Fed's announcements of interest rate too, see for example (Kontonikas *et al.*, 2013) who examined the response of US stock returns to federal fund rate's surprises between 1989 and 2012. They found that (outside the GFC period) stock prices increased as a response to unexpected federal fund rate cuts. So expansionary monetary policy implies more money growth and more demand on stocks, hence, higher stock price inflation. State dependence is identified with stocks exhibiting larger increases when interest-rate easing coincided with recessions, bear markets, and tightening credit conditions. However, an important structural shift occurred during the crisis, changing the stocks' response to FFR shocks and the nature of state dependence. Throughout the crisis period, stocks did not react positively to unexpected FFR cuts, which were interpreted as signals of worsening future economic conditions.

Expansionary monetary policy induces excess money supply, credit expansion, higher demand for assets and housing, in particular, eventually higher asset prices. Politicians tolerate, accept, and may like high housing prices more than

Why Do Central Banks Print More Money? 163

falling prices. Inflation, which is targeted, albeit differently, by many central banks in developed countries in our sample, affects asset prices too. For example, the inflation target is set by the elected government in New Zealand. The target could not be changed by the Reserve Bank. New Zealand politicians have changed the inflation target twice since 1989, and they might change it again. Most of the time, they increased the target, from 0–2 percent to 1–3 percent. The United Kingdom is similar in the sense that the government sets and could change the target, not in the United States, however. Although there should be less motivation for hedging when inflation is low and stable, people's demand for assets is very high in inflation-targeting countries. Many may consider this a wealth effect.

There is a literature on the optimal inflation target, although it is mostly New Keynesian, where the optimal target is never zero, but rather positive. Milton Friedman argued that the inflation rate should be negative so that the real rate of return on cash would be positive ($r = i - \pi$; since i is bounded and has to be ≥ 0, a negative inflation rate delivers a positive real rate r). With that rule, the Fed can make the real rate of return on cash to be anything it likes, including that equal to the rate of time preference. No central bank that I am aware of advocates such theory. Regardless of whether this rule or any other rules might be better than discretion, no central bank in developed countries takes Friedman's argument seriously. Central banks do not use policy rules – they never did.

Blanchard *et al*. (2010) favors a 4 percent inflation target. Central banks are very concerned about the effectiveness of monetary policy – that is, the nominal short-term interest rate to be precise – because of the Zero Lower Bound (ZLB). That might be *the* primary reason perhaps to argue for a positive, perhaps > 2 percent inflation target. Central banks may also believe that downward nominal wage rigidity is another reason. Note that inflation-targeting central banks do not target the quantity of money, and that is why money keeps growing; they target the short-term interest rate (the price of money). The New Keynesian argument may well provide support to higher than lower inflation target, see for example (Andrade *et al*., 2019), which is consistent with (Blanchard *et al*., 2010) who show that starting from pre-crisis values, a 1 percentage point decline in the natural rate r^* should be accommodated by an increase in the optimal inflation target of about 0.9 to 1 percentage point. But who knows what r^* is. There is an enormous uncertainty about this figure (see for example (Beyer and Wieland, 2019) and (Orphanides and Williams [2002]).

However, (Modigliani and Cohn, 1979) hypothesized that the stock market suffers from money illusion. Campbell and Vuolteenaho (2004) showed more evidence for the Modigliani and Cohn's hypothesis, and the persistent use of the "Fed model" by Wall Street suggests that the stock market incorrectly extrapolates past nominal growth rates without taking into account the impact of time-varying inflation. They found that the level of inflation explains almost 80 percent of the time-series variation in stock-market *mispricing*. However, we showed that inflation is uncorrelated with the quantity of money under successful inflation-targeting regimes. Their success of stabilizing inflation for a long time and the lack of correlation between money growth and inflation might have convinced policymakers that printing more money is harmless. Do policymakers suffer from money illusion too?

It is very difficult to test the correlation between stock prices, nominal and real, and money, nominal and real, because the former is relatively highly volatile. The standard deviation of the growth rate of nominal and real stock prices in the United States (Wilshire 5000 Total Market Full Cap Index) is at least ten times in order of magnitudes larger than the standard deviation of money growth. To plot the two, we standardized the data by deflating them by their standard deviations. Figure 7.23a plots the US annual *standardized* (i.e., the standard deviation is equal to one for both variables) growth rate of real broad money, where broad money is deflated by the CPI and the standardized rate of growth of real stocks prices. There is a reasonable positive association, but it is statistically insignificant.

The next figure, Figure 7.23b, is a 45° line scatter plot of these two variables. It shows a positive, albeit weak or insignificant association. Figure 7.23c is the 95 Percent Chi-Squared Confidence Ellipse test, which confirms that the correlation is positive but statistically insignificant.

Figure 7.24 is a 45° line scatter plot of the growth rates of the standardized real broad money and stock prices in the United Kingdom from 1960 to 2020. There are outliers, which cause the fit to falter even though we standardized the data. The standard deviation of the growth rate of real stock price is 380 compared with 11.5 for the growth rate of the real broad money. The correlation is nonetheless much higher than the US data in Figure 7.24.

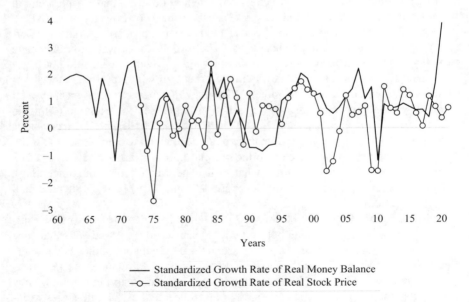

Figure 7.23a Standardized Growth Rates of Real Money Balances and Real Stock Price in the United States, 1973–2020

Stock Prices Data Source: FRED, from 1973

Board Money Data Source: World Development Indicators

Why Do Central Banks Print More Money? 165

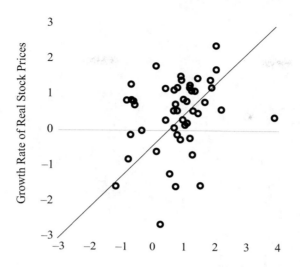

Figure 7.23b 45° Line Scatter Plot of US Standardized Growth Rates of Real Broad Money and Real Stock Prices, 1973–2020

Stock Prices Data Source: FRED, from 1973
Board Money Data Source: World Development Indicators

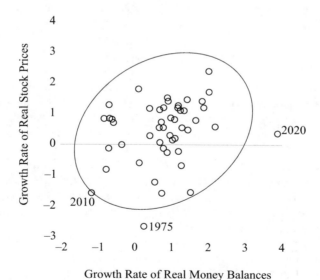

Figure 7.23c 95 Percent Chi-Squared Confidence Ellipse Test of US Standardized Growth Rates of Real Broad Money and Real Stock Prices, 1973–2020

Stock Prices Data Source: FRED, from 1973
Board Money Data Source: World Development Indicators

166 *Why Do Central Banks Print More Money?*

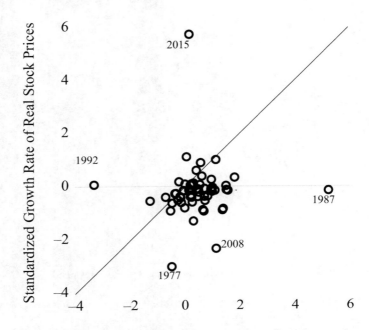

Figure 7.24 45° Line Scatter Plot of UK Standardized Growth Rates of Real Broad Money and Stock Prices, 1961–2020

Stock Prices Data Source: FRED

Board Money Data Source: World Development Indicators

Stock prices in many countries in our sample are not as reliable as the US and the UK data, and many countries either do not report stock price time series or their stock markets are thin. For example, most of New Zealander's wealth is in housing rather than shares. Therefore, excess money could be spent on another important asset – housing. Housing wealth is quite important politically and economically in developed countries. House owners are voters. Politicians encourage homeownership and make laws to encourage homeownership. Thus, the housing market is a crucial policy. Is money growth correlated with house price inflation as a sign of wealth? Figure 7.25 plots the row data, the housing price index, and broad money per unit of real output. The trend is obvious.

Cyclical correlations are plotted in Figure 7.26, which shows the cyclical fluctuations of broad money and housing prices in Denmark, Norway, Sweden, the United Kingdom, and United States. The Australian data are unreported. New Zealand has quarterly data, which we test separately. We use the Full Sample Asymmetric Frequency filter of (Christiano and Fitzgerald, 2003) to remove the noise and the trend from the house price data. The remaining are the fluctuations in the data between 2 and 8 years only. The housing price data are from the Bank for International

Why Do Central Banks Print More Money? 167

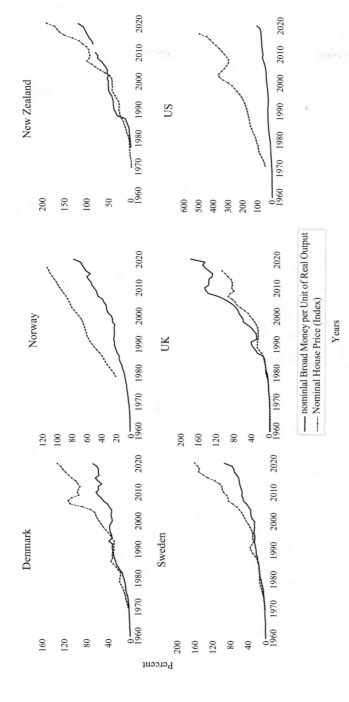

Figure 7.25 Housing Prices and Broad Money – Real GDP Ratios in Inflation-Targeting Countries (Except Australia)

Data Source: Housing Price: BIS; Broad Money: World Development Indicators

168 *Why Do Central Banks Print More Money?*

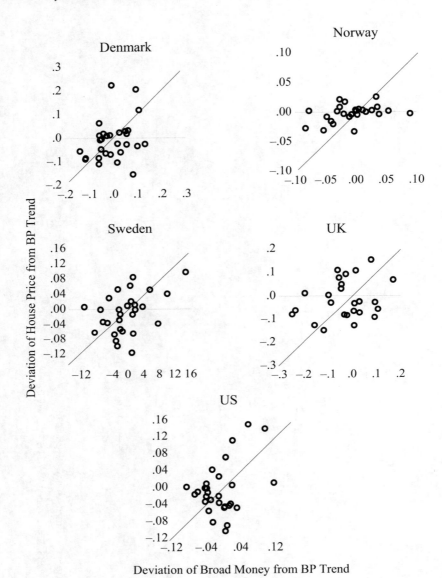

Figure 7.26 45° Line Scatter Plot of Cyclical Fluctuation of Broad Money and Housing Prices in Inflation-Targeting Countries

House Price *Data Source*: BIS
Broad Money Data Source: World Development Indicators

Settlements (BIS). The contemporaneous correlation in the United States is *marginally* negative (not plotted); however, it is positive when we lagged the house price cycle by 2 years, which is consistent with (Friedman, 1988). Although we are dealing with volatile asset prices, the fit is reasonable in all countries – the least is in Norway and remarkable in the UK data.

Figure 7.27 shows the 95 Percent Chi-Squared Confidence Ellipse test for the correlation. There is a statistically positive correlation between broad money and housing prices. We also tested the data in *real terms*, that is, real broad money

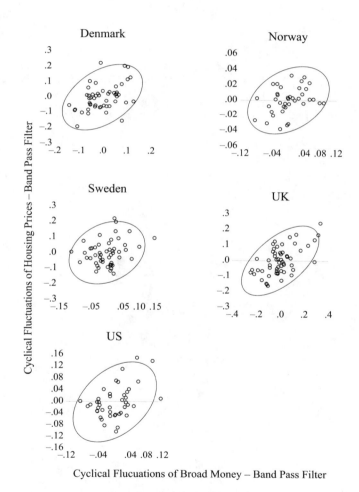

Figure 7.27 95 Percent Chi-Squared Confidence Ellipse Test of Cyclical Fluctuation of Broad Money and Housing Prices in Inflation-Targeting Countries

House Price *Data Source*: BIS

Broad Money Data Source: World Development Indicators

170 *Why Do Central Banks Print More Money?*

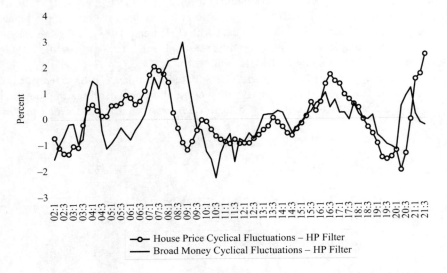

Figure 7.28 New Zealand Quarterly Business Cycle Fluctuations of Broad Money and Housing Prices

Data Source: Reserve Bank of New Zealand

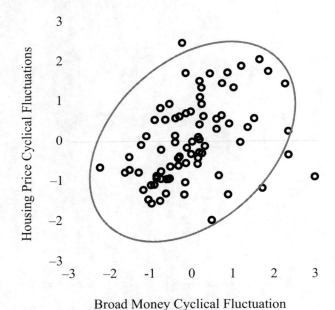

Figure 7.29 95 Percent Chi-Squared Confidence Ellipse Test of New Zealand Cyclical Fluctuation of Broad Money and Housing Prices in Inflation-Targeting Countries, March 2002 to September 2021

Why Do Central Banks Print More Money? 171

balance and real housing prices and found the results of the Chi-Squared test to be similar. We do not report the results.

Next, we test the quarterly New Zealand data. Figure 7.28 plots the data and shows that cyclical fluctuations of broad money and housing prices move together. The sample is from March 2000 to September 2021. Finally, we test the correlation between money and housing prices in New Zealand using the 95 percent Chi-Squared Confidence Ellipse test. Figure 7.29 shows the test values. The correlation is only marginally significant, nonetheless indicate close association between money and housing prices.

We conclude that the data are supportive of all three hypotheses that money growth in general could be motivated by seigniorage revenues, especially in developing countries and nonindependent central banks. In developed countries with independent central banks and inflation-targeting regimes, money growth is mostly a result of government deficit spending, and it is positively correlated with rising asset prices such as stocks and housing.

8 The Phillips Curve, Anticipated Inflation, and Output

Abstract

We discuss the evolution of and the theoretical issues surrounding the Phillips curve, which was originally (Phillips, 1958) a negative empirical relationship between the unemployment rate and the inflation rate. It has been the dominant theory of inflation in central banks in developed countries. Policymakers and politicians seem to like the idea that they could influence the economy by exploiting this relationship, that is, in order to create more employment, they inflate the economy. By late 1960s and through the 1970s, more theoretical analyses showed that such exploitation is fruitless because unanticipated aggregate demand shocks, that is, surprises, ignored by Phillips, is the only significant determinant of real output. Anticipated aggregate demand shocks, on the other hand, are ineffective in stimulating the economy. Every time the monetary authority attempts to stimulate demand, it increases real output (reduces unemployment) in the short run, then inflation expectations shift up the Phillips curve, and real output (unemployment) returns to their long-run equilibrium before the policy change. If the monetary authority continues to stimulate the economy, the Phillips curve keeps shifting up via expectations effects, and, in the long-run, the economy ends up with more inflation and no change in real output or unemployment; hence the Phillips curve is vertical in the long run, and no trade-off between inflation and output (unemployment) exists. Our Sample Generalized Variance tests indicate that the New Keynesian specification, change in inflation–output gap, is unstable in most of the 42 countries in our sample.

Monetary theories of inflation are contentious. There are stark differences of opinions between economists about the determinants of inflation. So far, we have only analyzed the QTM, where in the *long run*, inflation is caused by, or is highly correlated with, the growth rate of the quantity of money per unit of real output. Remember that we define inflation as a *continuing* increase in the price level, and the difference between the short run on one hand and the *long run* is a key to the arguments given before.

In our sample of 42 countries, we showed evidence that there is a strong long-run correlation between money and prices and money growth and inflation, especially in developing and developed countries, especially before inflation-targeting in the early

DOI: 10.4324/9781003382218-8

The Phillips Curve, Anticipated Inflation, and Output   173

1990s. Most interestingly, we found insignificant correlation between money growth and inflation in successful inflation-targeting regimes. The QTM explains the positive association between money growth and real output in the short run, that is, over the business cycle, presumably because prices are sticky. Here, the *short run* is a key to the argument. Thus, when the quantity of money grows, prices take more time to catch up, which causes real output to increase during that time interval. We found no evidence of significant positive relationship between money growth and real GDP in the long run, and there is very slim evidence for such correlation over the business cycle. On average, there is no effect of money growth on real GDP growth.

In my experience, most central banks and policymakers, especially in the advanced economies, however, hold strong non-Monetarists' views. To be more precise, it seems that most policymakers care more about the short run than the long run. Keynes is widely quoted to have said, *we are all dead in the long run*, therefore, people who believe in this statement suggest that we should not care about the long-run inflationary implications of money creation and hope for a short-run increase in real output and a reduction of unemployment. Many of us will remember that there have been times during our lifetime of very high inflation and hyperinflation, and people were very much alive and suffering. Did policymakers interpret Keynes' statement to mean it's okay to print as much money as they want because if inflation occurs in the long run it would not be a problem since we would be dead? I wonder. Do people care about their offspring? Sure they do. We care about the future generation. That said; the long run in the context of modern macroeconomic theory is rather not about calendar time. The long run is when expectations about the future state of the economy are realized, that is, the expected values are equal to the actual values; and when growth of all macroeconomic variables ceases.

This literature is voluminous, and I will try to cover the arguments briefly before I begin testing the Phillips curve. Friedman (1968) talked about the role of monetary policy in the context of the Phillips curve in a highly cited lecture at the American Economic Annual meeting. Lucas (1972a) is another classic reference to the expectations and the neutrality of money within the Phillips curve framework. Friedman explained what monetary policy could and could not do. Monetary policy might be able to stimulate the economy in the short run, but, in the long run, there would be *only* higher inflation as a result of such stimuli. So let's begin our journey with the Phillips curve from here. Keep in mind that the Phillips curve is the dominant model of inflation in central banks, especially in the advanced world.

Phillips (1958) shows an *empirical* relationship between the rate of (nominal) wage inflation and the unemployment rate in the United Kingdom. He found a downward-sloping relationship between nominal wage inflation (the rate of growth of nominal wages on the vertical axis) and the unemployment rate on the horizontal axis. Milton (Friedman, 1976, p. 215) stated that the argument about the relationship between inflation rate and the unemployment rate was first studied by Irving Fisher in 1926 (Fisher 1926). Fisher documented a significant positive relationship between inflation and unemployment. Friedman points out one major difference between the findings of Phillips and Fisher, which are 32 years apart – it was that Fisher took the rate of change of prices (inflation) to be the *independent*

174   *The Phillips Curve, Anticipated Inflation, and Output*

variable, that is, causality in this case runs from inflation to unemployment. Friedman quoted Fisher saying that when the dollar is losing value, or in other words when the price level is increasing, a business person finds the receipts rising as fast, on average. With this general rise of prices and not in expenses, because expenses consist, largely, of things, which are (counterfactually) fixed, employment is then stimulated – for some time at least.

Fisher and Friedman's views implied that producers misinterpret the shock, which lead to the *misperception model* (Lucas 1972b, 1973). The story is that both producers (and workers) observe a rise in spending for whatever reason or shock. The producers interpret it as an increase in the demand for their *own* products. In other words, they interpret higher spending as an increase in real demand for their own products. Naturally, they would respond by expanding production. They do so by hiring more workers. The economy expands as Fisher stated. Output and employment increase (unemployment falls) *first* due to the shortsightedness or misinterpretation of the shock by producers and workers. At this point, both the labor market and the output market have *nominal* wages and prices at equilibrium w^* and p^*, and, with excess demand for labor and goods, both wages and prices face upward pressures. Both wages and prices begin to increase to eliminate the excesses. Of course, the opposite of this scenario is true. A decline in spending or the money supply could also be misinterpreted as a decline in demand for a specific product. This is a dynamic process, which describes the fluctuations in the rate of spending about some average trend. However, this is just the beginning. You could imagine this downward sloping aggregate demand–upward sloping aggregate supply curve shifting impacting both real output (on the X-axis) and the price level (on the Y-axis).

At the time of Fisher, prices were stable. That was the trend. It was the Gold Standard then. He made a distinction between the *high* and *low* price on one hand, and the *rise* and *fall* in prices. Friedman emphasizes that Fisher was making a distinction between *anticipated* and *unanticipated* changes.

A very different approach was taken by Phillips, whereby *unemployment is the independent* variable, not prices. The rate of change of nominal wages is the dependent variable. Phillips argued that when the demand for a commodity or service is high relative to supply, we expect the price (wage) to rise, which is surely true. The rate of increase is greater, the greater the excess demand. It seems plausible that this should work for the rate of change of *nominal* wages, which are the prices of labor services (Phillips, 1958, p. 283). Therefore, we have static demand and supply curves. The point of intersection is the market equilibrium of wages and unemployment. It is where the employment quantity is the amount of labor demanded. Unemployment is zero. This is later called the *Natural Rate of Unemployment Hypothesis* (NRUH).[1]

Phillips says that at this point, *there is no pressure on wages*, that is, wages are stable. Thus, wages rise when the unemployment rate falls below this equilibrium point, and falls when unemployment increases above it. Essentially, there is a negative relationship between nominal wage growth and unemployment.

Friedman was critical of both Fisher and Phillips in taking it for granted that wages are a major component of total cost and that wages and prices would tend to

---

1 Friedman said that he borrowed this concept from (Wicksell's, 1898) natural rate of interest.

The Phillips Curve, Anticipated Inflation, and Output 175

move together. The fallacy in this according to him is that supply and demand are not functions of *nominal* wages. If we look at the data of wages and price today, we observe that wages did not rise at the same rate of prices. However, the *real wage* is the relevant variable in economic theory, not the *nominal wage*. Therefore, the theory does not predict what happens to *nominal* wages when employment changes. *The real wage could remain unchanged if the nominal wage and the price level are separately constant; when each is rising at the same rate or falling at the same rate.* The only way the real wage changes is if the price does not move at the same rate of the nominal wage, which is the next story in the battle of ideas between Keynesian and non-Keynesian economists.

Phillips' idea means that changes in *expected* nominal wages are equal to changes in *expected* real wages. There are two components of the Keynesian system that are essential for Phillips' argument. First, prices are rigid in the sense that people do not allow for the possibility of a price change when they plan; thus, the changes in nominal wages or nominal prices are the same as changes in real magnitudes. Second, real wages *ex-post* could be altered by anticipated or expected inflation. It could be that the Keynesian argument for a full employment arose out of the assumption that it was possible to get workers (at least in the 1930s when Keynes wrote the General Theory) (Keynes, 1936, pp. 9, 14, and 15) to accept lower *real wages* produced by inflation that they would not have accepted in the direct form of a reduction in nominal wages. Keynes (1936, p. 9) wrote, and I am quoting here, "whilst workers will usually resist a reduction in money-wages, it is not in their practice to withdraw their labor whenever there is a rise in the price of wage-goods." And on page 14, he wrote, "they [the workers] resist reductions of money-wages . . . whereas they do not resist reductions of real wages." (Keynes, 1936, p. 15) argued that since no trade union would dream of striking on every occasion of a rise in the cost of living, they do not raise the obstacle to any increase in aggregate employment attributed to them by the classical school.

Most important, however, is the fact that the Keynesian system was incomplete. There was a missing equation. The Phillips curve is not the missing equation that connected the real economy with the monetary economy. What is needed to complete the Keynesian system is an equation to determine the *equilibrium price level*. The Phillips curve is a relationship between the rate of change of wages or prices and unemployment. It does not determine the equilibrium price level. It is true too that the price level is indeterminate in inflation-targeting regime.

Policymakers, especially politicians, through time liked the idea of the *original* Phillips curve regardless of its fallacy. The fact that it tells them that they could reduce unemployment by allowing some inflation is quite enticing for politicians for obvious reasons: spend more, stimulate the economy, and the election results may well be favorable.

There were three reactions to the Keynesian model back in the 1960s. First is the general theoretical reaction, which brought about the fallacy in the *original* Phillips curve approach of identifying *nominal* and *real* wages. Second is the failure of the Phillips curve empirical relationship to hold in data for other countries. Fisher had found it to hold for the United States for the period before 1925. Phillips had found to hold for Britain for a long period. However, when people tried it for any

176 *The Phillips Curve, Anticipated Inflation, and Output*

other country, they failed to get it to fit. Furthermore, nobody was able to construct a *stable* empirical Phillips curve. The Phillips curve failed to hold over different periods of time. The stability of the Phillips curve is a testable hypothesis, and it could easily be tested statistically. Most macroeconomic textbooks have graphs for the Phillips curve, where it is clear that the curve has shifted over time and, when the points are connected, we observe fat loops. Essentially, it seems like the original Phillips curve is a mirage – it seems to exist but it is not.

We will examine the stability of the Phillips curve, but before we do that, note finally that, stagflation, which was a result of the oil supply shocks in the 1970s, rendered somewhat unbelievable the confident statements that many economists had made about the "trade-off" on the basis of the empirically fitted Phillips curve. We are probably facing similar supply shocks today, that is, COVID-19, the supply chain interruption, the Russia–Ukraine conflict, and its effect on food and oil prices, which should be tested when more data become available.

Short-Run and Long-Run Phillips Curves

The failure of the empirical Phillips curve resulted in attempts to rescue it by distinguishing between the short run and the long run. Samuelsson and Solow wrote Analytical Aspects of Anti-Inflation Policy in 1960. Stanley Fischer (1994) quoted them. He said that the Phillips curve was brought to the United States by Paul Samuelson and Robert Solow who, after presenting the menu view of the curve, warned that their discussion dealt only with the *short run* and that it would be wrong to think that the same trade-off between inflation and unemployment would be maintained in the longer run. Samuelson and Solow then gave examples of how the Phillips curve shifts. First, low inflation might shift the curve down because of its impact on expectations. It is fascinating that the two Laureates spoke of expectations long before Edumnd (Phelps, 1967) and Milton (Friedman, 1968) provided their views on the role of expectations on the validity of the Phillips curve. In fact, a tremendous amount of research emerged in the past 25 years documenting the flattening of the Phillips curve in successful inflation-targeting regimes. Blanchard (2016) for example, among many others, found that the slope of the US Phillips curve has declined. However, he found that there is more evidence for the original Phillips curve than the expectations-augmented newer version because inflation expectations have been anchored. This finding is true in a number of inflation-targeting countries. Second, Solow and Samuelson said that structural unemployment might increase as a result of higher unemployment so that the curve would shift up. There is no doubt that the Phillips curve is unstable in that sense; hence, it could not be used for forecasting and policy.

I continue to draw on (Friedman, 1976). Now imagine an aggregate demand and aggregate supply curves intersecting at a point of equilibrium for employment (or unemployment) and *real wages*. Because both potential employers and employees expect an implicit or explicit contract covering a long period, both must guess (forecast) in advance what real wage will correspond to the nominal wage. Assuming that expectations about the price level are slow with some time lag, we can,

The Phillips Curve, Anticipated Inflation, and Output 177

for a short period, revert to the original Phillips curve.[2] However, the equilibrium position is no longer a constant nominal wage, but a nominal wage changing at the same rate as the anticipated rate of change of prices Inflation. For a growing economy, we have to add the anticipated rate of change of productivity; e.g., see (Razzak, 2015) for empirical evidence using US data.[3]

When the demand and supply change due to the shock, first, there will be a change in the rate of change of nominal wages. Thus, there will be a change in the anticipated rate of change of real wages. Current prices may adjust as rapidly as or more rapidly than wages; thus real wages *actually received* may move in the opposite direction from nominal wages, but *anticipated real wages* will move in the same direction.

For example, assume that money wages increase by 2 percent a year. Workers will initially interpret this rise in wages as an increase in their *real* wages because they still anticipated constant prices, thus they will be willing to offer more labor (move up the labor supply curve) hence employment increases (the unemployment declines). Producers may have the same anticipation as workers about the general price level. However, producers have more information about the price of their own products. They will initially interpret a rise in aggregate demand as an increase in the demand for their own products, hence, a rise in the price of their own products. This means they thought that there was an increase in *relative prices*. It also means to them that the real wage they must pay to hire more labor will fall. Thus, they would hire more labor.

It would take some time for the employers and the workers to recognize and understand the nature of the shock because shocks are very difficult to identify and to interpret.

Even *ex-post*, the econometricians struggle to identify the nature of the shocks and their permanency. The producers and the workers would eventually understand that the shock increased the *general price level*, not their *relative prices*.

Eventually, the producers and the workers raise their estimate of the expected or anticipated inflation. Thus, the rate of increase of real wages falls, which will reduce employment (reduce labor supply). This leads to a reduction in labor supply (employment hours decline and unemployment increases). Therefore, there is a short-run trade-off between inflation and unemployment (or output), but no long-run trade-off. This is the trade-off alluded to by Samuelson and Solow earlier.

Employers and workers have different interpretations of the effect of the expansionary shock. Assume for example that the equilibrium points are associated with a constant price level. Workers care about the nominal wage they are being offered by the firm divided by a measure of the general price level, e.g., the CPI, which is what they pay for their purchases of goods and services. The workers think that the demand for labor has increased. The new equilibrium is the point of intersection of the initial

---

2 I think we have more evidence for wages being stickier than prices because of labor contracts, see, for example (Fischer, 1977).

3 (Razzak, 2015) provides evidence that the US macroeconomic data of real wages, unemployment, and labor productivity are consistent with the microeconomic theory that unemployment increases when real wages are higher than labor productivity; decreases when real wages are lower than labor productivity, and remains constant when real wages are equal to labor productivity.

178 *The Phillips Curve, Anticipated Inflation, and Output*

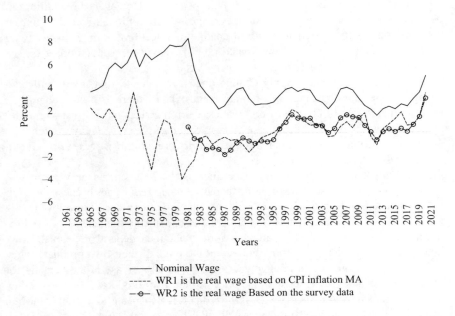

Figure 8.1 Nominal and Real Wage Growth Rates in the United States

upward sloping labor supply curve and the new higher downward sloping demand curve, which gives the higher real (and nominal) wage and more employment (or supply more hours of work, work more than one job, overtime work, and so on).

The employers, on the other hand, care about the prices of the goods and services they produce and the wage they pay to workers. The producer's demand for labor in terms of the nominal wage and his price would be unchanged. Thus, the intersection of this higher demand curve and the new supply of labor gives more employment and lower real wage. The producers think they face a higher demand for their own product, which would fetch higher prices, but pay less real wages. So the equilibrium labor quantity (employment) is the same as the worker's, but the *anticipated real wages* are different. This new equilibrium quantity of labor (employment) is temporary.

Producers would realize that the shock has increased the general price level, not their relative prices. Workers' realization of this fact would lower their expected real wages. Workers must now work fewer hours, that is, supply less labor, and employers must reduce their demand for labor. The curves will shift back in the long run. The anticipated price increase perceived by the workers and the anticipated price perceived by the producers converge, and both approach the rise in nominal wages. The result of government stimulus in the long run is more inflation and no increase in output over potential or a reduction in unemployment below the natural rate of unemployment.

Figure 8.1 plots three variables. First is the growth rate of nominal wages $\Delta ln W_t$ of the United States, which is the OECD private sector index. The other two

The Phillips Curve, Anticipated Inflation, and Output 179

variables measure real wages, WR_1 and WR_2. The real wage is $\Delta lnW_t - \pi_t^e$. Expected inflation π_t^e is measured as (1) a 2-year moving average of the CPI inflation and (2) the survey of inflation expectations reported by the Federal Reserve Bank of Philadelphia. The nominal and real wage growth rates move in directions that are consistent with Friedman's description. They move in opposite direction sometimes, especially when expected inflation is high in the 1960s through the 1980s, then they move closer as inflation expectations decline late in the sample.[4]

No Long-Run Money Illusion

In the presidential address to the American Economic Association in 1967, Milton Friedman argued that the long-run Phillips curve is vertical, which is based on the idea that economic agents have no money illusion in the long run. The paper was published in 1968, hence (Friedman, 1968). Edmund Phelps developed a seemingly similar idea (see, e.g., Phelps [1967, 1970]). His hypothesis was called, later, the *Accelerationist Hypothesis* or the NRUH. *Accelerationist* refers to monetary policy with the objective to hold unemployment below the horizontal intercept of the long-run vertical Phillips curve, which must lead to accelerated inflation. It is also widely known as the NAIRU – the *non-accelerated inflation rate of unemployment*. Many economists use this NAIRU concept interchangeably with the NRUH. These two concepts are different, however.[5] See also (Sargent, 1971) on this issue and (Lucas, 1972a) among many important references.

Begin from equilibrium in the wage–unemployment space again, with a certain wage inflation rate and an unemployment rate presented by the Phillips curve. A policy that aims at reducing the unemployment rate (move left on the horizontal axis towards the origin) must be accomplished by creating some inflation. Inflation results from some expansionary monetary policy. Reducing inflation must be accomplished by creating more unemployment. Most policymakers today tend to think this way. At this point, the expected inflation rate is zero. However, people's expectations about inflation change. This change in expectations constitutes a shift up in the short-run Phillips curve. Once it happens, the unemployment goes back (increase) to where it was in equilibrium. To keep unemployment down below, more inflation is needed. And, the short-run Phillips curve shifts up again. Thus, the only way the unemployment rate is kept below equilibrium is by an ever-accelerating inflation, which always keeps *current* inflation *above anticipated* inflation.

---

4 It is hard to measure expected inflation; therefore, it is hard to measure real wages, and it is highly likely that we have measurement errors. A general equilibrium model with model-consistent inflation expectation based on rational information set needs to be used to arrive at a better measure.

5 Think about the meaning of the "non-accelerating inflation rate . . ." It refers to a "unique" or "known" inflation rate, e.g., 2 percent, which is associated with unemployment. The fact of the matter is that in the *long run* the unemployment rate could be associated with *any* inflation rate, negative, zero, and X percent. We will provide some evidence for that later. Therefore, the natural rate of unemployment is not the same as the NAIRU.

180   *The Phillips Curve, Anticipated Inflation, and Output*

Friedman argued that the term "natural rate of unemployment" has been misunderstood. It does not refer to some *irreducible minimum of unemployment*. It refers to that rate of employment, which is consistent with the *existing real conditions* in the labor market. It can be lowered by removing obstacles in the labor market, that is, making it flexible. The purpose of the concept is to distinguish between monetary and nonmonetary aspects of the employment situation. At this point, I shall add that the NAIRU literally says that there exists *a unique* non-accelerated inflation rate that is consistent with unemployment. The fact, according to Friedman and most non-Keynesian economists, is that there is no such unique inflation rate. In the long run, the natural rate of unemployment rate is consistent with an infinite number of inflation rates. This precisely means the long-run Phillips curve is vertical.

The Phillips curve specification took several forms in the literature. Keeping with the Keynesian story, there are two Keynesian specifications. There is the original Phillips curve specification linking the *level of inflation* to the unemployment rate (no expectations) and the New Keynesian typical specification linking the *change in inflation* to unemployment. Let the Phillips curve be:

$$\pi_t = \alpha + \beta \pi_t^e + U_t, \tag{8.1}$$

where π_t is the CPI inflation rate, U_t is the unemployment rate, the superscript e on top of the inflation rate denotes the expectation operator, and α β are parameters to be estimated. The theory of expectations formation turned out to be crucial and complicates the Phillips curve policy implications. We will provide detail empirical examination in the next chapter. The coefficient β should be indifferent from unity, if Phelps's *Accelerationist* hypothesis is true; therefore, the unemployment rate is $-\alpha$, which is consistent with a vertical long-run Phillips curve when inflation is equal to expected inflation. Therefore, this value of U satisfies the NAIRU and the natural rate too. All other values of U either represent the short-term equilibrium or some stochastic component of the NAIRU. I am unaware of new surveys, but (Turnovsky, 1974) is a good "old" summary of all the empirical studies in the past. The majority of those old studies used time series data for different countries and covering different spans of time. Most estimates of β in Turnovsky were less than 1. There are important ramifications in case $\beta < 1$, which we will shed a lot of light on later.

The preferred New Keynesian specification is given by (Romer and Romer, 1997) who assume $\pi_t^e = \pi_{t-1}$, and such specification, that is, the change in inflation depends on the unemployment gap, is the standard specification of the NAIRU. So,

$$\pi_t = \pi_{t-1} + \gamma \left(U_t - U_t^* \right), \tag{8.2}$$

Thus,

$$\Delta \pi_t = \gamma \left(U_t - U_t^* \right), \text{ or,} \tag{8.3}$$

In terms of the output gap, we write:

$$\Delta \pi_t = \delta \left(Y_t - Y_t^* \right),$$

Blanchard (2016) has provided empirical support to the original Phillips curve specification. He estimated the US Phillips curve and showed that, and I am quoting him directly, "(1) Low unemployment still pushes inflation up; high unemployment pushes it down." Put another way, the US Phillips curve is alive. He said he wished he could say "alive and well," but it would be an overstatement: the relationship has never been very tight. (2) Inflation expectations, however, have become steadily more anchored, leading to a relation between the unemployment rate and the *level of inflation* rather than *the change in inflation*. In this sense, the relation resembles more the Phillips curve of the 1960s than the *Accelerationist* Phillips curve of the later period. (3) The slope of the Phillips curve, that is, the effect of the unemployment rate on inflation given expected inflation, has substantially declined. But the decline dates back to the 1980s rather than to the Global Financial Crisis. There is no evidence of a further decline during the Global Financial Crisis. (4) The standard error of the residual in the relation is large, especially in comparison to the low level of inflation.[6]

We test the correlation between the unemployment rate and the change in inflation, that is, the preferred New Keynesian specification, and the unemployment rate and the level of inflation, that is, the original Phillips curve, for the United States and Japan because we have data for unemployment, which are unavailable for the majority of countries in our sample. Figure 8.2a is the 95 Percent Chi-Squared Confidence Ellipse test for the US Phillips curves.

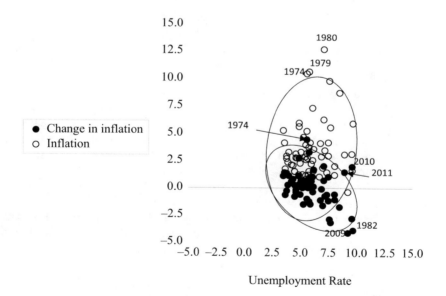

Figure 8.2a 95 Percent Chi-Squared Confidence Ellipse Test of the New Keynesian Preferred Specification of the Phillips Curve of the United States, 1960–2021

Data Source: World Development Indicators

---

6 There might be an argument for a non-linear or asymmetric Phillips curve specification such that negative output gaps have different effects than positive output gaps on inflation, which we will not examine. See (Razzak, 1995) for an example using New Zealand data.

182 *The Phillips Curve, Anticipated Inflation, and Output*

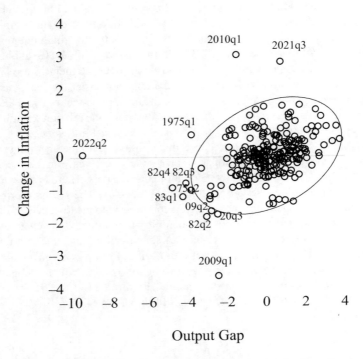

Figure 8.2b 95 Percent Chi-Squared Confidence Ellipse Test of the New Keynesian Preferred Specification of the Phillips Curve of the United States, March 1960 to June 2022

Data Source: World Development Indicators

The scatter plot tests are significantly different. The New Keynesian specification shows a significant downward sloping Phillips curve (in the change in inflation–unemployment space). The outliers of high unemployment are associated with recession dates, 1982 and 2009. There is no negatively sloped Phillips curve in the unemployment rate and *level* of the CPI inflation rate space. There is no evidence of the original Phillips curve as in (Blanchard, 2016).

We test the correlation between the *output gap* and the change in inflation and the output gap and the level of inflation using *quarterly* data from Mar 1960 to Jun 2022 in Figures 8.2b and 8.2c. Again, there is some evidence for the Phillips curve under the New Keynesian specification, but none under the original Phillips curve specification. In fact, in the inflation–unemployment rate, the Phillips curve is more vertical.

Figure 8.3 is the 95 Percent Chi-Squared Confidence Ellipse test of the Japanese Phillips curve, the unemployment rate, and CPI inflation taken from OECD Statistics. These tests are the exact opposite of the US data. There is no evidence for the New Keynesian Phillips curve specification and a well-defined and significant downward sloping Phillips curve under the original specification.

The Phillips Curve, Anticipated Inflation, and Output 183

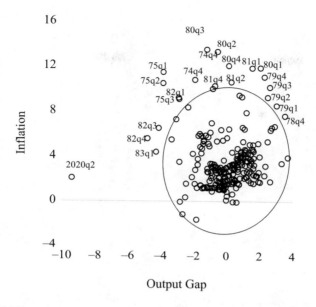

Figure 8.2c 95 Percent Chi-Squared Confidence Ellipse Test of the Original Specification of the Phillips Curve of the United States, March 1960 to June 2022

Data Source: World Development Indicators

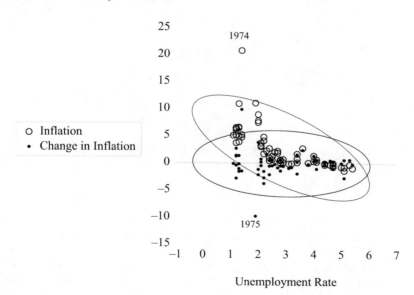

Figure 8.3 95 Percent Chi-Squared Confidence Ellipse Test of the New Keynesian Specification of the Phillips Curve of the Japan Inflation, 1960–2021

Data Source: OECD Statistics

184 *The Phillips Curve, Anticipated Inflation, and Output*

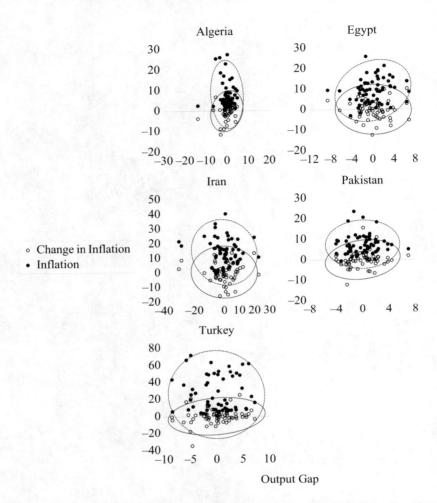

Figure 8.4 95 Percent Chi-Squared Confidence Ellipse Test of the Phillips Curve Specifications of the MENA Countries, 1960–2020

Data Source: World Development Indicators

For the rest of the countries, we test the Phillips curve specifications using the output gap (instead of unemployment) because the data for unemployment over our sample are unavailable for developing countries. Graphical presentations of the Phillips curve must be interpreted with care until more econometric tests are carried out. Figure 8.4 is the 95 Percent Chi-Squared Confidence Ellipse test for the MENA countries. In Algeria, the scatter plots resemble a significant vertical long-run Phillips curve in the unemployment–inflation specification. There is also a significant New Keynesian Phillips curve specification. There is no statistical evidence of such Phillips curve specification in Egypt; there is, however, some evidence in

The Phillips Curve, Anticipated Inflation, and Output 185

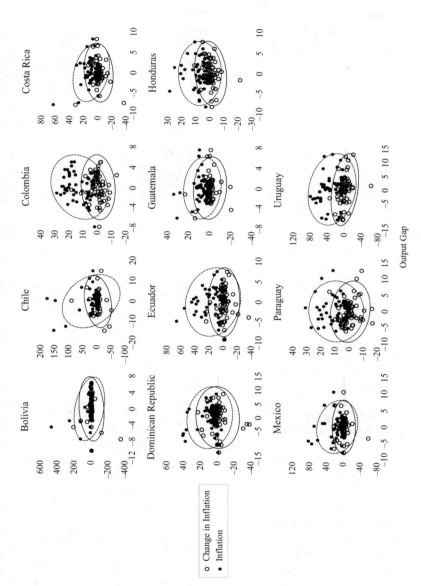

Figure 8.5 95 Percent Chi-Squared Confidence Ellipse Test of the Phillips Curve Specifications of the Latin and South American Countries, 1960–2020

Data Source: World Development Indicators

186 The Phillips Curve, Anticipated Inflation, and Output

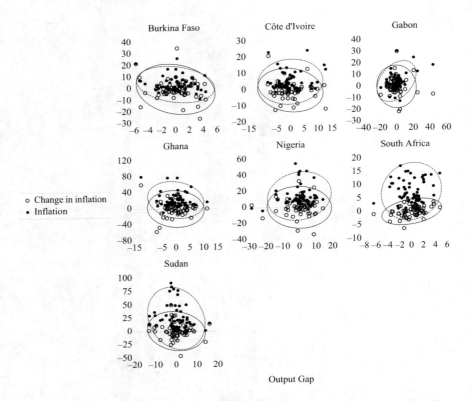

Figure 8.6 95 Percent Chi-Squared Confidence Ellipse Test of the Phillips Curve Specifications of the African Countries, 1960–2020

Data Source: World Development Indicators

favor of the original Phillips curve specification. There is no significant evidence of any Phillips curve of any specification in Iran, Pakistan, and Turkey.

Figure 8.5 is a scatter plot of the Latin and South American countries. For the original Phillips curve specification (output gap–inflation), we found no evidence in Bolivia, Chile, Costa Rica, the Dominican Republic, Ecuador, Guatemala, Honduras, Mexico, and Paraguay; there is weak statistical evidence in Colombia and Uruguay. There is no evidence for the New Keynesian Phillips curve anywhere in Latin and South American data in our sample.

Figure 8.6 for Africa shows insignificant Phillips curve, albeit Gabon has a positive correlation between the output gap and the change in inflation (the New Keynesian specification); and South Africa has a positive but statistically insignificant correlation between the output gap and inflation (the original specification).

Figure 8.7 tests the Asian countries' Phillips curve. Here, too, the Phillips curve is insignificant under both specifications, the original Phillips curve and the New Keynesian Phillips curve, albeit Malaysia, Singapore, and Thailand have insignificant upward sloping scatter plots.

The Phillips Curve, Anticipated Inflation, and Output 187

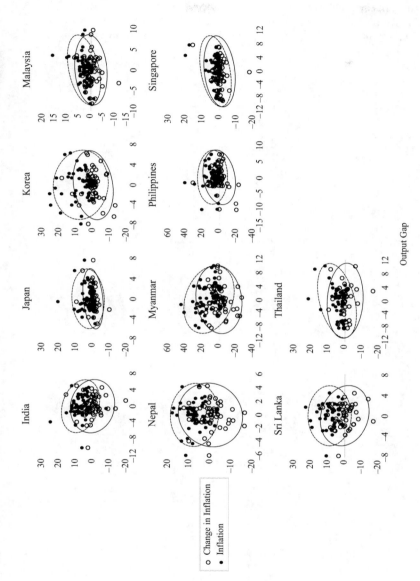

Figure 8.7 95 Percent Chi-Squared Confidence Ellipse Test of the Phillips Curve Specifications of the Asian Countries, 1960–2020

Data Source: World Development Indicators

188 The Phillips Curve, Anticipated Inflation, and Output

The Caribbean countries' data are plotted in Figure 8.8, and we still cannot find a significant evidence for the Phillips curve except for a positive but insignificant relationship in Trinidad and Tobago between the level of inflation and the output gap (the original specification).

Finally, we plot the inflation-targeting countries' data in Figure 8.9a and Figure 8.9b. These graphs cover the periods before and after inflation-targeting.

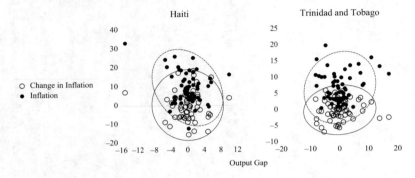

Figure 8.8 95 Percent Chi-Squared Confidence Ellipse Test of the Phillips Curve Specifications of the Caribbean Countries, 1960–2020

Data Source: World Development Indicators

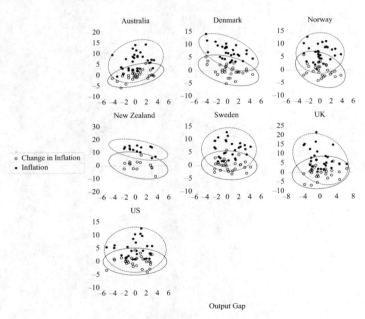

Figure 8.9a 95 Percent Chi-Squared Confidence Ellipse Test of the Phillips Curve Specifications of the Inflation-Targeting Countries Before Inflation-Targeting, 1960–1990

Data Source: World Development Indicators

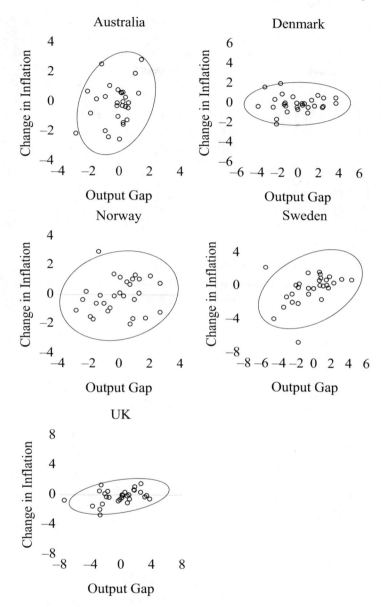

Figure 8.9b 95 Percent Chi-Squared Confidence Ellipse Test of the Phillips Curve Specifications of the Inflation-Targeting Countries Under Inflation-Targeting, 1992–2021*

Data Source: World Development Indicators

*The output gap data are up to 2020 and excludes New Zealand and the United States.

There is more evidence for a positive relationship, albeit insignificant, between the change in inflation and the output gap *after* inflation-targeting than *before* in Australia and Denmark, Sweden, and the United Kingdom (the New Keynesian specification), and a positive relationship between the level of inflation and the output gap (the original specification) in Australia and Denmark. Nonetheless, the statistical significance is small.

Figures 8.10 and 8.11 test the *quarterly* US data and quarterly New Zealand data under inflation targeting. There is a positive relationship between the level of inflation and the output gap (the original Phillips curve) over the period March 2012 to March 2022, albeit statistically insignificant. New Zealand has more data for the inflation-targeting period, from March 1988 to December 2021. The evidence for the original Phillips curve is relatively stronger.

The data of only a handful of countries in our sample of 42, mostly in developed countries, depict a positive, albeit not necessarily statistically significant Phillips curve.

The Phillips Curve Is a Mirage

Another issue is that the short-run Phillips curve has been unstable in the sense that the estimated slope coefficient changes over time. This has been documented in all

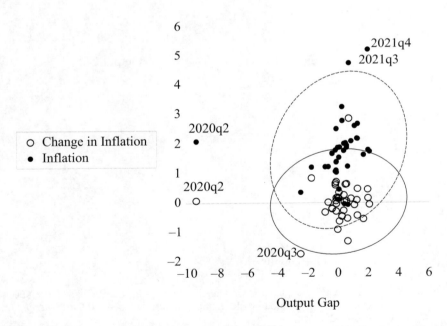

Figure 8.10 95 Percent Chi-Squared Confidence Ellipse Test of the Phillips Curve Specifications of the US Quarterly Data for Inflation-Targeting Period, March 2012 to December 2021

Data Source: World Development Indicators

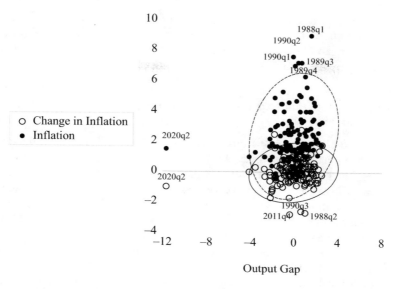

Figure 8.11 95 Percent Chi-Squared Confidence Ellipse Test of the Phillips Curve Specifications of the New Zealand Quarterly Data for Inflation-Targeting Period, June 1988 to December 2021

Data Source: Reserve Bank of New Zealand

Note: Real GDP data for 2022 are unavailable.

intermediate macroeconomic textbooks, where the curve turns positive, negative, and flat over time. The tests reported before also show different slopes. Most, if not all, central banks in the advanced world have short-run objectives only. Some of the central banks explicitly say that they target the inflation rate over the business cycle; all of them re-set monetary policy quarterly. Other central banks state a period of 2 years as a time horizon for their inflation target. There would be a problem with this instability of the Phillips curve if it is used as a guide for policy. Unstable Phillips curve cannot be used for forecasting. Forecasting errors would become policy errors. Policy errors are notoriously persistent. They are very costly to undo.[7]

There was no discussion or a mention of the Phillips curve in the RBNZ before 1994. There was no theory of inflation at all; yet, the RBNZ successfully brought inflation down to the target level before the deadline. A very senior policymaker at the RBNZ told me that it was unexpectedly easy to achieve the inflation target. That said, of course, there are some explanations to this, which have nothing to do with the Phillips curve. One possible explanation is that the public must have understood the commitment of the RBNZ to adhere to the law. The data plots seem

---

7 We are unsure if the Phillips curve is actually used as a guide for policy in all of the central banks in the world, but we could be pretty sure that central bank economists in the developed world take the Phillips curve seriously, and policymakers like the idea. It should not be surprising, however, if policymakers in most of the central banks in our sample do not know what the Phillips curve is.

192   *The Phillips Curve, Anticipated Inflation, and Output*

to suggest that expected inflation, *regardless of how it is measured,* explains all the variations in the inflation rate and not the output gap. The slope coefficient, that is, the output gap coefficient, is small. Regressions are often different from plots, however. We will test this hypothesis later in this chapter.

Formation of Inflation Expectation Is a Challenging Specification Problem

What is the theory of expectations, how to measure expectations, and the endogeneity of inflation expectations are the most challenging problems to deal with when estimating the Phillips curve. Not only these, but expectation formation is also an important problem of the Phillips curve. Note that there is no role for expectations in the original Phillips curve. Then we had (Phelps', 1967) expectations story and somehow ambiguous theory of expectation formation in (Friedman, 1968). Lucas and Sargent were specifically talking about *rational expectations* (RE) theory. For more on rational expectations, see for example, volumes 1 and 2 of (Lucas and Sargent, 1981a, 1981b, 1981c), which include many articles in nearly 700 pages. See also (Attfield *et al.*, 1985), which explains the theory and the macroeconomic empirical evidence nicely.

The problem of the measurement of anticipated or expected inflation is a difficult one because every test of the Phillips curve becomes a *joint test problem.* If the single-equation Phillips curve is tested using the *Accelerationist* theory for example, where expectations are adaptive or rational, then it is unclear that rejecting the null hypothesis that the coefficient is 1 indicates a rejection of the assumption of expectations' formations or rejection of the long-run Phillips curve.

Adoptive expectations mean that expectations are revised on the basis of the difference between actual and expected inflation. For example, if actual inflation is 2 percent and expected inflation is 4 percent, then expected inflation should be scaled down towards 2. The revision is by a fraction the difference between 2 and 4. Thus, expected inflation is an exponentially weighted average of the past rate of inflation. The weights usually get smaller as one goes back in time. Such expected inflation could also be a moving average. Muth's (1961) Exponentially Weighted Moving Average representations could be like this:

$$Z_t = \lambda \bar{\pi}_t + (1 - \lambda) Z_{t-1}, \tag{8.4}$$

where $0 < \lambda < 1$ weight, $\bar{\pi}_t$ is the sample mean. Or it could be a 2-year moving average in:

$$\pi_t = \beta \pi_t^e + \gamma \tilde{Y}_t + \varepsilon_t, \tag{8.5}$$

where, π_t is the inflation rate; the superscript e denotes the expectations operator; and $\sim$ denotes the output gap; if β is statistically different from 1, then the long-run Phillips curve is not vertical or equally true that this measure of

The Phillips Curve, Anticipated Inflation, and Output   193

expected inflation is wrong, and people follow different ways when forming their expectations.

Another way to measure inflation expectations in empirical analysis has been the use of survey data. We do not have survey data of inflation expectations for all countries in our sample. The United States and a few advanced countries do publish monthly surveys. The next chapter shows how to evaluate such data and test them for RE. That said, it is very difficult to have a measure of a rational expected inflation. The theory states that the rational economic agent basically runs a regression, whereby the information set includes *all* available information about inflation, that is, the explanatory variables, up to period $t-1$. It does not say what these variables are, and there is no general guide for picking such variables. The economic agents who watch and study the central bank making of monetary policy and its model maybe are able to discern some useful information. Aggregate demand shifters are the obvious ones. Maybe nominal GDP growth, nominal money growth, nominal government expenditures growth, long-run nominal interest rates, and lagged inflation perhaps are the most obvious.

Endogeneity

The other specification problem is that U or Y is taken to be exogenous, assuming they could persist for the long run. The question is whether one should follow Fisher and Friedman argument by specifying the Phillips curve by having U (or a function of it) on the LHS of the equation and inflation on the RHS. Reversing the Phillips curve this way would totally disturb central bankers and New Keynesian economists because they firmly believe that causality runs from $U - U^*$ or $Y - Y^*$ to π, not the other way around. Therefore, estimating an *OLS single-equation* Phillips curve runs into the textbook single-equation bias problem. This means that the estimated coefficients are biased and inconsistent. Instrumental variables may resolve the problems if appropriate instruments are used.

The Mismeasurement of the Output Gap and Expected Inflation

Expected inflation and the output gap are unobservable. The natural rate of unemployment too is unobservable. All the explanatory variables in the Phillips curve are subject to measurement errors. Thus, single-equation OLS typically leads to biased and inconsistent parameter estimates. Typically, the output gap is derived from a hypothetically specified production function or using a linear filter such the (Hodrick and Prescott, 1997) – HP filter, or, maybe, for example (Baxter and King, 1999) – Band-Pass filter, the (Christiano and Fitzgerald, 2003) – Optimal Band-Pass filter, and/or the (Beveridge and Nelson, 1981) filter. The HP filter is the most popular, which acts as a smoother (see Razzak [1997]). Razzak and Dennis (1995) provided evidence that allowing the smoothing parameter of the HP filter to vary with the demand and supply shocks over the sample improves the forecast of inflation. The slope coefficient is positive in the inflation – expected inflation–output

194   *The Phillips Curve, Anticipated Inflation, and Output*

gap space; that is, the short –run Phillips curve is upward sloping and the long-run Phillips curve is vertical if $\beta = 1$.

The Rational Expectations (RE), Policy Issues and the Phillips Curve

In the 1970s, Robert Lucas Jr. (1973, 1972a, 1972b) and Sargent (1973) and Sargent and Wallace (1974) among many others criticized the adaptive expectations' formation on the basis that it did not make sense to form expectations on the basis of a weighted average of past experience. If inflation is accelerating (has a continuous positive trend), then expected inflation will *always* be lagging behind. It means that people are *persistently wrong* about the expected inflation. There must be a richer information set that people use to forecast inflation.

Muth (1961) devised the original idea behind the rational expectations. His assumption is that people base their forecasts of inflation on an economic theory. This does not mean that they are right in every case, but that over a long period they will *on average* be right. So, sometimes the forecast could be wrong, but not all the time. This point has been missed by many economists who insist that people are irrational. Clearly, Muth did not claim that *all people* or every person is rational. People cannot be forming correct rational expectations about future inflation or other variables *all the time. On average*, however, they should be right. Rational people in this sense cannot make the same error twice. So if people form expectations as Muth says but the econometrician uses weighted average adaptive expectations when estimating the Phillips curve, the estimated β will be less than 1 even if the true value is 1, that is, underestimate it.

This literature is quite rich, deep, and wide in scope. A number of policy issues arose.

In Lucas and Sargent's work, in countries, where inflation is significantly *variable*, expectations responded to the changes in the current rate of inflation much more than in countries, where inflation is stable. This is clear today in the data of the successful inflation-targeting countries, where inflation has been stable around some target for a long period of time. Indeed, it has become harder to fit the Phillips curve in inflation-targeting countries and much harder to forecast inflation. The scatter plots test presented earlier show that this is true in inflation-targeting regimes and in many other countries. Think about inflation's variance declining significantly to a point that it could not be correlated with any other macro variables (the covariance approaches 0, hence the slope coefficient approaches 0). The conclusion is that if people are forming their expectations rationally, policy could not have any effect in the long run. The only way policy could alter the real economy (unemployment and output) is by engineering a surprise unexpected inflation.

Under inflation targeting or inflation forecast targeting as Lars Svensson put it (e.g., 2000), people know what the central bank does, and they incorporate this information in their information set when they make a forecast. Thus, the central bank cannot achieve any unemployment target other than the natural rate following such a *quasi-rule* as inflation targeting. The central bank can only change

The Phillips Curve, Anticipated Inflation, and Output   195

unemployment if it continuously changes the rule, which takes people by surprise for a while until they learn it and so on and so forth. This type of policy is destabilizing.

The Assumption of Price Stickiness

The RE theory assumes flexible prices. It predicts that systematic aggregate demand policies would be *ineffective* in stabilizing the *real* economy as in the Keynesian theory – that is, the *policy ineffectiveness* proposition. Recall that earlier we reported insignificant correlation between money and real output in the short run in almost all countries in our sample. Nonetheless, there is a general agreement, however, that some prices do not clear some markets so quickly, e.g., the labor market. In other markets, price adjustment is immediate, e.g., the exchange rate in floating regimes and the stock markets. There are subtle ways for which good prices change without the actual change in the sticker price, thus the price appears sticky, while it may not be actually sticky, for example, services provided by the manufacturer.

Akerlof and Yellen (1985), among others, argued that firms do not change their prices immediately after shocks as suggested by the RE theory due to what they called Bounded Rationality. It is costly, and it takes firms time to learn and adjust. In developed inflation-targeting countries, central banks use the Phillips curve or, more precisely, the augmented Phillips curve as a guiding theory of inflation's determination as a guide for policy. The idea is that excess demand (measured either by the deviation of unemployment from trend, which they referred to as the NAIRU or the output gap) causes inflation to deviate from expected inflation, that is, inflation falls (increases) if unemployment is above (below) its trend and increases (decreases) if output is above (below) its trend. This trade-off in some central bankers' minds exists in the long run, for most it is a short run trade-off only as argued by Solow, Samuelson, Friedman, and others, and yet for many other economists, this trade-off is unstable and could not be used for policy.

There are a couple of important models of RE with sticky prices, e.g., see McCallum (1980, 1981). The crucial finding here is that if the price-setter and the policymaker are defined on the same period (one period), the same results of the RE fully flexible price hold, that is, fully anticipated aggregate demand shifts have no real effects, hence policy remains ineffective in stabilizing the real economy. The policy effectiveness arises because producers commit to their setting of prices over a number of periods, whereas the policymaker is free to intervene to equilibrate the market. McCallum (1981) modified the (Sargent and Wallace, 1975) model to incorporate price stickiness. Each period, the market price adjusts to the equilibrium market price only if the equilibrium price is perceived to be far from the expected value because the cost of keeping such price unchanged exceeds the lump-sum cost of the revision. Otherwise, McCallum had the price equal to the price expected last period. He shows that under such assumption, the policy ineffectiveness proposition of (Sargent and Wallace, 1975) remains in place.

Fischer (1977) and Phelps and Taylor (1977) are the other two classic papers in this literature, which make the opposite assumption: firms or workers bind

196   *The Phillips Curve, Anticipated Inflation, and Output*

themselves to fix prices over a number of periods that are sufficiently long to permit the policymaker to intervene within the period. In these models, the Sargent and (Wallace, 1975) policy ineffectiveness proposition under RE does not hold. Here, if prices are sticky over periods of time longer than the policy horizon, anticipated aggregate demand shocks have real effect, hence policy could be stabilizing under RE.

The arguments about RE and policy raged during the 1970s and 1980s. Neary and Stiglitz (1983) provided the idea *of Rational Constraint Expectations*. The main point of this idea, however, is that when the constrained equilibrium exists in period *t* (usually in Keynesian models), the government spending multiplier (anticipated or unanticipated) is greater under RE than under no RE. The increase in the quantity of money has a real effect regardless of whether the shock is anticipated or not. They argued that the RE assumption in a quantity constrained model improves stabilization policies.

My own assessment is that most central banks in the world and especially in the developed countries struggle with how these theoretical issues, which are closely associated with the estimation of the Phillips curve, affect forecasts and policy. The forecasts will be biased if the parameter estimates are biased. Inflation forecasts have not been accurate. Forecast errors are large. Forecast error variance is wide and non-convergent. Policy errors are large and persistent.

The Micro-Foundation for Sticky Prices

Imagine a situation, whereby the aggregate demand shocks are highly volatile. In such times, it is hard to argue that producers would be willing to fix prices two periods in advance. Perhaps, producers set prices fixed in advance for only one period. Therefore, price stickiness itself is affected by the nature and permanency of the shocks, monetary and fiscal policies, and other determinants. Lucas and Sargent (1981a, 1981b, 1981c) said that to understand the implications of long-term contracts for monetary policy, one needs a model of the way those contracts are likely to respond to alternative monetary policy regimes. Hence, the *contract theory* emerged. For example, see Baily (1974), Azariadis (1975), and Gordon (1974). They argued that if producers are willing to take some of the risk from workers, they would be able to hire labor at a lower average wage. In a well-specified contract, producers could guarantee labor a fixed wage over some specified period, and when the economic conditions decline, the producer may lay off some labor, but the wage of those unaffected workers would not be reduced. When economic conditions improve, the laid off workers would be rehired at the same wage. They argued that such a contractual agreement might be appealing to workers because it provides some certainty and to producers because it allows them to hire relatively cheaper labor. This original idea was taken further in this literature. Those theories run into a problem of explaining why real wages rather than *nominal wages* could be fixed. Even though a contract of fixed wage of the type suggested before might be advantageous to both producers and workers, an unpredictable random aggregate demand shock could cause deviations from equilibrium, which calls for

The Phillips Curve, Anticipated Inflation, and Output   197

a quantity rule to determine actual output or unemployment. Thus, the producer is forced to hire more or less workers than planned to be the optimal quantity at the wage set. Under RE, the producers realize that such a shock could occur and that they would be forced to produce or hire workers at a suboptimal level.

Barro (1977) asked why producers should agree to a fixed contract, for which they know that under certain circumstances they would be forced to do something suboptimal *ex ante*. A similar situation could occur for consumers. Knowing that shocks may cause disequilibrium, why would they agree to a contractual agreement, which, under such circumstances, forces them to purchase a quantity of goods at the agreed suboptimal price? A contract like that is *ex ante* suboptimal. Barro argued that the only optimal situation is with a quantity rule that sets output or employment at the values they would take in the absence of unanticipated shocks. Drawing contracts with fixed prices and wage but not output or employment need a theoretical explanation. And, if quantities are fixed, they have to explain how quantity changes happen.

Blinder (1994) argues that any theory of how nominal money affects the real economy must explain how demand or supply functions derived from basic micro principles have money as an argument only in ratio to the general price level. Hence, if monetary policy is to have real effects, there must be some reason why changes in money are not followed promptly by equip-proportionate changes in prices. This is the sense in which some kind of "price stickiness" is essential to virtually any story of how monetary policy works.

Between Barro (1977) and Blinder (1994), and after, there has been a big theoretical literature on the micro-foundation of sticky prices and wages, and equally large empirical literature, which are beyond the scope of this book. We could not possibly cite all the work, but see for example, Hall *et al.* (1980), Hall (2005), Rotemberg (1982, 1996), Calvo (1983), Howitt (1986), Ball and Romer (1989), Farmer (1991), Ball and Mankiw (1994), McCallum and Nelson (2000), Eichenbaum and Fisher (2004), Ireland (2003), Walsh (2005), and Kehoe and Midrigan (2015) among a very large number of contributions.

It seems that nominal prices adjust relatively rather faster than nominal wages, and prices adjust faster (shorter lag) when high-inflation environments and when inflation is relatively more variable than when it is low and stable. It is a difficult empirical problem nonetheless. We have shown earlier that money is neutral and even super neutral in the long run and is not correlated with real GDP in most of the countries in our sample.

The Lucas Critique

Lucas (1976) provided a critique to the way we evaluate policy using econometrically estimated models with fixed coefficients. The misspecification problem is about the modeling of expectations. This critique applies to the Phillips curve of course and to the problem we are dealing with in this book. If expectations are rational, they will be determined by the process governing that particular variable; e.g., *expectations about monetary policy will be determined by the process*

198   *The Phillips Curve, Anticipated Inflation, and Output*

governing that policy. Therefore, a change in policy will change the way in which the public forms expectations about policy. The *policy invariant* assumption in evaluating fixed-estimated coefficient is a problem. Lucas provided no solution to this problem.

To illustrate the critique, consider a simple two-equation model,

$$\Delta ln M_t = \alpha X_{t-1} + u_t, \tag{8.6}$$

where M_t is money, X_{t-1} is a vector of variables whose last period values determine the rate of growth of money, and u_t is an unpredictable component of money growth whose mean is zero.

And

$$Y_t = \delta Z_t + \beta u_t + e_t, \tag{8.7}$$

where Y_t is real output, Z_t is a vector of variables that determine potential output, and e_t is an error term with mean zero.

Substituting for u_t from the money growth equation in the output equation, thus, we get,

$$Y_t = \delta Z_t + \beta \Delta ln M_t - \beta \alpha X_{t-1} + e_t \tag{8.8}$$

Suppose that an adviser to the policymaker does not know this specification. The adviser regresses Y_t on Z_t, $\Delta ln M_t$, and X_{t-1} as in:

$$Y_t = \theta_1 Z_t + \theta_2 \Delta ln M_t + \theta_3 X_{t-1} + v_t, \tag{8.9}$$

and estimates these $\theta's$ and interprets them as significant and plausible structures of the economy. The economy behaves according to the two-equation system not Eq. (8.9) *per se.* If this equation is used to advise the policymaker to change policy to stimulate the economy by increasing the quantity of money, for example, then non-rational expectations (8.9) will fail in the sense that $\theta's$ will change. For example, θ_3 is $\beta \alpha$, which is unknown to the adviser. Since this product coefficient changed so would θ_3.

Therefore, the estimated structure of the economy has not remained invariant to the policies. Because the policy is based on the premise that the structure of the economy remains unchanged in the face of different policies (e.g., changing the quantity of money or increasing the inflation target), it should not be difficult to understand that the policy advice will not work. As the coefficient α changes so would the expectations formation about the policy. The unexpected component of monetary policy u_t will equal its value in that period. Since the random component of monetary policy that affects real output has not been affected by the policy change, the policy change will have no effect on output.

Sims (1999), for example, argued that although the variances of the shocks have changed over time, the coefficients in VARs and monetary policy decisions rules

The Phillips Curve, Anticipated Inflation, and Output   199

seem to have remained unchanged during the post-WWII period. This has been a large research in monetary econometrics. Basically, Fed policy has not changed but rather the nature and the distribution of the shocks. The standard error of the innovations of the nominal interest rate, inflation, and unemployment changed significantly (see Cogley and Sargent [2005a]). However, Clarida *et al.* (2000) and Cogley and Sargent (2002) using different models found evidence that the coefficients of the VARs and monetary policy rules have drifted in the post-WWII period. It is hard to reach a solid conclusion on the basis of VAR evidence for many reasons, among them being that the statistical tests are weak in the sense that they do not reject the null of unit root very often.

Shocks, however, are random and, therefore, unpredictable. Shocks have been very difficult to identify, even *ex-post*, despite huge efforts by econometricians. Further, it is even harder to assume certain monetary policy rules. As far as we know, no policy rule has ever been implemented by any central bank.

Time Consistency and Inflation Bias

An important issue that arose from the assumption of rational expectations *is commitment and time consistency*. Kydland and Prescott (1977) showed that rule-based monetary policy provides superior outcomes to discretionary policy (in which the policy choice is updated each period) when the model contains forward-looking agents. If expectations are rational in this sense of Muth, the government should not expect a policy about the growth in the supply of money – past period inflation to result in real changes in output or unemployment because people cannot be fooled more than once. People, however, monetary policy notwithstanding, are expected to change their expectations in turn with the process announced for determining monetary policy and aggregate demand. Therefore, the government could make real changes, only if it cheats or surprises people. If governments cheat, economic agents will take note, but that kind of cheating increases uncertainty about economic policy. Thus, it has been argued that *quasi rules* such as inflation-targeting regimes that are legally binding may reduce such uncertainty. *Time inconsistency* is a result of the possibility of cheating. A policy is said to be time inconsistent if the authority, monetary or fiscal, reneges on its commitment to a certain policy – for example, promising not to increase taxes then raise taxes or not to stick to the inflation target or the money supply growth announced at the beginning of the period. Policymakers must understand how people form expectations.

Take for example a government policy that aims at stimulating or increasing private consumption. Consumption after all makes up two-third of GDP, maybe more in the United States. Under RE, people do not alter their current consumption unless they anticipate an increase in their real income – that is, the Permanent Income Hypothesis. Policymakers would be making a mistake if they assume that the stimulus would increase current income and hence current consumption. An *anticipated* tax cut or tax increase alters expected real income, hence current consumption. A government, which promises a tax cut tomorrow, affects current consumption if rational people believe the government, thus, governments reneging

200 *The Phillips Curve, Anticipated Inflation, and Output*

about their promised future tax cut cause time inconsistency since people have already spent the money. The same is true for investment spending or any other private decision made on the basis of an anticipated policy announcement.

Essentially, governments, which believe in *fine-tuning*, that is, managing the business cycle fluctuations via expansionary fiscal and monetary policies, could only succeed if it surprises people, that is, only unanticipated aggregate demand could have real effects. Thus, there is the so-called *inflation-bias* inherited in *discretionary* policies. There is a huge literature on these issues, which have been totally ignored by central banks. Central bankers simply could not exist or function under the assumptions of RE, policy rules, time inconsistency, flexible prices, and other neoclassical assumptions. Central banks adopt and fully adhere to the New Keynesian paradigm. For example, see (Barro and Gordon, 1983).

Reputation

The effect of the reputation of the central bank implies that the history of monetary policy matters. However, time-consistent equilibrium does not allow monetary policy to depend on its history and its outcomes. There is a game-theoretic literature, whereby the central bank's time inconsistency problem could be solved if the public follows a process of expectations about the central bank, hence reputation. The central bank in this case has no other choice but to confirm this policy path, otherwise the central bank would have a reputation coupled with the inferior outcomes. This theory predicts that a successful good reputational central bank may resolve the time inconsistency; nonetheless, there might be bad reputations too. There could be situations, where the central bank has the incentive to confirm expectations that lead to bad policy, for example, see (Chari *et al.*, 1988) expectations trap. In these traps, expectations of high or low inflation lead the public to take "self-protective actions," which then make accommodating those expectations by the central bank the optimal monetary policy. Under commitment, however, the equilibrium is unique, and the inflation rate is low on average.

Some economists argued for increasing the inflation target as a solution to the "near zero lower-bound interest rate" we observed in the past few years because the nominal interest rate was effectively zero. See for example (Blanchard *et al.*, 2010) and (Summers *et al.*, 2018). Many central banks pursued negative nominal interest rate policy, e.g., the Swiss National Bank, Denmark National Bank, and the ECB among others. These central banks including all other central banks in the developed world wanted more inflation only shortly before COVID-19 struck. They ran out of stimulus. They thought lowering the nominal interest rate motivates more consumption. It is clear that they think stimulating demand will bring about inflation. Inflation, unexpectedly, has come back strong now. What would the advice be now? Increasing the interest rate is the main policy action. These are typical episodes in advanced economies; continuous interventions by policymakers are the main cause of booms and busts, crisis, and instability.

The Phillips Curve, Anticipated Inflation, and Output 201

Rational Expectations and the Rules versus Discretion Argument

Woodford (2003) extended this concept to the New Keynesian framework. Taylor's (1993) is another well-known policy rule. Both Woodford and Taylor use interest rates as policy instruments to influence output and inflation instead of money. McCallum in a number of various papers, e.g., (1988), uses money, that is, nominal GDP-targeting rule as instruments, and that has been a heated debate on which one is more appropriate. There is a condition where both rules result in an almost identical outcome.[8] Therefore, there is sort of a general agreement that rules are preferred to discretionary policy among academics of all schools of thought; yet, central banks never used rules, and I suspect they would never do because they follow a fixed rule, which is fully transparent. One thing one has to understand is that these rules, e.g., Taylor's, are not the same as the X-percent money growth rule advocated by Milton Friedman. This rule implies that when the central bank finds out that inflation has deviated from the target by 1 percent in time t, it raises the short-term interest rate at time t by 1.5 percent.

The RE theory is supportive of monetary policy rules rather than discretion. It is straightforward to show that the *x-percent money growth rule* is an optimal rule using micro-founded macroeconomic models with RE, and when the expectation's formation is non-RE, such rule is not optimal. In such models, this rule would result in more variations in real output over the business cycle (around its potential level). Intuitively, the government would be able to fool people more often if expectations are non-RE, adaptive. When the price level expected next year is the same as this year, a permanent shock that reduces aggregate demand would prompt an immediate fall in prices and output. Such shock would not be foreseen by either the government or the public. The expected price level will fall gradually until it reaches the new equilibrium. Output will be below its potential. A central bank, which is committed to a preannounced policy of an X-percent growth of money, will be unable to stimulate aggregate demand in this case. However, under RE, the fall in aggregate demand would have been fully anticipated, and, thus, the shock would have no effect on real output. The adverse effect of the shock would be temporary, that is, it disappears after one period since RE implies that the effect of the shock is already fully priced out by the market; see (Sargent and Wallace, 1975) again. That being said, it is impossible to convince central banks to adhere to such fixed policy rules because it would diminish the power of the central bank significantly.

The fact that RE theory implies no prolonged recessions is counterintuitive to central banks' thinking. In the Phillips curve equation, reducing inflation must involve a recession. Should it?

Under non-RE formation assumption, that is, adaptive expectations, it is quite possible to follow a monetary policy rule that would consistently fool people. It is obvious that the central bank can make the growth rate of money a function of last period price level, which would ensure that the actual price level exceeds the

---

8 (Razzak, 2003) shows that the Taylor rule is not very different from McCallum's type rule if the velocity of money is a stable function of the short-term interest rate.

202 *The Phillips Curve, Anticipated Inflation, and Output*

expected price level; thus, output would be kept above its potential level. This kind of monetary policy would be effective even if it is fully announced provided that expectations are adaptive. Therefore, there is no reason for the government to cheat or renege on its commitment because it could fool people easily. Such a policy of making the growth rate of money a function of last period's price level could not work under RE; people could not be fooled. People would change their method of forming expectations taking into account monetary policy rule whatever the policy is. The only possible way for the government to increase output or reduce unemployment is by cheating on its announced policy intentions. Under RE, such conduct of monetary policy increases uncertainty.

The Variance of Demand Management Policy

Another issue that is highly implied by the theory of expectations formation is that the larger the variance of the random component of aggregate demand is, the smaller the effect on real output or unemployment. Under RE, the producer in a typical market knows the difference between a general increase and a relative increase in prices. The producer knows that an increase in the price level above the average is either due to an unpredictable increase in aggregate demand or a favorable relative demand shift in his or her market. If the price in the typical market increases above average, the reason could be partly attributed to a general increase in aggregate demand and partly to a relative demand shift. Under RE, there would be no change in production if the increase in the price level is fully attributed to an aggregate demand increase. The opposite is true.

Today, in 2023, there should be no doubt that *all prices* have increased above the average; thus, rational producers should not expand their own output, and rational workers should not supply more hours of work. In countries, where relative demand shifts are small on average and random fluctuations in aggregate demand are large and more frequent, rising prices would be rationally interpreted as a result of random increases in aggregate demand and should have little or no effect on output. The opposite is true in economies, where aggregate demand fluctuations are small and less frequent than relative demand fluctuations.

It is widely agreed that a monetary policy, which produces large fluctuations in real output and unemployment, is inferior to one, which provides stability. *Thus, aggregate demand policies should be as predictable as possible.* Government policies should aim at reducing random and unpredictable fluctuations in aggregate demand. The inflation-targeting developed countries have successfully managed to reduce random and unpredictable aggregate demand shocks from the early 1990s.

Estimation of a Single-Equation Phillips Curve

The scatter plots reported earlier in this chapter show that, except in a few cases, the variance of change in inflation is greater than the variance of the output gap. Next, we test the equality of the means and the variances of the change in inflation and the output gap in our sample countries. We report the mean and the standard deviation

The Phillips Curve, Anticipated Inflation, and Output   203

of the change in inflation $\Delta\pi_t$ and the output gap and test for the equality of the variances. The output gap could not conceivably be a significant explanatory variable in the Phillips curve if its variance is smaller than the variance of inflation or $\Delta\pi_t$.

Table 8.1 reports the tests for the MENA countries, where the variance of the output gap is smaller than the variance of the change in inflation in Egypt, Pakistan, and Turkey. Therefore, the output gap could not conceivably explain the variability of inflation in these three countries. In Algeria, the two variances are equal; hence, the output gap could explain the change in inflation according to the New Keynesian Phillips curve prediction.

Table 8.2 reports that only Honduras has a clear-cut equality of the variances of the change in inflation and the output gap. The output gap could not possibly explain inflation's variability in the Latin and South American countries. The scatter plots presented earlier are consistent with these statistics.

Table 8.3 shows that there is more evidence of equality of the variance of the change in inflation and the output gap in African than in the MENA and Latin and South Africa. Only Burkina Faso, Ghana, and Sudan show significant inequality. The prediction of the New Keynesian Phillips curve holds in four out of seven African countries. Again, these statistics are consistent with the scatter plots presented earlier.

Table 8.4 reports the tests for the Asian countries in our sample. It shows that Japan, Singapore, and Thailand have equal variances of change in inflation and the output gap. Therefore, the New Keynesian Phillips curve specification may only fit in these three countries.

For the two Caribbean countries', Table 8.5 shows that the change in inflation and the output gap have unequal variances, with the change in inflation's variance is greater than the variance of the output gap in Haiti, which makes the New Keynesian Phillips curve specification highly unlikely to fit the data. In Trinidad and Tobago, the output gap seems to vary more than inflation, which makes the New Keynesian Phillips curve highly likely to fit the data.

Table 8.1 Descriptive Statistics of the MENA Countries: Change in Inflation and the Output Gap, 1960–2020

	$\Delta\pi_t$		$\tilde{Y}_t$		H_0: Equal Variance			
	μ	σ	μ	σ	F	Siegel–Tukey	Levene	Brown–Forsyth
Algeria[i]	−0.08	4.0	−0.03	3.0	(0.0998)	(0.1133)	(0.7360)	(0.7438)
Egypt[ii]	0.07	4.8	0.08	2.8	(0.0001)	(0.0344)	(0.0026)	(0.0033)
Pakistan[iii]	0.13	3.8	0.01	2.2	(0.0000)	(0.6538)	(0.1079)	(0.1061)
Turkey[iv]	0.14	8.7	−0.006	3.6	(0.0000)	(0.0318)	(0.0028)	(0.0032)

$\Delta\pi_t$ is the change in CPI inflation. $\tilde{Y}_t$ is the output gap (deviations from an HP filter's trend). σ is the standard deviation. *P*-values are in parentheses. [i] $F_{60,50}$; Levene and Brown–Forsyth df are (1,110); [ii] $F_{58,60}$; Levene and Brown–Forsyth df are (1, 118); [iii] $F_{59,60}$; Levene and Brown–Forsyth df are (1, 119); [iv] $F_{58,60}$; Levene and Brown–Forsyth df are (1, 118).

204 The Phillips Curve, Anticipated Inflation, and Output

Table 8.2 Descriptive Statistics of the Latin and South American Countries: Change in Inflation and the Output Gap, 1960–2020

	$\Delta\pi_t$		$\tilde{Y}_t$		H_0: Equal Variance			
	μ	σ	μ	σ	F	Siegel–Tukey	Levene	Brown–Forsyth
Bolivia[i]	−0.10	59.5	−0.04	3.1	(0.0000)	(0.0198)	(0.0167)	(0.0167)
Chile[ii]	−0.31	19.2	−0.24	5.0	(0.0000)	(0.9504)	(0.0164)	(0.0161)
Colombia[iii]	−0.09	4.83	−0.02	2.5	(0.0000)	(0.3548)	(0.0258)	(0.0269)
Costa Rica [iv]	−0.03	8.25	−0.06	2.8	(0.0000)	(0.0246)	(0.0065)	(0.0067)
Dominican R[v]	0.13	10.3	0.025	4.5	(0.0000)	(0.4569)	(0.02580)	(0.0279)
Ecuador[vi]	−0.07	8.91	−0.03	3.4	(0.0000)	(0.3259)	(0.0088)	(0.0084)
Guatemala[vii]	0.06	6.24	−0.02	2.4	(0.0000)	(0.0977)	(0.0155)	(0.0154)
Honduras[viii]	0.03	4.52	−0.01	3.1	(0.0049)	(0.7290)	(0.3988)	(0.3914)
Mexico[ix]	0.03	10.9	−0.00	3.2	(0.0000)	(0.7225)	(0.0146)	(0.0149)
Paraguay[x]	−0.26	5.60	−0.04	3.7	(0.0018)	(0.0676)	(0.0210)	(0.0305)
Uruguay[xi]	−0.18	12.9	−0.05	5.3	(0.0000)	(0.0074)	(0.0020)	(0.0019)

$\Delta\pi_t$ is the change in CPI inflation. $\tilde{Y}_t$ is the output gap (deviations from an HP filter's trend). σ is the standard deviation. *P*-values are in parentheses. [i] $F_{59,60}$; Levene and Brown–Forsyth df are (1,119); [ii] $F_{49,60}$; Levene and Brown–Forsyth df are (1,109); [iii] $F_{59,60}$; Levene and Brown–Forsyth df are (1,119); [iv] $F_{59,60}$; Levene and Brown–Forsyth df are (1,119); [v] $F_{59,60}$; Levene and Brown–Forsyth df are (1,119); [vi] $F_{59,60}$; Levene and Brown–Forsyth df are (1,119); [vii] $F_{59,60}$; Levene and Brown–Forsyth df are (1,119); [viii] ($F_{58,60}$; Levene and Brown–Forsyth df are (1,118); [ix] $F_{59,60}$; Levene and Brown–Forsyth df are (1,119); [x] $F_{59,60}$; Levene and Brown–Forsyth df are (1,119); [xi] $F_{59,60}$; Levene and Brown–Forsyth df are (1,119).

Table 8.3 Descriptive Statistics of the African Countries: Change in Inflation and the Output Gap, 1960–2020

	$\Delta\pi_t$		$\tilde{Y}_t$		H_0: Equal Variance			
	μ	σ	μ	σ	F	Siegel–Tukey	Levene	Brown–Forsyth
Burkina Faso[i]	−0.25	8.6	0.02	2.2	(0.0000)	(0.0000)	(0.0000)	(0.0000)
Cote d'Ivoire[ii]	−0.14	5.3	−0.04	4.7	(0.2701)	(0.5288)	(0.9927)	(0.9284)
Gabon[iii]	−0.10	7.3	−0.17	9.4	(0.08720	(0.2626)	(0.3315)	(0.3394)
Ghana[iv]	−0.25	18.2	−0.08	4.0	(0.0000)	(0.0000)	(0.0000)	(0.0000)
Nigeria[v]	0.08	10.4	0.05	7.7	(0.0151)	(0.2793)	(0.1636)	(0.1664)
South Africa[vi]	0.02	1.96	0.04	2.0	(0.8825)	(0.8785)	(0.8418)	(0.8539)
Sudan[vii]	1.41	14.8	0.00	5.5	(0.0000)	(0.0009)	(0.0001)	(0.0001)

$\Delta\pi_t$ is the change in CPI inflation. $\tilde{Y}_t$ is the output gap (deviations from an HP filter's trend). σ is the standard deviation. *P*-values are in parentheses. [i] $F_{59,60}$; Levene and Brown–Forsyth df are (1,119); [ii] $F_{49,60}$; Levene and Brown–Forsyth df are (1,109); [iii] $F_{59,60}$; Levene and Brown–Forsyth df are (1,119); [iv] $F_{54,60}$; Levene and Brown–Forsyth df are (1,114); [v] $F_{57,60}$; Levene and Brown–Forsyth df are (1,117); [vi] $F_{60,59}$; Levene and Brown–Forsyth df are (1,119); [vii] $F_{58,60}$; Levene and Brown–Forsyth df are (1,118).

The Phillips Curve, Anticipated Inflation, and Output   205

Table 8.4 Descriptive Statistics of the Asian Countries: Change in Inflation and the Output Gap, 1960–2020

	$\Delta\pi_t$		$\tilde{Y}_t$		H_0: Equal Variance			
	μ	σ	μ	σ	F	Siegel–Tukey	Levene	Brown–Forsyth
India[i]	0.08	5.2	0.02	2.6	(0.0000)	(0.0294)	(0.0050)	(0.0050)
Japan[ii]	−0.09	2.4	0.04	2.3	(0.7129)	(0.0119)	(0.2065)	(0.2697)
Korea[iii]	−0.12	4.7	−0.14	2.7	(0.0001)	(0.9164)	(0.1562)	(0.1551)
Malaysia[iv]	−0.016	2.7	−0.012	3.4	(0.1131)	(0.0297)	(0.0786)	(0.0789)
Nepal[v]	−0.06	6.0	0.02	1.8	(0.0000)	(0.0002)	(0.0000)	(0.0000)
Myanmar [vi]	0.15	10.8	0.09	3.9	(0.0000)	(0.0000)	(0.0000)	(0.0000)
Philippines [vii]	0.017	7.6	0.00	3.4	(0.0000)	(0.0104)	(0.0078)	(0.0079)
Singapore [viii]	−0.009	3.7	−0.13	4.1	(0.3825)	(0.0000)	(0.0083)	(0.0105)
Sri Lanka [ix]	−0.009	5.7	0.08	2.3	(0.0000)	(0.0030)	(0.0003)	(0.0003)
Thailand[x]	−0.13	3.8	−0.02	3.8	(0.9915)	(0.0250)	(0.3106)	(0.3361)

$\Delta\pi_t$ is the change in CPI inflation. $\tilde{Y}_t$ is the output gap (deviations from an HP filter's trend). σ is the standard deviation. *P*-values are in parentheses; [i] $F_{58,60}$; Levene and Brown–Forsyth df are (1,118); [ii] $F_{58,60}$; Levene and Brown–Forsyth df are (1,118); [iii] $F_{58,60}$; Levene and Brown–Forsyth df are (1,118); [iv] $F_{60,59}$; Levene and Brown–Forsyth df are (1,119); [v] $F_{55,60}$; Levene and Brown–Forsyth df are (1,115); [vi] $F_{57,59}$; Levene and Brown–Forsyth df are (1,116); [vii] $F_{58,60}$; Levene and Brown–Forsyth df are (1,118); [viii] $F_{60,59}$; Levene and Brown–Forsyth df are (1,119); [ix] $F_{44,45}$; Levene and Brown–Forsyth df are (1,89); [x] $F_{60,59}$; Levene and Brown–Forsyth df are (1,119).

Table 8.5 Descriptive Statistics of the Caribbean Countries: Change in Inflation and the Output Gap, 1960–2020

	$\Delta\pi_t$		$\tilde{Y}_t$		H_0: Equal Variance			
	μ	σ	μ	σ	F	Siegel–Tukey	Levene	Brown–Forsyth
Haiti[i]	0.28	7.5	−0.001	3.4	(0.0000)	(0.0000)	(0.0000)	(0.0000)
T&T[ii]	−0.01	3.0	0.07	4.9	(0.0003)	(0.3085)	(0.0374)	(0.0458)

$\Delta\pi_t$ is the change in CPI inflation. $\tilde{Y}_t$ is the output gap (deviations from an HP filter's trend). σ is the standard deviation. *T & T* denotes Trinidad and Tobago. *P*-values are in parentheses. [i] $F_{59,60}$; Levene and Brown–Forsyth df are (1,119); [ii] $F_{60,58}$; Levene and Brown–Forsyth df are (1,118).

Next, we test the data for the developed countries. We will test two different samples, before and after inflation-targeting. New Zealand and the United States will be tested separately because New Zealand data are quarterly for the inflation-targeting period only. The United States started targeting inflation in 2012. Table 8.6 reports the tests for the period before inflation-targeting, and Table 8.7 reports the tests for the period after inflation-targeting.

Before inflation-targeting, we could not reject the null hypothesis that the variance of the change of inflation is equal to the variance of the output gap. Norway

206 *The Phillips Curve, Anticipated Inflation, and Output*

Table 8.6 Descriptive Statistics of the Inflation-Targeting Countries: Change in Inflation and the Output Gap Before Inflation-Targeting, 1960–1992

	$\Delta\pi_t$		$\tilde{Y}_t$		H_0:Equal Variance			
	μ	σ	μ	σ	F	Siegel–Tukey	Levene	Brown–Forsyth
Australia[i]	−0.04	2.25	−0.02	1.95	(0.4314)	(0.9038)	(0.7539)	(0.7542)
Denmark[ii]	−0.04	2.22	0.06	2.04	(0.5363)	(0.8403)	(0.7135)	(0.7575)
Norway[iii]	0.005	2.56	−0.10	1.74	(0.0245)	(0.0784)	(0.0448)	(0.0906)
Sweden[iv]	0.007	2.44	0.35	1.85	(0.1153)	(0.7882)	(0.4187)	(0.4049)
UK[v]	0.03	3.23	0.07	2.54	(0.1346)	(0.4765)	(0.2574)	(0.2942)
US[vi]	0.02	1.66	0.03	2.01	(0.1877)	(0.0110)	(0.0429)	(0.0411)

$\Delta\pi_t$ is the change in CPI inflation. $\tilde{Y}_t$ is the output gap (deviations from an HP filter's trend). σ is the standard deviation. *P*-values are in parentheses. [i] $F_{30,32}$; Levene and Brown–Forsyth df are (1,62); [ii] $F_{30,32}$; Levene and Brown–Forsyth df are (1,62); [iii] $F_{30,32}$; Levene and Brown–Forsyth df are (1,62); [iv] $F_{30,32}$; Levene and Brown–Forsyth df are (1,62); [v] $F_{30,32}$; Levene and Brown–Forsyth df are (1,62); [vi] $F_{52,50}$; Levene and Brown–Forsyth df are (1,102). The US sample is 1960 to 2012.

Table 8.7 Descriptive Statistics of the Inflation-Targeting Countries: Change in Inflation and the Output Gap Under Inflation-Targeting, 1993–2021

	$\Delta\pi_t$		$\tilde{Y}_t$		H_0:Equal Variance			
	μ	σ	μ	σ	F	Siegel–Tukey	Levene	Brown–Forsyth
Australia[i]	−0.006	1.30	−0.08	0.86	(0.0250)	(0.0358)	(0.0615)	(0.0567)
Denmark[ii]	−0.06	0.75	−0.01	2.02	(0.0000)	(0.0002)	(0.0000)	(0.0000)
Norway[iii]	−0.04	1.20	0.09	1.44	(0.3462)	(0.3461)	(0.2747)	(0.2767)
New Zealand*	−0.03	0.80	−0.01	1.65	(0.0000)	(0.0000)	(0.0000)	(0.0000)
Sweden[iv]	−0.06	1.40	−0.30	2.31	(0.0117)	(0.0242)	(0.0074)	(0.0149)
UK[v]	−0.12	0.81	−0.12	2.51	(0.0000)	(0.00001)	(0.0000)	(0.0001)

$\Delta\pi_t$ is the change in CPI inflation. $\tilde{Y}_t$ is the output gap (deviations from an HP filter's trend). σ is the standard deviation. *P*-values are in parentheses. * denotes New Zealand's quarterly data from March 1988 to December 2021. [i] $F_{27,27}$; Levene and Brown–Forsyth df are (1,54); [ii] $F_{27,27}$; Levene and Brown–Forsyth df are (1,54); [iii] $F_{27,27}$; Levene and Brown–Forsyth df are (1,54); [iv] $F_{27,27}$; Levene and Brown–Forsyth df are (1,54); [v] $F_{27,27}$; Levene and Brown–Forsyth df are (1,54).

is probably an exception. This result is probably supportive of the New Keynesian Phillips curve. It is likely that the developed countries have been exploiting the Phillips curve before the inflation-targeting policy regimes began.

Under inflation-targeting, the variance of inflation fell significantly relative to its past values. The variance of the output gap exceeded the variance of the change in inflation in all countries, except Australia. The New Keynesian Phillips curve is expected to fit the data more in Denmark, Norway, New Zealand, Sweden, and the United Kingdom and United States. See the scatter plots presented earlier.

The Phillips Curve, Anticipated Inflation, and Output   207

Australia's variance of the output gap is relatively smaller than the variance of the change in inflation, but we cannot strongly reject the null in some of the tests.

So far, we have shown that the variance of the output gap is statistically smaller than the variance of the change in inflation in the majority of countries in our sample, except Malaysia, Singapore, Gabon, Trinidad and Tobago, and the developed inflation-targeting countries are the only ones with such variations, where the variance of the output gap exceeds that of inflation. Therefore, we do not expect the New Keynesian Phillips curve specification to fit the data in all countries.

The Stability of the New Keynesian Phillips Curve Specification – Change in Inflation and the Output Gap

The aforementioned results lead us to believe that a single-equation New Keynesian Phillips curve specification could only be fit in a handful of countries out of 42. Now we examine the *stability* of the relationship between the change in inflation and the output gap, which is the preferred (Romer and Romer, 1997) New Keynesian specification.

Razzak (2013) provides a methodology to test instability in a multivariate economic system, which is a system comprising N variables, where $N \geq 3$. The idea is that we let a statistic ω, which could have any distribution, measure certain features of the vector X such as the variance.

If $\omega_\alpha (0 < \alpha < 1)$ denotes the $(1-\alpha)^{th}$ fractile of the distribution ω, then ω_α satisfies the equation:

$$Prob(\omega > \omega_\alpha) = \alpha \qquad (8.10)$$

Generally, we define a zone for ω under some common distribution by defining upper and lower critical limits such that ω stays within. In other words, when ω exceeds the critical limits, it is considered a significant value (i.e., falling in the tails of the distribution). This zone is a prediction interval.

Take a bivariate normal variable $X^T = [X_1, X_2]$, where each X is an *iid* Gaussian random variable, but the $cov(X_1, X_2) \neq 0$ and the superscript T denotes transpose. If $(1-\alpha)$ probability is maintained on each component, then the *probability* that all variables X_1 and X_2 are simultaneously falling within the upper and lower critical limits is

$$1 - \varphi = (1-\alpha)^p \qquad (8.11)$$

The probability of falling outside the critical limit is

$$\varphi = 1 - (1-\alpha)^p \qquad (8.12)$$

To satisfy a probability of $1-\varphi$ that both variables are falling within the critical limits on one sample when the parameters are the nominal values, α must be:

$$\alpha = 1 - (1-\varphi)^{1/p} \qquad (8.13)$$

208 *The Phillips Curve, Anticipated Inflation, and Output*

Consider a bivariate system, which includes X_1 (the change in inflation) and X_2 (the output gap), that is, $N = 2$. These are I(0) time series. The statistic, which we are interested in, is the variance or the dispersion of this bivariable system. The variance in this case is *not a scalar*, but rather a 2×2 matrix, whereby the function $\sigma_1^2 \sigma_2^2 - \sigma_{12}^2$ is called the *Generalized Variance*. σ_1^2 is the variance of the change in inflation, σ_2^2 is the variance of the output gap, and σ_{12}^2 is the covariance. The function $s_1^2 s_2^2 - s_{12}^2$ is called the *Sample Generalized Variance*, and s_1^2, s_2^2, and s_{12}^2 are the sample estimates of the true variances and covariance. See (Anderson, 1958). This is given by the statistic:

$$D = 2(n-2)\left(\frac{s_1^2 s_2^2 - s_{12}^2}{\sigma_1^2 \sigma_2^2 - \sigma_{12}^2}\right)^{\frac{1}{2}}, \tag{8.14}$$

where the statistic D is distributed $\chi_{(2(n-2))}^2$ random variable. For the time series X_1 (the change in inflation) and X_2 (output gap), we calculate D for windows of $n = 5$ observations (years). s_1^2 is the sample variance of the change in inflation, and s_2^2 is the sample variance of the output gap. The same is for the covariance s_{12}^2. The statistics σ_1^2, σ_2^2, and σ_{12}^2 are the *averages* of s_1^2, s_2^2, and s_{12}^2 for the intervals of size $n = 5$. The *probability* of D is:

$$u = \chi_{2(n-2)}^2 D. \tag{8.15}$$

For an easier interpretation, we could calculate a *Standardized* Sample Generalized Variance.

We compute:

$$R = \Phi^{-1}(u), \tag{8.16}$$

where Φ^{-1} is the *inverse Normal Distribution Function*, which defines the prediction interval; it measures the distance from the mean in terms of standard deviations.

We use the value $\mp 3\sigma$, *or for a tighter interval, one could take the value $\mp 2\sigma$*. These limits, under a standard normal distribution function, are *prediction* limits for the distributions of R. Note that a $\mp 3\sigma$ critical or confidence limit constitutes a band of 0.99730 prediction intervals for values of the statistic R according to the Tchebysheff's theorem.[9] In other words, values that fall in the tails of the distribution are statistically significantly different from values elsewhere under the distribution and represent *instability* in this case. We will calculate the statistic for every

9 Chebyshev's inequality (also known as Tchebysheff's inequality, Chebyshev's theorem, or the Bienaymé–Chebyshev inequality) states that in any data sample or probability distribution, nearly all the values are close to the mean value and provides a quantitative description of *nearly all* and *close to*. For any $k > 1$, the following example (where $\sigma = 1/k$) meets the bounds exactly. So, $\Pr(X = 1) = 1/2k^2$; $\Pr(X = 0) = 1 - 1/k^2$ and $\Pr(X = -1) = 1/2k^2$ for that distribution $\Pr(|X - \mu|) \geq k\sigma = 1/k^2$. Equality holds exactly for any distribution that is a linear transformation of this one. Inequality holds for any distribution that is not a linear transformation of this one.

The Phillips Curve, Anticipated Inflation, and Output 209

country's pair of the change in inflation and the output gap for periods 1962 to 2020 using 12 samples of size $n = 5$, that is, 1962–1966, 1967–1971, and the last interval is $n = 4$, from 2016 to 2020 because the output gap data ends in 2020.

For illustration, Table 8.8 reports the calculations for the MENA countries. We do not report tables for the rest of the countries to save space. Figure 8.12 plots the statistic $R(.)$ for the MENA countries. Figures 8.13, 8.14, 8.15, 8.16, and 8.17 plot the $R(.)$ statistics for the rest of the countries. The horizontal axis is the N samples

Table 8.8 The MENA Countries' Sample Generalized Variance

Algeria

OBS	n	s_1^2	s_2^2	s_{12}^2	D	u	Intervals	R
1	5	8.42	47.02	11.25	12.93	0.04	1972–1976	−1.70
2	5	15.36	3.67	−2.29	5.05	0.54	1977–1981	0.09
3	5	20.93	7.58	1.32	8.27	0.22	1982–1986	−0.78
4	5	17.86	2.97	2.71	4.68	0.59	1987–1991	0.22
5	5	45.07	4.87	2.05	9.73	0.14	1992–1996	−1.10
6	5	22.90	0.66	2.71	2.33	0.89	1997–2001	1.21
7	5	8.94	5.95	−2.37	4.92	0.55	2002–2006	0.14
8	5	1.60	1.97	0.78	1.01	0.99	2007–2011	2.17
9	5	12.14	1.30	0.61	2.57	0.86	2012–2016	1.08
10	6	6.37	13.47	−0.59	7.66	0.47	2017–2020	−0.08

$\sigma_1 = 15.96 \; \sigma_2 = 9.33 \; \sigma_{12} = 1.86$

Egypt

OBS	n	s_1^2	s_2^2	s_{12}^2	D	u	Intervals	R
1	5	38.90	23.98	8.20	19.22	0.00	1962–1966	−2.67
2	5	22.17	4.77	−5.81	6.68	0.35	1967–1971	−0.38
3	5	5.43	9.73	−3.49	4.74	0.58	1972–1976	0.19
4	5	45.09	1.21	0.67	4.64	0.59	1977–1981	0.23
5	5	27.26	1.15	−1.41	3.62	0.73	1982–1986	0.61
6	5	10.55	1.30	−1.75	2.49	0.87	1987–1991	1.13
7	5	30.62	0.39	−1.26	2.30	0.89	1992–1996	1.23
8	5	0.71	2.12	0.80	0.53	1.00	1997–2001	2.79
9	5	19.78	1.09	0.82	2.88	0.82	2002–2006	0.93
10	5	24.45	1.67	−0.41	4.06	0.67	2007–2011	0.44
11	5	4.93	0.91	−1.06	1.49	0.96	2012–2016	1.75
12	4	113.79	1.35	−5.93	5.98	0.20	2017–2020	−0.84
Averages								

$\sigma_1 = 28.64 \; \sigma_2 = 5.58 \; \sigma_{12} - 0.36$

Pakistan

OBS	n	s_1^2	s_2^2	s_{12}^2	D	u	Intervals	R
1	5	3.48	5.43	1.76	5.22	0.52	1962–1966	0.04
2	5	13.42	5.99	2.38	11.13	0.08	1967–1971	−1.38
3	5	105.35	0.97	7.75	12.25	0.06	1972–1976	−1.58
4	5	8.12	4.62	−1.10	7.84	0.25	1977–1981	−0.67
5	5	5.64	0.36	−0.19	1.89	0.93	1982–1986	1.47
6	5	3.20	0.49	0.29	1.42	0.96	1987–1991	1.81
7	5	2.97	1.52	−1.57	3.11	0.80	1992–1996	0.83

(Continued)

210 *The Phillips Curve, Anticipated Inflation, and Output*

Table 8.8 (Continued)

Pakistan								
8	5	4.85	0.37	0.59	1.38	0.97	1997–2001	1.84
9	5	4.49	10.59	0.28	8.67	0.19	2002–2006	−0.87
10	5	38.78	6.75	3.14	20.27	0.00	2007–2011	−2.81
11	5	4.35	1.49	0.87	2.98	0.81	2012–2016	0.88
12	4	6.59	10.28	2.00	7.67	0.10	2017–2020	−1.26
Averages		$\sigma_1 = 16.77$	$\sigma_2 = 2.47$	$\sigma_{12} = 1.13$				

Turkey								
1	5	12.81	4.19	−0.11	1.79	0.94	1962–1966	1.54
2	5	41.00	2.60	−6.02	2.60	0.86	1967–1971	1.07
3	5	23.92	11.93	−6.05	4.17	0.65	1972–1976	0.39
4	5	528.43	28.92	42.33	30.16	0.00	1977–1981	−3.97
5	5	62.72	4.07	0.01	3.90	0.69	1982–1986	0.50
6	5	82.51	6.81	5.66	5.76	0.45	1987–1991	−0.13
7	5	133.49	11.15	−22.84	9.50	0.15	1992–1996	−1.05
8	5	31.82	34.00	7.40	8.01	0.24	1997–2001	−0.71
9	5	60.85	26.62	23.88	9.76	0.14	2002–2006	−1.10
10	5	6.18	30.91	3.00	3.35	0.76	2007–2011	0.72
11	5	2.30	1.70	−1.31	0.56	1.00	2012–2016	2.75
12	4	11.20	12.93	8.33	2.14	0.71	2017–2020	0.55
Averages		$\sigma_1 = 83.10$	$\sigma_2 = 12.96$	$\sigma_{12} = 4.92$				

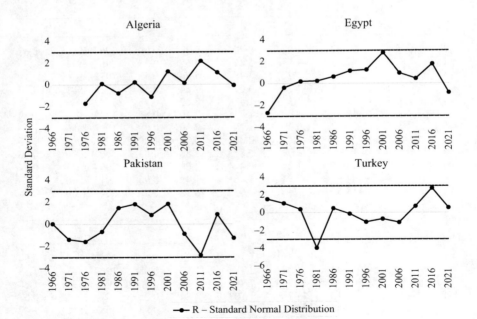

Figure 8.12 Sample Generalized Variance for the MENA Countries' New Keynesian Phillips Curve Specification, 1962–2020

The *Sample Generalized Variance* is stable for the MENA countries, except in one 5-year period for Turkey from 1977 to 1981, which is a period of high political crisis, *coup d'etat*, and oil price shock. No instability in the New Keynesian Phillips specification is detected in the other countries at the 99.7 percent level; however, there were significant instability at the 95 percent level in Egypt in 1962–1966 and in 1996–2000, in Pakistan in 2006–2010, and in Turkey in 2010–2015. Note that more instability could be detected at the 95 percent level, that is, $\pm 2\sigma$.

Figure 8.13 plots the test for Latin and South America. Consistent with the previous tests of the relationship between the change in inflation and the output gap, the Latin and South American countries exhibit a significant instability at the 99.7 percent level in the New Keynesian Phillips curve specification advocated by (Romer and Romer, 1997), except perhaps in the cases of Colombia and Honduras, which have instability at the 95 percent level $(\pm 2\sigma)$. In fact, all countries exhibited statistical instability at the 95 percent level.

For Africa, Figure 8.14 shows that the data exhibit instability in the New Keynesian Phillips curve specification at the 95 percent level; however, at the 99.7 percent level, Burkina Faso, Côte d'Ivoire, South Africa, and Sudan show stable variations.

Figure 8.15 for Asia shows that India, Malaysia, Myanmar, and Thailand have a relatively more stable change in inflation–output gap *Sample Generalized Variance* at the 99.7 percent level. At the 95 percent level, however, the Asia data show significant instability in all countries. The variances of the change in inflation and the output gap are identical as shown earlier when we tested them for equality. Sri Lanka had a highly significantly unstable Phillips curve for years, which is now in the news for a near collapse of the economy. Nepal too has volatility near the upper limit for a long time.

Figure 8.16 plots the Sample Generalized Variance for the change in inflation and the output gap for the two Caribbean countries in our sample, Haiti and Trinidad and Tobago.

These are interesting results because Haiti has so many adverse shocks to inflation; yet, only two 5-year instability periods are showing in this test, 1982–1986 at the 99.7 percent level and 2012–2016 at the 95 percent level. The Sample Generalized Variance is strikingly stable in Trinidad and Tobago.

Figure 8.17 plots the Sample Generalized Variance test for the inflation-targeting countries, except New Zealand, which is plotted in Figure 8.18.

Norway, Sweden, and the United States have relatively more stable *Sample Generalized Variance*, that is, stable New Keynesian Phillips curve specification between the change in inflation and the output gap at the 99.7 percent level. At the 95 percent level, all of the countries exhibited instability.[10]

---

10 Brexit in January 2020 caused real output in the United Kingdom to plummet. The output gap fell from 3.7 percent in 2019 to −7.3 percent in 2020. However, our R test statistic did not show significant instability in the relationship between $\Delta\pi_t$ and the output gap over the sample window 2015 to 2020. Future data may show something different.

212 *The Phillips Curve, Anticipated Inflation, and Output*

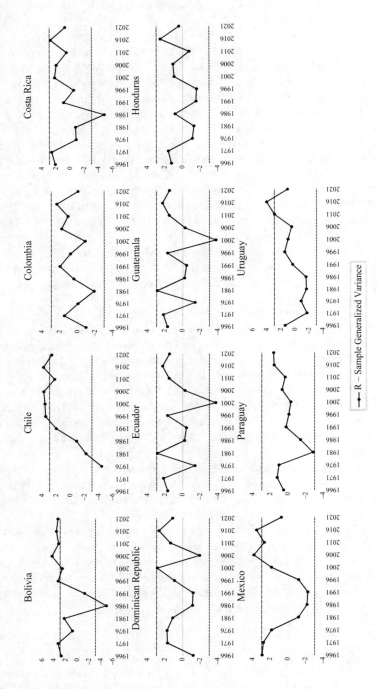

Figure 8.13 Sample Generalized Variance for Latin and South American Countries' New Keynesian Phillips Curve Specification, 1962–2020

The Phillips Curve, Anticipated Inflation, and Output 213

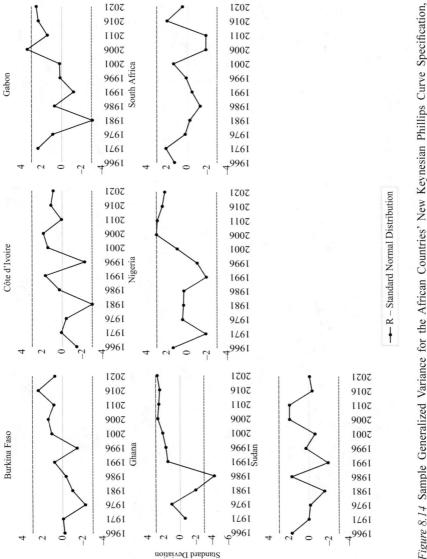

Figure 8.14 Sample Generalized Variance for the African Countries' New Keynesian Phillips Curve Specification, 1962–2020, where Gabon Data are from 1964 and Ghana's Data are from 1966

214 *The Phillips Curve, Anticipated Inflation, and Output*

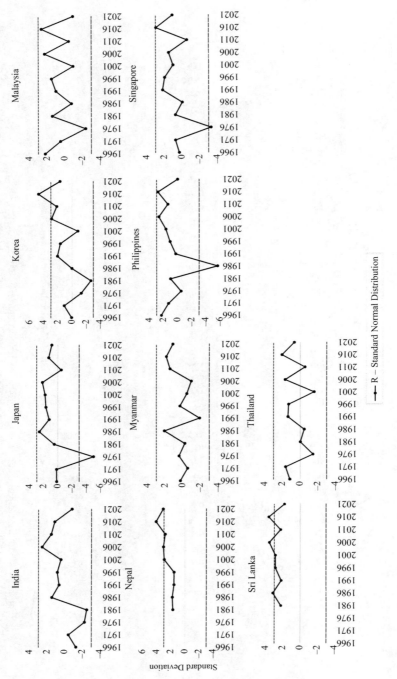

Figure 8.15 Sample Generalized Variance for the Asian Countries' New Keynesian Phillips Curve Specification, 1962–2020, where Nepal and Sri Lanka Have Shorter Samples (1976–2020)

The Phillips Curve, Anticipated Inflation, and Output 215

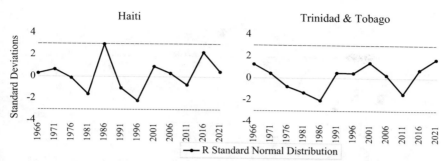

Figure 8.16 Sample Generalized Variance for the Caribbean Countries' New Keynesian Phillips Curve Specification, 1962–2020

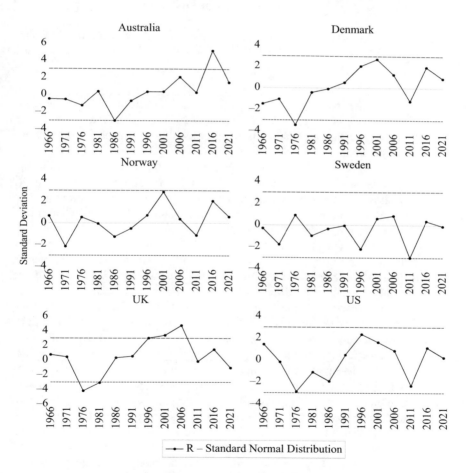

Figure 8.17 Sample Generalized Variance for the Inflation-Targeting Countries' New Keynesian Phillips Curve Specification, 1962–2020

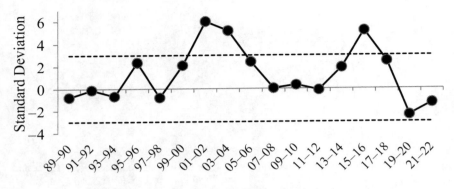

Figure 8.18 Sample Generalized Variance for New Zealand's New Keynesian Phillips Curve Specification, March 1989 to December 2021

Finally, we test New Zealand's quarterly data under the inflation-targeting regime. The sample is March 1989 to September 2021. Each interval is $n = 8$ quarters (2 years), and the last quarter is $n = 3$, which is most probably biased and should be ignored.

The results of testing the internal consistency of the New Keynesian Phillips curve specification, that is, change in inflation–output gap, for a sample of 42 countries, show that the majority of the countries have (1) the variances of their output gaps < the variances of their change in inflation; and (2) only a handful of countries have a stable Sample Generalized Variance, that is, the bivariate statistics of a system on change in inflation and the output gap are revealing. They imply that, first, the output gap does not explain the change in inflation, hence, second, it must be expected inflation that provides all the explanation of the change in inflation. We tried different measures of expected inflation, e.g., inflation minus a 2-year moving average, instead of lagged inflation. We also tried EWMA inflation instead of lagged inflation. We find no change in these results. Furthermore, problems such as the endogeneity and the mismeasurement of the output gap and expected inflation of these variables, since they are unobservable, imply that a single-equation OLS method to estimate the Phillips curve results in biased and inconsistent parameter estimates. We suppose that Instrumental Variable methods such as Two-Stage Least Square (2SLS) and the less efficient Generalized Method of Moments (GMM), to a lesser extent, could remedy the endogeneity and mismeasurement issues. However, they could not resolve the Lucas critique, that is, that the coefficients such as the coefficient on expected inflation and the output gap change when policy changes. The least required is to estimate a system of equations jointly, whereby there are some testable cross-equation restrictions. We attempt to do so in the next chapter.

9 Estimating the Phillips Curve

Abstract

We estimate simultaneous-equation systems for the United States (March 1960 to March 2022) and New Zealand (Mar 1992 to Jun 2022) and test theoretical cross-equation restrictions. The Phillips curve has serious specification and estimation issues. The explanatory variables, expected inflation and the output gap, are unobservable, hence measurement errors. Policymakers and economic agents in these two countries and maybe in other inflation-targeting countries must have strongly believed that inflation expectations have been anchored, thus they assumed that expected inflation tomorrow is proportional to inflation today, e.g., . This assumption when with explains their inability to foresee the most recent rise in inflation. The assumption results in systematic under-prediction of inflation. A New Keynesian active monetary policy affects inflation via the output gap with long and variable lags; hence, the central banks should act earlier and on the basis of anticipated inflation. The inability of the central bank to forecast inflation means they would be acting late and strong, based on observed rather anticipated rising inflation, which is a serious policy error. Policy errors are notoriously persistent and very costly to undo.

When estimating the Phillips curve, we consider a number of obvious specification and estimation issues. In the Phillips curve, there are two *endogenous* and *unobservable* explanatory variables: expected inflation and the output gap (or the deviations of the unemployment rate from the natural rate of unemployment); they must be either measured, estimated, or forecast, hence, measurement errors. Specification and estimation errors cause biased and inconsistent parameter estimates in Ordinary Least Squares (OLS). An Instrumental Variable estimator (IV) may be used to deal with these problems. However, as explained in the previous chapter, there are implications for the assumption or the specifications of expectation's formation, which should be tested empirically.

We test the Phillips curve under the assumptions that the anticipated (expected) inflation is (1) rational in the sense of the RE theory, whereby *more* information than past inflation is included in the central bank's specification of the Phillips curve and (2) backward, that is, inflation expectations is equal to lagged inflation. Keep in mind our evidence that the relationship between $\Delta \pi_t$ and the output gap is

DOI: 10.4324/9781003382218-9

218 *Estimating the Phillips Curve*

unstable. Here, we will *estimate* the coefficient instead of imposing it; we do not expect this coefficient to be equal to 1. We test the implication of *structural neutrality*, that is, anticipated aggregate demand shocks have no real effects, the *policy ineffectiveness* proposition, and that only *unanticipated* aggregate demand shocks (surprise monetary policy) have real effects. We also have to deal with the Lucas critique, which is daunting. Therefore, we will not consider the Phillips curve as a single reduced-form equation as it is typically done. We assume that the Phillips curve is a proxy of the short-run aggregate supply curve, specify an aggregate demand, estimate them jointly, and test the cross-equation *restrictions* of the RE theory along with the tests for expected inflation and the output gap.

We do not estimate the Phillips curve for developing countries, not only because the required data are not readily available, but also because we showed significant instability and lack of correlation in the data in the previous chapter. For the developed countries, we only estimate the Phillips curve for the United States and New Zealand because the scatter plots showed some evidence of correlation between inflation and the change in inflation and the output gap and because we have sufficient up-to-date *quarterly* data. For New Zealand, the sample covers the period of successful targeting of low and stable inflation only, from 1992 to 2022. For the United States, Volker's disinflation in the 1980s and Bernanke's explicit inflation-targeting in 2012 are the two publicly known inflation-targeting periods.

We use quarterly data for two reasons. First, central banks use quarterly data to estimate their models because they reset monetary policy quarterly. Second, there might be issues with *temporal aggregation*, which arises when the frequency of the data generation is lower than that of the data collection so that not all the realizations of the original stochastic processes are observable (see Marcellino [1999] and Rossana and Seater [2012]). They found the losses of information to be substantial. Monthly and quarterly data are governed by complex time series processes with much low-frequency cyclical variation, whereas annual data are governed by simpler processes with virtually no cyclical variation. Cycles of much more than a year's duration in the monthly data disappear when the data are aggregated to annual observations. Moreover, the aggregated data show more long-run persistence than the underlying disaggregated data. See also (Silvestrini and Veredas, 2008) who provide a survey article on temporal aggregation and show that the estimated quarterly model is richer, information-wise, as the number of observations used for estimation is four times larger than for the annual model.

Measuring Expected Inflation

The Phillips curve has very serious measurement challenges because the explanatory variables, expected inflation, and the output gap are unobservable. Measuring inflation expectations is the thorniest specification and measurement issue in estimating the Phillips curve.

The expectation's specification has a major impact on policy. One potentially useful way to measure expected inflation is to use survey data. Fewer developed countries including the US report survey data for inflation expectations. The sample of the survey is larger in the United States than for example, in New Zealand. Therefore, we

Estimating the Phillips Curve 219

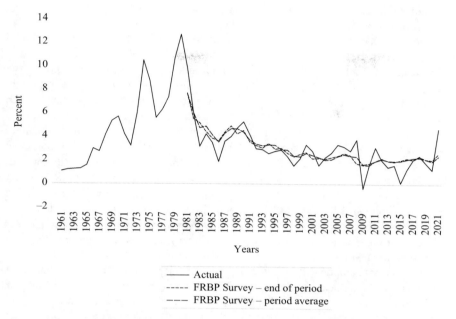

Figure 9.1 Actual CPI Inflation and US Survey of 1-Year-Ahead CPI Inflation

Data Source: US Survey of Professional Forecasters – FFRP

begin by testing whether the survey data are consistent with the RE theory. We will not use the survey data if they turn out to be inconsistent with RE because our aim is to test the implications for the Phillips curve. The most cited survey is the Federal Reserve Bank of Philadelphia (FRBP) survey of professional forecasters. It publishes the US CPI inflation annualized rates quarterly from 1981. We use the average of the quarterly data and the end-of-period (fourth quarter) data for the 1-year-ahead forecast and the actual inflation rate for the US CPI inflation in Figure 9.1.

The testing method for the survey data for rational expectations is straightforward. Let x_{t+f} be the realization of the random variable x for the period $t+f$ and x_t^f denotes the expectations of x_{t+f} at the end of the period t. If expectations are rational, then $x_t^f = E(x_{t+f} | I_t)$, where E is the expectations operator, and I is the information set.

$E(x_{t+f} - x_t^f | I_t) = 0$. The forecast error is given by $x_{t+f} - x_t^f = \eta_{t,f}$, which is uncorrelated with each variable in I_t. We are assuming that the economic agent knows the full information set. Alternatively, the agent may know a subset of the full information set. Thus, rationality implies, *unbiasedness*: $x_{t+f} = x_t^f + \eta_{t,f}$, and $E(\eta_{t,f} | x_t^f) = 0$; *efficiency*: $E(\eta_{t,f} | \eta_{t-i,f}) = 0$ $\forall i \geq f$, and *orthogonality*: $E(\eta_{t,f} | X_{t-i}) = 0$ $\forall i \geq 0$.

Put simply, the testing involves a few steps: (1) Regress the inflation rate on a constant term and the survey data; test the joint hypothesis that the constant term is 0 and the slope coefficient is 1. (2) Test whether the residuals of this equation are identically, independently distributed (*iid*) and serially uncorrelated. Finally, test

220 Estimating the Phillips Curve

whether the residuals are uncorrelated with the variables that could have been in the information set.

The RE theory does not provide a method for choosing the variables that should be included in the agent's information set. The guess is that the economic agent studies the central bank's models and policy and is able to discern what variables to use. These variables could be past inflation, the nominal interest rate; money growth; nominal GDP growth; and government expenditures growth, etc. We test the RE assumption. Table 9.1 reports the OLS regression of actual CPI inflation on a constant term and the survey. The results indicate that the constant term is insignificantly different from 0, the slope coefficient is insignificantly different from 1 as indicated by the P-values of F and Chi-Squared tests, and the residuals are serially uncorrelated and *iid*. So far, these tests are supportive of the predictions of the RE theory. Table 9.2 reports the results of regressing the residuals from the aforementioned regression on lags of nominal GDP growth, broad money growth, nominal government consumption expenditures, last years' federal fund rate (ffr) and the 10-year US Government bond yield, and last year's output gap. We are assuming that these variables are the most relevant macroeconomic variables in the information set used by the survey respondents to forecast the CPI inflation. The results show that all of the coefficients are statistically significantly different from 0; therefore, the survey of inflation expectations is correlated with the variables in the information set and does not imply or is being inconsistent with the predictions of the RE theory.

We showed earlier that the inflation–money correlation has almost vanished under successful inflation-targeting, and the output gap–change in inflation relationship is unstable. Many central banks managed to reduce the level and the variability of inflation, which altered the relationships between inflation and other macroeconomic variables such as money, government spending, and output. Policy affects the time series properties of the data; it may make the inflation data stationary, it may induce breaks in the data, and surely break up the correlation among the variables in the system. Recall the (Taylor, 2001) interview with Milton Friedman, which we had mentioned earlier in Chapter 5. Successful monetary policy intervention such as inflation targeting is akin to the thermostat Friedman described; it

Table 9.1 OLS Regression Test of the US CPI Inflation Survey Data $\pi_t = \beta_0 + \beta_1 \pi_t^e + \zeta$, 1981–2021

	Coefficient	t-Test	P-value $\beta_0 = 0$ $\beta_1 = 0$	P-value $\beta_1 = 1$
β_0	−0.28	−0.8152	0.4214	
β_1	1.06	0.9761	0.0000	
χ_1	–	–	–	0.5672
$\bar{R}^2$	0.71			
H_0 : No serial correlation $F_{4,26}$			0.4963	
H_0 : *iid*, Jarque–Bera			0.9528	

- HAC standard errors and covariance, pre-withering with lag = 1 from AIC max lag = 3, Bartlett kernel, Newey–West automatic bandwidth = 4.8442, NW automatic lag = 3
- Breusch–Godfrey LM test

Estimating the Phillips Curve 221

Table 9.2 OLS Regression Test of the Residuals $\zeta_t = \alpha_0 + \alpha_1 \Delta lny_{t-1} + \alpha_2 \Delta lnM_{t-1} + \alpha_3 \Delta lnG_{t-1} + \alpha_4 r^s_{t-1} + \alpha_5 r^l_{t-1} + \alpha_6 \tilde{Y}_{t-1} + \eta_t$, 1981–2021

	Coefficient	P-value
α_0	1.17	(0.0000)
α_0	0.22	(0.0000)
α_2	−0.09	(0.0002)
α_3	0.15	(0.0000)
α_4	0.31	(0.0000)
α_5	−0.64	(0.0785)
α_6	−0.08	(0.1176)
$\bar{R}^2$	0.38	
DW	2.57	

HAC standard errors & covariance, pre-whitening with lag = 3 from AIC with max lag = 3, Bartlett kernel, Newey–West with automatic bandwidth = 2.3857, NW automatic lag length = 3. y is nominal GDP, M is broad money, G is nominal government expenditures, r^s_t is the effective federal fund rate, r^l_t is the 10-year government bond yield, and $\tilde{Y}_t$ is the output gap. Asterisk denotes significance at the 95% level, and hash denotes significance at the 90% level.

breaks up the correlation between inflation and its determinants specified by the model used for policy. Eventually, the model fails. We cannot forecast inflation a year ahead, the historical data (whether in real time or not) are contaminated by continuous active policy tinkering, and we are totally uncertain about the nature and permanency of future shocks. In turn, econometricians and data analysts find it increasingly difficult to test models of inflation determination and to forecast inflation in countries, where the monetary authority actively manages demand and target inflation. The same thing could happen of course if central banks decide to target money growth, nominal GDP, the exchange rate, or any other nominal variable; the QTM becomes unstable too.

The empirical literature of the Phillips curve is truly massive because central banks produced lots of empirical research; therefore, here are a few examples of important references of estimations of various Phillips curve specifications by country. Among hundreds of papers, for example, see (Haldane and Quah, 1999) for the UK Phillips curve; for the Swedish Phillips curve, see (Karlsson and Österholm, 2019); and for New Zealand, see for example (Razzak, 1997) and (Razzak and Dennis, 1995) and (Razzak, 2015). For the Australian Phillips curve, see (Gruen *et al.*, 1999) and (Debelle and Vickery, 2007). For the United States, see (Blanchard, 2016). For the EU, see for example (Ball and Mazumder, 2021). For Canada, see (Debelle and Laxton, 1997).

Having found the survey data of inflation expectations inconsistent with the predictions of the RE theory, we steer away from single-equation estimators and estimate a system of equations using the Maximum Likelihood Method in order to test the restrictions implied by the RE theory including the Phillips curve. We focus on the RE versus New Keynesian specifications of expected inflation, RE theory implications, and the Lucas critique.

222   *Estimating the Phillips Curve*

The Estimation of the Phillips Curve

We propose to estimate a simultaneous-equation system using the Maximum Like-lihood Method.[1] One prediction of the RE theory under flexible prices is that only *unanticipated* aggregate demand shocks have real effects, *anticipated* ones don't. It also means that the central bank has to surprise people in order to affect the real economy, and only in the short run. I believe that politicians are more interested in the short-run than the long-run effects because they are short-lived but that is a different issue for now. Thus, *policy ineffectiveness* is an important prediction of the RE theory. However, Fischer (1977), Phelps and Taylor (1977), and Neary and Stiglitz (1983), among others, argued that anticipated aggregate demand shocks can or may also have real effect. We test these – structural neutrality – predictions too.

We propose a three-equation model. The first equation is the aggregate demand equation. For simplicity, we assume that nominal GDP growth equation under the RE theory is:

$$\Delta lny_t = \underbrace{\beta_{10} + \beta_{11}\Delta lny_{t-1} + \beta_{12}L^i\pi_t + \beta_{13}L^i\left(\Delta lnm_t\right)}_{anticipated\ AD\ Shock} + u_t, \tag{9.1a}$$

where y_t is nominal GDP (or nominal GDE), L is the lag operator, $\left(m_t\right)$ is broad money, and CPI inflation π_t, which is ΔlnP_t, P_t is the CPI, and u_t is the unantici-pated aggregate demand shock. Lucas (1973) has an aggregate demand function with only β_{10}, which is the estimated mean growth of nominal GDP. There are more potential demand shifters that could be included such as government spending growth rate and credit growth, but the lagged dependent variable Δlny_{t-1} probably accounts for such shifters. The assumption that the rational agents use all available information to them up to time $t-1$ is strong and ambiguous. It is difficult to have a general guideline about what information to include/exclude from the informa-tion set. The RE theory does not tell us what variables to use to make rational pre-dictions about inflation; it just says that the information set includes all available information up to period $t-1$. We assume that the economic agent has understood the inflation dynamic by studying the history of the central bank's policy and model and that these three variables are sufficient to explain aggregate demand shocks. Lagged nominal GDP also captures other variables we do not include in the equa-tion, e.g., lagged government spending and lagged total credit. Figures 9.2 and 9.3 are 45° line scatter plots of the growth rate of money and nominal GDP growth and inflation, and of inflation and nominal GDP growth.

With the exception of a few outliers, there is quite a strong association among nominal GDP growth, inflation, and broad money growth in the United States. Remember the sample from 1960 has not been entirely an explicit inflation-targeting

---

1 There is an argument against ML estimators because they require exact or correct specifications. It is that we really do not know the Data-Generating-Process. Many people argued that the General-ized Method of Moments (GMM) maybe a better alternative estimator. However, GMM has its own problems, from instrument's validity to efficiency issues. My take is that one should use both and compare the estimates. They would be very close. The most important point is that OLS and all single-equation estimators should be avoided for the reasons we have presented earlier, i.e., mismeas-urement of expected inflation and the output gap causes bias and inconsistency.

Estimating the Phillips Curve 223

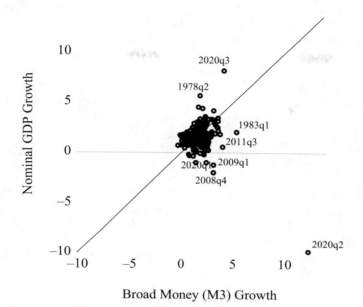

Figure 9.2 45° Line Scatter Plot of US Money and Nominal GDP Growth, March 1961 to March 2022
Data Source: FRED

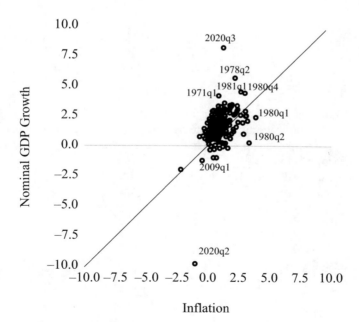

Figure 9.3 45° Line Scatter Plot of the US Inflation and Nominal GDP Growth, March 1961 to March 2022
Data Source: FRED

224 Estimating the Phillips Curve

regime. Explicit inflation-targeting began in 2012, but the Fed disinflated in the 1980s and stated publicly that it targets both low inflation and high (full) employment. We will test the null hypothesis that the coefficients in Eq. (9.1a) are equal to 0. The error term u_t is assumed to have classical assumption and represents the *unanticipated component* of aggregate demand, which plays a major role in the RE theory.

In model specification (2), it is assumed that the New Keynesian specification does not include money in the aggregate demand equation, and the aggregate demand is a function of lagged nominal GDP growth and lagged inflation, hence:

$$\Delta lny_t = \underbrace{\beta_{10} + \beta_{11}\Delta lny_{t-1} + \beta_{12}L^i\pi_t}_{\text{anticipated AD Shock}} + u_t \qquad (9.1b)$$

The difference between Eqs (9.1a) and (9.1b) is basically that money is not included in Eq. (9.1b), which is exactly what we want to test. The Fed in particular (and many central banks in developed countries) has not paid attention to the role of money in policy and ignored the economic implications of the increase in money growth; see (Poole, 1994) for example, who strongly criticized the Fed for not doing so.

The second equation in the model is for real output gap, which is specified as follows:

$$\tilde{Y}_t = \beta_{21}\tilde{Y}_{t-1} + \beta_{22}\left\{ \underbrace{\beta_{10} + \beta_{11}\Delta lny_{t-1} + \beta_{12}L^i\pi_t + \beta_{13}L^i\left(\Delta lnm_t\right)}_{\text{anticipated AD shock}} \right\}$$

$$+\beta_{23}\left\{ \underbrace{\Delta \ln\left(y_t\right) - \beta_{10} - \beta_{11}\Delta lny_{t-1} - \beta_{12}L^i\left(\pi_t\right) - \beta_{13}L^i\left(\Delta lnm_t\right)}_{u_t : \text{unanticipated AD Shock}} \right\}$$

$$+\beta_{24}\left\{L^i r_t^l - L^i r_t^s\right\} + \psi_t, \qquad (9.2a)$$

where the first and the second terms are substituted in from Eq. (9.1a). Here, we have cross-equation restrictions on the parameters. So the real output gap is influenced by the anticipated and unanticipated aggregate demand shocks, and the last term is the slope of the yield curve.

Similarly, under the New Keynesian specification:

$$\tilde{Y}_t = \beta_{21}\tilde{Y}_{t-1} + \beta_{22}\left\{ \underbrace{\beta_{10} + \beta_{11}\Delta lny_{t-1} + \beta_{12}L^i\pi_t}_{\text{anticipated AD shock}} \right\}$$

$$+\beta_{23}\left\{ \underbrace{\Delta \ln\left(y_t\right) - \beta_{10} - \beta_{11}\Delta lny_{t-1} - \beta_{12}L^i\pi_t}_{u_t : \text{unanticipated AD Shock}} \right\} + \beta_{24}\left\{L^i r_t^l - L^i r_t^s\right\} + \psi_t, \quad (9.2b)$$

where $\tilde{Y}_t$ is the *real* output gap measured by log real GDP deviation from a Hodrick–Prescott (HP) filter trend. There are a number of methods to estimate the trend. We choose the HP because it is commonly used in this literature.[2] So the output gap is a function of own lagged value to account for persistence, if any, and inside the first and second curly parentheses are the *anticipated* and *unanticipated* aggregate demand shocks from Eqs (9.1a) and (9.1b); hence, cross-equation restrictions are imposed and tested. We test $\beta_{21} < 1$, and $\beta_{22} = 0$. Under the RE theory assumption, anticipated aggregate demand shocks (anticipated monetary policy) have no real effect. However, only unanticipated aggregate demand shocks, that is, a surprise monetary policy, have a real effect, thus, $\beta_{23} > 0$; and it is significant under the RE theory specification.

The last explanatory variable is the slope of the yield curve defined as the difference between the 10-year government bond rate r_t^l and the federal fund rate *ffr* for the short-term interest rate r_t^s. There is a macroeconomic and finance literature on the relationship between the slope of the yield curve and GDP in the United States. These two literatures are outside the scope of this chapter. However, the general premise is that among the disagreements between finance and macroeconomics on the role of the slope of the yield curve is one about the direction of causality. There is a wide belief among economists and market analysts that the inversion of the yield curve, i.e., when the Fed increases the federal funds rate like now and the slope becomes negative, signals the Fed's intention to slow down the economy in order to bring inflation down. The long-term government bond rate is quite a complex variable to interpret. It may signal an increase in risk and anticipated inflation. There are forecasting issues and puzzles. For more on this issue, see Campbell (1995), Rudebusch and Williams (2009), and Diebold and Rudebusch (2013), for example.

Finally, the Phillips curve equation:

$$
\pi_t = \beta_{30} \underbrace{\left\{ \beta_{10} + \beta_{11}\Delta lny_{t-1} + \beta_{12}L^i\left(\pi_t\right) + \beta_{13}L^i\left(\Delta lnm_t\right) \right.}_{\pi_t^e}
$$
$$
\left. + \beta_{31}\tilde{Y}_t + \beta_{32}L^i\left(\Delta lnP_t^o\right) + \varepsilon_t, \right.
$$

(9.3a)

where the terms inside the curly bracket are the variables in the information set at time

$t-1$, see Eq. (9.1a). Under this RE specification, β_{30} should be equal to 1 so we test $\beta_{30} = 1$. Note that there is a joint-hypothesis problem here. A rejection of β_{30} equal to 1 means rejecting the long-run *vertical* Phillips curve and also rejecting the assumptions that inflation expectations are rational. Disentangling these two things is impossible, for me at least. Furthermore, note that these aggregate demand shifters are weakly correlated or uncorrelated with inflation in successful inflation-targeting courtiers and also when inflation is stable for a long period of time, which may make them poor predictors in macro models.

The price of oil *(Pᵒ)* affects the short-run aggregate supply curve and could have a significant *second round effect* on the inflation rate. Oil prices alone do not cause

---

2 The Baxter and King's (1999) Band-Pass filter removes a lot more noise from the data, but we lose some observations during the measurement. The optimal Band-Pass filter, of (Christiano and Fitzgerald, 2003), as a full-sample asymmetric frequency-domain filter is just as good.

226 *Estimating the Phillips Curve*

inflation. A second-round effect on inflation is associated with a relatively looser monetary policy. In Japan, for example, during the first oil price shock in 1973 and the second in 1979, inflation increased in 1973 but not in 1979. In the United States, monetary policy was very loose in 1979–1980 and until Volker's disinflation policy kicked in. We also test two dummy variables to account for these oil price shocks in 1973 and in 1979. The output gap must have a positive impact on the current inflation rate, thus, $\beta_{31} > 0$, so we test $\beta_{31} = 0$.

For the New Keynesian specification of the Phillips curve, we estimate the system of Eqs (9.1b), (9.2b), and (9.3b).

$$\pi_t = \beta_{30}\underbrace{\pi_{t-1}}_{\pi_t^e} + \beta_{34}\tilde{Y}_t + \beta_{35}L^i\left(\Delta lnP_t^o\right) + \varepsilon_t, \tag{9.3b}$$

where we test the hypothesis that $\beta_{30} = 1$. Blanchard (2016) shows that a similar backward specification holds well in the US data. He estimates a regression with time-varying coefficients, where the expected inflation is a linear combination of a long-term expected inflation, which depends on average lagged inflation and a short-term expected inflation that is a function of lagged average inflation. Such specification seems reasonable, even rational, but not necessarily correct, during periods of low and stable inflation. The policymaker and the economic agent, too, might believe that the best predictor of tomorrow's inflation is current inflation when inflation is kept low and stable for a long time.

Identifications of the system's parameters require that the order and rank conditions are satisfied. See Appendix 9.1. All the data are taken from the Federal Reserve Bank of St. Louis (FRED). We plot the data used in the estimation of the systems in Fig. 9.4.

Visually, there are spikes in nominal GDP, money, inflation, and the output gap at the end of the sample, and inflation and the interest rates have trends.[3]

Now we estimate the system of equations. We estimate model specification (1), which is Eqs (9.1a), (9.2a), and (9.3a) and model specification (2), which includes Eqs (9.1b), (9.2b), and (9.3b) separately using ML, with diagonal residual covariance matrix; the estimates are asymptotically normal with coefficient covariance computed using the partitioned inverse of the outer product of the gradient of the full likelihood (OPG) or the inverse of the negative of the observed Hessian of the concentrated likelihood. We use the Huber–White sandwich with both the OPG and the inverse negative Hessian and the optimization method Broyden–Fletcher–Goldfarb–Shanno (BFGS)–Marquardt. Table 9.3 reports two regression results.

---

3 The ADF test, with and without constant and trend, suggest that we cannot reject the null hypothesis of unit root in the *quarterly* federal fund rate and the inflation data. The *P*-values for the federal fund rate are 0.2178 and 0.2115 and for the inflation data, 0.4370 and 0.0468. The inflation data may or may not be I(0), probably fractionally integrated with d = 0.80.

Estimating the Phillips Curve 227

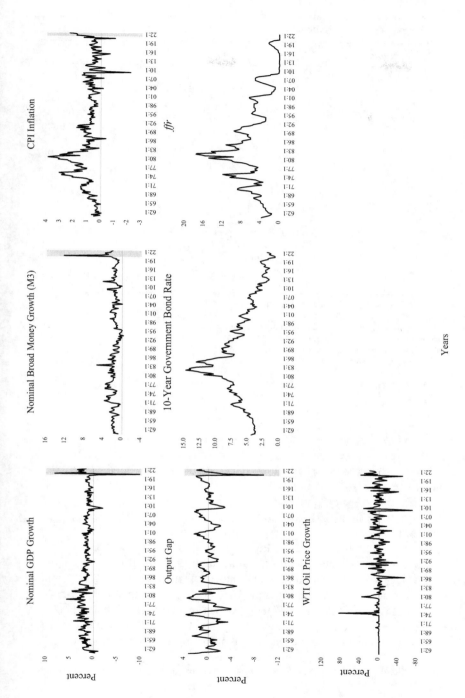

Figure 9.4 Quarterly Growth Rate of the Variables Used to Estimate the US Phillips Curve System (%)
Data Source: FRED

228　*Estimating the Phillips Curve*

Table 9.3 Maximum Likelihood Estimates of the *Quarterly* US Phillips Curve, September 1960 to March 2022

	Model (1)		Model (2)	
	Coef.	*Prob.*	*Coef.*	*Prob.*
β_{10}	0.65	0.0000	1.02	0.0000
β_{11}	0.07	0.0798	0.09	0.0240
β_{12}	0.57	0.0000	0.39	0.0000
β_{13}	0.14	0.0002	–	–
β_{21}	0.99	[0.7835]	1.03	[0.2265]
β_{22}	−0.03	0.5180	−0.08	0.0455
β_{23}	0.83	0.0000	0.81	0.0000
β_{24}	0.04	0.1037	0.10	0.0000
β_{30}	0.63	[0.0000]	0.91	[0.0093]
β_{31}	0.07	0.0008	0.06	0.0183
β_{32}	0.005	0.0339	−0.006	0.0882
β_{33}	0.31	0.0955	0.28	0.1144
β_{34}	1.00	0.0000	0.38	0.0330
LL	−664.6		−657.9	
DRC	0.038		0.032	

– The system of Eqs (9.1a), (9.2a), and (9.3a) with lag L^i, $i = 1$
– The system of Eqs (9.1b), (9.2b), and (9.3b) with lag L^i, $i = 1$
– Residuals covariance matrix restricted to be diagonal in FIML.
– Optimization method is BFGS. Step method is Marquardt.
– Coefficient covariance method is Huber–White.
– LL is log of the likelihood function.
– DRC is the determinant of the residuals covariance.
– The *P*-values of the Wald Chi-Squared test for testing the coefficient equal to 1 are in square brackets.

We tried more lags, but we report the estimates of a system with one lag (i.e., L^i, where $i = 1$) because we do not find significant differences in the magnitudes of the coefficients when the lag specifications change from 1 to 4, 6, and 8 lags. More lags run into degrees-of-freedom problems.

The coefficients β_{11} and β_{12} of the variables in the aggregate demand Eqs (9.1a) (model 1) and (9.1b) (model 2) are positive and statistically significant, and β_{13}, the coefficient of the growth rate of money, is significant in model (1).

In both specifications (1 and 2) of Eqs (9.2a) and (9.2b), the coefficient of the lagged output gap β_{21} is statistically insignificantly different from 1. The Wald statistic *P*-values to test the null that $\beta_{21} = 1$ indicate that we cannot reject the null. This size of the coefficient is larger than we anticipated, given that the output gap is I(0) by construction.[4] (Lucas, 1973) argued that this coefficient should be < 1. However, Lucas used the growth rate of real GDP, not the output gap in his regression. Nonetheless, this estimated coefficient is suspiciously large in magnitude.

4　All commonly used tests for unit root, with different specifications, indicate that we can reject the unit root in the HP-filter measure of the output gap.

Estimating the Phillips Curve 229

Most important is the fact that in models (1) and (2), the *anticipated* aggregate demand shock's coefficient β_{22} is statistically insignificant, more so in model (1), which is consistent with the predictions of the RE theory: *anticipated aggregate demand shocks do not have real effect*s. McCallumm (1981), which is a modified (Sargent and Wallace, 1975) model, incorporated price stickiness and explained why the *policy ineffectiveness* remains true under a New Keynesian sticky-price model too. Each period, the market price adjusts to the equilibrium market price only if the equilibrium price is perceived to be far from the expected value because the cost of keeping such price unchanged exceeds the lump-sum cost of the revision. Otherwise, McCallum had the price equal to the price expected last period. He shows that under such assumption, the *policy ineffectiveness* proposition of (Sargent and Wallace, 1975) remains intact, but not in our case.

In both model specifications, the *unanticipated* aggregate demand shock's coefficient β_{23} is large, 0.83, 0.81, and statistically significant, which is consistent with the predictions of the RE theory that only surprise monetary policy (unanticipated demand shocks) has real effects. The coefficient of the slope of the yield curve β_{24} is marginally significant in model (1), but it is twice as large in magnitude in model (2) and statistically significant.

The coefficient of expected inflation β_{30} is smaller than 1 in model (1) than model (2), the values being 0.62 and 0.91, respectively. The *P*-values of the Wald statistic reject the null hypothesis that β_{30} is equal to 1 in both models. A coefficient value less than 1 in model (1) suffers from a joint-hypothesis problem. The rejection of the hypothesis that β_{30} is equal to 1 is a rejection of both the long-run vertical Phillips curve and the assumption of RE theory. It is difficult to disentangle these two assumptions. We tried adding more variables such as total private credit growth and government consumption expenditures to the right-hand-side of Eq. (9.1a), which also appear in Eq. (9.3a), and re-estimated the system, but β_{30} remained equal to 0.62. The difference between the Phillips curve specifications in Eqs (9.3a) and (9.3b) is that inflation is a function of lagged inflation *only* in the latter equation, and the estimated coefficient is less than 1.

It is important to understand the implications of assuming $\pi_t^e = \alpha\pi_{t-1}$, with $\alpha < 1$. It means that the economic agents systematically lag behind in their expectations of inflation, that is, systematically underpredict inflation. When expected inflation is a function of lagged inflation $\pi_t^e = a\pi_{t-1}$ (or something like $\pi_t^e = a\pi_{t-1} + b\pi_{t-1}^e$), the expected inflation would be less than actual if $a < 1$ and $b < 1$. For example, let expected inflation be 0 in period 1, 1 percent in period 2, 2 percent in period 2, and 3 percent in period 3, and so on. Let $a = b = 0.50$. Expected inflation is 0 if last-period inflation is 0. Expected inflation in the next period is 1 while the actual is 2 percent, then 1.25 while the actual is 2.125 percent, and so on. Therefore, the economic agent or the central bank never learns or adjusts, contrary to the first-principle experiments in economics shown in (Vernon Smith and Bart Wilson, 2019), which describe agents' continuous adjustments of prices and quantities until they arrive at the optimal utility – maximizing market equilibrium levels. There is a

230 *Estimating the Phillips Curve*

reasonably large literature on learning and RE theory, see for example (Cogley and Sargent, 2005b) among many important articles.

It might be rational, however, for the Fed to assume that the expected inflation is proportional to last period's inflation because it successfully targeted low and stable inflation for a long time and when the correlation between money growth and inflation has been declining for a long time. This expectation formation would systematically underpredict future inflation, nonetheless. Figure 9.5 shows that during those years, the relationship between money growth and inflation deteriorated. We label the dates, where there is a significant distance from the 45° line.

The other important result is that the coefficient of the output gap β_{31}, however, is small in magnitude, 0.06 and 0.07, and statistically significant in both model specifications. It suggests that a 1 percent increase in the output increases inflation by 0.06–0.07 percent only. Therefore, most of the explanation of inflation is done by expected inflation, whether it is lagged inflation or a broader measure. The model fits the data.

The dummy variables for the first and second oil price shocks are significant, but the price of oil is insignificant under the New Keynesian specification in model (2). Oil prices affect the general price *level* but do not cause inflation; they might, however, have what we call a second-round effect, that is, affect the inflation rate,

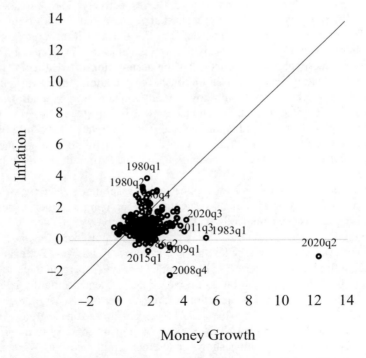

Figure 9.5 45° Line Scatter Plot of Money Growth and Inflation in the United States, March 1961 to March 2022

only when monetary and fiscal policies are accommodating (expansionary). Inflation could increase in times when policy is relatively loose at the time of the oil price shock.

Figure 9.6a plots the residuals of model (1), and Figure 9.6b plots the residuals of model (2). The Phillips curve equation in model specification (2) clearly shows it fits the data better than model specification (1) because lagged inflation has soaked up all the serial correlation. *We noted earlier that the US quarterly inflation data from 1960 to 2022 may not be stationary.*[5]

Re-estimating the system over the period up to December 2019, that is, excluding the last 3 years, which witnessed an explosive increase in money growth, the skewness and kurtosis statistics improve. The turbulent economic conditions from COVID-19 and the explosive fiscal and monetary expansions might explain the non-normality of the residuals, especially the kurtosis statistic in the full sample.

The Lucas critique requires a policy rule in the model in order to show how it would affect the coefficients of the model. The problem is that neither the Fed nor any other central bank has ever used instrument's rules. We could easily incorporate the Taylor rule or nominal GDP-targeting rule or even an X-percent money growth, but that will not add any new information or change any parameter significantly. Therefore, next, we want to show that expectation formation such as the New Keynesian specification of the Phillips curve, no matter how rational it might be, fails to predict rising inflation. We already know the algebra, which we discussed earlier, but we want to show the effect on the actual data.

We solve the models (1 and 2) and generate *in-sample dynamic stochastic projections* of inflation and the output gap from September 1960 to March 2022. The innovations are generated using normal random numbers by bootstrapping 10,000 times. The method is described in Appendix 9.2. Then we compare the predicted *mean dynamic stochastic projections*. Figure 9.7a and Figure 9.7b plot actual inflation, the mean dynamic stochastic projection, and the upper and lower 95 percent confidence intervals.

Under model (2) specification, *the projection drifts downward continuously with the standard errors widening as time increases*. Figure 9.8 plots actual inflation, the mean dynamic stochastic projections of model specification (1), and model specification (2) *without the confidence interval*s in order to show the differences.

Table 9.4 reports descriptive statistics. The differences are self-explanatory.

We may conclude that the Phillips curve specification, where inflation is a function of lagged inflation and the output gap, holds well in the US quarterly data; however, dynamic stochastic (in-sample) projections show significant uncertainty around inflation under such expectation's formation. The dynamic stochastic projection is inferior to that obtained from model specification (1), which has included only one additional variable, that is, money growth. Lucas and Sargent (1979) already concluded that backward looking modeling of inflation expectations could not be useful as guides for policy. Note that we are not evaluating a particular

---

5 The inflation data are not unit root, but maybe nonstationary fractionally integrated.

232 Estimating the Phillips Curve

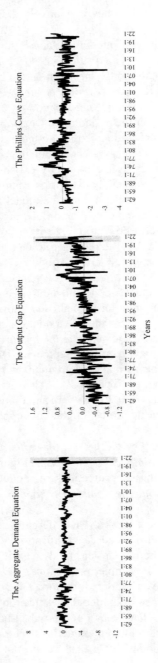

Figure 9.6a Residuals – Model Specification (1)

Estimating the Phillips Curve 233

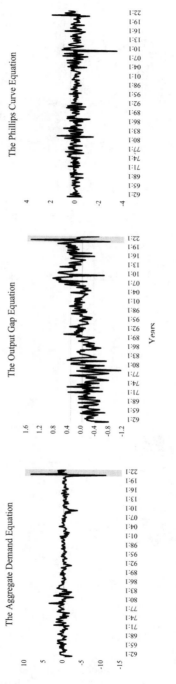

Figure 9.6b Residuals – Model Specification (2)

234 *Estimating the Phillips Curve*

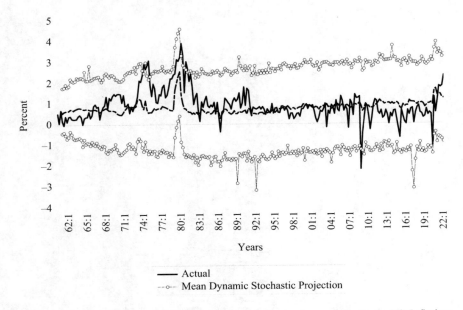

Figure 9.7a Actual and Mean Dynamic Stochastic Projections of Quarterly US Inflation: Model (1) – RE Specifications: Phillips Curve

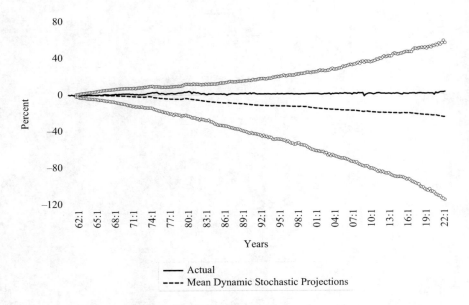

Figure 9.7b Actual and Mean Dynamic Stochastic Projections of Quarterly US Inflation: Model (2) – New Keynesian Specifications: Phillips Curve

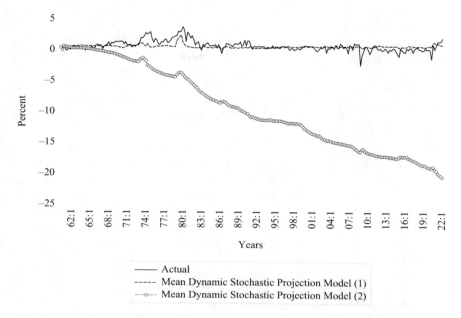

Figure 9.8 Actual Inflation and Mean Dynamic Stochastic Projections for Model (1) and Model (2)

Table 9.4 Descriptive Statistics of Dynamic Stochastic Projections of Models (1) and (2): Actual and Mean Dynamic Stochastic Projections

	Actual	Model (1)	Model (2)
Mean	0.91	0.79	−9.27
Median	0.70	0.76	−10.67
Maximum	3.91	2.55	0.69
Minimum	−2.18	0.07	−20.25
Standard deviation	0.75	0.27	6.49
Skewness	0.85	2.53	0.13
Kurtosis	5.80	14.77	1.63
Observations	248	248	248

past monetary policy action today using current data sets, which have been revised several times before. It is worth remembering that (Orphanides', 2001) argument of using *real time data* is more appropriate if one wants to evaluate past monetary policy.

These statistics suggest that if expected inflation in the Phillips curve is backward looking, measured by lagged inflation, the Fed cannot foresee rising inflation. Projected inflation would be drifting downward as the forecasting horizon increases. This might explain why no one saw inflation coming.

236 *Estimating the Phillips Curve*

Lucas (1977, p. 15) stated that as far as business cycles can be viewed as repeated instances of essentially similar events, it will be reasonable to assume that expectations are rational, that people have fairly stable arrangements for collecting and processing information, and that they utilize this information in forecasting the future in a stable way, free of systematic and easily correctable biases. It seems that the Fed, and economic agents who carefully study the Fed's policy reactions, learned about how inflation expectations have been anchored over the past decades and, perhaps, *rationally* decided to assume that the best forecast of tomorrow's inflation is today's inflation plus a random noise.

Blanchard (2016) showed evidence for the US Phillips curve, where inflation expectation is a function of lagged *average* inflation rate. Such expectations of formation equations would not enable the Fed to foresee rising inflation as far as the coefficient β_{30} is <1. It would not serve the policymaker either because *the lags are long and variable*, thus policy must be forward looking in order to affect the output gap first then inflation. One might conjecture that the lags are relatively longer in a system of low and stable inflation such as successful inflation-targeting system than say in non-inflation-targeting systems. Thus, monetary policy might take a much longer time to affect the real economy than say in a high-inflation environment. The Fed should have anticipated inflation earlier and raised the federal funds rate much earlier; assuming that raising the interest rate is the correct policy move.

Consider the following three possible explanations for why the Fed assumes expected inflation is equal or proportional to lagged inflation, ignoring information about money, government spending etc., in the information set. First, the Fed succeeded in targeting low and stable inflation for a long time and anchored inflation expectations; therefore, the policymaker might feel confident that the best predictor of tomorrow's inflation is today's.

Second, the Phillips curve predicts that inflation can only be brought down if the economy slows down or goes into a recession; therefore, a model with fully forward looking inflation expectations cannot generate the necessary (cycles) recessions they want. There is a required *inertia* in the New Keynesian models to generate business cycles, which could not be possible with RE. Furthermore, economic agents who watch the central bank, and supposedly learn about the process of how it models and targets inflation, may also rationally accept the Fed's view that the best predictor of tomorrow's inflation is today's inflation plus a random error. This belief arises from observing the Fed's credibly stabilizing inflation for a long period. Thus, the economic agents are equally unable to forecast the rise in inflation that we have been experiencing. Again, I remind you that these monetary lags could be relatively longer in inflation-targeting countries.

Third, the Fed pursues active discretionary monetary policy; therefore, it cannot afford to have fully forward-looking expectations formation and in particular rational expectations in the model, and it cannot even assume that agents form expectations rationally, because under rational expectations, monetary policy is *ineffective* in stimulating the economy. Note that even if the Fed follows a monetary policy *rule* rather than a discretionary monetary policy, it would remain unable to forecast the rise in inflation under such expectations formation model.

Estimating the Phillips Curve 237

Therefore, in addition to the specification of inflation expectation, an activist and doctrinaire monetary policy is not useful. No one knows, and we will not know the *true data-generating-process* of inflation. There are many different models of inflation other than the Phillips curve. However, even if the Fed decided to change its model, *active policies* will continue to alter the time series properties of the data. This activism breaks up the correlation between inflation and whatever explanatory variables are assumed. If the Fed uses the Phillips curve indeed, then to nip inflation in the bud, the Fed should have anticipated inflation earlier and tightened monetary conditions much earlier. They failed to do so. Assuming expected inflation to be proportional or equal to last period's inflation is not an innocuous assumption for monetary policy.

For robustness, we want to estimate the aforementioned system for another country. We estimate a similar system for New Zealand. New Zealand data are the most interesting. The Reserve Bank of New Zealand (RBNZ) has data from March 1988 to June 2022. The disinflation period from 1988 is striking, where inflation dropped very fast and the variance reduced significantly. Therefore, for estimating the Phillips curve, we choose a sample that covers the stable inflation period from March 1992 to June 2022. In 1992, the RBNZ completely stabilized inflation at a low level. We mentioned earlier in this book that New Zealand's inflation target was changed twice over that time by the government. The law gives the elected politicians the right to do so. The target was 0 to 2 percent from 1989 to 1996 then changed to 1 to 3 percent. Subsequent governments changed the objective of the RBNZ from the one primary objective of *price stability* to a wider objective, which included *stable exchange rate* once then to price stability and *maximum sustainable employment* recently. The exchange rate is highly variable in New Zealand, especially before 2002, because the RBNZ never intervened in this market under the Governorship of Don Brash, and the freely floating exchange rate fluctuated and acted as a shock absorber. For more, see the history of the REMIT and Policy Targets Agreements on the Reserve Bank of New Zealand website, 2022. Like the Fed and other central banks in inflation-targeting countries, the RBNZ did not foresee inflation rising; therefore, it tightened monetary conditions by raising the *official cash rate* (OCR) from 0.75 percent in early 2022 to reach 3 percent in August 2022.

We already showed that New Zealand's inflation over that sample is I(0), and the correlation between money growth and inflation is very weak. The correlation between money growth and nominal GDP growth is relatively stronger but still unjustified to have it as an explanatory variable in Eq. (9.1), see Figures 9.9a and 9.9b. Figure 9.9c plots the 95 Percent Chi-Squared Confidence Ellipse test for nominal government expenditures and nominal GDP growth and shows relatively stronger positive correlation. Government expenditure is a good alternative to money in the aggregate demand equation.

The system we estimate for New Zealand covers the period from March 1992 to June 2022. We "modified" the system, which we estimated for the United States as follows: there are a couple of differences in Eqs (9.1), (9.2), and (9.3), in both models (1 and 2). First, money is excluded entirely because the fit is poor as shown in the scatter plots before.

238 *Estimating the Phillips Curve*

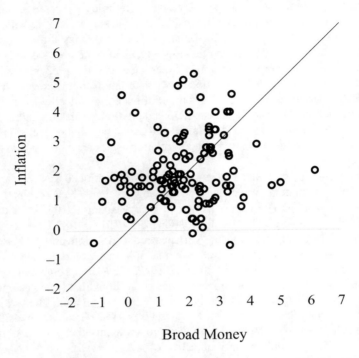

Figure 9.9a 45° Line Scatter Plot of New Zealand's Broad Money Growth and Inflation, March 1992 to December 2021

Data Source: RBNZ

We already explained why that is. Government expenditures are used instead of money. The RBNZ has financed the government budget deficits by issuing new money lately. Therefore, the coefficients in the aggregate demand equation are β_{10}, β_{11}, β_{12}, and β_{13} are those of a constant term, the lagged dependent variable (nominal expenditure's side nominal GDP), lagged inflation, and lagged government spending growth rate, respectively. The output gap equation does not include the slope of the yield curve because it is negatively correlated with the output gap, see Figure 9.10d. We do not have an explanation for this negative correlation; it could be a misspecification issue or a more complicated explanation beyond the scope of this essay.[6]

We have two dummy variables, and β_{32} is the coefficient of the dummy variable that takes a value of 1 during the GFC in Sep 2008. The Asian Financial Crisis (AFC) is not accounted for because inflation was declining rapidly. The coefficient

---

[6] Scatter plots of the OCR, the 90-day rate, and the 10-year government bond rate against the output gap show insignificant association. Even four-quarter lagged OCR is uncorrelated with the output gap. These are very peculiar results because the OCR is the RBNZ instrument. We do not report these scatter plots, but we are happy to provide them if requested.

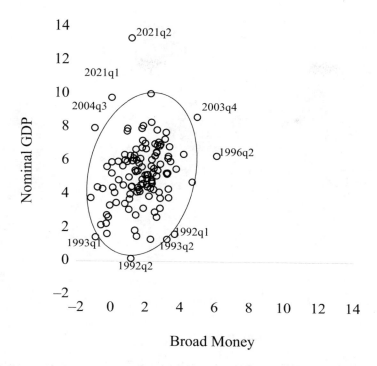

Figure 9.9b 95 Percent Chi-Square Confidence Ellipse Test of New Zealand's Broad Money and Nominal GDP Growth Rates, March 1992 to September 2021

Data Source: RBNZ

β_{33} is for the dummy variable that takes a value of 1 during the Christchurch earthquake in June 2011. Table 9.5 reports the results.

New Zealand's estimates favor the New Keynesian specification of the Phillips curve. The *anticipated* and *unanticipated* aggregate demand shock effects β_{22} and β_{23} are consistent with the predictions of the RE theory, whereby β_{22} is insignificant and β_{23} is significant. The coefficient β_{30} is significantly different from 1 in model (1), which is similar to the US case; therefore, we reject the hypothesis that there is a long-run vertical Phillips curve, but because it is a joint-hypothesis problem, we reject the RE assumption too. Hence, we are unable to disentangle these two things. In model (2), however, β_{30} is statistically indifferent from 1. The output gap is significant under both specifications with a small magnitude similar to those found in the US data, 0.06–0.08; thus a 1 percent increase or decrease in the output does not increase and decrease inflation by much – 0.06 percent to 0.08 percent. The GFC and Christchurch earthquake were inflationary.[7] Most of the explanation

---

[7] The Christchurch earthquake was a devastating event that disrupted the economy for a long time. The rebuilding process was costly.

240 *Estimating the Phillips Curve*

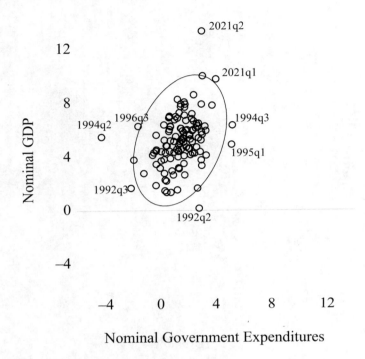

Figure 9.9c 95 Percent Chi-Square Confidence Ellipse Test of New Zealand's Growth Rates of Nominal Government Expenditures and GDP(e), March 1992 to December 2021

Note: GDP(e) is Expenditure Side Measure.
Data Source: RBNZ

of inflation is accomplished by expected inflation, whether it is lagged inflation or a broader measure.

We solve the model just like we did with the US model and show how mean dynamic stochastic projections look like under these two model specifications (1 and 2). Having expected inflation proportional to lagged inflation with a coefficient less than 1 always results in the underprediction of inflation and, thus, unanticipated rise in inflation. The monetary authority's response to unforeseen inflation is delayed, and the consequences of delayed policy tightening policy will be unpleasant. The RBNZ has started a series of strong policy tightening. Figures 9.10a, 9.10b, and 9.10c plot the actual mean dynamic stochastic projections of models (1), (2), and (1 and 2) together.

Table 9.6 reports the descriptive statistics of the actual and mean dynamic stochastic projections of models (1) and (2).

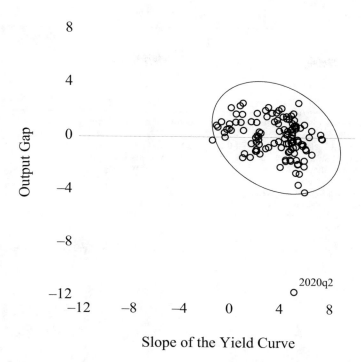

Figure 9.9d 95 Percent Chi-Square Confidence Ellipse Test of New Zealand's Slope of the Yield Curve and the Output Gap, March 1992 to December 2021

Data Source: RBNZ

Table 9.5 Maximum Likelihood Estimates of the *Quarterly* NZ Phillips Curve, March 1992 to June 2022

	Model (1)		Model (2)	
	Coefficient	Probability	Coefficient	Probability
β_{10}	0.44	0.1073	6.15	0.0000
β_{11}	0.01	0.2624	−0.14	0.2554
β_{12}	1.58	0.0000	–	–
β_{13} [i]	0.05	0.0438	–	–
β_{21}	0.73	0.0000	0.67	0.0000
β_{22}	−0.006	0.7621	0.003	0.9077
β_{23}	0.11	0.0000	0.12	0.0000
β_{30}	0.52	[0.0000]	0.96	[0.1898]
β_{31}	0.06	0.0363	0.08	0.0118
β_{32} [ii]	1.25	0.0000	1.21	0.0000
β_{33} [iii]	1.14	0.0000	1.05	0.0000

(*Continued*)

Table 9.5 (Continued)

	Model (1)		Model (2)	
	Coefficient	Probability	Coefficient	Probability
LL	−1313.8		−1456.0	
DRC	41.00		41.95	

[i] Lagged nominal growth rate of government expenditures instead of money.
[ii] Dummy variable for GFC.
[iii] Dummy variable for Christchurch earthquake in June 2011.
- The system of the *modified* Eqs (9.1a), (9.2a), and (9.3a) with lag L^i, $i = 1$, see the modifications be.
- The system of the *modified* Eqs (9.1b), (9.2b), and (9.3b) with lag L^i, $i = 1$, see the modifications before.
- Residuals covariance matrix restricted to be diagonal in FIML.
- Optimization method is BFGS. Step method is Marquardt.
- Coefficient covariance method is Huber–White.
- LL is log of the likelihood function.
- DRC is the determinant of the residuals covariance.
- The *P*-values of Wald Chi-Squared for testing the coefficient equal to 1 are in square brackets.

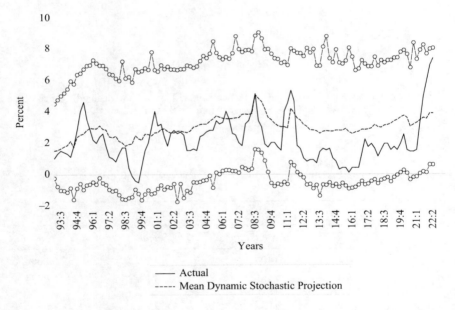

Figure 9.10a Actual and Mean Dynamic Stochastic Projections of New Zealand Quarterly Inflation: Model (1) – RE Specifications: Phillips Curve

The conclusion we have reached earlier using the US data remains unchanged, if expected inflation is proportional or equal to lagged inflation, that is, a backward-looking expectation, the New Keynesian Phillips curve specification fits the data well.

Estimating the Phillips Curve 243

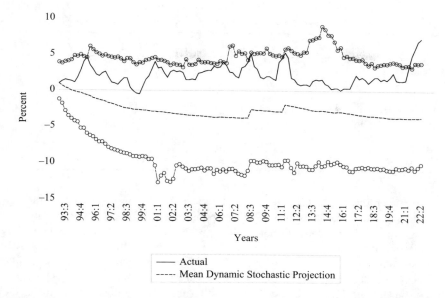

Figure 9.10b Actual and Mean Dynamic Stochastic Projections of New Zealand Quarterly Inflation: Model (1) – New Keynesian Specifications: Phillips Curve

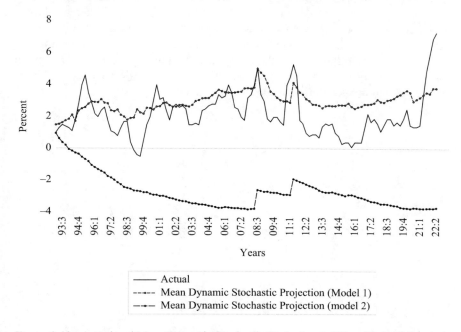

Figure 9.10c Actual and Mean Dynamic Stochastic Projections of New Zealand Quarterly Inflation: Model (1) – RE and Model (2) New Keynesian Specifications: Phillips Curve

244 *Estimating the Phillips Curve*

Table 9.6 Descriptive Statistics of New Zealand Actual Inflation and Mean Dynamic Stochastic Projections of Models (1) and (2), March 1993 to June 2022

	Actual	*Model (1)*	*Model (2)*
Mean	2.14	2.97	−2.73
Median	1.80	2.90	−2.91
Maximum	7.30	5.04	0.96
Minimum	−0.50	1.49	−3.81
Standard Deviation	1.38	0.63	1.07
Skewness	1.09	0.27	1.53
Kurtosis	4.82	3.77	4.89
Observations	118	118	118

However, even if this specification of expected inflation is considered rational because of the RBNZ's successful inflation targeting rendering inflation stable for a long time, it is the wrong formation of expectations because it leads to the under-prediction of inflation. Such a view, we believe, explains the unanticipated inflation we have seen lately in New Zealand. *Active* monetary policy means that the RBNZ has to tighten policy to reduce the output gap, which would reduce inflation according to the Phillips curve. It means that the RBNZ must act earlier to the anticipated inflation, because the policy *lags are long and variable*. Such speci-fication (i.e., expected inflation equals past inflation) would make it impossible for the RBNZ to predict rising inflation. When policymakers are taken by surprise with rising inflation at time t, they react late and strong to bring inflation down. In other words, they raise the policy interest late and more. Indeed, we are witnessing a strong reaction to inflation by the RBNZ and by almost all central banks in the inflation-targeting countries, and the ramifications could be devastating worldwide recessions and financial markets' instability if not crisis.

Appendix 9.1

Order and Rank Conditions for Identifying the System

The way to compute the order condition, which is a necessary but insufficient condition, is to list the number of variables and the number of equations like this:

Model (1)

Equation	Δlny_t	Δlny_{t-1}	$\tilde{Y}_t$	$\tilde{Y}_{t-1}$	π_t	ΔlnM_{t-1}	π_{t-1}	$r^l_t - r^s_t$	ΔlnP^o_t	d_73	d_79
1	*	*	0	0	0	*	*	0	0	0	0
2	*	*	*	*	0	*	*	*	0	0	0
3	0	*	*	0	*	*	*	0	*	*	*

The number of equations $G = 3$. Let k be the number of zeros in each row. These are the variables, which are not in the equation. The order condition implies that $k > G - 1$; therefore, the system is over-identified. The rank condition is to delete the row and pick up the column that has zeros. For the first row, we would be left with a matrix whose rank $> G - 1$.

Model (2)

	Δlny_t	Δlny_{t-1}	$\tilde{Y}_t$	$\tilde{Y}_{t-1}$	π_t	ΔlnM_{t-1}	π_{t-1}	$r^l_t - r^s_t$	ΔlnP^o_t	d_73	d_79
1	*	*	0	0	0	0	*	0	0	0	0
2	*	*	*	*	0	0	*	*	0	0	0
3	0	0	*	0	*	0	*	0	*	*	*

$k > G - 1$

For New Zealand:

246 *Estimating the Phillips Curve*

Model (1)

Equation	Δlny_t	Δlny_{t-1}	$\tilde{Y}_t$	$\tilde{Y}_{t-1}$	π_t	Δlng_{t-1}	π_{t-1}	d_GFC	$d_{Earth}Q$
1	*	*	0	0	0	*	*	0	0
2	*	*	*	*	0	*	*	0	0
3	0		*	0	*	*	*	*	*

$k > G - 1$

Model (2)

Equation	Δlny_t	Δlny_{t-1}	$\tilde{Y}_t$	$\tilde{Y}_{t-1}$	π_t	Δlng_{t-1}	π_{t-1}	d_GFC	$d_{Earth}Q$
1	*	*	0	0	0	0	*	0	0
2	*	*	*	*	0	*	*	0	0
3	0	0	*	0	*	0	*	*	*

Appendix 9.2
The Solver of the Model

- The method is fully described in EViews.
- We solve the model using Broyden method, which is a modified Newton's method. It involves the use of an approximation, rather than the true Jacobian when linearizing the model.
- We update the approximation at every iteration of the 5,000 iterations we used by comparing the residuals from the new trial values of the endogenous variables with the residuals predicted by the linear model on the basis of the current Jacobian approximation. This method is faster than Newton (see Dennis and Schnabel [1983]).
- We use analytic derivatives. The starting values are actual values. The model is solved both directions. We stop solving when we hit a missing value.
- In a stochastic simulation, we solve the equations of the model such that the residuals match to randomly drawn errors, and the coefficients and exogenous variables of the model change randomly. The solution generates a distribution of outcomes for the endogenous variables in every period. We approximate the distribution by solving the model many times using different draws (10,000) or the random components in the model then calculating statistics over all the different outcomes.
- Only values of the endogenous variables, which are obtained before the solution sample, are used in the dynamic solution of the projections. Lagged endogenous variables are calculated using the solutions calculated in previous periods, i.e., not from actual historical values. A series for the mean is calculated. We consider 1,000 repetitions reasonable to capture the true values; however, some random variation may be present between adjacent observations.
- The 95 percent confidence intervals are computed using (Jain and Chlamtac, 1985) updating algorithm. This updating algorithm provides a reasonable estimate of the tails of the underlying distribution as long as the number of repetitions is not too small.
- We use bootstrapped innovations; however, bootstrapped innovations drawn from a small sample provide a rough approximation to the true underlying distribution of the innovations. For the diagonal covariance matrix, the diagonal elements are set to zero. We do not scale the variances.

10 The "Newer" Theories and Models of Inflation

Abstract

We discuss a number of relatively new models of inflation and empirically test the policy recommendation of Modern Monetary Theory (MMT) to reduce inflation via higher taxes. We provide a micro-foundation model to derive an equilibrium labor supply, estimate a VAR, provide baseline dynamic stochastic projections of key economic variables of the model, and then compare the outcomes with scenarios of MMT policy recommendations.

After a very long pause since Phillips, Fisher, Friedman, and Phelps, many leading macroeconomists decided to either formulate new monetary theories or tweak the Phillips curve for the purpose of explaining inflation. This research includes, as far as I know, the New Phillips curve, the Sticky Information Phillips curve, a couple of P* models, the Fiscal Theory of Inflation (FTOI) and the Fiscal Theory of the Price Level (FTOPL), and the Modern Monetary Theory (MMT). We will describe and discuss these models and theories in this chapter, and test the implications of the MMT policy to reduce inflation.

The New Phillips Curve

The *new* Phillips curve is based on a proxy for marginal cost changes that are associated with excess demand (Gali and Gertler, 1999; Gali *et al*. 2001; Gali *et al*. 2005). In this model, inflation depends on the expected real marginal cost (or maybe the real marginal cost's deviations from the expected real marginal cost or the deviations from steady-state, however that might be measured), expected future inflation, and lagged inflation. Note that lagged inflation is still assumed to be an explanatory variable. Think of expected inflation being partly forward-looking and partly backward-looking, maybe a linear combination of the two. In many central banks' Dynamic Stochastic General Equilibrium Model (DSGE), which is a RE model, there are *rule-of-thumb* agents, who are *myopic* in the sense that their expectation formation is backward-looking. One could imagine a model with the share of the rule-of-thumb exceeding the share of forward-looking agents. In such a case, under-predicting inflation is an assured outcome. Backward-looking expected inflation is

DOI: 10.4324/9781003382218-10

The *"Newer" Theories and Models of Inflation* 249

the typical (Romer and Romer, 1997) specification, that is, lagged inflation. This kind of specification guarantees business cycle fluctuations away from equilibrium for more periods, which is something that could not be obtained under RE.

Gali *et al.* (2005) show that the coefficient on expected future inflation substantially exceeds the coefficient on lagged inflation. While the latter differs significantly from 0, it is quantitatively modest. In this modified model, firms set nominal prices on the basis of the expectations of future marginal costs. Rotemberg and Woodford (1997) impose certain restrictions on technology and the labor market and show that the marginal cost is a function of the output gap. Clarida *et al.* (1999) argue that the longer prices are fixed on average, the less sensitive is inflation to movements in the output gap. This model is harder to estimate than the New Keynesian Phillips curve because it has to specify the expected variable, and we know from estimating the Phillips curve earlier that the specifications of expectations affect the results significantly.

Gali *et al.* (2005) write the hybrid New Phillips curve like this:

$$\pi_t = \lambda mc_t + \gamma^f E_t \pi_{t+1} + \gamma^b \pi_{t-1} + \varepsilon_t, \tag{10.1}$$

where π_t is inflation and mc_t is the *real* marginal cost deviation from trend. Following (Calvo, 1983), each firm has a probability $1-\theta$ of being able to reset its price in any given period, independently of the time elapsed since its most recent price adjustment. Thus, a fraction θ of firms keep their prices unchanged in any given period. In contrast to Calvo, however, of those firms able to adjust prices in a given period, only a fraction, $1-\omega$, sets prices optimally on the basis of expected future marginal costs. A fraction of firms ω, on the other hand, instead uses a simple rule of thumb: they set prices equal to the average of newly adjusted prices last period plus an adjustment for expected inflation, based on lagged inflation π_{t-1}.

$$\lambda = (1-\omega)(1-\theta)(1-\beta\theta)\phi^{-1}, \tag{10.2}$$

$$\gamma^f = \beta\theta\phi^{-1}, \tag{10.3}$$

$$\gamma^b = \omega\phi^{-1}, \tag{10.4}$$

where, $\phi = \theta + \omega[1 - \theta(1-\beta)]^{-1}$, and the error term ε_t picks up errors in measurement or shocks to the desired mark-up. When $\omega \to 0$ in the limits, $\gamma^b \to 0$, and $\gamma^f = \beta$, and the New Phillips curve is fully forward looking. Gali *et al.* (2005) used different estimators and showed that the baseline GMM estimates $\gamma^b = 0.349$, $\gamma^f = 0.635$, and $\lambda = 0.013$. The closed form GMM estimates $\gamma^b = 0.374$, $\gamma^f = 0.618$, and $\lambda = 0.013$. A single-equation GMM estimator is, highly probably, an inefficient estimator.

The GMM estimator used by (Gali *et al.*, 2005) has been criticized. The authors discussed the criticism of their equation specification bias arising from the GMM estimator, which refuted and showed that their estimates are robust to more than

250 *The "Newer" Theories and Models of Inflation*

one estimator. They estimated the closed-form model and showed that the estimated reduced-form parameters are consistent with the structural parameters of the model. Sbordone (2005) estimates the closed form of a similar model (using an alternative estimation technique) and reported very similar results about the forward versus backward-looking inflation expectations. There has been a question about using nonlinear estimation methods, which they did and showed the results. After all, I agree with Gali *et al.* and Sbordone that FIML and GMM are not very different estimators essentially, and GMM might be inefficient. There is a very large literature on this issue. That said, I am still unsure why marginal cost is preferred to the output gap or the unemployment. Estimating the structural model as a system, or a VAR, SVAR, BVAR, might have been my preferred strategy. Estimating a single-equation reduced-form equation is less efficient than estimating a system of equations. This model, however, has not attracted the attention of central banks.

The explanations that wages, labor costs, or marginal costs based on labor costs explain inflation are controversial. My earlier confusion was what additional gains one could have by using the marginal cost instead of the output gap? Why would replacing the output gap with the marginal costs increase our understanding of inflation? The marginal cost itself could be a function of the output gap as (Rotemberg and Woodford, 1997) explain. Regressions show correlation, which is quite understood. However, causality is another issue; it requires a solid theory. We cited Freidman and Fisher theoretical reasoning earlier, which have causality running exactly the opposite direction of the original Phillips curve. However, central bankers do not seem to accept such formulation and without providing any careful evidence repeatedly claimed that wage growth drives inflation. Furthermore, it is unclear how wages, which are sticky in the Fischer, Phelps, and Taylor Keynesian contract theory, cause the price level. It seems that wages get adjusted upward to keep up with rising prices. Wage indexation is just another observation. Theoretically, and here we are talking about microeconomic theory, real wages are equal to the marginal product of labor at the firm level. When real wages is more than marginal productivity, the producer lays off labor and that causes unemployment; when real wages less than marginal productivity, the producer hires more labor until real wages equals marginal productivity; the producer stops hiring more labor. For example (Razzak, 2015) shows that this microeconomic theory holds perfectly well in the US *macroeconomic data*. In the Keynesian models, real wages are not equal to the marginal product of labor at any time. Therefore, the cyclical fluctuations' patterns are ambiguous. This ambiguity is difficult to confirm in the US data.[1]

Figure 10.1 is a plot of the cyclical fluctuations of the US real wages obtained using the Hodrick–Prescott (HP) filter. We pass log real wages through the filter, where real wages are measured by nominal labor compensations/CPI (1960 = 100). Output is real GDP, and the cyclical fluctuations are the output gap. Real wages appear *procyclical* from 1960 to 2000. After 2000, real wages were *countercyclical*. There are no periods of *acyclical* real wages. These changes might be the results of different dominant

---

1 Wage data are most difficult to find for the countries in our sample. The quality of the data is also questionable in developed countries.

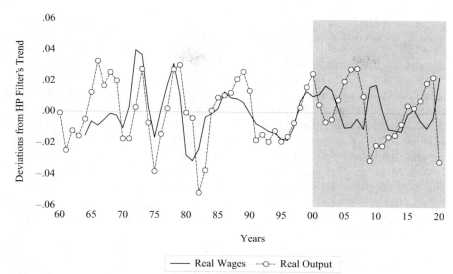

Figure 10.1 Cyclical Fluctuations of Real Wages and Real Output in the United States

Data Source: Wages are Total Compensations – FRED; Real GDP is from the World Development Indicators

shocks across periods, or policy effects, or both. The question is what happens to the expected price level such that expected real wages change like that?

Even if we accept the new formulation, where the marginal cost replaces the output gap in the Phillips curve and overcomes the problem of measurement, specification problems of the inflation expectation formation may still remain as we have shown in Chapter 9. The size of the coefficients on the backward and forward components of expected inflation may be affected by the sample size, the specification of the dynamic, and many other estimation issues. Therefore, it is not guaranteed that the forward-looking component is larger than the backward-looking one in every data set. If not, then the policymaker might run into the same underprediction of inflation and the subsequent policy consequences.

For estimation and specification issues, see (Whelan, 1999) who shows that the *Accelerationist* relationship between the change in price inflation and the unemployment rate is consistent with any type of microeconomic real-wage dynamics. However, these dynamics determine how supply shocks affect inflation. The evidence on supply shocks and inflation points against the traditional real-wage formulation.

Razzak (2003) estimates these specifications for Hong Kong and attempts to explain the deflationary period, which started before the Island became part of China in 1997, and shows that the New Phillips curve outperforms the original Phillips curve specification and other models of wage-price dynamics such as the one estimated by (Whelan, 1999). Because the marginal cost is basically unit labour cost, the model suggests that wage and productivity dynamics could play an important role in explaining price dynamics.

252　*The "Newer" Theories and Models of Inflation*

The Sticky Information Model

The other model is by (Mankiw and Reis, 2002, 2007), which brings the New Keynesian Phillips curve much closer to the expectation-augmented Phillips curve. They propose a replacement to the New Keynesian Phillips curve with one that has some dynamic, combined with the Calvo's price-setting framework. They suggest that information about the state of the economy diffuses slowly through the population either because it is costly to acquire information or it is costly to re-optimize, hence the sticky-information model. Today's price depends on expected prices that have been made in the past, not so much because of labor contracts but because some firms are still using old information to set prices (Fischer, 1977). Inflation depends on output, expectations of inflation, and expectations of output growth. The story Mankiw and Reis tell is that firms set prices of their goods every period. The firms gather information and re-compute prices slowly over time. In each period, a fraction of firms obtain new information about the state of the economy and compute a new path of optimal prices. The remaining firms continue to set prices on the basis of the old plans. Following Calvo, each firm has the *same* probability of being one of the firms updating their pricing plans regardless of how long it has been since its last update.

This model is a general equilibrium model with sticky information. Mankiw and Reis assumed rigidity in goods, labor, and financial markets, whereby agents infrequently update their information sets, when setting prices, wages, and consumption. These assumptions are sensible. They solve the model, examine the dynamics, and estimate the model for the United States. The model has five variables. They report that information stickiness is found in all markets and the stickiness is heightened for consumers and labor. The variance decomposition indicated that aggregate demand shocks account for the variance in inflation, output, and hours as expected. These proposals to replace the Keynesian Phillips curve have not attracted the Fed or other central banks. They seem to be stuck with the old Keynesian Phillips curve.

Razzak (2002) estimated the Mankiw–Rees model for New Zealand along with more than 60 different model specifications, nonetheless.[2] There should be no illusion that the same issues regarding the formation of inflation expectation, which we examined previously, would be present in these new modified models of the Phillips curve. The Phillips curve, where expected inflation is modeled as lagged inflation, underpredicts future inflation.

The P Model

There is more than one P^* model. P* is derived from the Quantity Theory of Money (QTM) under the assumption that the levels of velocity V_t and real output Y_t, though they deviate from their equilibrium levels V_t^* and Y_t^* for whatever reason (e.g., shocks), return reasonably quickly to their long-run equilibrium levels. The

---

2 (Razzak, 2002) is an application of (Granger and Jeon's, 2004) "Thick Modeling method" for forecasting inflation.

The "Newer" Theories and Models of Inflation   253

Fed's model assumes that velocity grows at a constant rate equal to its historical average, and, contrary to our evidence, output grows at a smooth *deterministic* trend. The inflation rate depends on the expected inflation rate and the deviations of the price level from P^* plus an error term.

There is another specification of the P* model, whereby the inflation rate is a function of expected inflation and the deviation of real-money balances from its long-run equilibrium. It combines the QTM and the expectation-augmented Phillips curve. Gerlach and Svensson (2003) argue that this model has a substantial predictive power for future inflation in Europe. The basic idea is to fit a Keynesian demand for real-money balances function, use the estimated long-run elasticity (the income and the interest rate elasticity) to compute the equilibrium values, then compute the money gap as the deviation of actual real-money from this long-run equilibrium.[3] (Razzak, 2002) also tested the predictability of these models using data for New Zealand. In all three models presented so far, the econometrician faces the same problems that arise from the specification of expected inflation.

The Fiscal Theory of Price Level and Inflation – FTOPL and FTOI

In order to understand this theory, we need to start with deriving the interaction between fiscal and monetary policy. In most of the developed countries, with or without explicit inflation-targeting policy, monetary policy is independent from fiscal policy. Central banks take fiscal policy as given. However, central banks do take into account the impact of spending, taxation, and debt, for example, seriously when formulating policy responses and when forecasting liquidity requirements. The central bank wants to know if there is enough cash for the government to pay its bills. The fiscal authorities are supposed to do the same.

Inflation and debt-financed fiscal spending is a classic issue of research; the former is a key objective of the central bank and the latter is a key variable in fiscal policy. Higher inflation reduces real debt. Independence notwithstanding, the two policies impact each other, and there is a scope for arriving at an optimal policy depending on the interactions of the two.

In this literature, one way to analyze the monetary–fiscal policy nexus is to study the government budget constraint, which describes the interaction of the two policies. In a very simple way, assume that there is a fiscal authority, which formulates taxing and spending decisions, and a central bank that controls the money supply. As in game theory analysis, it turned out that it matters who sets policy first because this affects the policy choices of the other player.

---

3 (Kool and Tatom, 1994) suggested a P* model for open economies. The model includes the foreign price level and imposes strong assumptions. It assumes that the exchange rate is fixed. $P^* = \dfrac{EP^* f}{ER^*}$, where E is the fixed nominal exchange rate and ER^* is the equilibrium exchange rate. $P^* f$ is the foreign P^*. It is rather difficult to estimate the equilibrium nominal exchange rate.

254 The "Newer" Theories and Models of Inflation

The Government Budget Constraint

I follow Christiano and Fitzgerald (2000) and Chugh (2015) very closely. Let the government's simplest budget constraint in period t be:

$$B_{t-1}^T + P_t g_t = T_t + P_t^b B_t^T + \Pi_t,\tag{10.5}$$

where B_{t-1}^T is the stock of government's bonds outstanding at the beginning of the period t; $P_t g_t$ is the price level P_t times the real amount of government spending g_t; T_t is the lump-sum taxes collected by the government; $P_t^b B_t^T$ is the nominal value of bonds sold in period t; and Π_t denotes the central bank's profit, which is transferred to the treasury by the end of the period. The face value of each bond is assumed to be 1.

The Central Bank Budget Constraint

Regardless of how the central bank's monetary policy is conducted, a simple budget constraint may look like this:

$$P_t^b B_t^M + \Pi_t = B_{t-1}^M + \Delta M_t,\tag{10.6}$$

The LHS of the equation has the outlays of the central bank, which are the government bonds B_t^M it buys at the market price P_t^b. We have shown earlier that there has been a significant increase in such purchases in developed countries during the period of COVID-19 because the government issued new debt financed by central bank fiat money. The second term on the LHS of the equation is the central bank's profit Π_t. On the RHS of the equation, we have the income of the central bank, which consists of matured bonds and newly created money – that is, the change in the nominal money stock. So, rearranging the equation gives the central bank's profit, $\Pi_t = B_{t-1}^M + \Delta M_t - P_t^b B_t^M$.

The Consolidated Government Budget Constraint

Putting the two constraints in Eqs (10.5) and (10.6) together gives:

$$B_{t-1}^T + P_t g_t = T_t + P_t^b B_t^T + B_{t-1}^M + \Delta M_t - P_t^b B_t^M\tag{10.7}$$

Note that we have B_t^T and B_t^M, where the former is the total amount of bonds issued by the fiscal authority, and the latter is the total amount of government bonds held by the private sector or the central banks. Note also that the central banks may keep these bonds on their balance sheets and just pay the government in newly printed money without selling them in the market. In fact, this has happened recently in New Zealand and other countries. So, $B_t = B_t^T - B_t^M$ is the amount of bonds not held by the central bank – that is, the *net* amount of debt held by the public.

The "Newer" Theories and Models of Inflation   255

Rewrite the aforementioned consolidated budget constraint as:

$$B_{t-1}^T + P_t g_t = T_t + P_t^b B_t + \Delta M_t, \tag{10.8}$$

which combines the fiscal authority and central bank activities that holds all the time. Central banks in developed countries pursue active monetary policy all the time. Let us assume that the central bank sets monetary policy before the fiscal policy is set at time t. The central bank chooses the amount of money supply M_t (as a matter of fact, central banks seem to do more than control the quantity of money; they also set the overnight interest rate). Maybe the central bank has an inflation target, where such a quantity of money is consistent with it! In this game, it is assumed that the fiscal authority plays second by reacting to such monetary policy. The fiscal authority must choose the appropriate levels of spending g_t, taxing T_t, and borrowing B_t (three instruments). It may not be able to freely choose all three levels. It might be able to choose two out of the three instruments, and the third is pinned down by the budget constraint. In this sense, the fiscal authority is a bit constrained in its policy because it could not choose all three instruments freely. However, if the central bank does not get to set the instrument first, the fiscal authority gets to choose all three fiscal instruments and leaves the central bank to decide on the money supply to ensure that the budget constraint holds.

The Intertemporal Government Budget Constraint

To analyze the dynamic, the *flow*-consolidated budget constraint shown before could be extended to be a lifetime budget constraint. The derivation is standard and all laid out in (Chugh, 2015). Divide the government budget constraint in Eq. (10.8) by the period price level P_t so that we have the real budget constraints:

$$\underbrace{\frac{B_{t-1}}{P_t}}_{\text{real g Debt}} = \underbrace{\underbrace{\frac{T_t}{P_t}}_{\text{Tax Revenues}} - g_t + \underbrace{\frac{P_t^b B_t}{P_t}}_{\text{Bond sales}}}_{\text{Net Real Revenues (deficits)}} + \underbrace{\frac{\Delta M_t}{P_t}}_{\text{Seignorage}}. \tag{10.9}$$

Simplify the notation such that *real terms* are in *lowercase*, with the term $\dfrac{\Delta M_t}{P_t}$ as the typical measure of seigniorage s_t. Thus,

$$\frac{B_{t-1}}{P_t} = \left[t_t - g_t + P_t^b b_t \right] + s_t. \tag{10.10}$$

Take the one-period lead of (10.10), then multiply through by P_{t+1}, then divide through by P_t, and make $P_{t+1}/P_t = 1 + \pi_{t+1}$, we get:

$$b_t = \left[(1 + \pi_{t+1}) t_{t+1} - (1 + \pi_{t+1}) g_{t+1} + (1 + \pi_{t+1}) P_{t+1}^b b_{t+1} \right] + (1 + \pi_{t+1}) s_{t+1}. \tag{10.11}$$

256 *The "Newer" Theories and Models of Inflation*

Substitute this value of b_t into the flow-consolidated budget constraint (10.10), collect the terms $1 + \pi_{t+1}$ together, and collect the seigniorage terms and the fiscal terms together to get:

$$\frac{B_{t-1}}{P_t} = \left[s_t + P_t^b \left(1 + \pi_{t+1}\right) s_{t+1} \right] + \left[\left(t_t - g_t\right) + P_t^b \left(1 + \pi_{t+1}\right)\left(t_{t+1} - g_{t+1}\right) \right]$$
$$+ \left[P_t^b \left(1 + \pi_{t+1}\right) P_{t+1}^b b_{t+1} \right].$$

(10.12)

Since the price of the bond is inversely related to the nominal interest rate, $P_t^b = 1 / 1 + i_t$, and from the Fisher equation, we have the *real interest rate* equal to the nominal rate minus expected inflation, $1 + r_t = (1 + i_t) / (1 + \pi_{t+1})$, we combine these two expressions to arrive at:

$$P_t^b \left(1 + \pi_{t+1}\right) = \frac{1 + \pi_{t+1}}{1 + i_t} + \frac{1}{1 + r_t}.$$ Substitute this expression in Eq. (10.12):

$$\frac{B_{t-1}}{P_t} = \left[s_t + \frac{s_{t+1}}{1 + r_t} \right] + \left[\left(t_t - g_t\right) + \left(\frac{t_{t+1} - g_{t+1}}{1 + r_{t+1}} \right) \right] + \left[\frac{P_{t+1}^b b_{t+1}}{1 + r_{t+1}} \right].$$

(10.13)

In these typical models, $1 + r = 1 / \beta$, where β is the consumer's *discount factor*, which measures the impatience of the consumer. Going forward k – periods in the future, there would be another term $\lim_{k \to \infty} \dfrac{P_{t+k}^b b_{t+k}}{\prod_{k=0}^{\infty} \left(1 + r_{t+k}\right)}$ which converges to zero.

Essentially, the intertemporal government budget constraint reduces to:

$$\frac{B}{P} = f\left(\frac{s}{r} + \frac{t - g}{r} \right)$$

(10.14)

Subscripts aside, the amount of real debt B/P is a function of the *sum of all future real* seigniorage revenues and primary fiscal surpluses (deficits). Having derived the intertemporal government budget constraint, we are in a position to discuss the fiscal theory of inflation and the fiscal theory of the price level.

The Fiscal Theory of Inflation – FTOI

Let's assume that B is the amount of nominal debt at time t, which the government owes and must repay. The central bank is assumed to have been able to commit to a future path of seigniorage revenues from date t forward. The central bank knows how much money it is going to print every period. There is another strong assumption to be introduced, and that is the quantity of money announced at the beginning of the period t, determining the price level P

The "Newer" Theories and Models of Inflation 257

at time t. Thus, P is fixed. As you can see here, the central bank started the game first; therefore, the fiscal authority must choose two of its three instruments, presumably its future primary fiscal surpluses $t - g$ such that the intertemporal government budget constraint is satisfied. Alternatively, the fiscal authority could have started setting fiscal policy first, that is, by choosing the future path of the primary fiscal surpluses and debt, and the central bank had to follow by deciding on the seigniorage revenues.[4]

Christiano and Fitzgerald (2000) and Chugh (2015) carefully explain the differences between *Ricardian and non-Ricardian* fiscal policies, which is a crucial assumption here. A fiscal policy is said to be Ricardian if the fiscal authority ensures that the intertemporal government budget constraints hold when setting the current and future fiscal policy. Under a Ricardian fiscal policy, the fiscal authority is constrained by the intertemporal government budget constraint: that it acknowledges its responsibility to set current and future fiscal surpluses to meet the constraint. Under the non-Ricardian assumption, the fiscal authority is unconstrained or unobligated to make the intertemporal government budget constraint hold.[5]

Ricardian and non-Ricardian assumption notwithstanding, let's continue with these assumptions. Theoretically, the story goes that the amount of seigniorage revenues committed currently and in the future by the central bank eventually determines inflation. The higher the amount of seigniorage revenues is set, the higher *expected* inflation. If the fiscal authority *starts first* by committing itself to a future of primary surpluses and debt, then such fiscal policy with a fixed price level at time t and the intertemporal government budget constraint implies a fiscal theory of inflation. Note that for this to be true, that is, for the fiscal theory of inflation to be true, the fiscal authority has *to start the game before the central bank*. That said, the printing of new money still affects the price level and inflation.

The Fiscal Theory of the Price Level – FTOPL

Suppose that the central bank is fully committed to its independent monetary policy and it sets up its instruments such that no matter what the fiscal authority does, it will not prompt it to change monetary policy, that is print more or less money. Essentially, neither the fiscal authority nor the central bank is willing to react to make the intertemporal government budget constraint hold. In such a situation, the price level, which is the only variable left, must jump to satisfy the intertemporal government budget constraint. The governments in the developed democracies do not default on their nominal debt obligations. So if the central bank is fully committed to its policy at all times, but the fiscal authority reacts by reducing its *current*

---

4 One could see that in reality, none of this could be true. There is no such a clear commitment anywhere. I have never seen such a calculated game played between the treasury and the central bank.

5 There is no evidence of a constrained fiscal policy in reality.

258 *The "Newer" Theories and Models of Inflation*

primary surplus, that is, at time t only, but *does not change the sequence of its future* primary surplus, that is, at time $t+1$ to $t+k$, then it is clear from the intertemporal government budget constraint equation that the price level must jump to make the RHS equal to the LHS. This is the Fiscal Theory of the Price Level in a nutshell.

A scenario like the just-cited case does not imply that the fiscal policy causes inflation. The rise in the price level is not "inflation" as we defined in the introduction of this book. Under the FTOPL, *unanticipated* fiscal shocks could immediately cause the price level to rise. This is a one-off increase in the price level, not a continuous increase, hence not inflationary. Under the FTOI, however, a change in *current and future* fiscal policy, which is a change in time t and $t+k$ sequences of the primary fiscal balances, causes an increase in current and future money supply, hence causing inflation at time t and the future. This is an important difference between the FTOI and the FTOPL to keep in mind. One could see that if the current US government, which has been in office since 2021, believes in the MMT, it might have committed itself to run budget deficits covering the period, at least until the next election.

There is an appealing reason to believe that the current inflation we are witnessing in the developed inflation-targeting countries is a result of the fiscal authorities' unexpected increase in the deficits. However, it is very difficult to disentangle the effects of fiscal policy on the price level and inflation. Put differently, it is hard to identify these two effects econometrically or empirically. Christiano and Fitzgerald's (2000) paper is a rich discussion of the theory and how one might test it.

Cochrane (2000) argues that monetary policy is irrelevant to the price level determination. Of course, some of the most important readings in the FTOPL include (Sims, 1994) and (Woodford, 1994, 1995, 1998a, 1998b, 2002). There were some important criticisms to the theory, see for example (McCallum, 2001), (Carlstrom and Fuerst, 2000), and (Buiter, 1999). Also see (Gordon and Leeper, 2006).

The current extraordinary increase in the inflation rates in developed countries, which have very successfully targeted low and stable inflation, may be a good reason to think more about the FTOPL as an appealing explanation. As a matter of fact, not CPI inflation but rather asset price inflation (housing and stocks) has been increasing for a very long time. The price level, however, has been rising continuously since the beginning of the inflation-targeting in the developed countries because *bygones-are-bygones* under inflation-targeting. The central bank ignores the increases in the price level. Moreover, fiscal deficits financed by debt creation have been evident for years. It seems that empirically testing these theories has not been successful. Christiano and Fitzgerald (2000) elaborate on the difficulties facing the econometrician when testing the theory.

The Modern Monetary Theory – MMT

Presumably, this is the most recent theory – not an inflation theory *per se*, but has implications of course given that it is a monetary theory. The only reference to it as far as I know is (Mitchell *et al.*, 2019). The book was critically reviewed by (Mankiw, 2020). Mankiw says that MMT begins with the government budget constraint

The "Newer" Theories and Models of Inflation   259

under a system of fiat money. According to (Mitchell *et al.*, 2019), the standard theory of the government budget constraint, which relates the present value of tax revenue to the present value of government spending and the government debt, is misleading. Thus, what we presented earlier is misleading according to them. They write that the most important conclusion reached by MMT is that *the issuer of a currency faces no financial constraints. A country that issues its own currency can never run out and can never become insolvent in its own currency.* It can make all payments as they come due (Mitchell *et al.* [2019, p. 13]). As a result, they say that for *most* governments, there is no default risk on government debt (p. 15). This is the bit that interests politicians, who want to spend fiat money to finance their programs.

Mankiw (2020) says that an MMT proponent will point out that the interest on debt can be paid by printing yet more money. But the ever-expanding monetary base will have further implications. Aggregate demand will increase due to a wealth effect, eventually spurring inflation. I am not sure that I understand or explain the wealth effect resulting from printing money. Maybe they mean government debt. Even so, a serious argument could be made about this assertion.[6] We argued in this book that an upward shift in aggregate demand (to the right) or a leftward shift in aggregate supply do not produce inflation; they merely increase the aggregate price level.

However, central bank's printed money to finance government debt is inflationary even if the central bank successfully targets a low and stable inflation rate. We showed that the correlation between government spending and inflation is quite high. Such monetary expansion causes asset price inflation (continuing increases in stock and housing prices) as we have shown and should be responsible for the high CPI inflation at some point because the lags are long and variable, and economic models usually break down and cease to predict inflation.

We want to test the MMT inflation's policy prescription. The proponents of the MMT suggest that if inflation increases as a result of printing money or deficit spending, an increase in taxes would bring it down.[7] Consider the following simple model; see (Razzak and Laabas, 2016), (Shimer, 2009), (Prescott, 2004), and (Nickell, 2003) for example.

---

6 For the wealth effect to work, the stock of real wealth must be allowed to vary with the price level. A fall in the domestic price level increases the real value of the government debt, hence a rise in the economy's aggregate wealth and consumption. However, there is an issue with treating interest-bearing government debt as net wealth to households. Interest payments on government debt are expected to be met with higher future taxes. The Ricardian Equivalence suggests that when the price level falls, the value of the real debt rises, and people would expect an increase in the present value of future tax liabilities. Barro (1974) argued, on the basis of this argument, that government debt is not net wealth to households. However, noninterest-bearing government debt could be considered net wealth. Laidler (1985) argued that an increase in the real value of such debt outstanding carries with it no corresponding increase in tax liabilities.

7 For optimal taxation theory, see (Diamond and Mirrlees, 1971; Diamond *et al.*, 1980). The proponents of MMT and politicians generally ignore economic theory of optimal taxation.

260 *The "Newer" Theories and Models of Inflation*

The Household

The household holds bonds and stocks, owns the capital stock, and rents it to the firm. The firm combines capital and labor to produce real output using a constant return-to-scale Cobb–Douglas production function. The household also pays taxes on the consumption goods, on investments, on labor income, and on capital income. All tax revenues, except those used to finance the pure consumption goods, are given back to households in the form of transfers. The transfers are lump sum (independent of household income). Public expenditures are generally substitutes for private consumption in the G7 countries. Prescott (2004) assumed that they substitute on a one-to-one basis for private consumption with the exception of military expenditures. The goods and services in question consist mostly of publicly provided education, health care, protection services, and judiciary services. Therefore, the model's household consumption is not the same as the Statistics of National Account (SNA) measure; rather it includes government consumption, less military spending, and less indirect taxes on consumption. The government budget constraint holds all the time.

The utility function is log-linear, which helps in the computation of

$$E\left\{\sum_{t=s}^{\infty} \beta^{t+s} \left(\ln C_{t+s} + \alpha \ln\left(l_{t+s}\right)\right)\right\}, \tag{10.15}$$

where E is the expectation operator at time t, C_t is consumption, and l_t is leisure. The parameter $\alpha > 0$ measures the nonmarket productive time of the household (e.g., the relative value of leisure). We assume that a person has 100 hours of productive time a week. The nonmarket productive time, that is, leisure is $100 - L_t$, where labor is average weekly hours worked per worker.[8] Capital stock evolves according to this equation:

$$K_{t+1} = \left(1 - \delta\right) K_t + I_t, \tag{10.16}$$

where K_t is the stock of physical capital, δ is the depreciation rate, and I_t is investment.[9]

The Firm

We assume a firm producing output, Y_t, using capital K_t and labor L_t in a Cobb–Douglas production function that exhibits a constant return to scale with the shares of capital and labor, θ and $\left(1-\theta\right)$, respectively. The variable A_t is labor-augmenting technical progress, which we assume to be exogenous for simplicity.

$$Y_t = A_t K_t^{\theta} L_t^{1-\theta}, \tag{10.17}$$

---

8 Production of goods and services during leisure time is untaxed.
9 The assumptions of whether the firm owns the capital and the household own the firm, or debt-financing, or renting capital do not affect the solution.

Next, we set the Lagrange multiplier optimization problem with the Lagrange multiplier λ and the discount factor β. In the budget constraint, we introduce a simple tax system similar to that in (Nickell, 2003) and (Prescott, 2004). Let τ_c be the consumption tax rate, τ_I is the investment tax rate, τ_L is the marginal labor tax rate, w_t is the real wage rate (W_t is the nominal wage rate), τ_k is the capital income tax rate, r_t is *nominal* interest rate, P_t^K is the purchase price of capital, and TR_t is transfers. Tax revenues, except those used to finance pure public good consumption, are returned to households as lump-sum transfer payments – that is, independent of the household's income.[10] Taxes could affect the prices of consumption and investment goods (e.g., investment tax credit).[11] The household owns bonds B_t and stocks S_t, where their prices are P_t^b and P_t^s, respectively (the superscript b denotes bonds, and s stocks), and d_t is dividend.

The budget constraint BC in real terms:

$$
\begin{aligned}
(1-\tau_L)W_t L_t + (1-\tau_k)(r_t - \delta)P_t^K K_t + \delta P_t^K K_t + B_{t-1} + (P_t^s + d_t) \\
S_{t-1} + TR_t = (1+\tau_c)P_t C_t + (1+\tau_I)P_t^I I_t + P_t^b B_t + P_t^s S_t
\end{aligned}
\tag{10.18}
$$

The multiple-period Lagrange multiplier is:

$$
\begin{aligned}
[lnC_t + \alpha \, ln(100-L_t) + \beta u(lnC_{t+1} + \alpha \, ln(100-L_{t+1}) + \beta^2 u(lnC_{t+2} + \alpha ln \\
(100-L_{t+2})] + \beta^3 u(\ldots) + \lambda_t[BC_t] + \beta\lambda_{t+1}[BC_{t+1}] + \beta^2 \lambda_{t+2}[\ldots]
\end{aligned}
\tag{10.19}
$$

Solving from the time-sequential Lagrange multiplier problems, and focusing on the variables, consumption–leisure ratio $C_t / (100-L_t)$ and capital–labor ratio K_t / L_t, the marginal rate of substitution (MRS) between leisure and consumption is:

$$
\frac{\dfrac{\alpha}{100-L_t}}{\dfrac{1}{C_t}} = \frac{1-\tau_L}{1+\tau_c}\frac{W_t}{P_t}.^{12}
\tag{10.20}
$$

---

10 The majority of public expenditures in G7 (i.e., education, health) are perfect substitutes for private consumption, except for military spending. This is especially true for the United States, see (Christiano and Eichenbaum, 1992). However, this assumption could be highly restrictive for other countries as explained in (Prescott, 2004).

11 This is a significantly simpler tax system than the systems used by the G7 countries. An accelerated depreciation and investment tax credits would affect the price of the investment good relative to the consumption good but would not alter the inference drawn in this case. Similarly, introducing a corporate sector, with dividends not taxed, as is generally the case in the EU, or taxed as ordinary income, as they are in the United States, would not alter any conclusion significantly because in this model, the most important parameters are the factor shares and the relative value of leisure. See (McGrattan and Prescott, 2005).

12 The price level could be set to 1, but we kept it as it will become clear at the end why we did that.

262 *The "Newer" Theories and Models of Inflation*

To simplify further, we introduce the tax rate τ :

$$\text{Let } \frac{\tau_c + \tau_L}{1+\tau_c} = \tau.$$ (10.21)

Adding 1 to both sides,

$$1 - \frac{\tau_c + \tau_L}{1+\tau_c} = 1 - \tau.$$ (10.22)

We arrive at:

$$\left(\frac{1-\tau_L}{1+\tau_c} \right) = 1 - \tau.$$ (10.23)

So the MRS becomes

$$\frac{\dfrac{\alpha}{100 - L_t}}{\dfrac{1}{C_t}} = (1-\tau)\frac{W_t}{P_t}.$$ (10.24)

Solving for labor from the aforementioned First Order Conditions for L :

$$L_t = \frac{1-\theta}{1-\theta + \left(\dfrac{C_t}{Y_t}\right)\left(\dfrac{\alpha}{1-\tau}\right)}$$ (10.25)

Taxes and labor (employment or hours worked) are inversely related. The ratio of consumption to GDP captures the *intertemporal substitution*. The tax rate captures the *intratemporal substitution*. If people expect the effective tax rate on labor income to be lower (higher) in the future, for example, they will increase (decrease) their *current* consumption.[13] The policymaker, who follows the MMT advice to increase taxes to reduce inflation, should know that people *expect* real income to decline; therefore, *current* consumption will decline. That may well reduce the aggregate price level, however, hours worked, that is, the supply of labor will also fall, and unemployment has to increase. This is nothing less than the standard Keynesian policy to deal with inflation.

To show that by estimating an unrestricted VAR:

$$y_t = A_1 y_{t-1} \cdots A_p y_{t-p} + \varepsilon_t,$$ (10.26)

where $y_t = \left(y_1, y_{2t}, \cdots y_{kt}\right)'$ is a $k \times 1$ vector of endogenous variables.

---

13 It is important to note that our analysis of the labor supply abstracts from demographic factors, which are known to affect the supply of labor.

The "Newer" Theories and Models of Inflation   263

There is also an exogenous constant term, $\varepsilon_t = (\varepsilon_{1t}, \varepsilon_{2t}, \cdots \varepsilon_{kt})'$ and is a $k \times 1$ vector of white-noise innovations with $(\varepsilon_t) = 0;\ E(\varepsilon_t \varepsilon_t') = \Sigma\varepsilon$, and $E(\varepsilon_t \varepsilon_s') = 0$ for $t \neq s$.

Let $(pk + d) \times 1$ be a vector:

$$Z_t = \left(y_{t-1}' \cdots y_{t-p}' \right)',$$

where d is a vector of exogenous variables.

And write the VAR as a compact form:

$$Y_t = BZ_t + \epsilon_t. \tag{10.27}$$

We choose the following *five* variables in the VAR, the nominal debt level, D_t, the real government budget surplus $(t_t - g_t)$, the consumption–output ratio C_t/Y_t, the CPI price level P_t, and total hours worked h_t. All variables are in *log term*.

The vector Y_t includes $(ln\,D_t, (lnt_t - lng_t), lnC_t/Y_t, lnh_t, lnP_t)$; ε_t is $(\varepsilon_{1t}, \varepsilon_{2t}, \cdots \varepsilon_{5t})$ both are matrices of the endogenous variables and are the innovations. The matrices $B = (A_1, A_2, \cdots A_5,\ constant)$ and $Z = (Z_{1t}, Z_{2t}, Z_{5t})$ are the matrix of coefficients and matrix of regressors, respectively.

The methodology consists of the following steps: (1) we estimate this VAR for the United Kingdom and Norway, which are the only two countries in our sample with readily available and sufficient time series data to test the MMT implications. The sample is 1980 to 2019. (2) We solve the model and compute *baseline dynamic stochastic projections* from 2020 to 2040. (3) We test a severe scenario whereby the real tax revenues doubled. We then measure the deviation of the dynamic stochastic projections of the CPI and hours worked from the baselines. Figure 10.2 plots the UK data, which we will use in estimating the VAR and shows the real fiscal policy instruments, that is, the components of the intertemporal government budget constraint.

Note that (1) the sample is restricted by the consumption–output data, which are up to 2019; and (2) consumption is the sum of the household and the government consumptions. There is a trend in the levels, especially interesting is the continuous budget deficit; the rise in the CPI and the debt; and the decline in hours worked. We test the time series for unit root using the same battery of tests we used earlier. These commonly used tests have low power as discussed many times in earlier; however, there is an agreement among most economists that the trends in these variables are stochastic. We test the null hypothesis that the variables' nominal debt, the budget surplus (taxes – spending), consumption–output ratio, hours, and the CPI are not cointegrated using the Johansen's Maximum Likelihood Test (see Johansen [1988, 1991, 1995] and Johansen and Juselius [1990]). The Johansen test is an appropriate test in a multivariate case like this one. We used a variety of trend-specifications and numbers of lags and found strong evidence for more than one cointegrating relationship (see Appendix 10.1). Therefore, we could estimate the VAR in log-levels. We estimated the unrestricted VAR with two lags. The sample is

264 The "Newer" Theories and Models of Inflation

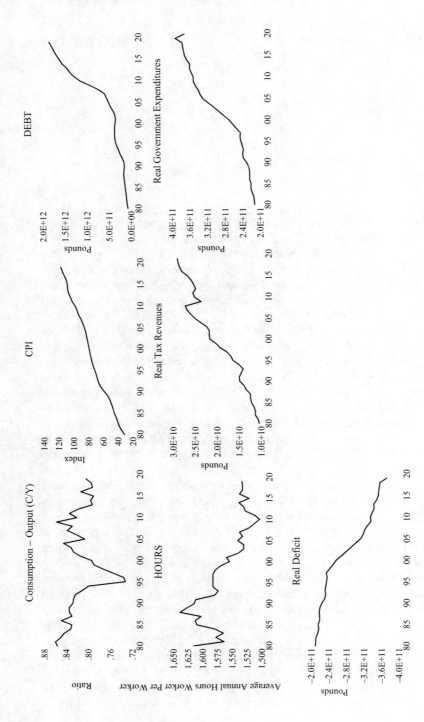

Figure 10.2 The UK Variables of the VAR

Data Source: World Development Indicators
Consumption–Output Ratio is from Penn World Table Sample: 1980–2019
Hours Worked are from OECD Statistics
Local Currency Units

The "Newer" Theories and Models of Inflation   265

relatively short for such exercise, which affects the lag length. Figure 10.3 plots the *generalized impulse response functions*. The order of the variables does not seem to matter. We tested that and found that the standard Choleski impulse response functions to be the same.[14]

These impulse response functions predict that nominal debt plummets on impact with the increase in surplus and vice versa. Debt increases in response to the C/Y shock and has a hump-shape impulse response function. The increase in government consumption is likely to be the main explanatory factor. The higher the deficit, the higher the debt is. The UK government has run budget deficits since 1960, so when we say surplus it is actually negative, that is, deficit. The labor supply (hours worked) falls slightly initially in response to the increase in debt, and the CPI does the same thing, and then, only slightly increases. The impulse response functions look very similar.

The surplus falls on impact in response to rising debt. The surplus drops significantly in response to a rise in the consumption–output ratio. Consumption includes government spending. As it increases, the surplus, that is, taxes less government spending, falls. The response of the surplus to the labor supply is shallow and insignificant. However, it increases for about 4 years in response to a jump in the CPI and then stabilizes close to 0.

The impulse response function of the consumption–output ratio in response to the debt shock is 0. The surplus dips initially, rises, and then declines to 0 in a humped-shape response. The response of consumption–output ratio to the labor supply shock is a slow fall. The CPI seems to have a negative initial response to the consumption–output shock.

The labor supply initial response to rising debt is a significant drop. It increases initially then it drops significantly and remains negative in response to the surplus. The increase in the surplus is an increase in taxes, which reduces hours worked in our model. The supply of labor increases only slightly in response to consumption–output shock and then takes a long time before it begins to increase and remains high. The supply of labor increases initially with the CPI, and then it falls permanently.

Finally, the impulse response functions of the CPI to debt and to the surplus are positive (taxes raise the CPI). The CPI initially dips then climbs up with high consumption–output ratio and permanently rises with the labor supply with a hump-shaped impulse response function.

The second step is to solve the model and to generate *baseline dynamic stochastic projections* from 2018 to 2040. We plot the mean dynamic stochastic projections along with the upper and lower confidence intervals in Figures 10.4, 10.5, 10.6, 10.7, and 10.8.

The standard errors grow wider with time, which is typical, given our sample size and that the variables have stochastic trends.

---

14 See (Koop *et al.*, 1996) and (Isakin and Ngo, 2020).

266 The "Newer" Theories and Models of Inflation

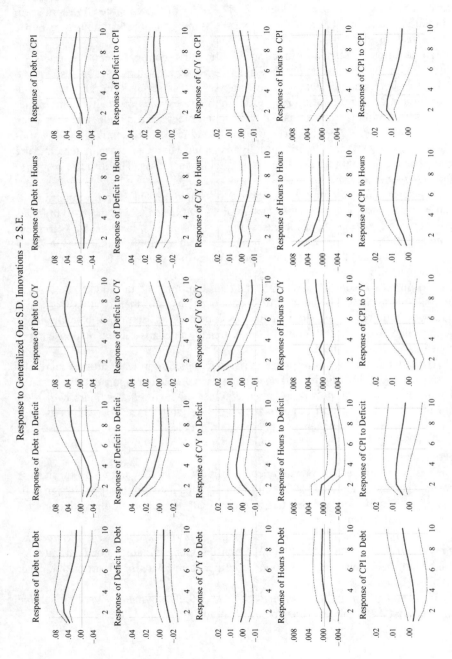

Figure 10.3 UK Generalized Impulse Response Functions of the Baseline VAR

The *"Newer" Theories and Models of Inflation* 267

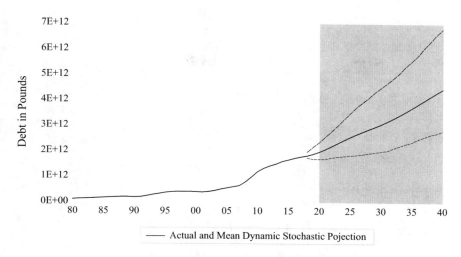

Figure 10.4 UK Mean Baseline Dynamic Stochastic Projections of *Log Nominal* Debt

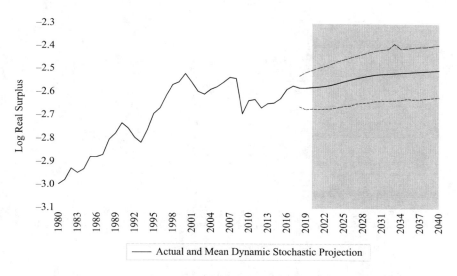

Figure 10.5 UK Mean Baseline Dynamic Stochastic Projections of *Log Real* Surplus (Log Real Taxes and Log Real Government Expenditures)

Note: Log real tax revenues < log real government expenditures (i.e., deficit).

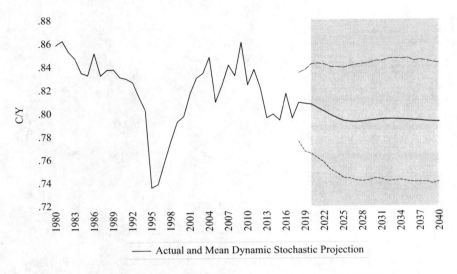

Figure 10.6 UK Mean Baseline Dynamic Stochastic Projections of *Real C/Y*

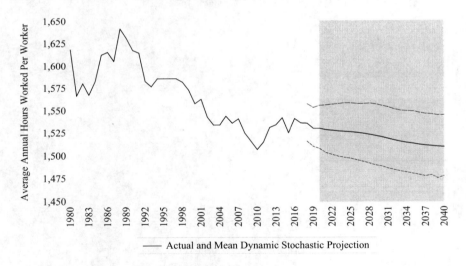

Figure 10.7 UK Mean Baseline Dynamic Stochastic Projections of Hours Worked

Now we can examine the MMT proposition to reduce inflation by raising taxes. Remember that the MMT theory proponents did not challenge the prediction held by the QTM that the increase in spending financed by fiat money eventually results in higher inflation. To bring inflation down, they suggest using fiscal not monetary policy. To test this proposition, we assume a severe scenario, whereby in 2019, which is the last observation, the UK government doubled real taxes *permanently* without a change in government spending.

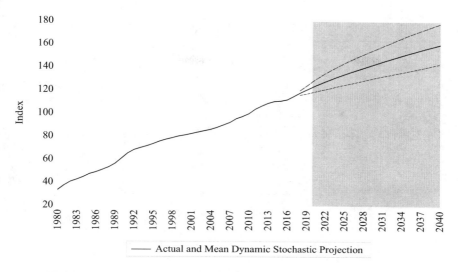

Figure 10.8 UK Mean Baseline Dynamic Stochastic Projections of the CPI

Sketch 10.1 illustrates. In theory, a permanent increase in the tax rate should shift the aggregate demand curve AD1 down to the left to AD2, whereby consumption and investment demand fall. The increase in the tax rate, however, reduces aggregate supply too from AS1 to AS2 through reduction in supply of labor, that is, hours worked per worker. Real output falls from Y1 to Y2. The price level is reduced from P1 to P2 only if the aggregate demand declines by more than the aggregate supply. However, if the aggregate supply curve shifts to the left by more than the decline in aggregate demand, AS3, output, will fall by more to Y3, but the price level increases to P3. This scenario is not considered by MMT. Therefore, it is the relative size of the shift of the aggregate demand and supply curve that determine what happens to the price level, and there is no guarantee that doubling taxes reduce the price level, isn't it?

To test the data, we re-estimate the same VAR from 1980 to 2019. Then we solve the model and examine the mean dynamic stochastic projections under the severe scenario of doubling total tax revenues, T.

Figures 10.9a and 10.10a and Figures 10.9b and 10.10b plot the mean dynamic stochastic projections of average annual hours worked per worker and the CPI, and their deviations from baseline projections.

The analysis is consistent with the prediction of MMT and as illustrated in Sketch 10.1. Both aggregate demand and aggregate supply shift, but the aggregate demand shift dominates. Both real output and the price level are reduced with the doubling of tax revenues. This outcome is not at all different from the outcome of Keynesian theory, whereby reducing inflation requires reducing real output, that is, slowing the economy or inducing a recession.

270 The "Newer" Theories and Models of Inflation

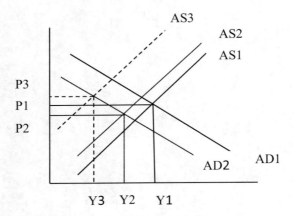

Sketch 10.1 Effect of Doubling the Tax Rate on Real Output and the Price Level

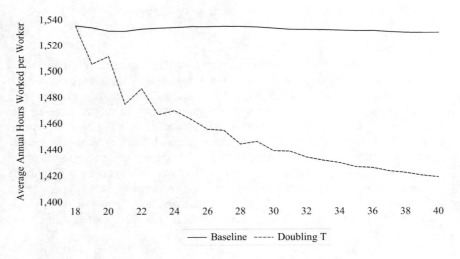

Figure 10.9a UK Mean Dynamic Stochastic Projections of Annual Average Hours Worked Per Worker, 2018–2040

Note: Hours worked are projected to fall significantly as taxes double.

Next, we examine the Norwegian data because Norway is the only other developed country, where we have the data to examine the predictions of the MMT (Figure 10.11).

Note again the rising trend of the CPI and debt and the decline in hours worked. These trends are similar in all developed inflation-targeting countries. The CPI is a unit root process, debt-financing, and the decline in work effort. We test the data

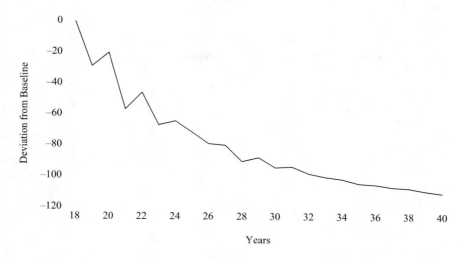

Figure 10.9b UK Mean Dynamic Stochastic Projection of Annual Average Hours Worked Per Worker: *Deviations from Baseline Mean*

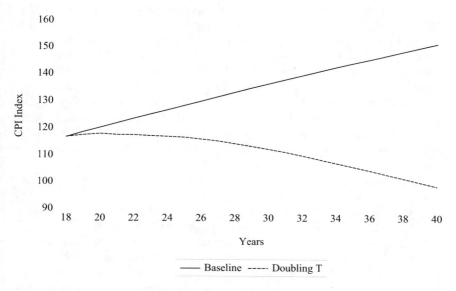

Figure 10.10a UK Mean Dynamic Stochastic Projection of CPI, 2018–2040

for unit root using the same commonly used tests we applied in this book earlier and proceed to test the null hypothesis that the variables are not cointegrated. The results are reported in Appendix 10.1. There are multiple cointegrating vectors. We estimate the VAR with two lags for the same reasons outlined earlier. The impulse response functions are plotted in Figure 10.12.

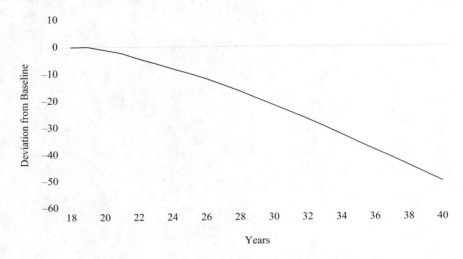

Figure 10.10b UK Mean Dynamic Stochastic Projection of CPI: *Deviations from Baseline Mean*

There are differences between these impulse response functions and those of the United Kingdom plotted earlier. The response of the debt to the rise in the deficit is muted. Equally insignificant is the response of debt to the consumption–output ratio. Hours worked, however, has a strong negative response to rising debt. Consumption–output ratio declines more in response to the deficit than to rising debt. It rises with the CPI and rises a little less in response to hours worked. The impulse response functions of hours worked show permanent decline in response to the increase in debt, decline in response to the deficit too, decline in response to the consumption–output ratio, and to the CPI. The CPI responses in Norway are significantly different from those of the United Kingdom; they jump and stay positive in response to the debt shock; increase in response to the deficit and to consumption–output ratio, and decline in response to hours.

Now we solve the VAR and generate dynamic stochastic baseline projections. Figures 10.13, 10.14, 10.15, 10.16, and 10.17 plot the projections.

We continue testing the MMT policy prescription to reduce inflation by examining a severe scenario, whereby we double tax revenues permanently. We estimate the VAR under the shock scenario, then solve the VAR, and generate dynamic stochastic projections. Then, we compare the deviations of each projection from the baseline. Figure 10.18 plots the deviations of the mean dynamic stochastic projection of hours worked under the scenario of doubling T from baseline. Doubling taxes reduce labor supply just as predicted by the model, and similar to the UK case. Doubling taxes, however, increases, not decreases the price level.

Figure 10.19 plots the deviations of mean dynamic stochastic projections of the CPI from the baseline under the scenario of doubling T. We get a story,

The "Newer" Theories and Models of Inflation 273

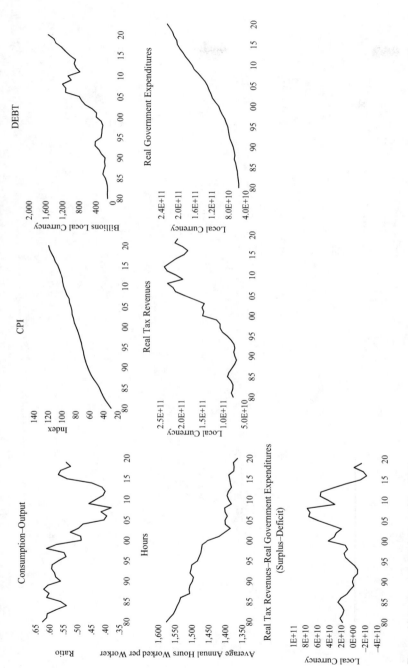

Figure 10.11 Norway Variables of the VAR
Data Source: World Development Indicators
Consumption–Output Ratio is from Penn World Table Sample: 1980–2019
Hours Worked is from OECD Statistics
Local Currency Units

274 The "Newer" Theories and Models of Inflation

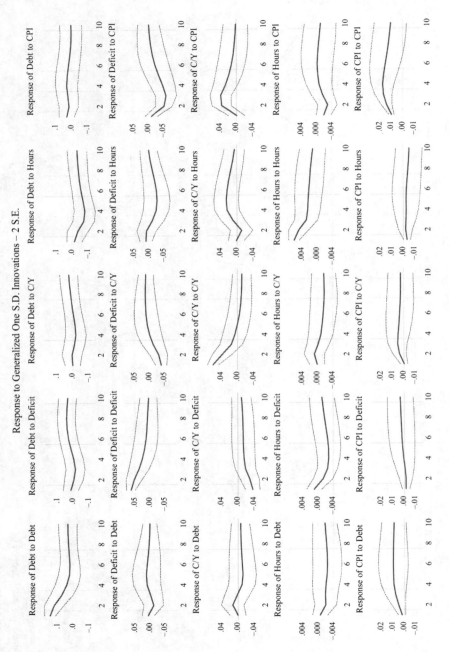

Figure 10.12 Norway Generalized Impulse Response Functions of the Baseline VAR

The "Newer" Theories and Models of Inflation 275

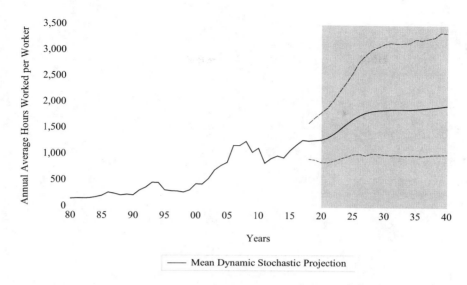

Figure 10.13 Norway Mean Baseline Dynamic Stochastic Projection of Nominal Debt

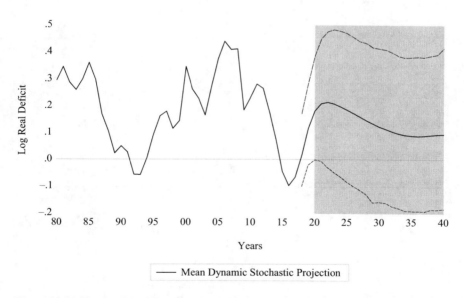

Figure 10.14 Norway Mean Baseline Dynamic Stochastic Projection of Log Real Deficit

276 The "Newer" Theories and Models of Inflation

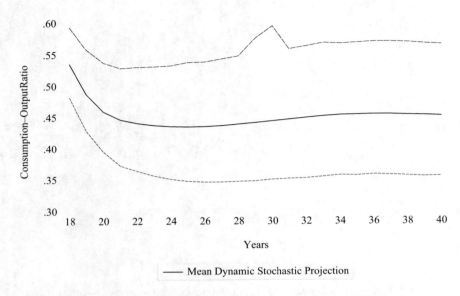

Figure 10.15 Norway Mean Baseline Dynamic Stochastic Projection of C/Y

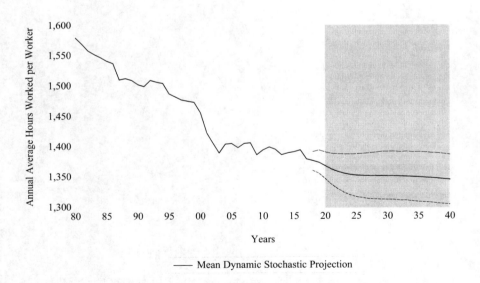

Figure 10.16 Norway Mean Baseline Dynamic Stochastic Projection of Hours Worked

The "Newer" Theories and Models of Inflation 277

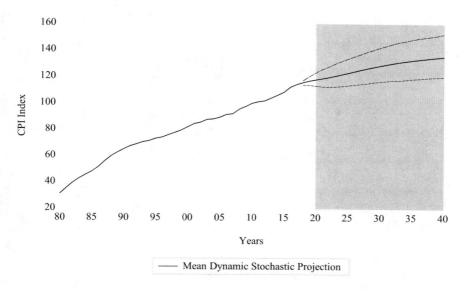

Figure 10.17 Norway Mean Baseline Dynamic Stochastic Projection of the CPI

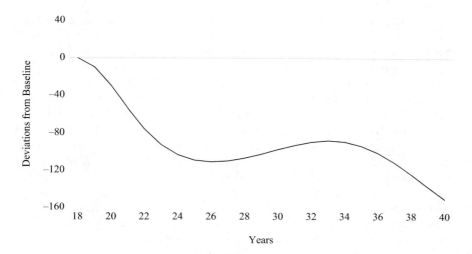

Figure 10.18 Norway Mean Dynamic Stochastic Projection of Hours Worked: *Deviations from Baseline Mean*

Note: As predicted, hours worked decline in response to the doubling of taxes.

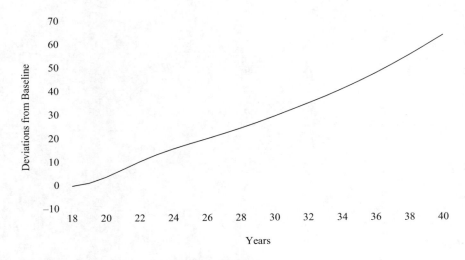

Figure 10.19 Norway Mean Dynamic Stochastic Projection of CPI: *Deviations from Baseline Mean*

very different from the United Kingdom's. Doubling taxes seems to increase the price level.

The increase in the price level after doubling taxes is an unintended policy outcome under MMT because MMT policy to reduce inflation does not consider the effect of taxes on aggregate supply. In Norway, an increase in taxes shifts the aggregate demand down just as theory predicts and lowers real output and the price level; however, unlike the United Kingdom, it shifts the aggregate supply to the left by more than demand, reduces the labor supply and real output, and increases the price level. The shift in aggregate supply dominates in this case, and the price level increases rather than decreases. See Sketch 10.1, which seems to indicate that doubling taxes has a smaller effect on aggregate demand, mainly consumption and investment demand than in the United Kingdom and has a stronger effect on labor supply and aggregate supply. Hours worked decline substantially. The last graph is for comparing the hours worked responses with doubling T in the United Kingdom and Norway. Figure 10.20 plots the deviations of mean dynamic stochastic projection of average annual hours worked per worker from the corresponding baselines in Norway and in the United Kingdom It is telling us that hours worked in Norway declines by more than that in the United Kingdom. Figure 10.21 shows the CPI's deviation from baseline projections for the United Kingdom and Norway.

For robustness, this stress-test exercise should be repeated using data from more countries when the data are available. However, these two cases should cast serious doubt about the efficacy of MMT policy recommendations to reduce inflation

The "Newer" Theories and Models of Inflation   279

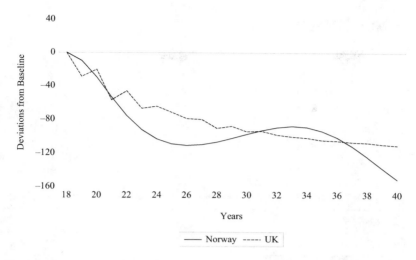

Figure 10.20 Comparing the Deviation of Average Annual Hours Worked from Baseline Doubling Taxes in Norway and the United Kingdom, 2018–2040

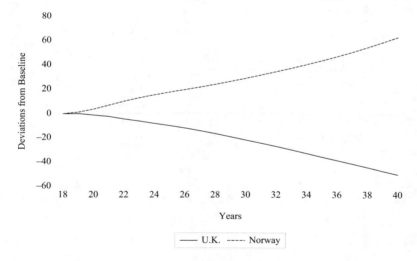

Figure 10.21 Comparing the Deviation of CPI from Baseline Doubling Taxes in Norway and the United Kingdom, 2018–2040

by increasing taxes. The outcome will be lower labor supply, lower employment, that is, higher unemployment, a recession possibly, but the effect on the price level is ambiguous because it depends on the relative shifts in aggregate demand and supply. This tax policy is not a typical demand management because taxes affect productivity via the effect on the supply of labor.

Appendix 10.1

Table A10.1 UK Cointegration Summary Statistics of a Number of Different Specifications

Sample: 1980–2040

Included observations: 35

Series: ln(debt), ln(surplus), $ln\left(\dfrac{C}{Y}\right)$, ln(hours), ln(CPI)

Lags interval: 1 to 4

Data Trend:	*None*	*None*	*Linear*	*Linear*	*Quadratic*
Test Type	No Intercept No Trend	Intercept No Trend	Intercept No Trend	Intercept Trend	Intercept Trend
Trace	4	5	5	5	5
Max-Eig	4	5	5	5	5

Critical values based on (MacKinnon *et al.*, 1999)

Information Criteria by Rank and Model

Data Trend:	*None*	*None*	*Linear*	*Linear*	*Quadratic*
Rank or	*No Intercept*	*Intercept*	*Intercept*	*Intercept*	*Intercept*
No. of CEs	*No Trend*	*No Trend*	*No Trend*	*Trend*	*Trend*
	Log Likelihood by Rank (Rows) and Model (Columns)				
0	513.67	513.67	518.20	518.20	525.13
1	564.55	566.90	571.42	571.42	578.14
2	594.61	597.29	601.78	615.92	620.89
3	607.32	625.65	629.26	644.28	649.11
4	614.84	637.23	637.91	656.25	659.01
5	614.84	644.63	644.63	664.49	664.49

The "Newer" Theories and Models of Inflation   281

Data Trend:	None	None	Linear	Linear	Quadratic
Rank or	No Intercept	Intercept	Intercept	Intercept	Intercept
No. of CEs	No Trend	No Trend	No Trend	Trend	Trend
	Akaike Information Criteria by Rank (Rows) and Model (Columns)				
0	−23.64	−23.64	−23.61	−23.61	−23.72
1	−25.97	−26.05	−26.08	−26.02	−26.18
2	−27.12	−27.16	−27.24	−27.94	−28.05
3	−27.27	−28.15	−28.24	−28.93	−29.09*
4	−27.13	−28.18	−28.16	−28.98	−29.08
5	−26.56	−27.97	−27.97	−28.82	−28.83
	Schwarz Criteria by Rank (Rows) and Model (Columns)				
0	−19.19	−19.19	−18.94	−18.94	−18.83
1	−21.08	−21.11	−20.97	−20.87	−20.85
2	−21.78	−21.73	−21.69	−22.29	−22.27
3	−21.49	−22.24	−22.24	−22.79	−22.87*
4	−20.91	−21.78	−21.72	−22.36	−22.42
5	−19.89	−21.09	−21.09	−21.71	−21.71

* denotes statistical significance.

Table A10.2 Norway Cointegration Summary Statistics of a Number of Different Specifications

Sample: 1980–2020

Included observations: 35

Series: ln(debt), ln(surplus), $ln\left(\dfrac{C}{Y}\right)$, ln(hours), ln(CPI)

Lags interval: 1 to 4

Data Trend:	None	None	Linear	Linear	Quadratic
Test Type	No Intercept No Trend	Intercept No Trend	Intercept No Trend	Intercept Trend	Intercept Trend
Trace	3	4	5	4	4
Max-Eig	3	4	3	4	4

Critical values based on (MacKinnon *et al.*, 1999)

Information Criteria
  by Rank and Model

(*Continued*)

282   The "Newer" Theories and Models of Inflation

Table A10.2 (Continued)

Data Trend:	None	None	Linear	Linear	Quadratic
Rank or	No Intercept	Intercept	Intercept	Intercept	Intercept
No. of CEs	No Trend	No Trend	No Trend	Trend	Trend
	Log Likelihood by Rank (Rows) and Model (Columns)				
0	408.92	408.92	412.33	412.33	417.32
1	442.98	444.48	447.86	454.20	459.18
2	461.01	475.75	479.06	488.72	493.42
3	470.45	491.79	495.05	510.82	515.37
4	474.42	500.76	500.89	526.78	530.24
5	475.67	504.73	504.73	530.61	530.61
	Akaike Information Criteria by Rank (Rows) and Model (Columns)				
0	−17.65	−17.65	−17.56	−17.56	−17.56
1	−19.03	−19.05	−19.02	−19.32	−19.38
2	−19.48	−20.21	−20.23	−20.67	−20.76
3	−19.45	−20.50	−20.57	−21.30	−21.44
4	−19.11	−20.38	−20.33	−21.58	−21.73*
5	−18.60	−19.98	−19.98	−21.17	−21.17
	Schwarz Criteria by Rank (Rows) and Model (Columns)				
0	−13.20	−13.20	−12.89	−12.89	−12.67
1	−14.13	−14.12	−13.91	−14.17	−14.04
2	−14.15	−14.79	−14.67	−15.02	−14.99
3	−13.67	−14.59	−14.57	−15.17	−15.22*
4	−12.88	−13.98	−13.89	−14.96	−15.06
5	−11.94	−13.09	−13.09	−14.06	−14.06

11 Reducing Inflation

Abstract

It is hypothesized that if the central banks in inflation-targeting countries want to reduce inflation, they set the policy interest rate above the natural interest rate r^* (Wicksell, 1898). However, r^* is unobservable. It has been estimated econometrically. The natural rate exists in the New Keynesian model as a statistic, that is, an empirical calculation that depends solely on observable data and not at all on estimated model parameters. Here, we derive the natural rate of interest from a structural micro-foundation model and compute it for the advanced countries in our sample. r^* depends on the consumption–leisure growth rates relative to capital–labor growth rates. It is zero in the steady state because all the growth rates are zero. However, the wider the gap, the higher r^* is. When consumption–leisure ratio grows faster (slower) than the capital–labor ratio, r^* tends to increase (decrease). The data and our calculations show that current monetary policy (as in November 2022) may be – on average – tighter than what is predicted by our calculations in Australia, Denmark, New Zealand, Sweden, the United Kingdom, and the United States. This may suggest that these central banks have higher estimates of the natural rates; have no estimates at all; or they are strongly overreacting to the unexpectedly high inflation.

Forbs *et al.* (2022) discuss how inflation in the United States (and elsewhere) should be reduced. They emphasize the role of liquidity. (Friedman, 1969) is probably a very important reference for the such policy. Although this is consistent with our findings, but the developed inflation-targeting countries do not adhere to such policy prescription. This is not how the Fed or the majority of central banks in the developed countries reduce inflation. The fact is that the Fed and most central banks in developed countries do not consider the quantity of money as an important determinant of inflation. We showed earlier that the correlation between money and inflation approaches zero when the central bank successfully targets a low and stable inflation rate in developed countries. (Woodford's, 2002) study is, more or less, what Fed does now. (Goodfriend and King, 2005) is a study of Volker's disinflation policy. In this approach, the price of money, i.e., the short-term interest rate is the key instrument for monetary policy, not the quantity of money. This literature is really voluminous, and we will not be able to cite every study. Here, we explain

DOI: 10.4324/9781003382218-11

284　*Reducing Inflation*

how the Fed reduces inflation. We also provide a new method to help policymakers in setting monetary policy.

To reduce inflation, most central banks and especially the advanced economies follow a New Keynesian recipe. They simply increase the overnight nominal interest rate, which presumably increases the (unobservable) real interest rate. A year or two later, the economy slows, that is, the output gap and expected inflation begin to fall. Recall that both expected inflation and the output gap are unobservable. The timing of the effects of this policy is uncertain to say the least. It gets more uncertain when the central banks ask that to what extent the overnight nominal interest rate should be increased? In theory, the short-term nominal interest rate should be set higher than the *natural real rate of interest*, which we call r^*. This r^* is unobservable; central banks think it is consistent with the level of real output that is equal to potential output and with the inflation rate that is equal to expected inflation.

(Hamilton *et al.*, 2015) define r^* as the *equilibrium real interest rate*, also often referred to as Wicksell's *natural rate* of interest. The difference between current-period rates and the equilibrium rate is a key channel through which central banks affect the economy. So when the short-term interest i_t is above r^*, inflation is expected to decline because this gap signals a tightening of monetary conditions.

(Woodford, 2003) encapsulates the New Keynesian approach to monetary policy; he extended and confirmed the finding of (Kydland and Prescott, 1977) that rule-based monetary policy provides superior outcomes to discretionary policy when the model contains forward-looking agents. There is no evidence that central banks make policy via explicit policy rules, however, their staffs do use them for policy analysis.[1] It is unclear whether central banks follow such a theory when they set the policy interest rate. The Fed, however, refers to (Laubach and Williams', 2003) estimated r_t^* from the data. It is easy to see that estimating r_t^* from the data would be subject to estimation and specifications errors, which could be large, adding more uncertainty to policy. To simplify this daunting policy issue, in this analysis, we show how an equilibrium real rate r^* may be calculated as a *statistic*, that is, an economic variable that does not depend on unknown parameters of an econometric model.[2]

This approach eliminates the specification errors, has no estimation errors associated with econometrics methods, and relies fully on the *observable* data to compute.

The Model

We follow the standard theory used in quantitative studies of the business cycle (see, e.g., Prescott [2004]), whereby the household maximizes a discounted log-linear and time-separable utility function in order to make decisions about consumption–savings and consumption–leisure choice.

1　See (Andrade *et al.*, 2021). The Reserve Bank of New Zealand (2020, p. 28) states that "the importance of predictable rules is now a centerpiece of monetary theory and policy." For current US policymaking, see for example Board of Governors of the Federal Reserve System (2022). The policymakers at the Fed do not follow policy rules but they say they consult the rule-analysis provided to them by their staff.

2　This econometric literature includes the important contributions of (Laubach and Williams, 2003), (Holston *et al.*, 2017), (Orphanides and Williams, 2002), (Beyer and Wieland, 2019), and (Koenig and Armen, 2015), where uncertainty of economic models is widely acknowledged.

Reducing Inflation 285

The Household

The household holds bonds and stocks, owns the capital stock, and rents it to the firm. The firm combines capital and labor to produce real output using a constant return-to-scale Cobb–Douglas production function. The household also pays taxes on the consumption goods, on investments, on labor income, and on capital income. All tax revenues, except those used to finance the pure consumption goods, are given back to households in the form of transfers. The transfers are lump sum. Public expenditures are generally substitutes for private consumption (one-to-one for private consumption with the exception of military expenditures). The goods and services in question consist mostly of publicly provided education, health care, protection services, and judiciary services. Therefore, the model's household consumption c_t is not the same as the SNA measure C_t ; rather it includes government consumption, less military spending, and less indirect taxes on consumption. The government budget constraint holds all the time.

The utility function is log-linear, which helps in the computation of

$$E\left\{\sum_{t=s}^{\infty} \beta^{t+s} \left(\ln c_{t+s} + \alpha \ln\left(l_{t+s}\right)\right)\right\}.$$ (11.1)

where E is the expectation operator at time t, c_t is household consumption, and l_t is leisure. The parameter $\alpha > 0$ measures the nonmarket productive time of the household (e.g., the relative value of leisure). We assume that a person has 100 hours of productive time a week. The nonmarket productive time that is, leisure, is $100 - L_t$, where labor is average weekly hours worked per worker. Capital stock evolves according to this equation:

$$K_{t+1} = \left(1 - \delta\right) K_t + I_t,$$ (11.2)

where K_t is the stock of physical capital, δ is the depreciation rate, and I_t is investment.

The Firm

The firm produces output, Y_t, using capital K_t and labor L_t in a constant return-to-scale Cobb–Douglas production function with the shares of capital and labor, θ and $(1-\theta)$, respectively. The variable A_t is labor-augmenting technical progress, which we assume to be exogenous for simplicity.

$$Y_t = A_t K_t^{\theta} L_t^{1-\theta},$$ (11.3)

Next, we set the Lagrange multiplier optimization problem with the Lagrange multiplier λ and the discount factor β. The budget constraint has a simple tax system (see Prescott [2004]). Let τ_c be the consumption tax rate, τ_I is the investment tax rate, τ_L is the marginal labor tax rate, w_t is the real wage rate (W_t is the nominal wage rate), τ_k is the capital income tax rate, r_t is *nominal* interest rate, P_t^K is the purchase price of capital, and TR_t is transfers. Tax revenues, except those used to finance pure public good consumption, are returned to households as lump-sum

286 *Reducing Inflation*

transfer payments.[3] Taxes could affect the prices of consumption and investment goods (e.g., investment tax credit).[4] The household owns bonds B_t and stocks S_t, where their prices are P_t^b and P_t^s, respectively (the superscript b denotes bonds, and s stocks), and d_t is the dividend.

The budget constraint BC_t is in *real* terms:

$$(1-\tau_L)W_tL_t + (1-\tau_k)(r_t - \delta)P_t^K K_t + \delta P_t^K K_t + B_{t-1} + (P_t^s + d_t)S_{t-1} + TR_t$$
$$= (1+\tau_c)P_tc_t + (1+\tau_I)P_t^I I_t + P_t^b B_t + P_t^s S_t \tag{11.4}$$

The multiple-period Lagrange multiplier is:

$$[lnc_t + \alpha ln(100 - L_t) + \beta u(lnc_{t+1} + \alpha ln(100 - L_{t+1})$$
$$+\beta^2 u(lnc_{t+2} + \alpha ln(100 - L_{t+2})]$$
$$+\beta^3 u(\ldots) + \lambda_t[BC_t] + \beta\lambda_{t+1}[BC_{t+1}] + \beta^2\lambda_{t+2}[\ldots] \tag{11.5}$$

Solving from the time-sequential Lagrange multiplier problems, and focusing on the variables, consumption–leisure ratio $c_t/(100 - L_t)$, and capital–labor ratio K_t/L_t, the MRS between leisure and consumption is:

$$\frac{\dfrac{\alpha}{100-L_t}}{\dfrac{1}{c_t}} = \frac{1-\tau_L}{1+\tau_c}\frac{W_t}{P_t}.^5 \tag{11.6}$$

To simplify further, we introduce the tax rate τ:

$$\text{Let } \frac{\tau_c + \tau_L}{1+\tau_c} = \tau. \tag{11.7}$$

Adding 1 to both sides,

$$1 - \frac{\tau_c + \tau_L}{1+\tau_c} = 1 - \tau. \tag{11.8}$$

We arrive at:

$$\left(\frac{1-\tau_L}{1+\tau_c}\right) = 1-\tau. \tag{11.9}$$

So the MRS becomes:

$$\frac{\dfrac{\alpha}{100-L_t}}{\dfrac{1}{c_t}} = (1-\tau)\frac{W_t}{P_t}. \tag{11.10}$$

---

3 This is especially true for the United States, see (Christiano and Eichenbaum, 1992).

4 This is a significantly simpler tax system than in the United States. However, it would not alter any conclusion significantly because in this model, the most important parameters are the factor shares and the relative value of leisure. See (McGrattan and Prescott, 2005).

5 The price level could be set to 1, but we kept it as it will become clear at the end why we did that.

We assume no financial market friction; therefore, we do not model the banking system, leverages, and the default rate. The model captures the linkages between the financial market and the rest of the economy via bond, stock, and the general price level. The stock–pricing equation is:

$$-\lambda P_t^s + \beta \lambda_{t+1}\left(P_{t+1}^s + d_{t+1}\right) = 0,$$ (11.11)

And for the bond price

$$-\lambda_t P_t^b + \beta \lambda_{t+1} = 0.$$ (11.12)

From finance theory and Eq. (11.12), the price of the bond is:

$$P_t^b = \frac{\beta \lambda_{t+1}}{\lambda_t}.$$ (11.13)

The term $\dfrac{\beta \lambda_{t+1}}{\lambda_t}$ is the "pricing kernel" of the economy. Thus, the price of the bond is equal to the pricing kernel × 1. The one is the payoff of the nominal bond assuming the face value of the bond = 1. The price of bonds, stocks, and the aggregate price are linked via the pricing kernel.

The stock price and the bond price are linked via

$$P_t^s = \frac{\beta \lambda_{t+1}}{\lambda_t}\left(P_{t+1}^s + d_{t+1}\right).$$ (11.14)

In real terms, divide by the CPI, and we get:

$$\frac{P_t^s}{P_t} = P_t^b \frac{\left(P_{t+1}^s + d_{t+1}\right)}{P_t}.$$ (11.15)

The variables with the subscripts $t+1$ in Eqs (11.11) to (11.15) are the expected values E_t. Although it does not affect the solution of our model, this relationship demonstrates, implicitly, that the pricing kernel binds the three prices, which represent the relationship between the macro economy and financial markets.

The FOCs from the firm side, basically, the marginal products whose ratio gives the MRTS between capital and labor equal to the factor input price ratio.

$$\theta\left(\frac{Y_t}{K_t}\right) = \lambda_t\left(1 - \tau_k\right)r_t + \tau_k \delta P_t^K,$$ (11.16)

And

$$\left(1 - \theta\right)\left(\frac{Y_t}{L_t}\right) = \lambda_t\left(1 - \tau_L\right)w_t,$$ (11.17)

Solving for w_t, and equating to Eq. (11.10), we get:

$$\left(1 - \tau_k\right)r_t + \tau_k P_t^K \delta = \left(\frac{\theta}{1-\theta}\right)\left(\frac{1-\tau_L}{1-\tau}\right)\left(\frac{K_t}{L_t}\right)^{-1}\left(\frac{\alpha c_t}{100 - L_t}\right).$$ (11.18)

288   *Reducing Inflation*

Subtract $\tau_k \delta$ from both sides and divide both sides by $1 - \tau_k$, we get:

$$r_t = \left(\frac{\theta}{1-\theta}\right)\left(\frac{1-\tau_L}{(1-\tau)(1-\tau_k)}\right)\left(\frac{K_t}{L_t}\right)^{-1}\left(\frac{\alpha c_t}{(100-L_t)}\right) - \frac{\tau_k \delta P_t^K}{1-\tau_k} \tag{11.19}$$

Let the constant terms be

$$\Gamma_1 = \frac{\theta}{1-\theta}\frac{\alpha(1-\tau_L)}{(1-\tau)(1-\tau_k)}, \quad {}^6 \tag{11.20}$$

and

$$\Gamma_2 = \frac{\tau_k \delta}{1-\tau_k}. \tag{11.21}$$

Let

$$l_t = 100 - L_t. \tag{11.22}$$

Thus, Eq. (11.19) reduces to

$$r_t = \Gamma_1 \times \left(\frac{K_t}{L_t}\right)^{-1} \times \frac{c_t}{l_t} - \Gamma_2 P_t^K. \tag{11.23}$$

Take log, lag the equation by one period, and take the difference as:

$$\Delta lnr_t = \left(\Delta lnc_t - \Delta lnl_t\right) - \left(\Delta lnK_t - \Delta lnL_t\right) + \Delta lnP_t^K. \tag{11.24}$$

In the long-run equilibrium with arbitrage and no uncertainty, $\ln\left(r_t / r_{t-1}\right)$ is r_t. Assuming that the purchase price of capital increases at the same rate of inflation, thus $ln(P_t^K / P_{t-1}^K)$ is π_t. Taking π_t to the other side, Eq. (11.24) becomes:

$$r_t - \pi_t = r_t^* = \left(\Delta lnc_t - \Delta lnl_t\right) - \left(\Delta K_t - \Delta L_t\right). \tag{11.25}$$

The RHS variables are the growth rates of four *observable* variables that we can compute easily; r_t^* depends on the consumption–leisure growth rates relative to capital–labor growth rates. r^* is zero in the steady state because all the growth rates are zero. However, the wider the gap the higher r^* is. When consumption–leisure ratio grows faster (slower) than the capital–labor ratio, r_t^* tends to increase (decrease).[7] The calculation of r_t^* is straightforward and depends on four *observable* variables. See the data file.

---

6 There are either small or no changes in taxes. However, if changes are significant, the tax rates could be kept in the model. The shares of capital and labor are almost constant.

7 For the asset prices in Eq. (11.16), $R_t^S - \pi = R_t^B - \pi_t + R_{P_{t+1}^S + d_{t+1}}$, where the LHS, the real return from the stock market, is equal to the real return from safe bonds plus the return from future price and dividend movements.

We will compute r_t^* for the United States first and compare our results with Laubach and Williams-type estimate, r_t^{HLW}; then we will compute r_t^* for a number of countries where data are readily available.

r_t^* for the United States

For the United States, we use annual data from 2000 to 2019 to compare r_t^* with r_t^{HLW} over time. Appendix 11.1 presents the data. Woodford (2003) emphasizes the gap between the natural rate and the short-term nominal interest rate as a key channel through which the Fed can affect the economy. Figure 11.1 plots the three gaps, $r_{1t}^* - i_t$, $r_{2t}^* - i_t$, and the Holston–Laubach–Williams' $r_t^{*HLW} - i_t$, where i_t is the effective federal fund rate. We use working age population to measure labor in r_{1t}^* and employment in r_{2t}^*. The plot suggests that the correlation between our computed gaps and r_t^{*HLW} gap was higher before 2010. From 2010 to 2019, the gaps increased and turned positive with $r_{2t}^* - i_t > r_{1t}^* - i_t > r_t^{*HLW} - i_t$.

Table 11.1 reports the descriptive statistics. On *average*, our interest gaps turned positive after 2009. The gaps are much wider than $r_t^{*HLW} - i_t$. A higher positive gap implies that i_t is set much lower than r_t^*, hence the easy monetary policy. Therefore, more anticipated inflation is associated with $r_{2t}^* - i_t$ than the other two gaps. Note that the gaps at time t *do not* provide sufficient information about the magnitude and the timing of future inflation because monetary policy lags are long and variable. Therefore, all we know in 2019 is that more inflation is anticipated. Printing money to finance increasing fiscal spending will have an impact on r^*. It will increase, if the growth rate of consumption–leisure is greater than the growth rate of capital–labor ratio and decrease if capital–labor growth is higher.

Note that financial markets affect the natural rate of interest. The model accounts for the financial markets (Eqs 11.14 and 11.15). Under uncertainty, the natural rate of interest is correlated with the real rate of returns on stocks (the real returns on capital) even though the latter is significantly higher and highly volatile. To show that, we plot the 95 Percent Chi-Squared test for the correlation between the natural rate r_{1t}^* and the real rate of return on stocks in Figure 11.2. Figure 11.3 plots the scatter plot between the natural rate r_{2t}^* and the real rate of return on stocks.

We do not have detailed data for all other countries. However, the Penn World Table and FRED report some selective usable data to compute r_t^* for Australia, Denmark, New Zealand, Sweden, and the United Kingdom. The variables are: real consumption of households and government at constant 2017 national prices (in mil. 2017 US$); capital stock at constant 2017 national prices (in mil. 2017 US$); number of persons engaged (in millions); and average annual hours worked by persons engaged and working age population (age 15–64). Figure 11.4 plots r_t^* for these countries.[8] Table 11.2 reports the descriptive statistics.

---

8 Real consumption for these countries is unadjusted for military expenditures and indirect taxes like the US. case because we do not have the data. Therefore, the level of real consumption is greater than it should've been. We also use employment to measure labor instead of working-age population.

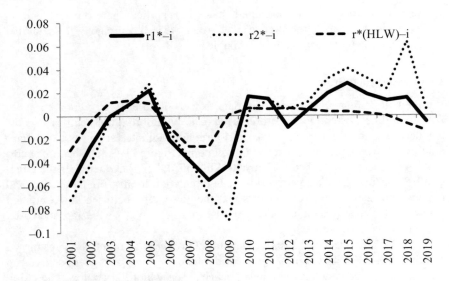

Figure 11.1 The US Federal Fund Rate – r* Gaps

Table 11.1 Computed r_t^* and Interest Rate Gaps for the United States

		r_{1t}^*	r_{2t}^*	r_t^{*HLW}	i_t	$r_{1t}^* - i_t$	$r_{2t}^* - i_t$	$r_t^{*HLW} - i_t$
2001–2009	Mean	0.009	0.0004	0.026	0.032	−0.023	−0.032	−0.007
	STD	0.018	0.0273	0.005	0.019	0.029	0.023	0.017
2010–2019	Mean	0.016	0.0332	0.006	0.004	0.012	0.040	0.001
	STD	0.011	0.2040	0.002	0.006	0.012	0.019	0.007

r_t^*, r_{1t}^*, and r_{2t}^* are our computed natural rates; r_t^{*HLW} is Holston–Laubach–Williams natural rate; i_t is the federal fund rate.

Denmark has the lowest natural rate of interest on average while New Zealand has the highest, and it is the most volatile in the group. Kurtosis indicates tailed-non-normal distributions. All countries experienced a significant decline in r^* during the 2009 recession because the consumption–leisure, employment, and investment growth rate fell significantly. The nominal policy interest rate in November 2022, which we report in the last column, indicates significant tightening relative to our computed r_t^* statistics in all countries. All central banks revealed that they would increase the policy rates even more in the future and until they see inflation falling. These central banks' statements may suggest that they have higher estimates of the natural rates than ours, or no estimates at all, or these are strong overreactions to their unexpected high inflation rates.

Reducing Inflation 291

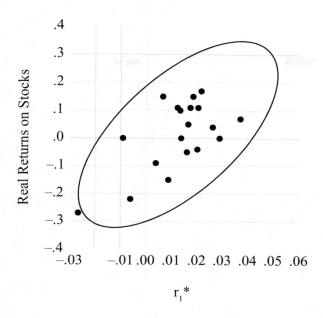

Figure 11.2 Chi-Square Correlation Test of Real Rate of Return on Stocks and the Natural Rate r_{1t}^*

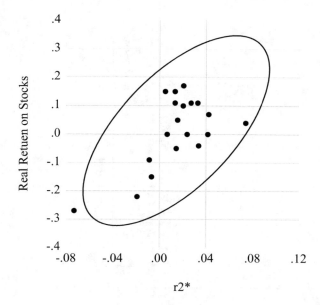

Figure 11.3 Chi-Square Correlation Test of Real Rate of Return on Stocks and the Natural Rate r_{2t}^*

292 Reducing Inflation

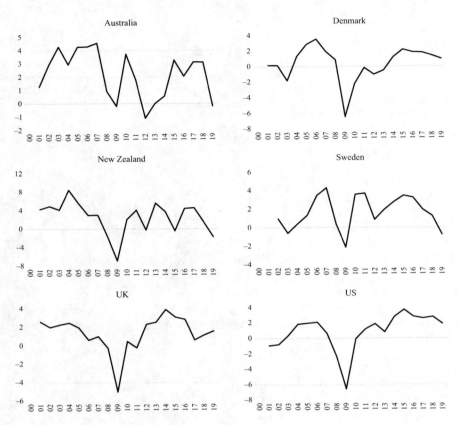

Figure 11.4 Computed r_t^* for Selective Advanced Countries

Table 11.2 Descriptive Statistics of Computed r_t^* for Selective Countries, 2000–2019

Countries	Mean	Max	Min.	Std. Dev.	Skew.	Kurt.	i_t^i
Australia	2.18	4.56	−1.09	1.78	−0.32	1.80	3.10
Denmark	0.41	3.53	−6.48	2.24	−1.51	5.75	1.90
New Zealand	2.53	8.44	−6.89	3.49	−0.98	4.01	4.25
Sweden	1.67	4.29	−2.12	1.80	−0.37	2.25	2.50
UK	1.28	3.90	−5.01	1.93	−1.85	7.25	3.00
US	0.87	3.76	−6.57	2.37	−1.70	6.14	3.83
All	1.49	8.44	−6.89	2.41	−0.91	5.37	

(^{i}) The nominal policy interest rate in November 2002.

Appendix 11.1
Data Appendix

WAP_t	Working age population (15–64)	OECD Statistics
e_t	Total employment (full time plus part time)	OECD Statistics
$\dfrac{h_t}{e_t}$	Hours worked per worker	OECD Statistics
L_t	$\left(\dfrac{e_t}{WAP_t} \times \dfrac{h_t}{e_t}\right) / 52$ is average weekly Hours worked – labor supply	
C_t	Real household and government consumption at constant 2011 national prices (in mil. 2011 US\$)	Penn WT 10.1
G_t^M	Real military spending	World Bank Data
T_t^i	Indirect tax rate on consumption consists of sales tax plus tax on use of goods plus custom duties collected for the EU plus custom duty plus excise plus tax on specific goods plus tax on specific services	OECD Statistics
$c_t = C_t - G_t^M - t_t^i$	Model consumption	
K_t	Capital stock at constant 2011 national prices (in mil. 2011 US\$)	Penn World, Table 10.1
P_t^K	The capital price deflator	Penn World, Table 10.1
P_t^s	Total share prices for all shares for the United States, Index 2015 = 100	FRED
i_t	3-month interest rate. For the US, the effective federal funds rate	FRED and OECD
Y	Real GDP	Penn World, Table 10.1

294 *Reducing Inflation*

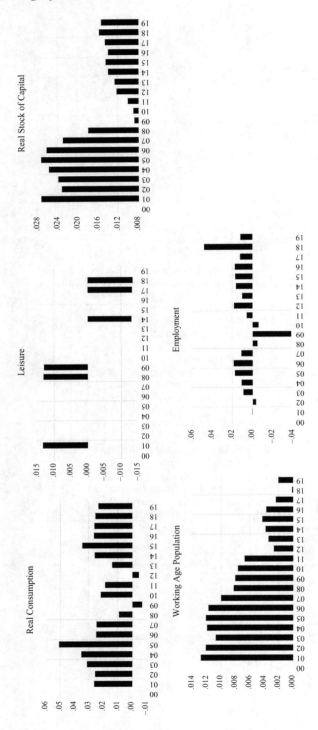

Figure A11.1 The US Data Growth Rates Required to Compute r^*

12 Summary and Conclusion

There are a number of different economic theories of inflation, which are based on different assumptions and tell different stories. We tested the oldest theory, the Quantity Theory of Money (QTM) using time series data for 42 countries from 1960. The log of the CPI and the log of broad money are cointegrated, that is, they share a common long-run trend. Dynamic OLS regressions of the log level of broad money on log of CPI confirm that there is a long-run relationship between these two variables in most countries, the lags are long, and there is an approximately one-to-one relationship between the log of broad money and the log of CPI in many countries.

Conditional on various shocks such as the two main oil price shocks, GFC and AFC, and country-specific shocks such as draughts, natural disasters, wars, domestic financial and banking crisis, and political crises, the relationship between the growth rate of broad money and the inflation rate varies across the world. There is a significant impact of money growth on inflation, which is one-to-one in a number of countries such as the United States; however, countries with low and stable inflation (e.g., Asian countries) have weak relationships between money growth and inflation. There is a weak correlation between money growth and inflation in the developed countries that target inflation explicitly especially during the successful inflation-targeting periods, that is, Friedman's thermostat story is the logical explanation for such weak correlations (Taylor, 2001). Shocks such as oil price shocks and other country-specific shocks can amplify inflation when they coincide with loose policies. Money growth seems to be significantly associated with high asset prices, housing, and stocks. Ignoring the effect of the quantity of money on goods, services, and asset prices, and money growth on inflation in conducting monetary policy is shortsighted.

In the long run, money neutrality holds in the data. We find no evidence that money could stimulate real output in the short run either, which casts doubt on price rigidity. There is evidence, however, that money growth and the real output gap are positively correlated in Singapore, Gabon, South Africa, Trinidad and Tobago, New Zealand, and the United States from 1960 to 1985 only. The general lack of correlation between money growth and output over the business cycle raises a question about the central bank' money-growth policies. We tested three hypotheses and found significant evidence for; first, central banks

DOI: 10.4324/9781003382218-12

296   Summary and Conclusion

make seigniorage revenues; second, money is highly correlated with government deficit spending; and finally, there is an illusion that money props asset prices, hence wealth. We find significant correlation between the monetary base and seigniorage revenues in countries where data are available; significant correlation between broad money and seigniorage revenues; significant correlation between the growth rate of government spending and the growth rate of broad money; and finally there is a strong evidence that money growth is highly correlated with asset price (stock and housing prices) inflation.

The second oldest theory of inflation is the celebrated Phillips curve. The Phillips curve has been intertwined with a number of very important macroeconomic, macro-econometric, and monetary policy literatures. We discussed many of the issues. Our Sample Generalized Variance bivariate test statistic of the New Keynesian specification of the Phillips curve, whereby the change in inflation $\Delta\pi_t$ is a function of the output gap, indicates that such a relationship is unstable in almost all the countries in our sample.

Furthermore, we tested the data for the United States from March 1960 to March 2022 and for New Zealand from March 1992 to December 2021. The United States explicitly targeted inflation from 2012, and New Zealand stabilized inflation at a low level for the entire period from 1992. We argued that the *Accelerationist* Phillip curve, where inflation is a function of two unobservable variables, expected inflation and the output gap, is subject to some serious specification and estimation problems. Measurement errors cause bias and inconsistency in OLS single-equation parameter estimates. These two variables are also endogenous; thus OLS parameter estimates will be biased and inconsistent. In order to tie the Phillips curve to the literature on expectations formation, e.g., rational expectations versus backward adopted expectations, we estimated the Phillips curve in a system of equations, that is, demand and supply, using the Maximum Likelihood method and imposed and tested theoretical restrictions.

The specification of expected inflation is the most problematic specification issue and has important policy consequences. We tested two specifications. One is, where the expected inflation is proportional to last period's inflation: $\pi_t^e = \alpha\pi_{t-1}$; and the other, where expected inflation is a function of more variables including money growth, government spending growth, and lagged inflation, and lagged nominal GDP growth.

Our estimates of a simultaneous-equation system with theoretical cross-equation restrictions show that the data support the predictions of the rational expectations theory. Namely, monetary policy is ineffective, that is, anticipated aggregate demand shocks do not have real effect, while surprises, that is, unanticipated aggregate demand shocks, do. However, the data rejected the hypothesis that the coefficient of expected inflation is equal to 1. This, however, is a joint hypothesis problem. The data reject the long-run *vertical* Phillips curve and the assumption of rational expectations. Disentangling these two issues is impossible, and this particular test seems to be jointly uninformative. Nonetheless, the data also fits the short-run Phillips curve in the United States and New Zealand in the sense that both expected inflation and the output are statistically significant. Expected inflation, whether it is

Summary and Conclusion 297

lagged inflation or a function of a wider set of variables as in rational expectations, has a significantly larger coefficient than the coefficient of the output gap.

As a result of fitting the short--run Phillips curve to the data, we explain why the Fed and the Reserve Bank of New Zealand, among other inflation-targeting advanced central banks, failed to anticipate the recent rise in inflation. We solve the model, make in-sample dynamic stochastic projections, and compare the projections of the New Keynesian specification of expected inflation with those of the rational expectations' specification. We show that the projections of the New Keynesian specification underpredict inflation and have wider standard errors than the projections of the model with rational expectations.

We think that there are at least three reasons for the inflation-targeting central banks in the advanced countries for assuming such backward-looking expectations' specification. First, the central banks of the developed countries in our sample have successfully stabilized inflation at a low rate. Therefore, they might have presumed that the best forecast of tomorrow's inflation is today's. On the surface, it seems natural and maybe rational to assume so. However, this assumption is not innocuous. They neglected the simple mathematical fact that such specification, that is, $\pi_t^e = \alpha\pi_{t-1}; \alpha < 1$, always underpredicts inflation.

Second, if the Phillips curve is the *modus operandi*, then the central bank can only reduce inflation if it slows down the economy, that is, creates a recession. A model of rational expectation specification would be unable to generate recessions to fit the New Keynesian story. Inertia in New Keynesian models is necessary to tell a New Keynesian story.

Third, a model with full rational expectation specification results in *policy ineffectiveness*, which is not helpful for central banks with *active monetary policy*.

So even if backward-looking inflation expectation seems rational because of the success to target inflation at a low and stable rate, it would always underpredict inflation. Furthermore, such assumption would not be helpful for active monetary policy because, in such models, the central bank increases the short-term interest at time t in order to slow down the economy at time $t + k$. This is because *monetary policy lags are long and variab*le, and because it anticipates future inflation. So when it fails to predict inflation or if it underpredicts inflation systematically, it fails to take a timely action. The central bank then acts late and much stronger, that is, raises short-term interest rate significantly, when it suddenly faces inflation, which has adverse real consequences.

Our final finding is that Modern Monetary theory policy prescription to reduce inflation by raising taxes has severe adverse economic consequences. We solve a micro-foundation model for equilibrium hours worked as a function of taxes, consumption–output ratio, and other parameters. Then, we use data for the United Kingdom and Norway, which are inflation-targeting countries to estimate a VAR, solve it, and produce baseline dynamic stochastic projections to the year 2040. We examine severe hypothetical scenario involving doubling taxes permanently and show the mean dynamic projections of key macroeconomic variables relative to baseline.

Economic theory predicts that a permanent increase in the tax rate causes the aggregate demand curve to shift down thus reducing investment demand and

298 *Summary and Conclusion*

consumption, hence reducing real output. At the same time, the increase in the tax rate shifts the aggregate supply curve to the left (reduce it), reducing the real output because of the reduction in hours worked. The price falls only if aggregate demand shifts down by more than the aggregate supply curve, that is, aggregate demand shift dominates. Therefore, the final effect of the increase in taxes on the price level depends on the relative magnitudes of these aggregate demand and supply shifts. The MMT inflation's reduction policy recommendation seems oblivious to the fact that higher taxes shift the aggregate supply curve in addition to the aggregate demand curve. While the UK data are consistent with the MMT prediction that higher taxes reduce the price level, the Norwegian data do not. The price level increases in Norway because the labor supply response to raising taxes is very large. It shifts the aggregate supply curve to the left by more than it shifts the aggregate demand.

Our analysis indicates that there is one main cause of inflation, and that is bad policies which propagate through the quantity of money and inflation expectations mostly and, to a lesser extent, through other variables such as the output gap. Bad luck (bad shocks), e.g., global and country and regional-specific adverse supply shocks such as oil price shocks, amplify inflation if they coincide with highly expansionary fiscal and monetary policy.

Policymakers tinker with policy instruments continuously in order to stabilize the quantities and prices in an active New Keynesian policy environment. Consumers, producers, and investors, too, are just as uncertain as the policymakers. They all make adjustments. The producers want the optimal price for what they sell, but won't get it right first and have to adjust; consumers want to buy the optimal quantity at the most satisfactory price, but won't get it the first time and have to adjust; and so on do forth until the equilibrium price and quantity are reached. They try to understand the effect of the policy and shocks on their decisions too. This is a very complex uncertain dynamic. Under uncertainty, however, the adjustments are cautious. Policy rules as opposed to active discretion may reduce the uncertainty and allow market participants to make more optimal decisions. Following policy rules rather than discretion may enhance market efficiency. However, since we never had any historical episodes of policy rules, we would not know what will happen. Would a model with backward-looking inflation expectations predict a rise in inflation in a regime of policy rule?

John B. Taylor wrote in his blog "Economic One" of 17 June 2022 that rules are back in the Monetary Policy Report last March. He quoted Federal Reserve Chair Jerome Powell from his March 2 and March 3 testimony at the House and Senate who said, "we'll have it in the next [Monetary Policy Report] one . . ." He was responding to questions at hearings of the House Financial Services Committee on March 2 and of the Senate Banking Committee on March 3 about why he and the Federal Reserve Board omitted the section on monetary policy rules in the just released February 2022 Monetary Policy Report. Well, he was true to his word. The Monetary Policy Report released today has put the section on policy rules, including the Taylor rule as number one on the list, back in. It stated that simple monetary policy rules, which relate a policy interest rate to a small number of other economic variables, can provide useful guidance to policymakers. And that simple monetary policy rule considered here calls for raising the target range for the federal funds rate significantly.

This all sounds very good, however, I am less convinced about the seriousness of the Fed and any other central bank regarding their intentions to use "instruments" rules. Instead, I envisage a future whereby central banks use Artificial Intelligence (AI) to forecast inflation. It is very promising because, among many other things, AI is a study of rational agents. AI could be used to choose the conditioning variables included in the information set optimally. There is evidence that AI forecasts are relatively better than many forecasting methods in the sense that they are unlike our prejudiced, judgmental, and highly subjective forecasts, see for example, (Coulombe *et al.*, 2022), (Maccarrone *et al.*, 2021), and (Hall, 2018). Machines do not possess such inherited biases as we do. Therefore, I expect AI forecasts to have relatively smaller forecast errors, less variability, and bias, hence small policy errors. I think that AI forecasts of inflation would improve current monetary policy.

References

Agrrawal, P., Doug Waggle, and Daniel H. Sandweiss. (2017). Suicides as a Response to Adverse Market Sentiment (1980–2016), *PLoS One*, Public Health Implications of Changing Climate. Open Access. https://doi.org/10.1371/journal.pone.0186913

Akerlof, George A. and Janet L. Yellen. (1985). Can Small Deviations from Rationality Make Significant Differences to Economic Equilibria? *American Economic Review*, 75(4), 708–720. JSTOR 1821349.

Alvarez, F., Francesco Lippi, and Aleksei Oskolkov. (2022a). The Macroeconomics of Sticky Prices with Generalized Hazard Functions, *The Quarterly Journal of Economics*, 137(2) (May), 989–1038.

Alvarez, Jorge, John C. Bluedorn, Niels-Jakob Hansen, Youyou Huang, Evgenia Pugacheva, and Alexandre Sollaci. (2022b). *Wage-Price Spirals: What is the Historical Evidence?* IMF Working Paper No. 2022/221, Washington, DC: IMF, pp. 1–28.

Anderson, T. W. (1958). *Introduction to Multivariate Statistical Analysis*, New York: John Wiley.

Andrade, P., J. Galí, H. Le Bihan, and J. Matheron. (2021). Should the ECB adjust its Strategy in the Face of a Lower r^*? *Journal of Economic Dynamics and Control*, 132, 104–207. ISSN 0165–1889. https://doi.org/10.1016/j.jedc.2021.104207.

Andrade, P., J. Galí, H. Le Bihan, and J. Matheron. (2019). The Optimal Inflation Target and the Natural Rate of Interest, *Brookings Papers on Economic Activity* (Fall), 173–255.

Attfield, C. L. F., D. Demery, and N. W. Duck. (1985). *Rational Expectations in Macroeconomics: An Introduction to Theory and Evidence*, New York: Basil Blackwell, ISBN 0–631–13663-X, and ISBN 0-631-13964-8-pbk.

Azariadis, C. (1975). Implicit Contracts and Underemployment Equilibria, *Journal of Political Economy*, 83, 1180–1202.

Baillie, Richard T., Ching-Fan Chung, and Margie A. Tieslau. (1996). Analysing Inflation by the Fractionally Integrated ARFIMA – GARCH Model, *Journal of Applied Econometrics*, 11(1) (January), 23–40.

Baily, M. N. (1974). Wages and Employment under Uncertain Demand, *Review of Economic Studies*, 41, 37–50.

Ball, L. and D. Romer. (1989). Are Prices Too Sticky? *The Quarterly Journal of Economics*, 104(3) (August), 507–524. https://doi.org/10.2307/2937808

Ball, L. and N. Gregory Mankiw. (1994). A Sticky-Price Manifesto, *Carnegie-Rochester Conference Series on Public Policy*, 41, 127–151. ISSN 0167–2231. https://doi.org/10.1016/0167-2231(94)00016-6

Ball, L. and S. Mazumder. (2021). A Phillips Curve for the Euro Area, *International Finance*, 24(1), 2–17.

References   301

Barro, R. J. (1993). *Macroeconomics*, 4th Edition, New York: Wiley.

Barro, R. J. (1977). Long Term Contracting, Sticky Prices, and Monetary Policy, *Journal of Monetary Economics*, 3, 305–316.

Barro, R. J. (1974). Are Government Bonds Net Wealth? *Journal of Political Economy*, 82(6), 1095–1117. doi:10.1086/260266

Barro, R. J. and David B. Gordon. (1983). Rules, Discretion and Reputation in a Model of Monetary Policy, *Journal of Monetary Economics*, 12(1), 101–121.

Barsky, Robert B., Christopher L. House, and Miles S. Kimball. (2007). Sticky-Price Models and Durable Goods, *American Economic Review*, 97(3), 984–998.

Baxter, M. and R. King. (1999). Measuring Business Cycles Approximate Band-Pass Filters For Economic Time Series, *Review of Economics and Statistics*, 81(4), 575–593.

Beveridge, S. and Charles Nelson. (1981). A New Approach to Decomposition of Economic Time Series into Permanent and Transitory Components with Particular Attention to Measurement of the 'Business Cycle', *Journal of Monetary Economics*, 7(2), 151–174.

Beyer, R. C. M. and V. Wieland. (2019). Instability, Imprecision, and Inconsistent Use of Equilibrium Real Interest Rate Estimates, *Journal of International Money and Finance*, 94, 1–14.

Bils, M. and P. J. Klenow. (2004). Some Evidence of the Importance of Sticky Prices, *Journal of Political Economy*, 112(5), 947–985.

Blanchard, O. (2016). *The US Phillips Curve: Back to the 60s?* Washington, DC: Peterson Institute for International Economics (PIIE) Policy Brief, January 1–16.

Blanchard, O., G. Dell'Ariccia, and P. Mauro. (2010). Rethinking Macroeconomic Policy, *Journal of Money, Credit and Banking*, 42, 199–215.

Blinder, A. S. (1994). *On Sticky Prices: Academic Theories Meet the Real World in Monetary Policy*, (ed.) G. Mankiw, Monetary Policy, Conference January 21–24, 1993, National Bureau of Economic Research, The University of Chicago Press, pp. 117–154. ISBN: 0-226-50308-9. www.nber.org/books/greg94-1

Blinder, A. S. (1997). Distinguished Lecture on Economics in Government What Central Bankers Could Learn from Academics – and Vice Versa, *Journal of Economic Perspectives*, 11(2), 3–19.

Boivin, Jean, Marc P. Giannoni, and Ilian Mihov. (2009). Sticky Prices and Monetary Policy: Evidence from Disaggregated US Data, *American Economic Review*, 99(1), 350–384.

Breitung, Jörg. (2000). The Local Power of Some Unit Root Tests for Panel Data, in B. Baltagi (ed.), *Advances in Econometrics, Vol. 15: Nonstationary Panels, Panel Cointegration, and Dynamic Panels*, Amsterdam: JAI Press, pp. 161–178.

Brown, M. B. and A. B. Forsythe. (1974a). "Robust Tests for the Equality of Variances," *Journal of the American Statistical Association*, 69, 364–367.

Brown, M. B. and A. B. Forsythe. (1974b). "The Small Sample Behavior of Some Test Statistics which Test the Equality of Several Means," *Technometrics*, 16, 129–132.

Buiter, H. Willem. (1999). *The Fallacy of the Fiscal Theory of the Price Level*, unpublished manuscript, the Bank of England, London, UK.

Calvo, Guillermo. (1983). Staggered Prices in a Utility-Maximizing Framework, *Journal of Monetary Economics*, 12(3), 383–398.

Campbell, John Y. (1995). Some Lessons from the Yield Curve, *Journal of Economic Perspectives*, 9(3) (Summer), 129–152.

Campbell, John Y. and Tuomo Vuolteenaho. (2004). Inflation Illusion and Stock Prices, *American Economic Review*, 94(2), 19–23. doi:10.1257/0002828041301533

Carlstrom, Charles and Timothy Fuerst. (2000). The Fiscal Theory of the Price Level, *Federal Reserve Bank of Cleveland Economic Review*, Q1, 22–32.

302 *References*

Chari, V. V., L. Christiano, and M. Eichenbaum. (1988). Expectations Traps and Discretion, *Journal of Economic Theory*, 81(2), 462–492.

Christiano, L. J. and M. Eichenbaum. (1992). Current Real Business Cycle Theories and Aggregate Labor Market Fluctuations, *American Economic Review*, 82 (June), 430–450.

Christiano, L. J. and M. Eichenbaum. (1990). Unit Roots in Real GNP: Do We Know, and Do We Care? *Carnegie-Rochester Conference Series on Public Policy*, 32 (Spring), 7–62.

Christiano, L. J. and Terry J. Fitzgerald. (2003). The Band Pass Filter, *International Economic Review*, 44(2), 435–465.

Christiano, L. J. and Terry J. Fitzgerald. (2000). *Understanding the Fiscal Theory of the Price Level*, NBER Working Paper No. 7668, Cambridge, MA: National Bureau of Economic Research, 1050 Massachusetts Avenue, p. 02138. www.nber.org/papers/w7668.

Chugh, Sanjay K. (2015). *Modern Macroeconomics* Cambridge, MA and London: MIT Press.

Clarida, Richard, Jordi Gali, and Mark Gertler. (2000). Monetary Policy Rules and Macroeconomic Stability: Evidence and Some Theory, *Quarterly Journal of Economics*, 115(1), 147–180.

Clarida, R., Jordi Gali, and Mark Gertler. (1999). The Science of Monetary Policy: A New Keynesian Perspective, *Journal of Economic Literature*, 37(4), 1661–1707.

Cochrane, J. (2000). *Money as Stock: Price Level Determination with No Money Demand*, NBER Working Paper 7498, Cambridge, MA: National Bureau of Economic Research, 1050 Massachusetts Avenue, p. 02138.

Cochrane, J. (1991). *Comments*, Cambridge, MA: NBER Macroeconomics Annual.

Cogley, Timothy and Thomas J. Sargent. (2005a). Drift and Volatilities: Monetary Policies and the Outcomes in the Post WWII U.S., *Review of Economic Dynamics, Elsevier for the Society for Economic Dynamics*, 8(2) (April), 262–302.

Cogley, Timothy and Thomas J. Sargent. (2005b). The Conquest of US Inflation: Learning and Robustness to Model Uncertainty, *Review of Economic Dynamics*, 8(2), 528–563. ISSN 1094–2025. https://doi.org/10.1016/j.red.2005.02.001.

Cogley, Timothy and Thomas J. Sargent. (2002). Evolving Postwar War II U.S. Inflation Dynamics, NBER Chapters, in *NBER Macroeconomics Annual 2001*, Cambridge, MA: National Bureau of Economic Research, Inc, Vol. 16, pp. 331–388.

Conover, W. J., M. E. Johnson, and M. M. Johnson. (1981). A Comparative Study of Tests for Homogeneity of Variance with Applications to the Outer Continental Shelf Bidding Data, *Technometrics*, 23, 351–361.

Coulombe, Philippe Goulet, Maxime Leroux, Dalibor Stevanovic, and Stéphane Surprenant. (2022). How is Machine Learning Useful for Macroeconomic Forecasting? *Journal of Applied Econometrics*, 37(5), 920–964.

Debelle, Guy and Douglas Laxton. (1997). Is the Phillips Curve Really a Curve? Some Evidence from Canada, the United Kingdom, and the United States, *IMF Staff Papers*, 44, 249–282.

Debelle, Guy and James Vickery. (2007). Is the Phillips Curve A Curve? Some Evidence and Implications for Australia, *Economic Record*, 74(227), 384–398.

Dennis, J. E. and R. B. Schnabel. (1983). *Secant Methods for Systems of Nonlinear Equations, Numerical Methods for Unconstrained Optimization and Nonlinear Equations*, London: Prentice-Hall.

Diamond, P. A. and J. A. Mirrlees. (1971). Optimal Taxation and Public Production I: Production Efficiency, *The American Economic Review*, 61(1), 8–27. www.jstor.org/stable/1910538

References   303

Diamond, P. A., L. J. Helms, and J. A. Mirrlees. (1980). Optimal Taxation in a Stochastic Economy: A Cobb – Douglas Example, *Journal of Public Economics*, 14(1), 1–29. ISSN 0047–2727. https://doi.org/10.1016/0047-2727(80)90002-X

Dickey, D. A. and W. A. Fuller. (1979). Distribution of the Estimators for Autoregressive Time Series with a Unit Root, *Journal of the American Statistical Association*, 74, 427–431.

Diebold, Francis X. and Atsushi Inoue. (2001). Long Memory and Regime Switching, *Journal of Econometrics*, 105(1), 131–159. ISSN 0304–4076. https://doi.org/10.1016/S0304-4076(01)00073-2. www.sciencedirect.com/science/article/pii/S0304407601000732

Diebold, Francis X. and G. Rudebusch. (2013). Yield Curve Modelling and Forecasting, in *The Series the Econometric and Tinbergen Institutes Lectures*, Princeton University Press. https://doi.org/10.1515/9781400845415

Dornbusch, R. and Frenkel, J. A. (1973). Inflation and Growth: Alternative Approaches, *Journal of Money, Credit and Banking*, 5(1), 141–156. https://doi.org/10.2307/1991068

Eichenbaum, M. and J. Fisher. (2004). *Evaluating the Calvo Model of Sticky Prices*. NBER WP Number 10617, MA: National Bureau of Economic Research, July. doi:10.3386/w10617

Elliott, Graham, Thomas J. Rothenberg, and James H. Stock. (1996). Efficient Tests for an Autoregressive Unit Root, *Econometrica*, 64, 813–836.

Engle, Robert F. and C. W. J. Granger. (1987). Co-integration and Error Correction: Representation, Estimation, and Testing, *Econometrica*, 55, 251–276.

Farmer, Roger E. A. (1991). Sticky Prices, *The Economic Journal*, 101(409), 1369–1379 https://doi.org/10.2307/2234890

https://www.federalreserve.gov/monetarypolicy/policy-rules-and-how-policymakers-use-them.htm

Fisher, Irving. (1926). A Statistical Relationship between Unemployment and Price Changes, *International Labor Review*, 785–792, and reprinted in the *Journal of Political Economy* in March/April (1973), 496–502.

Fisher, Irving. (1911). *The Purchasing Power of Money, Its Determination, and Relation to Credit, Interest, and Crisis. Introduction in Political Economy in Yale University, New Heavens, USA*, New York: The McMillan Company.

Fischer, Stanley. (1994). The Future of Central Banking, in F. Capie, S. Fischer, C. Goodhart, and N. Schnadt (eds.), *The Tercentenary Symposium of the Bank of England*, Cambridge: Cambridge University Press (Online 1995). https://doi.org/10.1017/CBO9780511983696

Fischer, Stanley. (1983). *Inflation and Growth*. NBER, WP 1235. 1050 Massachusetts Avenue Cambridge, MA 02138.

Fischer, Stanley. (1977). Long-Term Contracts, Rational Expectations, and the Optimal Money Supply Rule, *Journal of Political Economy*, 85(1), 191–205.

Fisher, R. A. (1932). *Statistical Methods for Research Workers*, 4th Edition, Edinburgh: Oliver & Boyd.

Forbs, Steve, Nathan Lewis, and Elizabeth Ames. (2022). *Inflation: What It Is, Why It's Bad, and How to Fix It*, New York: Encounter Books.

Friedman, Milton. (1988). Money and the Stock Market, *Journal of Political Economy*, 96(2), 221–245.

Friedman, Milton. (1976). *Price Theory*, Chicago, IL: Aldine Publishing.

Friedman, Milton. (1969). *The Optimal Quantity of Money and Other Essays*, Chicago, IL: Aldine Publishing.

Friedman, Milton. (1968). The Role of Monetary Policy, *American Economic Review*, LVIII(1) (March), 1–17.

304 *References*

Friedman, Milton and Anna J. Schwartz. (1963). *A Monetary History of the United States, 1867–1960*, Princeton, NJ: Princeton University Press.

Gali, J., M. Gertler, and J. David López-Salido. (2005). Robustness of the Estimates of the Hybrid New Keynesian Phillips Curve, *Journal of Monetary Economics*, 52(6), 1107–1118. ISSN 0304–3932

Gerlach, S. and Lars E. O. Svensson. (2003). Money and Inflation in the Euro Area: A Case for Monetary Indicators, *Journal of Monetary Economics*, 50(8), 1649–1672. ISSN 0304-3932, https://doi.org/10.1016/j.jmoneco.2003.02.002

Goodfriend, Marvin and Robert G. King. (2005). The Incredible Volcker Disinflation, *Journal of Monetary Economics*, 52(5), 981–1015. ISSN 0304–3932

Gordon, D. F. (1974). A Neoclassical Theory of Keynesian Unemployment, *Economic Inquiry*, 12, 431–459.

Gordon, D. F. and Eric Leeper. (2006). The Price Level, the Quantity Theory of Money, and the Fiscal Theory of the Price Level, *Scottish Journal of Political Economy*, 53(1), 4–27.

Granger, C. W. J. (1983). *Cointegrated Variables and Error Correcting Models*, WP 83–13, San Diego: University of California.

Granger, C. W. J. and P. Newbold. (1974). Spurious Regressions in Econometrics, *Journal of Econometrics*, 2, 111–120.

Granger, Clive W. J. and Yongil Jeon. (2004). Thick Modeling, *Economic Modeling*, 21(2), 323–343.

Gruen, David., Adrain Pagan, and Christopher Thompson. (1999). The Phillips Curve in Australia, *Journal of Monetary Economics*, 44(2), 223–258.

Guthrie, G. and Julian Wright. (2000). Open Mouth Operations, *Journal of Monetary Economics*, 46(2), 489–516. ISSN 0304–3932. https://doi.org/10.1016/S0304-3932(00)00035-0

Haldane, A. and D. Quah. (1999). UK Phillips Curves and Monetary Policy, *Journal of Monetary Economics*, 44(2), 259–278.

Hall, Aaron Smalter. (2018). Machine Learning Approaches to Macroeconomic Forecasting, *Economic Review, The Federal Reserve Bank of Kansas City*, Publication Information: 4 Quarter, 63–81. doi:10.18651/ER/4q18

Hall, Robert. (2005). Employment Efficiency and Sticky Wages: Evidence from Flows in the Labor Market, *The Review of Economics and Statistics*, 87(3), 397–407.

Hall, Robert E., M. Neil Baily, L. H. Summers, J. Duesenberry, F. Modigliani, W. Nordhaus, J. Tobin, R. Gordon, P. Kenen, T. Juster, and R. Marris. (1980). Employment Fluctuations and Wage Rigidity, *Brookings Papers on Economic Activity,* 1980(1, Tenth Anniversary Issue), 91–123, 125–141.

Hamilton, J. D., E. S. Harris, J. Hatzius, and K. D. West. (2015). *The Equilibrium Real Funds Rate: Past, Present and Future*, Proceedings of the US Monetary Policy Forum. National Bureau of Economic Research, 1050 Massachusetts Avenue Cambridge, MA 02138.

Haslag, J. H. (1998). Seigniorage Revenue and Monetary Policy: Some Preliminary Evidence, Federal Reserve Bank of Dallas, *Economic and Financial Policy Review*, (Q III), 10–20.

Henderson, David R. (2021). Inflation: True and False. Defining Ideas, *Hoover Institution Journal*. www.hoover.org/research/inflation-true-and-false

Hodrick, R. J. and E. C. Prescott. (1997). Postwar U.S. Business Cycles: An Empirical Investigation, *Journal of Money, Credit, and Banking*, 29, 1–16.

Holston, K., T. Laubach, and J. Williams. (2017). Measuring the Natural Rate of Interest: International Trends and Determinants, *Journal of International Economics*, 108 (Supplement 1), S59–S75.

References 305

Howitt, P. (1986). The Keynesian Recovery, *The Canadian Journal of Economics/Revue canadienne d'Economique*, 19(4), 626–641.

Im, K. S., M. H. Pesaran, and Y. Shin. (2003). Testing for Unit Roots in Heterogeneous Panels, *Journal of Econometrics*, 115, 53–74.

Ireland, P. N. (2003). Endogenous Money or Sticky Prices? *Journal of Monetary Economics*, 50(8), 1623–1648. ISSN 0304–3932. https://doi.org/10.1016/j.jmoneco.2003.01.001

Isakin, M. and P. V. Ngo. (2020). Variance Decomposition Analysis for Nonlinear Economic Models, *Oxford Bulletin of Economics and Statistics*, 82(6), 1362–1374.

Jain, Raj and Imrich Chlamtac. (1985). The P2 Algorithm for Dynamic Calculation of Quantiles and Histograms Without Storing Observations, *Communications of the ACM*, 28(10), 1076–1085.

Johansen, Søren. (1995). *Likelihood-based Inference in Cointegrated Vector Autoregressive Models*, Oxford: Oxford University Press.

Johansen, Søren. (1991). Estimation and Hypothesis Testing of Cointegration Vectors in Gaussian Vector Autoregressive Models, *Econometrica*, 59, 1551–1580.

Johansen, Søren. (1988). Statistical Analysis of Cointegration Vectors, *Journal of Economics Dynamics and Control*, 12, 231–254.

Johansen, Søren and Katarina Juselius. (1990). Maximum Likelihood Estimation and Inferences on Cointegration – with Applications to the Demand for Money, *Oxford Bulletin of Economics and Statistics*, 52, 169–210.

Jordi Galí, Mark Gertler, and J. David López-Salido. (2001). European Inflation Dynamics, *European Economic Review*, 45(7), 1237–1270. ISSN 0014–2921.

Karlsson, S. and P. Österholm. (2019). A Note on the Stability of the Swedish Phillips Curve, *Empirical Economics*, 59, 2573–2612.

Kapetanios, George, Yongcheol Shin, and Andy Snell. (2003). Testing for a Unit Root in the Nonlinear STAR Framework, *Journal of Econometrics*, 112(2), 359–379. ISSN 0304–4076. https://doi.org/10.1016/S0304-4076(02)00202-6

Kehoe, P. and Virgiliu Midrigan. (2015). Prices are Sticky After All, *Journal of Monetary Economics*, 75, 35–53. ISSN 0304–3932. https://doi.org/10.1016/j.jmoneco.2014.12.004

Kejriwal, Mohitosh and Pierre Perron. (2008). The Limit Distribution of the Estimates in Cointegrated Regression Models with Multiple Structural Changes, *Journal of Econometrics*, 146(1), 59–73. ISSN 0304–4076. https://doi.org/10.1016/j.jeconom.2008.07.001

Keynes, J. M. (1936). *The General Theory of Employment, Interest, and Money*, London: Macmillan.

Koenig, E. F. and A. Armen. (2015). *Assessing Monetary Accommodation: A Simple Empirical Model of Monetary Policy and Its Implications for Unemployment and Inflation*, Dallas, TX: Federal Reserve Bank of Dallas Staff Papers, No. 23.

Kontonikas, Alexandros, Ronald MacDonald, and Aman Saggu. (2013). Stock Market Reaction to Fed Funds Rate Surprises: State Dependence and the Financial Crisis, *Journal of Banking & Finance*, 37(11), 4025–4037. ISSN 0378–4266. https://doi.org/10.1016/j.jbankfin.2013.06.010

Kool, C. J. M. and J. Tatom. (1994). The P-Star Model in Five Small Economies, *Federal Reserve Bank of St. Louis Quarterly Review*, 11–29.

Koop, G., M. H. Pesaran, and S. M. Potter. (1996). Impulse Response Analysis in Nonlinear Multivariate Models, *Journal of Econometrics*, 74, 119, 147.

Kwiatkowski, Dennis, Peter C. B. Phillips, Peter Schmidt, and Yongcheol Shin. (1992). Testing the Null Hypothesis of Stationary against the Alternative of a Unit Root, *Journal of Econometrics*, 54, 159–178.

306 *References*

Kydland, F. E. and E. C. Prescott. (1977). Rules Rather than Discretion: The Inconsistency of Optimal Plans, *Journal of Political Economy*, 85(3), 473–491, https://doi.org/10.1086/260580

Laidler, D. E. W. (1985). *The Demand for Money: Theories, Evidence, and Problems*, New York: Harper & Row, Publishers.

Laubach, T. and J. C. Williams. (2003). Measuring the Natural Rate of Interest, *Review of Economics and Statistics*, 85(4), 1063–1070.

Leeper, Eric. (1991). Equilibria Under Active and Passive Monetary and Fiscal Policies, *Journal of Monetary Economics*, 27, 129–147.

Levene, H. (1960). Robust Tests for the Equality of Variances, in I. Olkin, S. G. Ghurye, W. Hoeffding, W. G. Madow, and H. B. Mann (eds.), *Contribution to Probability and Statistics*, Palo Alto, CA: Stanford University Press.

Levin, A., C. F. Lin, and C. Chu. (2002). Unit Root Tests in Panel Data: Asymptotic and Finite-Sample Properties, *Journal of Econometrics*, 108, 1–24.

Lowry, S. Todd. (1996). Reviewed Works: An Austrian Perspective on the History of Economic Thought. Volume 1, *Journal of Economic Literature*, 34(3) (September), 1336–1340.

Lucas, Rober, E. Jr. and Thomas Sargent. (1981a). After Keynesian Macroeconomics, in Robert Lucas and Thomas Sargent (eds.), *Rational Expectations and Econometric Practice*, Minneapolis: Minnesota University Press, Vol. 1, pp. 1–367.

Lucas, Rober, E. Jr. and Thomas Sargent. (1981b). After Keynesian Macroeconomics, in Robert Lucas and Thomas Sargent (eds.), *Rational Expectations and Econometric Practice*, Minneapolis: Minnesota University Press, Vol. 2, pp. 371–689.

Lucas, Rober, E. Jr. and Thomas Sargent. (1981c). After Keynesian Macroeconomics, in Robert Lucas and Thomas Sargent (eds.), *Rational Expectations and Econometric Practice*, Minneapolis: Minnesota University Press, Chapter 16, pp. 295–319.

Lucas, Robert, E. Jr. (1980). Two Illustrations of the Quantity Theory of Money, *American Economic Review*, 1005–1014.

Lucas, Robert, E. Jr. (1977). Understanding Business Cycles, in K. Brunner and A. H. Meltzer (eds.), *Stabilization of the Domestic and International Economy*, Amsterdam: North Holland.

Lucas, Robert, E. Jr. (1976). Econometric Policy Evaluation: A Critique, in Karl Brunner and Alan Meltzer (eds.), The Phillips Curve and Labor Market, *Carnegie – Rochester Series on Public Policy*, 1(1), 19–46.

Lucas, Robert, E. Jr. (1973). Some International Evidence on Output-Inflation Tradeoffs, *American Economic Review* (June), 326–334.

Lucas, Robert E. Jr. (1972a). Expectations and the Neutrality of Money, *Journal of Economic Theory* (April), 103–124.

Lucas, Robert, E. Jr. (1972b). Econometric Testing of the Natural-Rate Hypothesis, in Otto Eckstein (ed.), *The Econometrics of Price Determination*, Board of Governors of the Federal Reserve System, Washington, USA. pp. 50–59.

Lucas, Robert, E. Jr. and Thomas Sargent. (1979). After Keynesian Macroeconomics, *Federal Reserve Bank of Minneapolis Quarterly Review*, 3(2), 1–16.

Maccarrone, Giovanni, Giacomo Morelli, and Sara Spadaccini. (2021). GDP Forecasting, Machine Learning, Linear or Autoregression? *Frontiers in Artificial Intelligence*, 4, Article 757864, 1–9. doi:10.3389/frai.2021.757864

MacKinnon, James G. (1996). Numerical Distribution Functions for Unit Root and Cointegration Tests, *Journal of Applied Econometrics*, 11, 601–618.

MacKinnon, James G., Alfred A. Haug, and Leo Michelis. (1999). Numerical Distribution Functions of Likelihood Ratio Tests for Cointegration, *Journal of Applied Econometrics*, 14, 563–577.

Mankiw, N. Gregory. (2020). *A Skeptic's Guide to Modern Monetary Theory*, Working Paper No. 26650, Cambridge, MA: NBER, National Bureau of Economic Research, p. 02138. www.nber.org/papers/w26650

Mankiw, N. Gregory and R. Reis. (2007). Sticky Information in General Equilibrium, *Journal of the European Economic Association*, 5(2–3) (May 1), 603–613. https://doi.org/10.1162/jeea.2007.5.2-3.603

Mankiw, N. Gregory and R. Reis. (2002). Sticky Information Versus Sticky Prices: A Proposal to Replace the New Keynesian Phillips Curve, *The Quarterly Journal of Economics*, 117(4) (November), 1295–1328. https://doi.org/10.1162/003355302320935034

Marcellino, Massimiliano. (1999). Some Consequences of Temporal Aggregation in Empirical Analysis, *Journal of Business & Economic Statistics*, 17(1), 129–136. doi:10.1080/0 7350015.1999.10524802 To link to this article. https://doi.org/10.1080/07350015.1999. 10524802

McCallum, Bennett T. (2001). Indeterminacy, Bubbles, and the Fiscal Theory of Price Level Determination, *Journal of Monetary Economics*, 47(1), 19–30. ISSN 0304–3932

McCallum, B. T. (1993). Unit Roots in Macroeconomic Time series: Some Critical Issues, *Federal Reserve Bank of Richmond Economic Quarterly*, 79(2) (Spring), 13–43.

McCallum, B. T. (1988). Robustness Properties of a Rule for Monetary Policy, *Carnegie – Rochester Conference on Public Policy*, 29, 173–204.

McCallum, B. T. (1981). Price-Level Stickiness and the Feasibility of Monetary Stabilization Policy with Rational Expectations, in Lucas, Robert E. Jr. and Thomas Sargent (eds.), *Rational Expectations and Econometric Practice*, Minneapolis: University of Minnesota Press, Chapter 14, pp. 277–284.

McCallum, B. T. (1980). Rational Expectations and Macroeconomic Stabilization Policy, *Journal of Money, Credit and Banking*, 12, 395–402.

McCallum, B. T. and E. Nelson. (2000). Monetary Policy for an Open Economy: An Alternative Framework with Optimizing Agents and Sticky Prices, *Oxford Review of Economic Policy*, 16(4) (December), 74–91. https://doi.org/10.1093/oxrep/16.4.74

McGrattan, Ellen R. and Edward C. Prescott. (2005). Taxes, Regulations, and the Value of U.S. and U.K. Corporations, *The Review of Economic Studies*, 72(3) (July), 767–796. https://doi.org/10.1111/j.1467-937X.2005.00351.x

Mishkin, Frederick, S. (2001). *The Transmission Mechanism and the Role of Asset Prices in Monetary Policy*, Working Paper 8617, December, Cambridge, MA: NBER. doi:10.3386/w8617

Mitchell, William, L. Randall Wray, and Martin Watts. (2019). *Macroeconomics*, London: Red Globe Press.

Modigliani, Franco and Richard Cohn. (1979). Inflation, Rational Valuation, and the Market, *Financial Analysts Journal*, 35(3), 24–44.

Muth, J. (1961). Rational Expectations and the Theory of Price Movements, *Econometrica*, 315–335.

Neary, J. P. and Joseph E. Stiglitz. (1983). Toward a Reconstruction of Keynesian Economics: Expectations and Constrained Equilibria, *Quarterly Journal of Economics*, 98 (Supplement), 199–228.

Neter, John, Michael H. Kutner, Christopher J. Nachtsheim, and William Wasserman. (1996). *Applied Linear Statistical Models*, 4th Edition, Chicago: Times Mirror Higher Education Group, Inc. and Richard D. Irwin, Inc.

Newcomb, Simone. (1885). *Principles of Political Economy*. Harpers & Brothers, New York.

308 References

Newey, Whitney and Kenneth West. (1994). Automatic Lag Selection in Covariance Matrix Estimation, *Review of Economic Studies*, 61, 631–653.

Ng, Serena and Pierre Perron. (2001). Lag Length Selection and the Construction of Unit Root Tests with Good Size and Power, *Econometrica*, 69, 1519–1554.

Nickell, S. (2003). *Employment and Taxes*, Working Paper No. 1109, December, CESIFO. http://dx.doi.org/10.2139/ssrn.489443

Orphanides, A. (2001). Monetary Policy Rules Based on Real-Time Data, *American Economic Review*, 91(4), 964–985.

Orphanides, A. and J. C. Williams. (2002). Robust Monetary Policy Rules with Unknown Natural Rates, *Brookings Papers on Economic Activity* (2), 63–145.

Orphanides, Athanasios and Robert M. Solow. (1990). Chapter 6 Money, Inflation and Growth, in *Handbook of Monetary Economics*, Elsevier, Vol. 1, pp. 223–261. ISSN 1573–4498, ISBN 9780444880253. https://doi.org/10.1016/S1573-4498(05)80009-8. www.sciencedirect.com/science/article/pii/S1573449805800098

Perron, Pierre. (1989). The Great Crash, the Oil Price Shock, and the Unit Root Hypothesis, *Econometrica*, 57, 1361–1401.

Phelps, Edmund S. (2006). *Evidence Based Economics*, Project Syndicate. www.project-syndicate.org/commentary/evidence-based-economics

Phelps, Edmund, S. (1970). Money Wage Dynamics and Labor Market Equilibrium, in E. S. Phelps (ed.), *Microeconomic Foundations of Employment and Inflation Theory*, New York: Norton.

Phelps, Edmund S. (1967). Phillips Curves, Expectations of Inflation and Optimal Unemployment over Time, *Economica*, 34(135), 254–281.

Phelps, Edmund S. and John B. Taylor. (1977). The Stabilizing Powers of Monetary Policy under Rational Expectations, *Journal of Political Economy*, 85, 165–190.

Phillips, A. W. (1958). The Relation between Unemployment and the Rate of Change of Money Wage Rates in the United Kingdom, 1861–1957, *Economica* (November), 283–299.

Phillips, P. C. B. (2003). Laws and Limits of Econometrics, *Economic Journal*, 113(486), C26–C52.

Phillips, P. C. B. and M. Loretan. (1991). Estimating Long-Run Equilibria, *Review of Economic Studies*, 58(3), 407–436.

Phillips, P. C. B. and P. Perron. (1988). Testing for a Unit Root in Time Series Regression, *Biometrika*, 75, 335–346.

Poole, William. (1994). Monetary Aggregates Targeting in a Law-Inflation Economy, *Conference Series; [Proceedings]*, 38, 87–135.

Prescott, E. C. (2004). Why Do Americans Work So Much More Than Europeans? *Federal Reserve Bank of Minneapolis Quarterly Review*, 28(1), 2–3.

Razzak, W. A. (2015). Wage, Productivity, and Unemployment: Microeconomics Theory and Macroeconomics Data, *Applied Economics*, 47(58), 6284–6300.

Razzak, W. A. (2013). Predicting Instability, *Applied Economics*, 45(23), 3305–3315.

Razzak, W. A. (2007). A Perspective on Unit Root and Cointegration in Applied Macroeconomics, *International Journal of Applied Econometrics and Quantitative Studies*, 1–4, 78–102.

Razzak, W. A. (2003). *Wage – Price Dynamics, the Labour Market and Deflation in Hong Kong*, Working Paper No. 24, Hong Kong: Hong Kong Institute for Monetary Research, the Hong Kong Monetary Authority.

Razzak W. A. (2002), *Monetary Policy and Forecasting Inflation with and without the Output Gap*, Discussion Paper No. DP2002/03, Wellington, New Zealand: Reserve Bank of New Zealand.

References 309

Razzak, W. A. (1997). The Hodrick-Prescott Technique: A Smoother Versus a Filter: An Application to New Zealand GDP, *Economics Letters,* 56, 163–168.

Razzak, W. A. (1995). *The Inflation-Output Trade – Off: Is the Phillips-Curve Symmetric,* Discussion Paper G95/7, Wellington, New Zealand: Reserve Bank of New Zealand.

Razzak, W. A. (1994). *Is Inflation non-Stationary or a Long-Memory,* Research Note N94. 111, Wellington, New Zealand: Reserve Bank of New Zealand.

Razzak, W. A. and R. Dennis. (1995). *The Output Gap Using the Hodrick-Prescott Filter with a Non-Constant Smoothing Parameter: An Application to New Zeal,* Wellington, New Zealand: Reserve Bank of New Zealand G95/8.

Razzak, W. A. and B. Laabas. (2016). Taxes, Natural Resource Endowments, and the Supply of Labor: New Evidence, in M. Mustafa Erdoğdu and B. Christiansen (eds.), *The Handbook of Research on Public Finance in Europe and the MENA Region,* Hershey, PA: IGI Global Research Publishing, Chapter 23, pp. 520–544.

Razzak, W. A. and I. Moosa. (2018). Monetary Policy, Corporate Profit and House Prices, *Applied Economics,* 30(28), 3106–3114. doi:10.1080/00036846.2017.1418073, Online January 4.

Reserve Bank of New Zealand. (2020). *Monetary Policy Handbook.* www.rbnz.govt.nz/monetary-policy/about-monetary-policy/monetary-policy-handbook

Romer, Christina and David Romer. (1997). *Reducing Inflation: Motivation and Strategy,* Chicago, IL: University of Chicago Press. ISBN 0-226-72484-0

Rossana, Robert and John J. Seater. (2012). Temporal Aggregation and Economic Time Series. Journal of Business, *Economics and Statistics,* 441–451.

Rotemberg, J. (1996). Prices, Output, and Hours: An Empirical Analysis Based on a Sticky Price Model, *Journal of Monetary Economics,* 37(3), 505–533. ISSN 0304–3932. https://doi.org/10.1016/0304-3932(96)01264-0

Rotemberg, J. (1982). Sticky Prices in the United States, *Journal of Political Economy,* 90(6), 1187–1211.

Rotemberg, J. and M. Woodford. (1997). An Optimization-Based Econometric Framework for the Evaluation of Monetary Policy, *NBER Macroeconomics Annual,* 297–347.

Rudebusch, G. (1993). The Uncertain Unit Root in Real GNP, *American Economic Review,* 83 (March), 264–272.

Rudebusch, G. and J. Williams. (2009). Forecasting Recessions: The Puzzle of the Enduring Power of the Yield Curve, *Journal of Business & Economics Statistics,* 27(4), 492–503.

Said, Said E. and David A. Dickey. (1984). Testing for Unit Roots in Autoregressive Moving Average Models of Unknown Order, *Biometrika,* 71, 599–607.

Saikkonen, Pentti. (1992). Estimation and Testing of Cointegrated Systems by an Autoregressive Approximation, *Econometric Theory,* 8, 1–27.

Sargent, Thomas, J. (1973). *Rational Expectations, the Real Rate of Interest, and the Natural Rate of Unemployment,* Brookings Papers on Economic Activity No. 2, Washington, DC: Brookings Institution, pp. 429–472.

Sargent, Thomas J. (1971). A Note on the Accelerationist Controversy, *Journal of Money, Credit, and Banking* (August), 721–725.

Sargent, Thomas J. and Bruce Smith. (1987). Irrelevance of Open Market Operations in Some Economies with Government Currency Being Dominated in Rate of Return, *American Economic Review,* 77 (March), 78–92.

Sargent, Thomas J. and Bruce Smith. (1986). *The Irrelevance of Government Foreign Exchange Operations.* Manuscript. Forthcoming in The economic effects of the government budget, (eds.) Elhanan Helpman, Asaff Razin, and Efraim Sadka. Cambridge, MA: M.I.T. Press.

310   References

Sargent, Thomas J. and Neil Wallace. (1975). Rational Expectations, the Optimal Monetary Instrument and the Optimal Money Supply Rule, *Journal of Political Economy*, 83, 241–54.

Sbordone, Argia M. (2005). Do Expected Future Marginal Costs Drive Inflation Dynamics? *Journal of Monetary Economics*, 52(6), 1183–1197. ISSN 0304–3932

Sheskin, David J. (1997). *Parametric and Nonparametric Statistical Procedures*, Boca Raton: CRC Press.

Shiller, R. J. (1997). Why Do People Dislike Inflation? In Christina Romer and David Romer (eds.), *Reducing Inflation: Motivation and Strategy*, Chicago: University of Chicago Press, pp. 13–16.

Shimer, R. (2009). Convergence in Macroeconomics: The Labor Wedge, *American Economic Journal: Macroeconomics*, 1(1) (January), 280–297. doi:10.1257/mac.1.1.280

Shimotsu, Katsumi and Peter C. B. Phillips. (2006). Local Whittle Estimation of Fractional Integration and Some of its Variants, *Journal of Econometrics*, 130(2), 209–233. ISSN 0304–4076. https://doi.org/10.1016/j.jeconom.2004.09.014. www.sciencedirect.com/science/article/pii/S0304407605000527

Shimotsu, Katsumi and Peter C. B. Phillips. (2005). Exact Local Whittle Estimation of Fractional Integration, *Annals of Statistics*, 33(4) (August), 1890–1933. https://doi.org/10.1214/009053605000000309

Silvestrini, A. and D. Veredas. (2008). Temporal Aggregation of the Univariate and Multivariate Time Series Models: A Survey, *Journal of Economic Surveys*, 22(3), 458–497. https://doi.org/10.1111/j.1467-6419.2007.00538.x

Sims, Christopher. (1999). *Drifts and Breaks in Monetary Policy. Mimeo*, Princeton, NJ: Princeton University.

Sims, Christopher. (1994). A Simple Model for the Determination of the Price Level and the Interaction of Monetary and Fiscal Policy, *Economic Theory*, 4, 381–399.

Smith, V. L. and B. J. Wilson. (2019). *Humanomics: Moral Sentiments and the Wealth of Nations for the Twenty-First Century*, Cambridge: Cambridge University Press.

Solano, P., Enrico Pizzorno, Anna M. Gallina, Chiara Mattei, Filippo Gabrielli, and Joshua Kayman. (2012). Employment Status, Inflation and Suicidal Behaviour: An Analysis of a Stratified Sample in Italy, *International Journal of Socio Psychiatry*, 58(5), 477–484. doi:10.1177/0020764011408651

Stock, J. H. (1991). Confidence Intervals for the Largest Autoregressive Root in U.S. Macroeconomic Time Series, *Journal of Monetary Economics*, 28 (December), 435–459.

Stock, J. H. and Mark Watson. (1993). A Simple Estimator of Cointegrating Vectors in Higher Order Integrated Systems, *Econometrica*, 61, 783–820.

Summers, Lawrence, D. Wessel, and John David Murray. (2018). *Rethinking the Fed's 2 Percent Inflation Target*, Washington, DC: Brookings Institute, Hutchins Center on Fiscal & Monetary Policy, June 1–22.

Svensson, E. O. Lars. (2000). Open-Economy Inflation Targeting, *Journal of International Economics*, 50(1), 155–183. https://doi.org/10.1016/S0022-1996(98)00078-6

Taylor, J. B. (2001). *An Interview with Milton Friedman, Macroeconomic Dynamic*, Cambridge: Published online by Cambridge University Press.

Taylor, J. B. (1993). *Macroeconomic Policy in a World Economy*, New York: W. W. Norton.

Turnovsky, S. J. (1974). On the Role of Inflationary Expectations in a Short-Run Macro-Economic Model, *Economic Journal*, 317–337.

Vogelsang, Timothy J. (1993). Unpublished computer program.

References 311

Wachtel, Paul and Iikka Korhonen. (2004). *Observations on Disinflation in Transitional Economies*, BOFIT Discussion Paper No. 5/2004. Bank of Finland, Helsinki.

Wallace, Neil. (1981). A Modigliani-Miller Theorem for Open-Market Operations, *American Economic Review*, 71 (June): 267–274.

Walsh, C. (1995). Optimal Contracts for Central Bankers, *American Economic Review*, 85(1) (March), 150–167.

Walsh, C. E. (2005). Labor Market Search, Sticky Prices, and Interest Rate Policies, *Review of Economic Dynamics*, 8(4), 829–849. https://doi.org/10.1016/j.red.2005.03.004

Whelan, K. (1999). *Real Wage Dynamics and the Phillips Curve*, Washington, DC: The Federal Reserve Board of Governors.

Wicksell, K. (1898). *Interest and Prices: A Study of the Causes Regulating the Value of Money*. Translated by R. F. Khan with an Introduction by Bertil Ohlin. The Library of the Congress Card Number 65–16993, New York: Sentry Press.

Woodford, M. (2003). *Interest and Prices: Foundations of a Theory of Monetary Policy*, Princeton: Princeton University Press.

Woodford, M. (2002). Optimal Policy Inertia, *The Manchester School*, 67(S1), 1–35. https://doi.org/10.1111/1467-9957.67.s1.1

Woodford, M. (1998a). Doing Without Money: Controlling Inflation in a Post – Monetary World, *Review of Economics Dynamics*, 1, 173–219.

Woodford, M. (1998b). Control of the Public Debt: A Requirement for Price Stability? In G. Calvo and M. King (eds.), *The Debt Burden and its Consequences for Monetary Policy*, International Economic Association Series, London: Palgrave Macmillan. https://doi.org/10.1007/978-1-349-26077-5_5

Woodford, M. (1995). Price Level Determinacy without Control of Monetary Aggregate, *Carnegie – Rochester Series on Public Policy*, 43, 1–46.

Woodford, M. (1994). Monetary Policy and Price Level Determinacy in a Cash-in-Advance Economy, *Economic Theory*, 4, 345–389.

Index

Note: Page numbers in *italics* indicate a figure and page numbers in **bold** indicate a table on the corresponding page.

45° line scatter plots, *144, 146, 149, 153–154, 165, 223*
45° scatter plots, *33–37, 104, 119, 126–129, 131–133*

accelerationist hypothesis (Phelps), 180, 192
accelerationist Phillips curve, 5, 181, 296
accelerationist relationship, 251
active monetary policy, 297
   meaning, 244
   reasons, 2
active policies, impact, 237
actual inflation/mean dynamic stochastic projections, descriptive statistics (New Zealand), **244**
actual/mean dynamic stochastic projections (quarterly US inflation), *234–235*
   descriptive statistics, **235**
acyclical real wages, periods (absence), 250
adaptive expectations, 201–202
additive outlier (AO), 107
   break type, 59
ADF tests, **108–111**
   breaks, inclusion, 58
   specification, 107
   statistics, 33
ADF t-stat, minimization, 58
advanced countries, neutral interest rate total (r^*_t), *292*
Africa inflation
   descriptive statistics, **19**
   rate, *18*
African countries
   broad money averages, **117**
   broad money, chi-squared confidence ellipse test, *158*

broad money, descriptive statistics, **77**
Chi-Squared Confidence Ellipse test, 155
CPI trend, **39**
crises, 75–80
dynamic OLS, **47–48**
dynamic OLS (DOLS) estimated broad money, **78**
generalized variance sample, *213*
inflation, goodness of fit, *80*
inflation variability, growth (equivalence), **78**
Log (CPI), 45° scatter plots, *35*
mean inflation, growth (equivalence), **77**
money/output, relationship, 125
money per unit of output growth rate, inflation (relationship), *75*
money per unit of output growth rate, inflation time series, *76*
New Keynesian Phillips Curve specification, generalized variance sample, *213*
nominal government consumption expenditures, chi-squared confidence ellipse test, *158*
ordinary least squares, **47–48**
output gap, descriptive statistics, **204**
Phillips Curve specifications, chi-squared confidence ellipse test, *186*
real GDP growth rates, **117**
aggregate demand
   policies, predictability, 202
   unanticipated component, 224
aggregate demand shocks, impact, 218
aggregate income, importance, 122, 125
Akaike Information Criterion (AIC), lead/lag setting, 41

Index 313

Algeria
  inflation rate, 61
  money growth, reduction, 119
  real GDP ratio growth, inequality, 62
annual average hours worked per worker
  UK mean baseline dynamic stochastic
    projections, *270*
  UK mean dynamic stochastic
    projections, *271*
annual hours worked from baseline,
    deviation comparison (Norway/
    UK), *279*
ANOVA. *see* Kruskal-Wallis
    one-way ANOVA
ANOVA F-test, **63**, **69**, **77**, **83**, **87**, **94**
anticipated aggregate demand shocks, 224
  coefficient, 229
anticipated inflation, 172
anticipated real wages, 177
anticipated tax cut/increase, impact, 199–200
anti-inflation policy, analytical aspects, 176
artificial intelligence (AI), central bank
    usage, 299
Asian countries
  broad money averages, **117**
  broad money, chi-squared confidence
    ellipse test, *159*
  broad money, descriptive statistics, **82–83**
  CPI trend, **39–40**
  data, 81–88
  dynamic OLS, **49–50**
  dynamic OLS (DOLS) estimated broad
    money, **85**
  generalized variance sample, *214*
  inflation change, descriptive
    statistics, **205**
  inflation, goodness of fit, *84*
  inflation variability, growth
    (equivalence), **83**
  Log (CPI), 45° scatter plots, *36*
  mean inflation, growth (equivalence), **83**
  money growth, reduction, 119
  money/output, relationship, 125–126
  money per unit of output growth rate,
    inflation (relationship), *81*
  money per unit of output growth rate,
    inflation time series, *82*
  New Keynesian Phillips Curve
    specification, generalized variance
    sample, *214*
  nominal government consumption
    expenditures, *159*
  ordinary least squares, **49–50**
  output gap, descriptive statistics, **205**

Phillips Curve specifications, chi-squared
    confidence ellipse test, *187*
  real GDP growth rates, **117**
Asian countries, inflation
  descriptive statistics, **19**
  rate, *19*
Asian Financial Crisis (AFC), 10, 59, 83,
    86, 95, 295
  accounting, absence, 238–239
asset prices, excess money (relationship),
    162–171
Augmented Dickey-Fuller test, 22, 31
Australia
  broad money/nominal government
    consumption expenditures,
    chi-squared confidence ellipse test/
    scatter plots, *160*
  fitted values/residuals, *96*
  inflation change/output gap relationship,
    evidence, 190
  inflation-targeting, 91
  output gap, variance, 206
  petrol/gas prices, daily change, 121–122

backward-looking expectations, 297
Band-Pass filter, usage, 125, 193
Bank for International Settlements (BIS),
    166, 168–169
Barro, R.J., 1, 197, 200, 259, 301
Bartlett test, 62
baseline dynamic stochastic projections,
    computation, 263
baseline mean deviations, Norway mean
    baseline dynamic stochastic
    projection, *277*
baseline VAR, generalized impulse
    response functions (Norway), *274*
Baxter and King filter, 193
Bernanke, Ben, 218
Beveridge and Charles Nelson filter,
    usage, 125
Bienaymé-Chebyshev inequality, 208
bivariate normal variable, 207
bivariate system, consideration, 208
Blanchard, O., 176, 181, 182, 221, 226,
    236, 301
Blinder, Alan, 11
Bodin, Jean, 4, 26
Bolivia
  data, 70
  inflation, 15
    money growth, relationship, 66
  output gap-inflation, evidence
    (absence), 186

314 *Index*

bootstrapped innovations, usages, 247
Brash, Don, 89
Breitung, Jörg, 59, 301
broad money, *30, 31*
  chi-squared confidence ellipse test/
    scatter plots (Denmark), *160*
  chi-squared confidence ellipse test/
    scatter plots (Sweden), *161*
  cyclical fluctuation, scatter plot, *168*
  dynamic OLS estimated broad
    money, **65**
  inflation-targeting countries, real GDP
    ratios, *167*
  Log (CPI), 45° scatter plots, *33–37*
  MENA countries, *156*
  US quarterly fluctuations, *134*
  variances, equality, 66
broad money averages
  African countries, **117**
  Asian countries, **117**
  Caribbean countries, **118**
  developed inflation-targeting
    countries, **118**
  Latin/South American
    countries, **116**
  MENA countries, **116**
broad money, descriptive statistics
  African countries, **77**
  Asian countries, **82–83**
  Caribbean countries, **87**
  inflation-targeting countries, **94**
  Latin/South American countries, **69**
  MENA countries, **62**
broad money fluctuations
  Singapore, *130*
  Trinidad/Tobago, *131*
broad money growth (New Zealand), *238*
  rates, *239*
broad money/housing prices, quarterly
    business cycle fluctuations (New
    Zealand), *170*
broad money per unit of real GDP,
    stationary construction, 58
broad money per unit of real output/
    inflation, growth rate averages,
    104–106
Brown-Forsyth test, 62
Broyden-Fletcher-Goldfarb-Shanno
    (BFGS)-Marquardt optimization
    method, 226
budget constraint (BC), 254
  real terms, 261, 286
budget deficit. *See* United Kingdom
  financing, 10

Burkina Faso
  broad money per unit of output growth
    rate/inflation rate, inequality, 79
  money per unit of output growth,
    inflation inequality, 79
  New Keynesian Phillips Curve
    specification, 211
  output gap/inflation change, variance
    (inequality), 203
Burkina Faso, inflation rate, 17
BVAR, 250

Calvo, Guillermo, 121, 197, 249, 252, 301
capital income tax rate, 285
capital-labor ratio, 261, 288, 289
Caribbean countries
  broad money averages, **118**
  broad money, descriptive statistics, **87**
  CPI trend, **40**
  data, 86–89
  dynamic OLS, **51**
  dynamic OLS (DOLS) estimated broad
    money, **88**
  generalized variance sample, *215*
  growth patterns, volatility, 119
  inflation change, descriptive
    statistics, **205**
  inflation, goodness of fit, *88*
  inflation variability, growth
    (equivalence), **87**
  Log (CPI), 45° scatter plots, *36*
  mean inflation, growth (equivalence), **87**
  money per unit of output growth rate,
    inflation (relationship), *86*
  money per unit of output growth rate,
    inflation time series, *86*
  New Keynesian Phillips Curve
    specification, generalized variance
    sample, *215*
  ordinary least squares, **51**
  output gap, descriptive statistics, **205**
  Phillips Curve specifications, chi-squared
    confidence ellipse test, *188*
  real GDP growth rates, **118**
  Sample Generalized Variance, 211
Caribbean countries, inflation
  descriptive statistics, **20**
  rate, *20*
Central Bank of Japan, money injection, 6
central bank, reputation/credibility, 104
central banks
  budget constraint, 254
  money printing, increase (reasons), 135
  reputation, effect, 200

central banks, seignorage revenues, 295–296
Chebyshev's inequality, 208
Chile
    inflation-targeting country, 70
    inflation-targeting period, 73
    inflation volatility, 15
    output gap-inflation, evidence (absence), 186
Chi-Squared Confidence Ellipse test, 155, 181
    Africa, *128*
    African countries, *158*
    Asia, *130*
    Asian countries, *159*
    Australia, *160*
    broad money/government consumption expenditure (MENA countries), *156*
    broad money/government consumption expenditure (Turkey), *150*
    Caribbean countries, *131*
    Denmark, *160*
    developed inflation-targeting countries, *132*
    inflation-targeting countries, broad money/housing prices (cyclical fluctuation), *169*
    Latin/South American countries, *127*, *157*
    MENA countries, *126*
    monetary base/government consumption expenditures (Turkey), *150*
    New Zealand, *132*
    New Zealand, broad money/nominal GDP growth rates, *239*
    New Zealand, nominal government expenditures/GDPe, *240*
    Norway, *161*
    scatter plots, 142
    Sweden, *161*
    usage, 125, 147
    US broad money/government consumption expenditures, *149*
chi-squared correlation test
    natural rate (r_{1t}) (r_{2t}), *291*
    stocks, real rate of return, *291*
Chi-Squared tests, P-values, 220
Chi-Square tests, redoing, 133–134
Christiano and Fitzgerald filter, 193
    full sample asymmetric Christiano and Fitzgerald filter, usage, 125
civil unrests, impact, 77

closed form GMM estimates, 249
Cobb-Douglas production function, 260
cointegrating vectors, presence, 271
cointegration, 41
    relation, estimation, 56
    tests, 41
Cold War political issues, impact, 77
Colombia, inflation data abnormality, 66
commitment
    RE assumption, 199
    reneging, 202
confidence ellipse test, *128*, *132*, *150–152*, *156–161*, *169–170*, *181–191*, *239–240*. *see also* Chi-Squared Confidence Ellipse test
confidence intervals, absence, 231
consolidated budget constraint, 255
consolidated government budget constraint, 254–255
consumer impatience, measurement, 256
Consumer Price Index (CPI), 2, *14*, *32*
    baseline deviation, comparison (Norway/UK), *279*
    baseline mean deviations, Norway mean baseline dynamic stochastic projection, *278*
    baseline mean deviations, UK mean dynamic stochastic projection, *272*
    Gabon, *154*
    I(2) time series, 24
    Korea, *151*
    Log (CPI), 45° scatter plots, *33*, *34*, *35*, *36*
    log difference, 19, 22
    Malaysia, *153*
    money quantity, relationship, 11–12
    negative initial response, 265
    New Zealand CPI quarterly inflation rate (1988–2022), *25*
    Norway mean baseline dynamic stochastic projection, *277*
    one-year ahead CPI inflation, US survey, *219*
    trend, increase, 270–271
    trends, **37–40**
    UK mean baseline dynamic stochastic projections, *269*
    UK mean dynamic stochastic projections, *271*
    United Kingdom, *143*
    United States, *148*
    volatility, reason, 3

316 *Index*

Consumer Price Index (CPI) for All Urban
    Consumers, *3*
Consumer Price Index (CPI) inflation, *219*
    OLS regression, 220
    rate, 104, 106, 180
    survey, OLS regression test, **220**
    trend/relationship, 142
consumption-leisure ratio, 261
consumption-output data, sample
    restriction, 263, 265
consumption-output ratio, 265
consumption-output shock, CPI negative
    initial response, 265
Copernicus, Nicolaus, 4, 26
core inflation
    measure, volatility, 3
    plotting, 3
    standard deviations, 3
    US core inflation rate, *4*
Costa Rica
    broad money variances, inequality, 66
    output gap-inflation, evidence
        (absence), 186
Côte d'Ivoire
    money per unit of output growth,
        inflation inequality, 79
    New Keynesian Phillips Curve
        specification, 211
Côte d'Ivoire, price/money relationship, 52
countercyclical real wages, 250
countries, currency issuance, 259
COVID-19
    impact, 200
    relief programs, 145
    supply chain interruption, 176
cyclical broad money fluctuations
    Gabon, *129*
    South Africa, *129*
C/Y, Norway mean baseline dynamic
    stochastic projection, *276*
C/Y shock, response, 265

data
    natural variation level, 2–3
    symbols, 293
Data Generating Process (DGP), 31
debt, response, 272
deficit
    financing. *see* budget deficit; government
        deficit.
    real deficit, presence, 136
    real surplus (deficit), measurement, 147
    spending, 259
    spending, financing, 12

demand management policy, variance, 202
Denmark
    broad money/housing prices, cyclical
        fluctuations, 166
    broad money/nominal government
        consumption expenditures,
        chi-squared confidence ellipse test/
        scatter plots, *160*
    Chi-Squared Confidence Ellipse test, 155
    dynamic OLS estimated growth, inflation
        (relationship), **97**
    fitted values/residuals, *97*
    inflation change/output gap relationship,
        evidence, 190
    inflation-targeting, 91
Denmark National Bank, negative nominal
    interest rate policy, 200
deterministic trend, 32
developed inflation-targeting countries, 33
    broad money averages, **118**
    data, 89–104
    descriptive statistics, **22**
    estimates, 42
    money output, scatter plot/chi-squared
        confidence ellipse test, *132*
    policy prescription, 283
    real GDP growth rates, **118**
Dickey and Fuller test, 22, 29
discount factor, 256, 285
discretion argument, rules (contrast),
    201–202
discretionary policies, 200
disinflation, 218, 226, 283
Dominican Republic
    inflation rate, 15
    output gap-inflation, evidence
        (absence), 186
    slope coefficient, estimation, 73
draughts, impact, 77
dummy variables, test, 226
dynamic OLS (DOLS), 56
    African countries, **47–48**
    Asian countries, **49–50**
    broad money, leads/lags, 41
    Caribbean countries, **51**
    DOLS-estimated long-run elasticities,
        money neutrality (consistency), 52
    estimated slope coefficients, *103*
    estimates, summary statistics, **55**
    inflation-targeting countries, **53–54**
    Latin/South American countries, **44–46**
    MENA countries, **43**
    regression estimates, report, 95
    regressions, fitting, 70

Index 317

slope coefficients, estimate, *55*
  usefulness, 56
dynamic OLS (DOLS) estimated
  broad money
  African countries, **78**
  Asian countries, **85**
  Caribbean countries, **88**
  inflation-targeting countries, **96**
  Latin/South American countries, **71–72**
  MENA countries, **65**
dynamic OLS (DOLS) estimated growth,
  inflation (relationship)
  Denmark, **97**
  New Zealand, **99**
  Norway, **98**
  Sweden, **100**
  United Kingdom, **101**
  United States, **102**
Dynamic Stochastic General Equilibrium
  (DSGE) Model, 248
Dynamic Stochastic Projections, 10
  descriptive statistics, *235*

economic agents, lag, 229–230
economic/financial problems, impact, 77
economics, first-principle experiments,
  229–230
economic theory, predictions, 297–298
economy
  pricing kernel, 287
  structure, estimation, 198
Ecuador
  economic crises (1998–1999), 66
  output gap-inflation, evidence
    (absence), 186
Ecuador, inflation rate, 15
efficiency, 219
efficient estimators, 56
Egypt
  Arab Spring dummy variable,
    insignificance, 63
  output gap/inflation change, variance
    (contrast), 203
  Phillips Curve specification, evidence
    (absence), 184
  trend steepness, 60
Elliott, Graham, 303
endogeneity, 193
endogenous variables
  measurement, 114
  values, 247
Engel curve, 6
Equation of Exchange, 26–27
equilibrium real interest rate *(r*)*, 284

equities, deflated prices, 162
European Central Bank (ECB)
  data, 22
  negative nominal interest rate policy, 200
European Union (EU) inflation-targeting
  success, *23*
EWMA inflation, usage, 216
excess money, asset prices (relationship),
  162–171
exchange, equation. *see* Equation of
  Exchange
Exchange Rate Comfort Zone, 89
Exchange Settlement Account System
  (ESAS), 90–91
exogenous constant term, usage, 2632
exogenous variables, values, 114–115
expansionary monetary policy, impact,
  162–163
expectation-augmented Phillips curve,
  11–12, 176, 252
expected future inflation, coefficient, 248
expected inflation
  measurement, 216, 218–221
  mismeasurement, 193–194
expected nominal wage changes,
    expected real wage changes
    (equivalence), 175
explicit inflation-targeting, initiation, 224
Exponentially Weighted Moving Average
  representations, 192
ex-post real interest rate, 6, 8

federal fund rate *(ffr)* (FFR), 162, 220
Federal Reserve Bank of Dallas, 137
Federal Reserve Bank of Philadelphia
  (RFBP)
  inflation expectations, survey, 178
  professional forecaster survey, 219
Federal Reserve Bank of St. Louis
  (FRED)
  data, 10, 226
  Poole statement, 91
  report, 289
Fed model, usage, 163
fiat money, usage, 26
financial market friction, absence
  (assumption), 287
fine-tuning, government belief, 200
firm
  inflation reduction model, reduction,
    285–289
  MMT, relationship, 260–279
fiscal theory of inflation (FTOI), 248, 253,
  256–257

318 *Index*

fiscal theory of price level (FTOPL), 248, 253, 257–258

Fiscal Theory of the Price Level. *see* price level

Fischer, Phelps, and Taylor Keynesian contract theory, usage, 250

Fisher, Irving, 4, 26–27, 59, 125, 173–175, 193, 256, 303

flow-consolidated budget constraint, display, 255–256

FOCs, 287

frequency filters, usage, 125

Friedman, Milton, 26, 163, 176, 179, 201
  interview, 57, 220

F-test, 62

F test, *P*-value, 220

full sample asymmetric Christiano and Fitzgerald filter, usage, 125

future shocks, permanency, 221

G7 economies, public expenditures (impact), 261

Gabon
  Consumer Price Index (CPI), *154*
  cyclical broad money fluctuations/real output gap, *129*
  government consumption expenditures, scatter plot, *154*
  monetary base, scatter plot, *154*
  money base/seigniorage, *141*
  money/nominal government expenditures growth rates, association, 155
  money/output, relationship, 125
  money per unit of output growth, inflation inequality, 79
  non-normal residuals, 79
  output gap, variance, 207
  seigniorage, volatility, 142

GDP growth rate
  inflation, negative correlation, 7
  real GDP ratio, *30, 31*

generalized impulse response functions, plotting, 265

Generalized Method of Moments (GMM), 216, 222
  estimates/estimator, 249

Generalized Variance, 208

generalized variance, sample
  African countries, *213*
  Asian countries, *214*
  inflation-targeting countries, *215*
  Latin/South American countries, *212*
  New Zealand, *216*

generalized variance, sample (MENA countries), **209–210**

general price level (increase), shock (impact), 177

General Theory, 175

Germany, inflation rate, 8

Ghana
  output gap/inflation change, variance (inequality), 203
  price/money relationship, 52

Global Financial Crisis (GFC), 1, 15, 17, 59, 95
  evidence, 181
  period, 162

GLS-ADF Elliot test, 22, 31

government budget constraint, 254
  consolidated government budget constraint, 254–255
  intertemporal government budget constraint, 255–256

government consumption expenditures, 142–161
  growth, correlation, 137
  monetary base/government consumption expenditures, chi-squared confidence ellipse test, *151*
  scatter plot (Malaysia), *153*
  scatter plot/monetary base (New Zealand), *145*
  United States, scatter plot, *149*

government deficit
  financing, 136
  spending, money (correlation), 296
  spending, result, 171

government spending growth rates, broad money (correlation), 155

Great Depression, monetary policy error, 8

Gross Domestic Expenditure (GDE)
  Gabon, *141*
  Korea, *140*
  Malaysia, *140*
  New Zealand, *138*
  Turkey, *141*
  United Kingdom, *139*
  United States, *138*

gross domestic product (GDP)
  consumption, 199

growth
  inflation variability, equivalence, **63**
  mean inflation, equivalence, **63**
  money per unit of output growth rate, inflation (relationship), *67, 68*

Index 319

Guatemala
  inflation rate, 15
  output gap-inflation, evidence
      (absence), 186
  political/economic instability, 73

Haiti
  Chi-Squared Confidence Ellipse test,
      absence, 155
  instability, 88
  Sample Generalized Variance, 211
Hamilton, J.D., 284, 304
Hanke-Krus table, 8
heteroskedasticity-and-autocorrelation-
      consistent (HAC) estimators,
      usage, 41
Hodrick and Prescott (HP) filter
  trend, 224
  usage, 125, 193, 250
Holston-Laubach-Williams symbol,
      usage, 289
Honduras
  money growth/inflation relationship, 66
  output gap-inflation, evidence
      (absence), 186
  regression, non-normal residuals, 73
hours worked
  baseline mean deviations, Norway
      mean baseline dynamic stochastic
      projection, 277
  Norway mean baseline dynamic
      stochastic projection, 276
  UK mean baseline dynamic stochastic
      projections, 268
household
  inflation reduction model,
      relationship, 285
  MMT, relationship, 260
housing prices, inflation-targeting
      countries
  cyclical fluctuation, scatter plot, 168
housing prices, inflation-targeting countries
      (real GDP ratios), 167
Huber-White sandwich, usage, 226
Hume, David, 4, 26
Hungary (hyperinflation), 8
hyperinflation, 8–9

I(0) error process, capturing, 112
I(0) inflation rate, production, 24
impulse response function, 265
independently and identically distributed
      (iid) error, 107

independently and identically distributed
      (iid) residuals, 58
India
  inflation/growth rate of broad money per
      unit of real output, correlation, 81, 83
  money growth (variance), 81
ineffective monetary policy, 236
inflation
  Africa inflation rate, 18
  amplification, 298
  Asian countries, inflation rate, 19
  average rate, 23
  bias, time consistency (relationship),
      199–200
  conquest, explicit targeting (usage), 21
  CPI inflation, 219
  data (1960–2021), 13
  data (time series properties), policy
      (impact), 91
  definition, 1
  distortions, 6
  DOLS regression, 103–104
  elevation (1970s/1980s), 3
  expectation, formation (challenges),
      192–193
  expectation, measurement, 193
  expectations, 249–250
  expected inflation, mismeasurement,
      193–194
  findings, 10–11
  forecast targeting, usage, 194–195
  GDP growth rate, negative correlation, 7
  models, theories, 248
  monetary phenomenon, 26
  money growth, relationship, 57
  money per unit of output growth rate,
      relationship. see money per unit of
      output growth rate.
  one-year ahead CPI inflation, US
      survey, 219
  problems, 6, 8
  production, 259
  quarterly data, 24
  quarterly US inflation, actual/mean
      dynamic stochastic projections,
      234–235
  reduction, 178, 283–284
  reduction model, 284–289
  reduction, tax increase (MMT
      proposition), 268
  scatter plot (US), 230
  stationary data, 220
  stationary rendering, 6, 22, 57, 58

320 *Index*

target, optimum, 163
theories, 4–6
time series, appearance, 73
time series, output growth rate (money per unit) relationship, *61*
time series, visual inspection, 58
trend, display, 15, 226
true data-generating process, 237
US inflation growth, scatter plot, *223*
variability, inflation-targeting (impact), 57
volatility, 66, 69–70
inflation-bias inheritance, 200
inflation change
  New Keynesian Phillips Curve specification stability, 207–216
  output gap, relationship (stability), 207
inflation change, descriptive statistics
  African countries, **204**
  Asian countries, **205**
  Caribbean countries, **205**
  inflation-targeting countries, **206**
  Latin/South American countries, **204**
  MENA countries, **203**
inflation, goodness of fit
  African countries, *80*
  Asian countries, *84*
  Caribbean countries, *88*
  Latin/South American countries, *74*
  MENA countries, *64*
inflation rate
  lagged average inflation rate, 236
  second round effect, 226
  stabilization (New Zealand), 91
inflation-targeting, 65
  bygones-are-bygones, 258
  explicitness, 119
  impact, 57
  monetary base, growth rates, *145*
  period, 145
  policies, success, 114
  quasi-rule, 194–195
inflation-targeting countries. *see* developed inflation-targeting countries
  broad money, descriptive statistics, **94**
  broad money/housing prices, cyclical fluctuation (chi-squared confidence ellipse test), *169*
  broad money/housing prices, cyclical fluctuation (scatter plot), *168*
  CPI trend, **40**
  dynamic OLS (DOLS), **53–54**

dynamic OLS (DOLS) estimated broad money, **96**
dynamic OLS (DOLS) estimated growth, inflation (relationship), **97**, **98**
generalized variance sample, *215*
inflation change, descriptive statistics, **206**
inflation rate, 20
inflation variability, growth (equivalence), **94**
Log (CPI), 45° scatter plots, *37*
mean inflation, growth (equivalence), **94**
money per unit of output growth rate, inflation (relationship), *90*
money per unit of output growth rate, inflation time series, *92*
New Keynesian Phillips Curve specification, generalized variance sample, *215*
ordinary least squares, **53–54**
output gap, descriptive statistics, **206**
Phillips Curve specifications, chi-squared confidence ellipse test, *188*, *189*
QTM equation, 95
real GDP ratios, *167*
inflation-targeting period (US quarterly data), Phillips Curve specifications (chi-squared confidence ellipse test), *190*
inflation variability, growth (equivalence)
  African countries, **78**
  Asian countries, **83**
  Caribbean countries, **87**
  inflation-targeting countries, **94**
  Latin/South American countries, **70**
  MENA countries, **63**
Information Criteria, 32
innovation outlier
  break type, 59
  test, 107
Instrumental Variable (IV) estimator, usage, 217
intercept, absence, 32, 34
intercept break max ADF t-stat, 58
intercepts/slopes, DOLS estimates (summary statistics), **55**
interest, natural rate. *see* natural rate of interest
interest rate
  gaps, computation (US), **290**
  trend, display, 226
International Monetary Fund (IMF) data, 10

Index 321

International Monetary Fund-International
    Financial Statistics (IMF-IFS)
    report, 137–139
intertemporal government budget
    constraint, 255–256, 263
intertemporal substitution, 262
intratemporal substitution, tax rate
    capture, 262
inverse negative Hessian, usage, 226
inverse Normal Distribution Function, 208
invertible ARMA errors, 107
    process, capturing, 112
Iran
    Chi-Squared Confidence Ellipse test, 155
    DOLS regression, estimation
        inability, 64
    inflation rate, 61–62
I(1) time series, 24
I(2) time series, 24

Jacobian approximation, 247
Jain and Chlamtac updating algorithm, 247
Japan
    Central Bank of Japan, money
        injection, 6
    inflation/growth rate of broad money per
        unit of real output, correlation, 83
    inflation (Phillips Curve), New
        Keynesian specification
        (chi-squared confidence ellipse
        test), *183*
    output gap/inflation change, variance
        (equality), 203
Jarque-Bera *P*-value, 64, 70, 73
    indications, 79
    normality, 79
Johansen's Maximum Likelihood, usage,
    263, 265
joint test problem, 192

Keynesian economics, sticky price
    prediction, 114
Keynes, J.M., 11, 113, 173, 175, 305
Korea
    broad money, chi-squared confidence
        ellipse test, *152*
    Consumer Price Index (CPI), *151*
    government consumption expenditures,
        151, 152
    government consumption expenditures,
        chi-squared confidence ellipse
        etst, *152*
    IMF-IFS, 139

inflation/growth rate of broad money per
    unit of real output, correlation, 83
monetary base, *151*
money base/seigniorage, *140*
money/nominal government expenditures
    growth rates, association, 155
nominal government consumption
    expenditures, *151*
real government consumption
    expenditures, *151*
seigniorage, volatility, 142
KPSS test, 22, 31, 32
Kruskal-Wallis one-way ANOVA, 62
kurtosis, usage, 290
Kwiatkowski, Dennis, 305
Kwiatkowski test, 22, 31

labor-augmenting technical progress, 285
labor market, nominal wages/prices, 174
labor supply
    initial response, 265
    reduction, 177
lagged average inflation rate, 236
lagged inflation, 296
lagged nominal GDP
    growth, 296
    growth, function, 224
    impact, 224
lag/lead truncation parameter, 56
lag polynomial, 107
Lagrange multiplier optimization
    problem, 261
Latin American countries
    banking/financial/debt/political
        crises, 73
    broad money averages, **116**
    broad money, descriptive statistics, **69**
    chi-squared confidence ellipse test/
        scatter plot, *157*
    CPI trend, **38**
    data, test, 66–75
    dynamic OLS, **44–46**
    dynamic OLS (DOLS) estimated broad
        money, **71–72**
    inflation change/output gap, descriptive
        statistics, **204**
    Log (CPI), 45° scatter plots, *32*
    mean inflation, growth (equivalence), **69**
    money growth, reduction, 119
    money/inflation, volatility, 66, 69–70
    New Keynesian Phillips Curve
        specification, generalized variance
        sample, *212*

322　*Index*

ordinary least squares (OLS), **44–46**
Phillips Curve specifications, chi-squared
confidence ellipse test, *185*
real GDP growth rates, **116**
scatter plot, 184, 186
Latin American countries, inflation
descriptive statistics, *17*
goodness of fit, *74*
level, *16*
variability, growth (equivalence), **70**
lead/lag dynamics, 87
Levene test, 62
Levin, A., 59, 305
LHS, 193, 254, 258
Lin, C.F., 59, 305
linear OLS regressions, 24
linear trend
absence, 32
fitting, 34
significance, 64
Locke, John, 4
Log (CPI), 45° scatter plots, *33–37*
log nominal debt, UK mean baseline
dynamic stochastic projections, *267*
log real deficit, Norway mean baseline
dynamic stochastic projection, *275*
log real surplus, UK mean baseline
dynamic stochastic projections, *267*
long-differenced data, trend (reason), 22
long-run equilibrium, 253
long-run money illusion, 12
absence, 179–190
long-run Phillips Curve, 176–179
Friedman argument, 179
long-run trends, 35
CPI, relationship, 2
sharing, 295
long-run vertical Phillips Curve,
rejection, 225
long-term common trend, sharing, 52
long-term government bond rate, variable
(complexity), 225
low-frequency cyclical variation, 218
Lucas critique, 197–199
policy rule requirement, 231
resolution, impossibility, 216
Lucas, Jr., Robert, 194

Malaysia
Consumer Price Index (CPI), *153*
Consumer Price Index (CPI), log, 148
DOLS regression, 42
monetary base, scatter plot, *153*

money base, growth rate, 148
money base/seigniorage, *140*
money growth/inflation, associations
(weakness), 81
money/nominal government
expenditures growth rates,
association, 155
nominal/real government consumption
expenditures, *153*
output gap, variance, 207
seigniorage, volatility, 142
trends, similarities, 148
upward sloping scatter plots, 186
Mankiw, N. Gregory, 5, 258, 259, 306
Mann-Whitney test, generalization, 62
marginal cost, increase, 125
marginal labor tax rate, 285
marginal rate of substitution (MRS),
261, 286
Maximum Likelihood (ML), 10
Maximum Likelihood Method, 221, 296
maximum sustainable employment, 237
McCallum, B.T., 58, 195, 201, 229,
258, 307
mean dynamic stochastic projections,
deviations, 272, 278
mean inflation, growth (equivalence)
African countries, **77**
Asian countries, **83**
Caribbean countries, **87**
inflation-targeting countries, **94**
Latin/South American countries, **69**
MENA countries, **63**
Mexico
money growth/inflation relationship, 66
output gap-inflation, evidence
(absence), 186
price/money relationship, 52
QTM support, 73
microeconomic real-wage dynamics, 251
micro-foundation, 12, 196, 297
micro-founded macroeconomic models,
usage, 201
Middle East and North Africa (MENA)
countries, 59–66
broad money, averages, **116**
broad money, chi-squared confidence
ellipse test, *156*
broad money, descriptive statistics, **62**
CPI trend, **37–38**
dynamic OLS, 43
generalized variance, sample, **209–210**
inflation, **62**

Index 323

inflation, change (descriptive statistics), **203**
inflation, goodness of fit, *64*
inflation rate, 13, 15, 17
inflation variability, growth (equivalence), **63**
Log (CPI), 45° scatter plots, *33*
mean inflation, growth (equivalence), **63**
money-output stochastic ratio, **37–38**
money per unit of output growth rate, inflation time series, *61*
New Keynesian Phillips Curve specification, generalized variance (sample), *210*
nominal government consumption, chi-squared confidence ellipse test, *156*
OLS, **43**
output gap, change (descriptive statistics), **203**
output growth rate (money per unit), inflation (relationship), *60*
Phillips Curve specifications, chi-squared confidence test, *184*
real GDP growth rates, **116**
real GDP ratio growth, **62**
real GDP ratio growth-inflation relationship, **65**
Sample Generalized Variance, stability, 211
unit of real output model, broad money, *64*
Middle East and North Africa (MENA) Group, inflation, *14*
military coups, impact, 77
mismeasurement. *see* expected inflation; output gap
misperception model, 174
misspecification problem, 197–198
modern monetary theory (MMT), 5, 136, 258–279
firm, relationship, 260–279
household, relationship, 260
inflation policy implications, 10
inflation, reduction policy, 298
prediction, 269
proposition, examination, 268–269
modern monetary theory (MMT) policy, 297
outcome, 278
prescription, testing (continuation), 272
recommendations, efficacy, 278–279
monetary base, scatter plot

Gabon, *154*
Korea, *151*
Malaysia, *153*
Turkey, *150*
United States, *149*
monetary expansion, 259
monetary policy
impact, 236
ineffectiveness, 296–297
looseness, 162
rules, 199
Monetary Policy Report (2022), 298
money
base (quantity), targeting (absence), 136–137
broad money, *30, 31*
central bank printing, increase (reasons), 135
doctrine, neutrality, 114
government deficit spending, correlation, 296
government printing, 29
illusion, 6, 163–164
long-run money illusion, absence, 179–190
output, relationship, 125
prices, relationship (testing), 29
quantity, 27
quantity, CPI (relationship), 11–12
quantity, increase (impact), 120–134
quantity theory, 26
velocity, 27, 201
volatility, 66, 69–70
money growth, 220
average, *119*
equation, 198
inflation, correlation, 95, 103
scatter plot (US), *230*
US money growth, scatter plot, *223*
x-percent money growth rule, 201
money growth, inflation (relationship), 57
cross-sectional evidence, 106
money growth rates, average
African countries, *122*
Asian countries, *123*
Caribbean countries, *124*
inflation-targeting countries, *124*
Latin/South American countries, *121*
MENA countries, *120*
money neutrality, 12, 113, 295
DOLS-estimated long-run elasticities, consistency, 52
formal representation, 114–115

324 *Index*

money-output ratios, 29
money output, scatter plot/chi-squared
     confidence ellipse test
  Africa, *128*
  Asia, *130*
  Caribbean countries, *131*
  developed inflation-targeting
    countries, *132*
  Latin/South American countries, *127*
  MENA countries, *126*
  New Zealand, *132*
money-output stochastic ratio
  African countries, **39**
  Asian countries, **39–40**
  Caribbean countries, **40**
  inflation-targeting countries, **40**
  Latin America, **38**
  MENA countries, **37–38**
  South America, **38**
money per unit of output growth rate,
    inflation (relationship)
  African countries, *75*
  Asian countries, *81*
  Caribbean countries, *86*
  inflation-targeting countries, *90*
  Latin/South American countries, *67, 68*
  MENA countries, *60*
money per unit of output growth rate,
    inflation time series
  African countries, *76*
  Asian countries, *82*
  Caribbean countries, *86*
  inflation-targeting countries, *92*
  MENA countries, *61*
money per unit of real output, 29
MRTS, 287
multiple-period Lagrange multiplier, 286
Muth, J., 192, 194, 199, 307
Myanmar
  inflation/growth rate of broad money per
    unit of real output, correlation, 83
  money growth/inflation, associations
    (weakness), 81
  money growth, variance, 81
  price/money relationship, 52
  slope coefficients, 42, 52

natural rate (r_{1t}) (r_{2t}), chi-square correlation
    test, *291*
natural rate of interest, 284
Natural Rate of Unemployment Hypothesis
    (NRUH), 174, 179
natural real rate of interest, 2823
natural real rate of interest *(r*)*, 284

Nepal
  CPI level, 13
  government spending growth rates,
    broad money (correlation), 155
  Phillips curve, instability, 211
  time series, 29
neutral interest rate total ($r*_l$), 289
  computation (advanced countries), *292*
  computation (US), **290**
  descriptive statistics, **292**
neutral interest rate total ($r*_l$) (US),
    289–292
neutrality
  evidence, 115
  meaning, 113
neutral system, 115
Newey-West method, 41
New Keynesian framework, concept
    (extension), 201
New Keynesian models, inertia, 236
New Keynesian Phillips Curve
  estimation, 249
  instability, 211
New Keynesian Phillips Curve
    specification, 182
  stability, 12, 207–216
New Keynesian Phillips Curve
    specification, generalized variance
    sample
  African countries, *213*
  Asian countries, *214*
  Caribbean countries, *215*
  Latin/South American countries, *212*
  MENA countries, *210*
  New Zealand, *216*
New Keynesian preferred specification,
    chi-squared confidence ellipse test,
    181–182
New Phillips Curve, 5, 248–251
New Zealand
  actual inflation/mean dynamic
    stochastic projections, descriptive
    statistics, **244**
  binding monetary policy regime,
    adoption, 13, 17–18
  broad money growth/inflation, scatter
    plot, *238*
  broad money/housing prices, cyclical
    fluctuation (chi-squared confidence
    ellipse test), *170*
  broad money/housing prices, quarterly
    business cycle fluctuations, *170*
  broad money/nominal GDP growth rates,
    chi-square confidence ellipse test, *239*

broad money, scatter plot, *146*
chi-squared confidence ellipse test, *132*
consumption expenditures, government growth rates (descriptive statistics), **147**
CPI quarterly inflation rate (1988–2022), *25*
dynamic OLS (DOLS) estimated growth, inflation (relationship), **99**
fitted values/residuals, *99*
GDP(e), growth rates (chi-square confidence ellipse test), *240*
generalized variance sample, *216*
government consumption expenditures, growth rates, 145
government consumption expenditures, scatter plot, *146*
inflation rate, 89
inflation target, change, 163
inflation, targeting, 9, 89
inflation-targeting period (quarterly data), Phillips Curve specifications (chi-squared confidence ellipse test), *191*
Mankiw-Rees model, 252
monetary base, increase, 139
monetary base, scatter plot, *146*
money/nominal government expenditures growth rates, association, 155
money/output data, correlation, 125
money output, scatter plot/chi-squared confidence ellipse test, *132*
New Keynesian Phillips Curve specification, generalized variance sample, *216*
nominal government expenditures, growth rates (chi-square confidence ellipse test), *240*
output gap, variance, 206
petrol/gas prices, daily change, 121–122
quarterly data, 133
quarterly inflation, actual/mean dynamic stochastic projections, *242, 243*
quarterly money base, increase/ seigniorage, *138*
quarterly NZ Phillips Curve, maximum likelihood estimates, **241–242**
real output, scatter plot/chi-squared confidence ellipse test, *132*
seigniorage-NGDE ratio, 139
wealth, 166
year-on-year quarterly data, scatter plots, *93*
year-on-year quarterly time series data, *93*

Ng and Perron test, 22, 31
Nigeria
  Chi-Squared Confidence Ellipse test, 155
Nigeria, non-normal residuals, 79
nominal debt, Norway mean baseline dynamic stochastic projection, *275*
nominal GDP (NGDP), 137, 224
  growth, 193, 220
  growth rates, chi-square confidence ellipse test (New Zealand), *239*
  growth (US), scatter plot, *223, 223*
nominal government consumption (Norway), 155, 158
nominal government consumption (UK), *143*
nominal government consumption expenditures
  Asian countries, *159*
  Australia, *160*
  Denmark, *160*
  growth rate, *144*
  Korea, *151*
  MENA countries, *156*
  Norway, *161*
  Sweden, *161*
  United States, *148*
Nominal Gross Domestic Expenditure (NGDE), 137
  descriptive statistics, **142**
nominal interest rate, 261
  policy, central bank pursuit, 200
nominal money, impact, 197
nominal wage growth rates (US), *178*
nominal wages, change (anticipated rate), 176–177
non-accelerated inflation rate of unemployment (NAIRU), 179–180, 195
noninflation-targeting countries, correlations, 137
nonlinear unit root, 31
nonmarket productive time, 285
non-RE formation assumption, 201–202
non-Ricardian fiscal policies, 257
non-stationary mixed variables, handling, 59
Norway
  baseline VAR, generalized impulse response functions, *274*
  broad money/housing prices, cyclical fluctuations, 166
  broad money/nominal government consumption expenditures, chi-squared confidence ellipse test/ scatter plot, *161*

326 *Index*

CPI, baseline mean deviations (mean baseline dynamic stochastic projection), *278*
CPI, mean baseline dynamic stochastic projection, *277*
C/Y, mean baseline dynamic stochastic projection, *276*
data, examination, 270–271
dynamic OLS estimated growth, inflation (relationship), **98**
fitted values/residuals, *98*
hours worked, mean baseline dynamic stochastic projection, *276*
inflation-targeting, 91
log real deficit, mean baseline dynamic stochastic projection, *275*
nominal debt, mean baseline dynamic stochastic projection, *275*
oil production, 158
output gap, variance, 206
VAR variables, *273*
null hypothesis, 32–33
acceptance, 66, 205

Official Cash Rate (OCR), 90, 115
oil price, insignificance, 230–231
oil price shocks, 64, 211, 298
oil shocks, impact, 77
one-period lead, usage, 255
one-year ahead CPI inflation, US survey, *219*
open market operation, 136
Open Mouth Operation, 90
order and rank conditions, 226, 245
Ordinary Least Squares (OLS), 33. *see also* dynamic OLS
African countries, **47–48**
Asian countries, **49–50**
Caribbean countries, **51**
inflation-targeting countries, **53–54**
Latin/South American countries, **44–46**
MENA countries, **43**
parameter estimates, 217
regression, R^2 statistics/DW statistics, 52
regression test, **220**, **221**
single-equation OLS method, usage, 216
single-equation Phillips Curve, 193
Organization of Economic Constructions and Development (OECD)
data, 10
seignorage revenue reliance, 137
Orphanides, Athanasios, 235, 307

orthogonality, 219
outer product of the gradient (OPG), 226
output, 172
market, nominal wages/prices, 174
money per unit of output growth rate, inflation (relationship), *60, 67, 68*
quantity theory, 26
output gap, 5, 10–11, 195
inflation change, correlation, 182
mismeasurement, 193–194, 216, 222
variance, 202–203, 206–207
output gap change, descriptive statistics
African countries, **204**
Asian countries, **205**
Caribbean countries, **205**
inflation-targeting countries, **206**
Latin/South American countries, **204**
MENA countries, **203**
output gap change, New Keynesian Phillips Curve specification stability, 207–216
overnight interest rate, 255

Pakistan
DOLS slope efficiency, 64
inflation rate, 13
broad money per unit of real output, growth rate (relationship), 60–62
output gap/inflation change, variance (contrast), 203
real GDP ratio growth, inequality, 62
Paraguay
output gap-inflation, evidence (absence), 186
price/money relationship, 52
QTM support, 73
P*, derivation, 252
Penn World Table report, 289
Permanent Income Hypothesis, 199–200
personal consumption expenditures, *4*
Phelps, Edmund, 11, 176, 180
Philippines
DOLS regression, 42
government spending growth rates, broad money (correlation), 155
inflation/growth rate of broad money per unit of real output, correlation, 83
money growth/inflation, associations (weakness), 81
money growth, variance, 81
price/money relationship, 52
Phillips and Perron test, 22, 31

Phillips Curve, 4–5, 172, 296
  equation, 225, 231
  estimation, 217, 221–244
  expectation-augmented Phillips curve,
    11–12
  long-run Phillips Curve, 176–179
  mirage, 190–192
  New Keynesian Phillips Curve
    specification, stability, 207–216
  New Keynesian preferred specification,
    chi-squared confidence ellipse test,
    181–184
  New Keynesian specification,
    239–240
  New Phillips Curve, 248–251
  policymaker preference, 175
  rational expectations/policy issues,
    relationship, 194–195
  short-run Phillips Curve, 176–179
  Sticky Information Phillips curve, 5
  system (estimation), quarterly growth
    rate (variables, usage), *227*
  testing, 173
Phillips Curve specifications, chi-squared
    confidence ellipse test
  African countries, *186*
  Asian countries, *187*
  Caribbean countries, *188*
  inflation-targeting countries, *188, 189*
  Latin/South American countries, *185*
  MENA countries, *184*
P model, 252–253
policy evaluation, Lucas critique,
    197–199
policy ineffectiveness, 222, 229, 297
  proposition, 195
policy interest rate, central bank setting, 5
policy invariant assumption, 198
policy issues, rational expectations/Phillips
    Curve (relationship), 194–195
policy lags, characteristics, 244
Policy Targets Agreements, 237
Poole, William, 91
portfolio theory, usage, 162
postwar macroeconomic policymaking, 11
potential output, 2
  determination, 198
  real output level, equivalence, 284
Powell, Jerome, 298
price level, 13
  fiscal theory, 5, 136
  increase, shocks (impact), 137
  tax rate doubling, effect, *270*

prices
  increases, continuation (prolonged
    period), 1
  money, relationship (testing), 29
  quantity theory, 26
  recomputation, 252
  stability, objective, 237
price-setting framework (Calvo), 252
Price Stability ACT (1990), 89
price stickiness
  acceptance, 121
  assumption, 195–196
  evidence, 121
pricing kernel, 287
projection, downward drift, 231
P-values, 34
  indication, 66

Quantity Theory of Money (QTM), 4, 11,
    26–27, 172, 252–253
  correlation prediction, 60
  equation, 41, 43
  equation, estimates, 89
  identity, writing, 27
  implications, 27
  instability, 221
  model, 66
  oil imports, 87
  P* derivation, 252–253
  prediction, data consistency, 52
  testing, 35
  time series data, usage, 295
quarterly inflation, actual/mean dynamic
    stochastic projects (New Zealand),
    242, 243
quarterly NZ Phillips Curve, maximum
    likelihood estimates, **241–242**
quarterly US inflation, actual/mean
    dynamic stochastic projections,
    234–235
quarterly US Phillips Curve, maximum
    likelihood estimates, **228**
quasi rules, 194–195, 199

r^*. *see* equilibrium real interest rate; natural
    real rate of interest
r_{1t}. *see* natural rate
r_{2t}. *see* natural rate
rank conditions. *see* order and rank
    conditions
rational agents, information usage, 222
Rational Constraint Expectations, 196
rational expectations (RE)

328　*Index*

assumption, 199
impact, 197
policy issues/Phillips Curve, relationship, 194–195
rules, discretion argument (contrast), 201–202
theory, 192, 195, 222
theory, assumption, 229
real broad money/stock prices, 164
US standardized growth rates, scatter plot, *165*
real budget surplus (UK), *143*
real C/Y, UK mean baseline dynamic stochastic projections, *268*
real deficit, presence, 136
real GDP, 58, 173
average, *119*
deviation, 2
increase, money quantity increase (impact), 115–134
stimulation, 134
real GDP growth rates, averages
African countries, **117**, *122*
Asian countries, **117**, *123*
Caribbean countries, **118**, *124*
developed inflation-targeting countries, **118**
inflation-targeting countries, *124*
Latin/South American countries, **116**, *121*
MENA countries, **116**, *120*
real GDP ratio, *30, 31*, 41
decline, *7*
growth, **62**
real government consumption (UK), *143*
real government consumption expenditure
Korea, *151*
United States, *148*
real interest rate, calculation, 256
real marginal cost deviation, 249
real money balances/stock price, growth rates (US), *164*
real output gap, 224
Gabon, *129*
Singapore, *130*
South Africa, *129*
Trinidad/Tobago, *131*
US quarterly fluctuations, *134*
real output, scatter plot/chi-squared confidence ellipse test
Africa, *128*
Asia, *130*
Caribbean countries, *131*

developed inflation-targeting countries, *132*
Latin/South American countries, *127*
MENA countries, *126*
New Zealand, *132*
real output, tax rate doubling (effect), *270*
real seigniorage revenues, sum, 256
real surplus (US), *148*
real surplus (deficit), measurement, 147
real time data, usage, 235
Real-Time Gross Settlement (RTGS) basis, 90–91
real wage growth rates (US), *178*
real wages, procyclical appearance, 250
real wages/real output, cyclical fluctuations (US), *251*
real wealth, 6
inducing, 162
stock, variation, 259
regional-specific adverse supply shocks, impact, 298
regression, linear trend (fitting), 34
regression slope coefficient, war dummy variable (absence), 63
relative prices, 178
increase, 1, 177
REMIT, history, 237
reputation, 12, 104
impact, 200
Reserve Bank of New Zealand (RBNZ)
budget deficit financing, 238
data, 139, 237
disinflation process, 89
inflation rate stabilization, 91
interest rate adoption, 115
Phillips Curve, mention (absence), 191–192
Policy Targets Agreements, 237
policy tightening, 240
quarterly data, usage, 42
seigniorage revenues-nominal GDP ratio, 139
residuals
model specification, *232–233*
OLS regression test, **221**
return-to-scale Cobb-Douglas production function, usage, 260, 285
RHS, 193, 254, 258
Ricardian Equivalence, 259
Ricardian fiscal policies, 257
Romer, Christina/David, 180, 207, 211, 249, 309
r^*_t. *See* neutral interest rate total

R test statistic, 211
rule-of-thumb agents, 248
rules, discretion (contrast), 12, 201–202
Russian disinflationary policy, success, *9*
Russia-Ukraine conflict, impact, 176

Sample Generalized Variance, 208
  bivariate test statistic, 296
  stability, 211, 216
  test, 12, 211
Sargent, Thomas J., 136, 194–196, 201,
    229, 309
Satterthwaite-Welch t-test, **63**, **69**, **77**, **83**,
    87, **94**
second round effects, 226
  concern, 1
secular inflation, 1
  dominance, 58
seigniorage
  descriptive statistics, **142**
  Gabon, *141*
  Korea, *140*
  Malaysia, *140*
  New Zealand, *138*
  real seigniorage revenues, sum, 256
  revenues, 136–142
  revenues, OECD country reliance, 137
  Turkey, *141*
  United Kingdom, *139*
  United States, *138*
seigniorage-NGDE ratio, 139
self-protective actions, 200
shareholder value at risk (SVAR), 250
Shiller, Robert, 6
shock, impact, 177–177
short-run money, Chi-Squared test, 125
short-run Phillips Curve, 176–179
  fitting, 297
short-term interest rate, 284
short-term nominal interest rate, central
    bank increase, 5
Siegel-Tukey test, 62
Sims, Christopher, 5, 198, 258, 310
Singapore
  government spending growth rates,
      broad money (correlation), 155
  inflation/growth rate of broad money per
      unit of real output, correlation, 83
  money/output, relationship, 125–126
  output gap/inflation change, variance
      (equality), 203
  output gap, variance, 207
  upward sloping scatter plots, 186

single-equation GMM estimator,
    inefficiency, 249
single-equation Phillips Curve, estimation,
    202–207
Smith, Adam, 136
Smith, Vernon, 230
smooth deterministic trend, output
    growth, 253
South Africa
  broad money per unit of output growth
      rate/inflation rate, inequality, 79
  cyclical broad money fluctuations/real
      output gap, *129*
  inflation targeting, adoption, 79
  money/output, relationship, 125
  New Keynesian Phillips Curve
      specification, 211
  output gap-inflation, correlation, 186
South American countries
  banking/financial/debt/political crises, 73
  broad money averages, **116**
  broad money, descriptive statistics, **69**
  chi-squared confidence ellipse test/
      scatter plot, *156*
  CPI trend, **38**
  data, test, 66–75
  dynamic OLS, **44**–**46**
  dynamic OLS (DOLS) estimated broad
      money, **71**–**72**
  inflation change/output gap, descriptive
      statistics, **204**
  Log (CPI), 45° scatter plots, *34*
  mean inflation, growth (equivalence), **69**
  money growth, reduction, 119
  money/inflation, volatility, 66, 69–70
  New Keynesian Phillips Curve
      specification, 184
  New Keynesian Phillips Curve
      specification, generalized variance
      sample, *212*
  ordinary least squares (OLS), **44**–**46**
  Phillips Curve specifications, chi-squared
      confidence ellipse test, *185*
  real GDP growth rates, **116**
South American countries, inflation
  descriptive statistics, **17**
  goodness of fit, *74*
  level, *16*
  variability, growth (equivalence), **70**
spectral density, 56
Sri Lanka
  Phillips Curve, instability, 211
Sri Lanka, money growth (variance), 81

330 *Index*

stable exchange rate, inclusion, 237
stagflation, 2
Standardized Sample Generalized Variance, calculation, 208
state dependence, 162
stationary alternatives, tests (weakness), 22, 142
stationary mixed variables, handling, 59
stationary residuals, 52
stationary variable, unit root variable (regression), 58
Statistics of National Account (SNA) measure, 260, 285
sticky information model, 252
Sticky Information Phillips curve, 5
sticky prices
    micro-foundation, 196–197
    prediction, 114
sticky-price theory, 125
sticky wages, micro-foundation, 197
stochastic trends, 22, 58, 142, 265
stock market mispricing, time-series variation, 163–164
stock-pricing equation, 287
stocks, real rate of return (chi-square correlation test), *291*
structural neutrality
    implication, 218
    test, 222
Sudan
    New Keynesian Phillips Curve specification, 211
    output gap/inflation change, variance (inequality), 203
    price/money relationship, 52
superneutrality, evidence, 115
supply shocks, impact, 251
surprise monetary policy, impact, 218
Svensson, Lars, 194–195
Sweden
    broad money/housing prices, cyclical fluctuations, 166
    dynamic OLS (DOLS) estimated growth, inflation (relationship), **100**
    fitted values/residuals, *100*
    inflation change/output gap relationship, evidence, 190
    inflation-targeting, 91
    output gap, variance, 206
    price/money relationship, 52
Swiss National Bank, negative nominal interest rate policy, 200

tailed-non-normal distributions, indication, 290
tax rate, introduction, 262
Taylor, John, 57
Taylor rule, usage, 298–299
Tchebysheff's theorem, 208
temporal aggregation, 218
Thailand
    DOLS regression, 42
    inflation/growth rate of broad money per unit of real output, correlation, 83
    output gap/inflation change, variance (equality), 203
    slope coefficients, 42
    upward sloping scatter plots, 186
Theory of Moral Sentiments, The (Smith), 136
time consistency
    inflation bias, relationship, 199–200
    RE assumption, 199
time inconsistency, 199
time series data, usage, 295
time series processes, 218
time series properties, policy (impact), 57
Tobago
    broad money/output gap, short-run fluctuations, 128
    Chi-Squared Confidence Ellipse test, absence, 155
    inflation rate, 89
    instability, 88
    output gap/inflation (contrast), 203
    output gap, variance, 207
    price/money relationship, 52
    Sample Generalized Variance, 211
    slope coefficients, 42, 52
trend
    absence, 34, 70
    behavior, 107
    broad money deviation, 125
    continuous positive trend, 194
    CPI price level, sharing, 10–11
    deterministic trend, 32
    display, 15, 147, 226, 263
    increase, 270–271
    inflation, 17, 22, 22–24, 58
    positive level, 29
    prediction, difficulty, 2
    real marginal cost deviation, 249
    sharing, 135
    similarities, 148
    specifications, 59, 263
    steepness, 60

Index 331

stochastic trends, 22, 58, 142, 265
unemployment deviation, 195
trending data, models (usage), 107
trend-stationary model, 107
Trinidad
  broad money fluctuations/real output gap, *131*
  broad money/output gap, short-run fluctuations, 128
  Chi-Squared Confidence Ellipse test, absence, 155
  inflation rate, 89
  instability, 88
  output gap/inflation (contrast), 203
  output gap, variance, 207
  price/money relationship, 52
  Sample Generalized Variance, 211
  slope coefficients, 42, 52
true data-generating process, 237
Turkey
  broad money/government consumption expenditures, chi-squared confidence ellipse test, *150*
  double-digit inflation, 64
  inflation rate, 61–62
  inflation rate, variability, 61–62
  inflation, variability, 13
  monetary base, 147
  monetary base/government consumption expenditures, chi-squared confidence ellipse test, *150*
  money base/seigniorage, *141*
  money growth, reduction, 119
  money/nominal government expenditures growth rates, association, 155
  output gap/inflation change, variance (contrast), 203
  real GDP, negative correlation, 125
  Sample Generalized Variance, stability (absence), 211
  seigniorage-GDE ratio, 139
  slope coefficient, change, 73
  trend steepness, 60
Two-Stage Least Square (2SLS), 216

unanticipated aggregate demand shocks, 224, 229
unanticipated fiscal shocks, impact, 258
unbiasedness, 219
unemployment
  hypothesis, natural rate. *see* Natural Rate of Unemployment Hypothesis.

natural rate, 2, 5, 179
non-accelerating inflation rate, 2
United Kingdom
  annual average hours worked per worker, mean baseline dynamic stochastic projections, *270*
  annual average hours worked per worker, mean dynamic stochastic projections, *271*
  baseline VAR, generalized impulse response functions, *266*
  broad money/housing prices, cyclical fluctuations, 166
  budget deficit, 142
  cointegration summary statistics, **280–282**
  CPI, *143*
  CPI, baseline mean deviations (mean dynamic stochastic projection), *272*
  CPI, mean baseline dynamic stochastic projections, *269*
  CPI, mean dynamic stochastic projections, *271*
  dynamic OLS (DOLS) estimated growth, inflation (relationship), **101**
  fitted values/residuals, *101*
  hours worked, mean baseline dynamic stochastic projections, *268*
  inflation change/output gap relationship, evidence, 190
  inflation-targeting, 91
  inflation-targeting, monetary base (growth rates), *145*
  inflation-targeting, scatter plot, *144*
  log nominal debt, UK mean baseline dynamic stochastic projections, *267*
  log real surplus, mean baseline dynamic stochastic projections, *267*
  money base/seigniorage, *139*
  money/nominal government expenditures growth rates, association, 155
  nominal/real government consumption, *143*
  output gap, variance, 206
  Phillips Curve, 221
  real broad money/stock prices, standardized growth rates (scatter plot), *166*
  real budget surplus, *143*
  real C/Y, mean baseline dynamic stochastic projections, *268*
  seigniorage-NGDE ratio, 139
  VAR variables, *264*

332 Index

United States
 broad money/housing prices, cyclical
  fluctuations, 166
 broad money, scatter plot/chi-squared
  confidence ellipse test, *149*
 core inflation rate, *4*
 CPI, *148*
 CPI inflation annualized rates, FRBP
  publication, 218
 CPI inflation survey, OLS regression
  test, **220**
 data growth rates, requirement, *294*
 dynamic OLS (DOLS) estimated growth,
  inflation (relationship), **102**
 federal fund rate (r* gaps), *290*
 fitted values/residuals, *102*
 government consumption expenditures,
  scatter plot, *149*
 government consumption expenditures,
  scatter plot/chi-squared confidence
  ellipse, *149*
 inflation growth/nominal GDP growth,
  scatter plot, *223*
 inflation, scatter plot, *230*
 inflation-targeting, 90–91, 205
 inflation-targeting period (quarterly
  data), Phillips Curve specifications
  (chi-squared confidence ellipse
  test), *190*
 interest rate gaps, computation, **290**
 M3 deviations, 134
 macroeconomic data, 250
 monetary base, scatter plot, *149*
 money base, increase/seigniorage, *138*
 money growth/nominal GDP growth,
  scatter plot, *223*
 money growth, scatter plot, *230*
 money/nominal government expenditures
  growth rates, association, 155
 neutral interest rate total (r^*_t), 289–292
 neutral interest rate total (r^*_t),
  computation, **290**
 nominal government consumption
  expenditures, *148*
 nominal wage growth rates, *178*
 Phillips Curve, chi-squared confidence
  ellipse test, *181–183*
 Phillips Curve, estimation, 180–181
 Phillips Curve, evidence, 236
 Phillips Curve system (estimation),
  quarterly growth rate (variables,
  usage), *227*
 price/money relationship, 52

 quarterly data, Phillips Curve
  specifications (chi-squared
  confidence ellipse test), *190*
 quarterly fluctuations, broad money/real
  output gap, *134*
 quarterly inflation rate, *3*
 quarterly Phillips Curve, maximum
  likelihood estimates, **228**
 real broad money/stock prices,
  standardized growth rates
  (scatter plot), *165*
 real government consumption
  expenditures, *148*
 real money balances/stock price, growth
  rates, *164*
 real surplus, *148*
 real wage growth rates, *178*
 real wages/real output, cyclical
  fluctuations, *251*
 real wealth, *7*
 seigniorage-NGDE ratio, 139
 stock returns, responses, 162
unit of real output model, broad money
  (MENA countries), *64*
unit root, null hypothesis, 31–34
unit root tests, 31–35
unit root tests, breaks
  (inclusion), 107
 ADF tests, **108–111**
unrestricted VAR, estimation, 262
Uruguay
 inflation data abnormality, 66
 money growth/inflation
  relationship, 66
 QTM support, 73

value at risk (VAR), 250
variables, quarterly growth rate, *227*
Vector Autoregression (VAR), 10, 198
 baseline VAR, UK generalized impulse
  response functions, *266*
 coefficients, 198–199
 estimation, 263, 297
 re-estimation, 269
 solving, 272
 variables (Norway), *273*
 variables (UK), *264*
velocity, 4
 changes, 125
 levels, 252–253
 treatment, 27
velocity of money. *see* money
Volker, Paul (disinflation), 218, 226, 283

Index   333

Wald *P*-value, 41
Wallace, Neil, 136, 194–196, 201, 229, 309
war dummy variable, absence, 63
weak test, failure, 32
white-noise innovations, 2623
Wicksell, K., 174, 310
Wilshire 5000 Total Market Full Cap
   Index, 164
Wilson, Bart, 230
Woodford, M., 5, 201, 258, 283–284, 289,
   310–311

World Bank, World Development
   Indicators data, 10, 142

X-percent money growth rule, 201, 231

year-on-year quarterly CPI inflation
   rate, 3
yield curve, slope, 224–225

Zero Lower Bound (ZLB), 163
Zimbabwe, inflation rate, 8

Printed in the United States
by Baker & Taylor Publisher Services